KT-526-178

*Managing Systems
Development*

370013526 0

100940

1999

100

0

Managing Systems Development

Second edition

Jeffrey S. Keen

OXSTALLS CAMPUS LIBRARY

CHELTENHAM & GLOUCESTER
COLLEGE OF HIGHER EDUCATION
Oxstalls Lane, Gloucester GL2 9HW
Tel: (0452) 426718 004.068
KEE

JOHN WILEY & SONS

Chichester · New York · Brisbane · Toronto · Singapore

Copyright © 1981, 1987 by John Wiley & Sons Ltd.

All rights reserved.

No part of this book may be reproduced by any means, or transmitted, or translated into a machine language without the written permission of the publisher.

Library of Congress Cataloging-in-Publication Data:

Keen, Jeffrey S.
  Managing systems development.

  (Wiley series in information processing)
  Includes index.
  1. Electronic data processing departments—Management.
I. Title. II. Series.
HF5548.2.K39 1987   658′.05   86–15948

ISBN 0 471 91244 1

British Library Cataloguing in Publication Data:

Keen, Jeffrey S.
  Managing systems development.—2nd ed.

  —(Wiley series in information processing).
  1. Business—Data processing
  I. Title
  651.8   HF5548.2

ISBN 0 471 91244 1

Phototypesetting by Thomson Press (India) Limited, New Delhi
Printed and bound in Great Britain

To
Marilyn, Alexandra, and Olivia

Contents

APPENDIXES

Preface to first edition

I have worked in the computer industry for over twenty years in many varied capacities. Time and again, when acting as a consultant, or in a trouble-shooting role, or when in general contact with numerous computer installations, I came up against the same difficulties and mistakes in the way that organizations manage their DP. It seems unfortunate that so many managers must learn the hard way, struggling through similar learning processes. The aggregate money wasted by all these organizations is frightening!

How then can a data processing professional improve his own and his department's performance? Apart from on-the-job experience (which is often too late, or too slow) a popular method is to attend training courses (which may cover only a narrow spectrum), or to employ consultants (who also may have a limited brief). Currently available books rarely seem to be applicable in practice when an organization is experiencing difficulties. The market lacks a definitive text which covers both the theory and practice of system development and project management.

The combined topics of computing and management in current literature, often tend to be concerned with technical computing (for the specialist); with introductory computing for the business layman; or with ways computers can be used by management in its organization. There are not many books that relate the management aspects of the development of computerized business systems to the problems of business line management. Similarly, available literature fails to show how the technical requirements of the computer industry affect the practical way in which organizations are structured to use their computers commercially and effectively.

This book, therefore, attempts to illuminate some of the many problem areas in the managerial aspects of developing and installing computerized business systems. The text represents an accumulation, over a period of several years, of my ideas based on observations of both good and bad DP departments, coupled with copious notes made whilst working at numerous installations. These ideas have been augmented and refined as a result of general conversations with colleagues in the DP industry, notes taken whilst attending conferences or courses, and occasionally on reading thought-provoking articles. Also included are notes and feedback from presentations I have given to first-time user management (in organizations having their own computer) and to senior

xi

management of organizations acquiring their own first computer. The intension is to pass on practical advice (which to the author's knowledge is not readily available in other publications), and not to quote or paraphrase other authors.

As an aid for the practical manager, the text covers the planning and management of the entire development cycle of computer systems. This problem is examined not only from the viewpoint of the system development function within the computer department, but also from the organization's business requirements and the management of the development projects set up by the organization to develop computerized systems. Practical solutions are given to justifying and budgeting systems and projects, planning them with accurate estimates and minimum risks, motivating staff and measuring progress, and also to the interesting subject of politics within an organization and a DP project in particular.

The reader should be primarily a DP professional. As the text aims towards an advanced level, hopefully even the most experienced will learn something worthwhile from these pages. Teachers and students of DP may also find this book useful as supplementary reading for further education courses. This book is, therefore, addressed to all levels of management within a computer department and new or aspiring managers.

Although it is written from the viewpoint of organizations that manage their own DP, the issues raised should interest all computer manufacturing and servicing companies—in fact, anyone involved in making computers work.

With the advent of distributed data processing systems, and low cost computer hardware, more local management are forced to be responsible for their computerized business systems. It is intended that the text should appeal to this wider range of managers by facilitating their acquisition of expertise in DP management.

The reader should be able to extract and adopt those concepts that he feels are relevant to improve effectiveness in his own installation, and in his own job. After reading this book, managers should be in a position to appreciate the areas in which they could become involved personally, and what form their participation should take. Because of the connections between chapters, it is recommended that first the book be read in its entirety. The writing of this book will have been justified if it is not read just once for general interest, but if it finds its place as a daily reference to assist management in its work.

The text has been kept brief and concise for easy management assimilation. It has been assumed that the practical manager is too busy to check each section of the text against cross-references to other publications in order to 'substantiate the academic authenticity' of recommendations. As this book relates to management concepts, the detailed technical aspects of computing are not introduced. Similarly, the technical or management aspects of running live production work, or upgrading or replacing existing computers are not considered, as the purpose of the book is to cover the development side of computerized systems, as distinct from the hardware and its environment.

Certain project management aspects relating to the special case of commercial tendering, the negotiation of contracts and the legal aspects associated with projects of this nature, have been excluded deliberately. This omission has been felt necessary, because these general subjects have been well aired in other publications, and they do not relate to the major methods of in-house DP development within most organizations.

The management philosophies discussed here should apply to the majority of projects, irrespective of their actual 'product' or of the computerized system being developed. Throughout this book, the text is equally applicable to developing new systems, as well as to enhancing existing ones. To avoid repetition, cumbersome phraseology, and to improve clarity of the concepts being discussed, the text refers simply to new systems. No lack of emphasis is intended for enhancement work; only where differences apply is the subject raised explicitly.

The book is structured so that chapters proceed sequentially from topic to topic in a flow, that starts at the highest levels of management and then works down to the lower levels. Similarly, the topics appear logically in a chronological sequence. Several appendices provide practical checklists, which could be useful to managers when setting assignments, or when reviewing work.

When practical, each chapter covers the types of problems faced by small, medium, or large computer installations. The projects that these installations are called upon to deal with, will have varied problems or priorities. Where appropriate, the text discusses not only the management approaches that are required for different sized organizations, computer departments or projects, but also the change of emphasis that may arise during each phase of a project. Practical examples are liberally dispersed to illustrate points raised.

For the reader's convenience, many key words and descriptive phrases appear in italic, and the reader is advised of the connotation placed on certain terms used. The words 'organization', 'company', and 'corporation' may be interchanged, as can the words 'directors', 'senior management', and 'presidents/vice-presidents'. The terms 'a computer department', 'DP department', or just simply 'an installation' embraces the corporate DP function, whilst an 'information systems division', or 'management services division' exists in organizations whose computer department has a wider brief than just computing. The part of the computer department responsible for running jobs on the actual hardware is termed an 'operations department' or 'DP operations'. In common usage, the word 'system' is vague and can apply to many things. Where appropriate, the text refers to the different types of systems.

Bournemouth   JEFFREY S. KEEN

Preface to second edition

Since publication of the first edition of *Managing Systems Development*, the DP scene has continued to advance rapidly. Computing has taken on a broader role than just data processing, which is reflected in the phrase, currently in vogue, *information systems* (or information processing). Additionally, computing is evolving from a back-room administration and accounting tool into a more corporate and strategic role that is essential to improve an organization's competitive edge.

Summarized below are the main areas of change that influence the development of application systems. Although most of these topics were mentioned in the previous edition of *Managing Systems Development*, they are now given greater emphasis with the incorporation of additional practical comment, based on experience.

The *microcomputer* has had a major impact on both hardware and software, with the growing importance of *micro–mainframe links* to the corporate database. The allied technologies of *viewdata* and *communications* have provided further tools for the application system developer, as has the gradual introduction of *office automation* concepts. *Data-bases* have grown in popularity, with the market taking a greater interest in *relational*, rather than hierarchical or other systems. *Fourth generation languages* (often associated with a proprietory database management system) have gained wide acceptance as a means for improving the productivity of systems development work, often in conjunction with their use for *prototyping*. The latter is one of many techniques that require management to take a new look at the *system development project life cycle*. In particular, many new *development methodologies* are gaining acceptance. These lead to the *automation of the system development process*, with the resultant substantial productivity gains. Coupled with this is a clearer role for the *quality assurance* and *data administration* functions, which are tending to converge.

Not only do the users of the traditional data processing department benefit from all the previously mentioned trends, but *end-user computing* (whereby users are responsible for some of their own development of information systems) is gaining acceptance as a sound approach. The growth in *decision support software* enhances this trend, with *expert systems* (a form of decision support software) moving from the academic to the commercial world. *Information centres* have been established by many organizations to encourage this process of end-user computing, acting as a corporate focal point, and disseminating the necessary expertise to the end users. As organizations become dependent on their computers, with a growing number of skilled people being given friendlier access, the twin threats of *security and privacy* assume increasing importance.

All the above topics require management consideration and action. It is hoped that this edition of *Managing Systems Development* will provide relevant and practical advice to those managers involved with the development of information systems.

Chapter 1

Introduction

SOURCES OF TROUBLE IN MANAGING DATA PROCESSING

Most managers of DP have experienced some, if not most, of the types of troubles that are illustrated in Figure 1.1. Before attempting to recommend solutions it is sensible to start with some analysis and so a selection of these

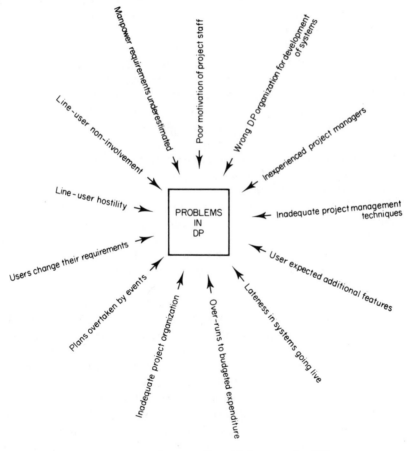

Figure 1.1   Sources of trouble in managing DP

troubles will be explored in order to achieve an understanding of how and why many of them arise. Effort and money are only expended on computerized systems so that the line user departments and not the computer department may benefit. Accordingly, it is good policy for the line departments to be given a degree of control over the *business* aspects of their computer projects, preferably at senior management level. Some senior line managers have preferred to remain only minimally involved in the development and implementation of computerized systems, making the DP professional's job more difficult. In other instances, well-meaning senior management involvement has swung the other way, with too much attention being paid to the wrong details. Frustrated DP management, lower DP productivity, or the development of unsuitable systems are often a result.

A frequently-heard complaint is that some computer line users may be unhelpful, being reluctant to assume their responsibilities. They may be critical of the management of computer departments which are supposed to benefit them. Frequently this is because their previous experience has been unfortunate. Promised objectives have been achieved only partially, or the original planning and estimating was over optimistic. Accordingly, the line users are now mistrustful.

A common cause of these shortcomings is that, conventionally, a computer analyst is given responsibility for the development and implementation of a substantial business application system. In practice, he may not have the essential management tools for managing projects, or sufficient management status to guarantee success. Also he may not have had the correct business experience to enable him to exercise the right judgement when compromises have to be made. In addition, the analyst may have had insufficient experience in managing projects (a) to appreciate the numerous components of a project which require planning and control, or (b) to divide a project into precise, quantifiable units or checkpoints.

In the rapidly fluctuating climate of modern business, various people may try to force the computer department to accept impractical tasks and deadlines. The result may be that rushed, unjustified, and *ad hoc* jobs are run on the computer, contrary to good computing practice and effective strategic management. Adverse comments on the quality of output may then be received from the board downwards.

The recent dramatic growth in minicomputers, microcomputers, and in distributed data processing has made a significant impact on the management aspects of developing business systems which utilize these new technologies. Reductions in cost, coupled with the communications ability of these small computers allowing them to be sited in remote locations, affects management in several ways. First, managers who previously were only on the fringe of DP may now have to take a more direct responsibility with the development and running of systems on their own satellite computer. Secondly, the great reduction in the cost required to install and run one of these computer systems need to be matched by lower development costs. This in turn, means aiming for reduced management overheads, using cheaper resources, and possibly employing a lower grade of staff than for, say, larger projects. This may then lead to an undesirable reduction in DP standards, and to the disregard (or unawareness) of management techniques which have been learned whilst working on mainframes, but may still be relevant to these limited budget development projects.

A further difficulty experienced in some organizations is that small cheaper computers invite individual divisions or departments to rush out and buy their own, sometimes without prior consultations with the established centralized computer department. The subsequent unco-ordinated mushrooming of computers throughout an organization may not only cause embarrassment to the DP management (who are often faced with a 'fait accompli', or are informed when it is too late to propose superior alternatives), but also it may be symptomatic of a lack of strategic DP plans for satisfying the organization's needs in a more effective and controlled manner.

Summary of the sources of problems

In summarizing the above, we see that there is a broad spectrum of problems which will be discussed in this book. They range from the possibility of the line department users not assuming their responsibilities (for various reasons), to senior managers declining to become involved as they are not sure what they are supposed to control and how they are to control it; or the wrong manager with inappropriate qualities is delegated to take control. Included in this is the conflict of business pressures requiring quick results which may be contrary to good development standards.

Lower down the management hierarchy, the wrong level of person is often held responsible for developing a computerized system, who is possibly not acquainted with the appropriate planning and control techniques. Poor motivation of DP staff may sometimes ensue. Finally, distributed computing may mean that managers new to DP might be made responsible for installing their own mini or microcomputer system. Coupled with this, a strain may be placed on the traditional control exercised by the centralized computer department.

SYNOPSIS OF EACH CHAPTER

Chapter 1: Introduction

Some analysis of relevant problem areas in DP work

Chapter 2: Corporate Aspects of Developing Computer Systems

The text first examines the reasons why an organization could need a new computerized system, but warns of the difficulties of adhering to these corporate ideals and objectives during the (lengthy) process that builds the new system. It then looks at the earliest stages of managing the development process.

Having defined what are the benefits of a project approach, and related it to the political framework of an organization, advice is given on setting up a corporate project, which develops the computerized system, and how this project is subsequently managed at the highest levels.

Chapter 3: Projects and the Computer Department

Effective organization of the computer department is discussed, suggesting how it should interact with corporate projects, how best to facilitate the system development process, and how it incorporates ideas relating to joint line user and computer department projects. Ways of handling live production work and post live system and enhancement are also discussed.

Chapter 4: Costs, Benefits, and Budgets

This chapter on budgets distinguishes between the corporate budget, the computer department's budget, the DP operations budget and the budget of an individual project. Also detailed is a comprehensive method of budgeting that could form a basis for justifying the project, and for its subsequent financial control.

Chapter 5: The Management of Developing Different Types of Systems

The next level of management responsibility for the system development process is explained. Advice is given on defining in quantifiable terms, the relative sizes, complexities and risk factors of projects. This could be useful when justifying projects, and in the recommended project planning and control process. Consideration is also given to the project's end-product in conceptual terms, which relate to other application systems within the computer industry, and to the technologies planned to be employed. These discussions form the basis for strategic decisions that must be made by the system development management function.

Chapter: 6 The Particular End-Product

The text moves from generalities to specifics, and defines the planning required for a particular end-product. This is important because the latter is difficult to define in black and white terms, and in large integrated systems, may become amoeba-like, being difficult to keep within continual grasp and under complete control.

Chapter 7: How the End-Product will be Constructed and Controlled

A feature of the book is the extensive treatment of the predictability of the components of a project, which require planning, monitoring, and controlling (i.e. management in its widest sense). This chapter elaborates on *how* the end-product (as defined above) will be constructed and controlled, how changes in specification are kept in check, how the development process will be administered and supported, and how the data requirement and the files are designed.

Chapter 8: Standards and Techniques

The topic of 'standards' causes many DP professionals to 'switch off'. This chapter continues the theme of how the end-product will be built, by taking a *practical* view of the minimum DP standards required, and couples them with useful techniques that facilitate systems development. Discussions regarding the thorny problem of documentation conclude this chapter.

Chapter 9: Testing

An explanation is given as to why testing may take up half of a project's resources, and advice is offered in formulating a testing strategy, quantifying the number of errors anticipated, planning what steps should be taken in testing, and who should complete them. Techniques to facilitate testing both new systems and maintenance are included, as well as suggestions relating to which testing utilities and aids may be usefully employed.

Chapter 10: Project Planning and Re-Planning

An extensive chapter on project planning starts by defining the purpose and extent of planning, and how a manager should and should not use planning. Detail is given of a structured approach to planning, when it should occur, and how *practical* plans are both iterative and evolving. No plan is complete without detailed consideration of the possible risks, and the ways of minimizing them with contingency plans during the implementation of the project. Finally, an examination is made of the consequences of the (parochial) project's planning on the rest of the DP department, and the organization as a whole.

Chapter 11: Project Organization and Structure

Up to now, manpower has been treated as a resource, not as individual people requiring skilled management. This chapter starts by identifying the staffing constituents of a project, the skills required and a general reporting structure. The discussions include information on how projects themselves are organized and structured, examples of how these change for different phases of development, and on the importance of practical considerations of management styles, personal relationships and the resulting political situations that arise when implementing a project. Examples are given of larger and smaller projects.

Chapter 12: People Management

This chapter commences with an analysis of the desirable personal qualities required at all levels of DP management. Traditional methods of motivating staff are augmented by some additional observations, and practical advice, relevant to DP, is given on such topics as corporate personnel policies, staff deployment, career development, training, recruitment, and appraisals.

Chapter 13: Project Control

An analysis is conducted of what is project control, why it is only a sub-set of project management, who is responsible for project control, and why each level of management sees project control in a different light. Various control techniques are covered, together with recommendations on their relevance to different types of management plans. The knotty, but universal problem of measuring progress is tackled, and this leads to specifying the requirements of quantitative project control systems, that give reliable end dates well in advance. Examples of these are given, together with advice on what to do when difficulties occur, and on the subject of written upwards reporting.

Chapter 14: DP/User Relationships and the Conclusion

The important topic of professionalism is covered, and coupled with the relationship between users and the computer department. Typical problem areas are highlighted (including communication and improving users' awareness of DP), together with possible solutions. The book concludes by bringing together the more important themes being advocated, and suggests that the responsibility for introducing these improvements to his own organization must primarily rest with the DP professional.

Chapter 2

Corporate aspects of developing computer systems

The reasons are examined why an organization, or part of it, could need a new computerized system, but warnings are given of the difficulties in adhering to these corporate ideals and objectives during the (lengthy) process that builds the new system. The earliest stages of managing the development process are discussed. A definition is given as to what constitutes a project and relates it to the political framework of an organization. Advice is given on setting up a corporate project which develops the computerized system, and how this project is subsequently managed at the highest levels. Although an emphasis may appear to be made on new systems, there is no reason why a project cannot involve enhancements to existing systems.

THE CORPORATE OBJECTIVE(S)

As this book relates to the management of developing systems, a reasonable starting point is to examine some of the reasons why an organization might wish to develop a computerized system, and to illustrate some of the derived benefits for the business functions involved. The corporate heart of the business requirements relating to computing is examined, and those management decisions which can be taken locally by the relevant line managers are indicated. The discussions mainly relate to the beginning of the system development cycle, and they elaborate on the overall corporate planning process.

Why introduce a computer application system?

There are several categories of benefits to be derived from commercial computer application systems, ranging from improved profitability to handling large volumes of data. At this stage we are not too concerned with the type of computerized system that produces these benefits, as the latter are similar whether say a batch, a distributed data processing, a real-time, or a micro-computer system, is contemplated. As anyone battle-worn in system development knows, developing even an apparently simple system is fraught with difficulties. An organization will only be motivated to embark on the traumatic system development path if the anticipated benefits at the end of the road are worth it. Are these reasons for developing an application system absolute

7

(i.e. couched in black and white terms) as many observers would claim, or are they relative and diffuse ideals created out of the organization's political framework? Let us examine how corporate objectives relating to DP evolve, and how checks and balances form part of the process.

Identifying potential corporate systems

How does an organization systematically find potential computer applications and set corporate priorities? The problem is a mixture of identifying (1) self-contained existing functions which require to be mechanized or enhanced, and (2) more significant key areas, where an application could have an important effect on the organization's profits or on its survival. The latter applications frequently have a high cost-effectiveness when implemented. Organizations employing corporate planning techniques, or management by objectives, or even long-term business plans will be acquainted with the following criteria for identifying key applications.

The fundamental question for senior executives is to determine the purpose and direction of the organization. These executives must impose any legal or moral restraints. Frequently, this purpose is related to the profitability to shareholders, but hospital boards, police authorities, education authorities, government bodies, etc. who can be significant commercial computer users, obviously have a different emphasis on fundamental purpose. Having determined this purpose and its associated long-term objectives, it is possible to identify internal corporate strengths and weaknesses, together with external opportunities and threats.

The next stage is to identify approximately six vital areas that are essential, in order that the organization achieves its purpose. Not all of these areas can utilize computer applications, as they could include diversifying into a new product, raising capital, or acquiring a new factory. The problems within these vital areas must therefore, be analysed in order to establish whether computer applications are appropriate and cost effective. This is not as straightforward as it appears. For example, if a vital problem area is cash flow, a proposal for developing a fast computerized order and despatch application system may not necessarily induce the customers to pay their bills any quicker than with the old system.

Consequently, it is not only necessary to determine carefully the cost benefits of any major application system, but also its practical relation to corporate problem areas; its purpose to the organization; and most important, the measure for judging the application's success in terms of corporate profitability, or survival. Obviously, this overall sequence is time-consuming, difficult, and requires experience. As the process is carried out infrequently, it may be possible for an organization to utilize consultants, or perhaps involve, to a limited extent, a computer hardware manufacturer, to supply the necessary expertise.

Finding new computerized systems in general

Having discussed corporate application systems, many worthwhile systems either may not come into this category or the organization might not have the necessary long-term strategic planning mechanism. Accordingly, the process of how new application systems are initiated could be more of an art than a precise science. In practice, there is a share of responsibility between project managers, systems development managers, DP managers, senior line management, and the line departments. The actual motivating factor depends mainly on personalities. A healthy state is indicated by the line department users frequently requesting practical new applications. There are numerous sources of inspiration for new application systems, and these are listed below:

1. Some projects are set up specifically to investigate potential new computer application systems.
2. An ongoing project may have been set up to initiate and implement say, retailing systems, and accordingly this should provide a continuous stream of new relevant systems.
3. An organization could be motivated into looking for new computer applications as a result of their competitors or industry adopting similar systems.
4. Some organizations will have a separate systems planning function within the computer department concerned with new ideas and applications. It may be staffed by full-time consultants or technical specialists reporting say, to the systems development manager.
5. Some larger development projects engage the above 'ideas' people full-time into the project.
6. The hardware and software suppliers' sales representatives constantly will be endeavouring to sell new applications as the means of selling more equipment. In fact, apart from the normal technical information, the hardware supplier can be used for obtaining information about the computing of other companies who are in the same industry, including details of their applications and problems they have experienced. This is a good method of initiating ideas for new computer application systems. In general, the hardware manufacturer does not always have detailed technical knowledge concerning the application, but this knowledge is usually sufficient at the initial stages of the system development process. Even more important is that the hardware or software supplier has the contacts, enabling further 'follow-ups' and visits to be arranged with other companies so that first-hand practical detail may be obtained.
7. In certain organizations, initiating new systems may be carried out by a business systems analyst, or an O and M department. This approach is not recommended unless there is doubt as to whether a computer solution is required. A good approach is for the head of the computer department, in discussions with his managers, to give the initial study to senior systems analysts, possibly promoted from other existing projects. The analysts assigned to this appraisal can be business, technical, computing or clerically

orientated, depending on the new system under consideration. In general, systems analysts often consider that project initiation is one of the more desirable jobs and regard it a promotion. (This also has the secondary benefit in that junior systems analysts can be promoted in existing projects to replace these more senior people). A good systems analyst will create an interactive dialogue with the line user(s). Using his experience he will ask the right questions, marry the answers to the latest technology and techniques, and put application ideas to the potential users, and in turn will receive useful and practical comments and reactions.

It is apparent that the spark which kindles the initiation and justification of a new computer system can originate from many different sources. The motivation for the subsequent development depends on the drive of particular individuals, as well as the enthusiasm of the organization.

The manager responsible for system development, and his staff, should ask for a wide brief in investigating new applications. However, to be successful in the long term, they need a breadth of vision and great depth of experience.

The need for corporate involvement at the highest levels

Having ascertained a set of objectives and a potential application system, the initial claimed benefits may include one or more of the following:

Improving productivity; reducing office equipment costs; coping with increased volumes; peak-load processing; improving accuracy; better customer service; improving cash flows; improving management information and control; reducing levels of stock.

Sometimes a computerized system (or an enhancement to it) is essential because there is no alternative method of carrying out the function.

On contemplating the above categories of benefits, several points are illustrated. First, a computer application system is introduced in order to allow a line department to improve its cost-effective performance, and consequently improve the organization's total profitability. It is only the line (not the computer) department that can produce this profitability. The computer department can only act as a catalyst or assist the line. For this reason the line user must be deeply involved in, and committed to, all aspects of *his* computer applications.

Secondly, the greatest benefits derived from a computerized system usually occur in areas related to fundamental corporate objectives, such as reduced operating costs, increased market share, or improved cash flow. These categories of anticipated benefits need to be identified and justified at the highest corporate levels unlike, say, the more easily identified and defined payroll, bought ledger, or statement applications, which can carry out existing functions cheaper, faster, or more accurately. Larger companies, in particular, may need several different divisions involved (e.g. marketing, production, distribution, and head office administration) in order to implement a fundamental corporate objective. Cutting across company boundaries is a characteristic of project management, and is another reason for stressing the need for a corporate involvement in developing computer application systems, preferably at the highest levels. However, this will be discussed later.

DP management's confirmation

Although the list of anticipated benefits for a proposed system are firmly user orientated, there is a definite need for DP management to be in a sufficiently influential position to confirm that the proposed benefits are attainable. It is the more senior DP professional who should have the experience of knowing in advance the limitations of a system once it has been implemented. Where necessary, he needs to dampen the enthusiasm of a user manager who may be expecting too much. The senior DP professional, in this situation, has the dual role of a business consultant as well as his more normal technical management responsibility. To this end, Appendix 1 sets out some practical comments on each category of system benefits, suggests the level of management held responsible for each category, and highlights possible reasons why anticipated benefits may not be achieved in practice.

An example of anticipated benefits which were not achieved
A national builders' merchant was concerned that its customers were taking an average of nearly three months from the date of delivery to pay. Invoices were being sent several weeks after delivery of goods, and statements were sent monthly. Even a discount for prompt payment did not encourage settlement of accounts. The Board decided to change from the decentralized (but generally well-run) clerical system, to a centralized fully-computerized pre-invoice system, which included a facility for invoices to be sent to a customer's head office for payment, on or before the customer's branch office or building site received the goods.

When the system eventually went live, it coincided with a credit squeeze and depression in the building industry. Customers paid no quicker, and in fact, used the system as a means of obtaining free credit, and in particular, gave the excuse of not settling until queries on an invoice had been resolved. There were also delays caused by customers reconciling part delivery goods received notes to invoices. In fact, the anticipated benefit of improved cash flow did not materialize, and the situation was the same as when the clerical system was in existence.

THE DIFFICULTY OF KEEPING TO THESE OBJECTIVES

Having ascertained and agreed realistic objectives for a new computerized system, all subsequent management actions relating to both the development process and to the running of the final application system must, in theory, relate to these original corporate objectives. Such management actions include setting up development projects; justifying facilities available in the system; allocating budgets; and managing the project's resources. However, this section illustrates the difficulty the DP manager experiences in adhering to these objectives, and even in attempting to review progress against these objectives.

The conflict between user benefits, DP benefits and corporate benefits

It is one thing determining a business need and proposing a system to meet it. It is another thing to execute the proposals. For example, even if user and DP management agree the obvious importance of introducing a new system, the method of implementation may cause conflict. In practice, what may appear as a benefit to a user may be bad news for the DP manager. The following example illustrates the general problem.

An example of the conflict between user, DP, and corporate benefits
An electronics company decided to diversify from producing small commercial products to manufacturing relatively complex industrial equipment. Orders were coming in faster than anticipated, and the clerical production control system (which was devised for this product) could not cope. Although the company had an adequate computerized production/ stock control system for its existing products, it was known to be unsuitable for the new complex equipment. There was complete agreement from all parties for the need for a computerized system. The (forceful) management responsible for launching the new product were demanding their own tailor-made system, with their own data files, run on their own mini-computer, and developed within a few months by a software house. This system would not be useful for the rest of company. The electronics company's own DP department preferred (for operational reasons, as well as to facilitate interfacing with other systems) only one production system which could be achieved by modifying the existing production control system. However, budgetary and resource limitations, together with technical considerations, suggested that 18 months was a more realistic target than within a few months.

The corporate benefit, in this example, was the compromise solution whereby the DP department would make some quick changes as part of maintenance to enable the user to run, on an interim basis, a part-clerical and part-computerized production system, pending the development of a fully-computerized system that integrated with the company's other systems and data bases.

Agreeing an objective is relatively easy; implementing it is a series of difficult compromises. The answer is rarely black and white, but results from political manoeuvrings in which individuals press for the 'best' corporate benefit, as they see it.

Going astray during the lengthy development process

Having ascertained a business objective, and having agreed a strategy for implementing the required new system, DP management can still easily lose sight of the overall objectives. This especially applies to larger projects, which usually require a lengthy development process. There are several causes that may include a changed business climate, or changes of management personnel, or changed requirements during the extensive period (often months or years) necessary to develop the system. Another example of deviation from objectives, is that during the development process, a project can easily convert a staff shortage problem into a mammoth recruiting and DP training exercise of perhaps, graduates or line personnel. This may deflect the project's management from the task at hand. Similarly, to overcome a technical problem, significant resources, say, can be shifted into developing file handling routines, or testing programs. In the eyes of the project's staff, these become the major factors in the project, whose principal objectives appear now to get these technical aspects working at all costs.

The following example illustrates how this phenomenon may arise.

An example of going astray during the (lengthy) development process
A large insurance company had a poor field credibility, caused by errors in statements and in the commission paid. Quite rightly, the managing director chaired a high-level DP steering committee which agreed that a fully-computerized commissions system was not only vital to improving the company's business, but also there was a saving of 32 clerical staff. This was confirmed by the Management Services Department, and the project's go-ahead was ratified without any difficulty at board level.

During the course of the eventual two-year development period, memories faded and three major areas of difficulty arose which caused the project to deviate from the original clear-cut business objectives. A substantial staff deficiency in programmers and system designers identified early on by the project manager, caused him inadvertently, during this period of pressure, to see the project's primary objective as an extensive recruiting and training exercise. On the other hand, the senior systems designer (and the chief programmer) saw as the primary objective of the project, (especially as their deadlines slipped) the development of some in-house file handling software, which they regarded as essential for the efficient running of the live system on the mainframe. The third difficulty was caused by the system development manager's strong desire to use several new structured programming techniques. However, insufficient training was given in their use, development was consequently slowed down, and, in particular, documentation was found to be unusable for coding and for testing. The pressures of rectifying this situation caused the systems development manager to lose sight of the project's original objectives and he saw the primary problem as that of implementing new techniques.

The system was by now several months' late. A few weeks before going live, during a casual conversation between the project manager and the user's senior manager, the latter let slip that there would be no clerical savings after all, and during the prolonged system development period, corporate, industry and government requirements had resulted in many more new reports having to be produced which were not planned as part of the computerized system. Furthermore, the current clerical system had been improved significantly and user management felt it was now secure. On the other hand, credibility in the new computerized system had sunk to a low (1) with the sales force in the field, because the system did not go live on the original (or the revised) target date, and (2) with the user, because controls, in the system were suspect.

However, it had become apparent to the head of management services, and via him to the financial director, that the main purpose of the system was now completely different. During system tests, many anomalies came to light regarding data pertaining to policy details and premium payments which came from several feeder systems. The primary purpose of the commissions system was now to stop agents and brokers 'bending' the rules, and as a means of recovering excessive over-payments of commissions.

This example illustrates how a project's purpose changed during development, from precise business objectives, via three sets of DP objectives, to a completely new business objective.

How does one attempt to overcome this difficulty of keeping to objectives, and avoid going astray? In principle, the answer is obvious: review against objectives. This leads to further questions (such as who does the reviewing?, how is it done?, when is it performed?, and with what information?). The answers to this, the business review, shall be deferred to later in this chapter.

STRATEGIC PLANNING

Evolving from objectives, management's thoughts concentrate on formulating a sound strategy for implementing a new system. This section on strategic planning again only serves as an introduction to the concepts. It is more appropriate to discuss solutions in later chapters, where strategic planning leads to tactical decisions which in turn, may include such factors as an in-house or bureau approach; maintaining existing systems or developing new ones; introducing the system in one go or staging the introduction of facilities, etc.

Strategic planning is not only an essential part of sound business practice, but also a means of motivating staff to produce maximum output, as well as designing sound computer systems for the future. A computer team, project or department, cannot function to its ultimate capabilities without a strategy. The situation is comparable to the proverbial 'ship without a helm'. It is essential for the manager to create, (in conjunction with his staff) ambitions, goals, objectives, or strategies—call them what you will. They all point to where the team is going. It is possible that some of these attainments will never be reached, but this is immaterial.

Examples of the consequences of poor strategic planning

The symptoms of not having any sound DP strategy may include the following:

1. Small insignificant *ad hoc* systems with minimum co-ordination and integration.
2. User management demanding excessive quick one-off jobs.
3. Possible management ideas of what could be done in the future, but no plans of how to do it.
4. Within about 3 to 4 years of introducing DP, a whole host of systems existing that are inadequate for changed markets, new products, or new government requirements.
5. The members of the department or the project being even more disgruntled than the average systems analysts or programmers, and probably being sent on numerous irrelevant training courses to keep them happy. Few of these courses may apply to the person's immediate career development, for the courses are too sophisticated to be applicable to the immediate needs of the department or project.
6. The whole computer department rapidly becoming *event driven* by the line users and their senior management, who require results quickly and cannot understand why an apparently simple job will take several months to complete. This state is usually symptomatic of a poor overall computer system development philosophy. Eventually the computing department's management will be forced to justify to senior management their response to every user request.
7. A high computer staff turnover, which is a possible sign of a strategic problem, but even more important, it may be noticed that the best people are leaving.
8. In an attempt to keep staff, the salaries of the computer department tend to increase faster than the computer industry average.

In practice, the highest levels of an organization down to the computer department or a project, must introduce strategic planning to include not only what the organization's data processing will look like in say three to five years' time, but also positive ideas on structure of the teams; organization; control; standards; staff development—in fact, everything concerned with working in a proper and professional manner.

Use of the supplier

The hardware and/or software suppliers' technical experts should not only be used for advising on the best use of hardware, they should also become involved in planning the system, the file structure, the programming, and the software strategies. This mainly applies to new, major, or state of the art applications; where the objective is to minimize risk, speed up implementation, reduce the eventual run-times, or obtain maximum utilization of say, a new direct access device.

It is highly desirable and reassuring if the hardware supplier signs-off its agreement to a project's strategy and tactics inasmuch detail as possible. In general, a careful balance has to be struck between involving the hardware supplier too much (and being unable to stand on one's own feet, or being oversold), and not using the supplier correctly or sufficiently to obtain the above benefits.

WHY BOTHER WITH A PROJECT?

It should be apparent that profitable computer applications are a substantial *corporate responsibility*, and it is the line user that produces and receives the benefits. Additionally, as the development of any application may have a duration of several years, not only must the relevant line departments be involved *continuously* with this development process, but they may possibly *supply* 30% of the necessary resources. A good method of combining this continuous corporate responsibility with a line department's supply of resources is by the organization setting up a project, with a sophisticated project management philosophy, which implements the proposed computerized application.

What is a computer development project?

This section is an introduction to the meaning of the term 'project'. In common terminology, the word 'project' could be applied to any human activity involving the development, and hopefully the subsequent achievement, of a specified one-off end-product. This book restricts the use of the word 'project' by:

(a) applying the term solely to the development of systems running on computers
(b) limiting the term 'project' to a formal management methodology that involves phased and structured management, planning and control
(c) implying that only substantial (and not trivial) applications are being developed.

This usage means that a project is not any clearly delineated task just lasting a few days, but a significantly complex assignment requiring several people and a project management approach. A project is something substantial that is often measured in man years (as opposed to man days) or thousands of dollars or pounds—even in smaller companies.

When is a formal project approach appropriate?

When is it appropriate for senior management to adopt a formal project approach? As an overview to some formalized guidelines, it is the author's experience that:

1. the successful conclusion to developing computer application systems bears a strong relationship to the adoption of a formal project approach
2. the degree of project formality that is required to be adopted bears a strong relationship to the presence and extent of certain development factors which include:

(a) the size and number of *interactions* of the development process (e.g. the number of departments involved)
(b) the *technical complexity* (e.g. a conventional local batch system with a 24 hour turn-round, or a more demanding geographically spread interrogation system with a few seconds response time)
(c) the *complexity* of the *business* application system, (e.g. a straightforward production of a file listing, or a stock control system using operational research techniques for optimizing stock levels)
(d) the *newness* of the proposed technology (e.g. the first user of a new generation of hardware or an operating system)
(e) the *risk* of financial loss to a customer or user. This may even apply to a

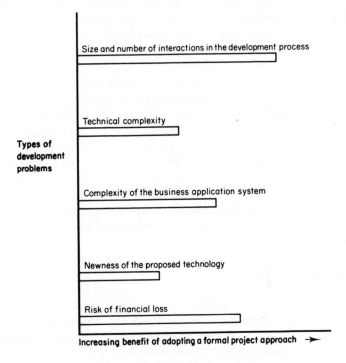

Figure 2.1   A pictorial overview of anticipated management problem areas during the development of an application system (N.B. The benefits are cumulative for each type of problem)

small research project where the consequential financial gains could be large if say, a new product emerges.

3. the total benefits of adopting a formal project approach are *cumulative* on the presence and extent of these factors, 2(a)–(e). Figure 2.1 illustrates this conceptually, for assessing a particular system to be developed.

At this stage in the argument, it is not necessary to quantify these factors, which are subjects in their own right and are elaborated in subsequent sections.

The benefits of project management

The main reason for introducing a project approach is akin to taking out an insurance policy for success. Even though this decision results in cost overheads for project management, these might easily outweigh the consequences of having to pay possible overrun penalties, or the large effect of adverse publicity if the project should fail.

How would the development process take place without a project? The main difference would be a lack of a *centralized management intelligence*. People who have attempted extensive building works at home by engaging separate self-employed plumbers, carpenters, plasterers, brick-layers, etc. will possibly have sympathetic views on the need to assign centralized management. In an organization developing a large application system, the alternative to a centralized project management approach might consist of a *committee* of representatives from the participants, including the user departments and sub-contractors. Unfortunately, the system being developed usually only represents a small part of these individual people's job; as well as a small percentage of the organizations turnover; and a minor part of each committee member's responsibilities. Human nature, being what it is, will ensure that these people are not well briefed at committee meetings, or are not personally committed. Similarly it is difficult to negotiate trade-offs, or to *optimize* cost, time and performance if the meetings become (1) politically charged and (2) comprise participants who may possess insufficient detail. In addition, if these committees (of senior management) meet frequently, the *cost* of this approach to a project could, in fact, be greater than the cost of an alternative project management overhead.

Committees are an easy way of off-loading personal responsibilities, especially in organizations with much internal politics. It is then difficult to assign blame for a failure—'it was always the committees decision!'. Similarly, it is an obvious ploy to adopt a committee approach when management is unsure of what to do. Committees are also notorious for slowing down progress! Another disadvantage of a committee approach is that there is usually not a separate controlled budget for the system under development. Line departments could spend an uncontrolled amount on alleged project activities. Project management, on the other hand, necessitates a centralized project budget and thus prevents unnecessary and unauthorized expenditure. The project approach might, therefore, exercise additional *cost control* on both user line department managers, as well as on managers in the computer department.

A final benefit for project management is also cost-related. It is derived from savings in *time*. Assuming delivery of an end-product is earlier than by other means, a project should reduce the servicing of capital employed, as well as bring in positive cash flows sooner. In addition, assuming that a project efficiently organizes its activities, delays between interacting departments should be minimized, reducing wasted time, and unnecessary costs.

The disadvantages of project management

Apart from the extra cost and overheads of project management, there is a project set-up and disbanding cost, coupled with the associated difficulties of recruiting and laying-off manpower. A disadvantage that should not be under-rated is that projects, almost by definition, cut across individual departments, possibly many users, and several suppliers as well. This may well result in much antagonism from the rest of the organization, and even split staff loyalties between their departments and their project.

An example of the benefits of project management

A complex stock control system was being developed by a manufacturer of military equipment, with an experienced systems analyst assigned to lead the development of the system. Halfway through development, the DPM thought that communication would improve if a task force, comprising the main people involved with the stock system, met once a week. Soon this task force became the controlling mechanism, and as each week passed, more and more people were co-opted on to the committee as the (integrated) system affected more and more user departments and DP skills. Eventually, the committee comprised 15 vital representatives (from the purchasing department, the manufacturing division, the field maintenance division, the auditors, the marketing department, the army, the software package supplier, the hardware manufacturer, the systems development department, computer operations, the programming team leader). This well-meaning committee met once a week for four hours per week (60 man-hours per week), and as time ran out, rarely reached the end of the agenda. Different members accused each other of causing delays, or alternatively of not being aware that they were the cause of a problem area. Procedural problems ensued regarding agreement of the last week's minutes, or not circulating the minutes quickly enough to outside parties (30 copies were distributed), or giving action assignments to people who were not at a meeting, or being ineffective if a representative from a vital area was not present that day.

As installation time approached, this committee grew further away from the detailed workings of the stock control system and were making decisions that were impossible to implement. They were dictating tasks without considering the effects on budgets, resources, other priorities, who would be responsible for actioning these tasks, or who had the authority to implement these dictates. They had also overlooked three essential and lengthy activities (mainly relating to data capture).

At this late stage, the task force committee was too firmly entrenched to be dissolved, but a single person (appointed by the DPM, and a project manager other than in name) was made responsible for implementing the system. He identified all the necessary activities and chased up people as appropriate. In the circumstances though, he reported to this committee each week, until the system eventually went live, and the majority of the company's products had been converted and controlled by the new system.

When to set up a project

Up to now we have examined the methods for finding a potentially profitable computerized system, and then discussed how the development of this system can be improved by setting up a corporate project with a tangible identity. Two interlinked questions present themselves—when should the project formally be set up? Who should be given the responsibility for the direct management of the project?

Basically, the project should be set up formally, after sufficient preliminary work has been done to enable senior management to have sufficient information on costs, benefits, profitability, and technical feasibility. They can then have the confidence to justify further system development effort, in the knowledge that the user departments and the computer department have agreed and are committed to the development project with a quantified budget. To define this point in time in absolute terms is impossible. In practice, it is somewhere between the end of the corporate planning phase (sometimes referred to as an initial appraisal or a pre-project business survey) and before the end of the feasibility study which is the next phase in the development process.

Appointing a project manager

At about the same time as setting up a corporate project, it is necessary to appoint a suitable project manager, who is charged by the organization to be responsible for the project's implementation, and form a management focal point. With regard to timing, it is important that the project manager is appointed as early as possible, preferably before the project has been formally established, in order to enable him to influence the approach, justification, and proposed budget for the project. This recommendation is usually valid because, in practice, a worthwhile and profitable project is apparent, unofficially, long before a formal decision is made.

A major difficulty is appointing a project manager with the appropriate

(a) business experience
(b) DP technical and system experience
(c) project management experience relevant to the characteristics of the project in question.

In most cases, a project manager meeting the above criteria will only be found from within the computer department. To facilitate this person's acceptance across the organizations structure, a senior DP department manager should brief senior line managers on the man's suitability under each of the above three headings.

Terms of references for project managers

In setting up a project, the numerous managers involved may wish to define the project manager's tasks and responsibilities. Appendix 2 contains generalized terms of reference for project managers, and covers most types of projects. Because of the complex reporting relationship, terms of reference may be helpful to avoid misunderstandings and confusion. Without them the project manager may be tempted to play politics with his many senior managers, enhancing his own position but causing frustration within the organization.

The overall approach should be to combine the terms of reference with the project's objectives that were agreed at the project's justification, e.g. the project's planned cost benefits, or the applications' potential quantifiable operating ratios (e.g. stock turnover improved from 6 to 9 times per annum). The philosophy is to inject these business objectives into the project manager and, via him, into the rest of the people in the project.

Measures for success

As the most important aspect of a project is its success, it is necessary to state what constitutes a successful project. When a project finally has been implemented, it is hoped that the following ideal aims will have been achieved:

1. completion within *agreed* manpower and resources
2. completion within *agreed* timescale
3. completion within *agreed* cost
4. *agreed* facilities provided
5. *agreed* service performance provided
6. senior management and line user department as well as computer staff, both inside and outside the project, being satisfied.

The word 'agreed' refers to the documents produced at the early stages of a project when the justification was made and the organization decided to set up the project. This in turn, as we have seen, relates to the project manager's brief and his expected performance.

INTER-COMPANY POLITICS AND PROJECTS

To whom does a project report?

Having set up a project, it is appropriate to discuss the project's reporting structure, which as we shall see, is not black and white, has a tendency to establish itself without directives, is highly complex, and is not necessarily identical to the project manager's own reporting structure.

Preferably, the project manager (and project) should have full-line reporting to a manager within the computer department. This means that the computer department pays the project manager's salary and that of his staff, and is involved with their appraisals. However, the project's budget is not necessarily included in the computer department's budget. A senior person at the level of the *systems development manager*, (or in some installations a DP manager, or a projects manager) should have this *full-line* responsibility for overseeing the projects within the computer department. It is not advisable for the project to have full-line reporting to a non-professional computer manager. Often he will not understand the project's computing problems, nor will he gain the respect of all the DP staff. It may be appropriate for the project to report to a senior line manager of a user department for short periods, or in an emergency. An example of this could be to resolve a problem, where most of the difficulties are with the users. However, after correcting the problem areas, the project and the project manager should go back to the computer department.

Even though the line users are represented in the project, continual reporting of progress to the line management is essential for their satisfaction; especially as the users are required to sign off their acceptance of the work done at the completion of project phases. Consequently the project must have a (dotted line) responsibility to the several *senior line managers* in the relevant user departments.

In most organizations, projects have to report regularly to a *steering* (or a project review) *committee*. The main benefits of this reporting are that it keeps the board of directors and senior line management informed and satisfied; reviews progress against business objectives; enables a detached view to be taken; provides a forum for resolving problems between line departments; and some good new ideas may arise.

In larger installations, the fourth group of people to whom a project may be responsible, are the managers who provide (possibly from a pool), the project's manpower. (These could include the whole range of systems analysts; O and M analysts; application programmers; internal consultants; management services specialists; hardware specialists; software specialists; communications specialists; and data-base specialists, as well as user staff). Consequently, the project manager may have to report indirectly to these *career managers* from whom he might have to request resources throughout the project; justify the need for these resources; and subsequently account for the way they are used, and the technical standards they adopt. Eventually, he must hand them back to the pool (hopefully well motivated, in good shape, and better experienced than before being assigned to the project).

A fifth influencing factor is the *DP operations manager* and the operations aspects of the project. Obviously, the people within the DP operations department will have some responsibility in deciding what form the application systems should take before they eventually receive it for running as a live production job. This operations group also will influence the project's use of certain DP resources during the course of development. These resources will probably include hardware and software specialists, as well as machine-time for testing, bulk data-entry, and magnetic tape and disc files.

A project may also 'report' to the *project managers* of other interacting projects. By definition, these interacting projects are effected by the application system, and their management may wish to influence its development. As some project managers could be more senior than others, this reporting could become emotionally strained at times.

Often the *hardware supplier* has an overseeing role, and may wish to influence events. In ensuring its products are used correctly to their maximum benefit, and to create useful 'reference sells', the hardware supplier may monitor management and technical performance.

Sometimes, as an alternative to the above, the entire management of a project is made the responsibility of a turnkey company, consultancy or a supplier. In these cases, the responsibility for the project is usually in the supplier's or software house's sales organization, where the objective is not to sell just hardware, software, and services, but to create a project that also ensures a successful implementation of their products. The total liability for failure, and the value of the risk to the supplier is a measure of the size and importance of the project. Consequently, the project could be the responsibility of a sales line manager (within the supplier's company), with the project size dictating whether it is reporting to an area, regional, or divisional manager who has the final word in appointing the project manager. It can be argued that in these cases, the project manager reports to the *appropriate sales line manager* (with a full-line responsibility), and the project manager's salary and part of the project's budget could come from the suppliers line manager's own budget.

An additional factor is that sometimes the project manager must report, for his own *career development* purposes, to a central support manager. The project manager is only required as a resource for the duration of the project. After the project is completed, the project manager returns to a pool, and hopefully he will be given a suitable larger project. This central support manager looks after the interest of the project managers; ensuring that they receive the best career development training and experience; organizing their performance appraisals; and arranging their promotions and salary increases.

Some larger projects may involve numerous users who are separate companies (e.g. brokers), or several government departments, or even multinational governments and companies. This is a current tendency, partly brought about by communication based systems, and the reporting structure of these projects is more akin to democracy in a United Nations Organization!

The project within an organization's political framework

It is apparent from the above, that not only might a project report in up to nine different ways, but also, in each of them, there are several managers involved, each with his own particular requirements. In fact, for a project developing a large integrated system, more than 20 managers and directors could be involved in the project's upward reporting structure! This is illustrated in Figure 2.2 and this situation may make life interesting for the project manager.

These 20 people do not just have a straightforward reporting connection with the project and its project manager. A situation has arisen whereby normal human inter-relationships can develop *among* these 20 people. In practice, each of them will have his own opinions; particular points of interest; priorities; methods of approach; and his own personal ambitions. In an attempt to influence the project in any way, an element of lobbying, discussions, and agreements have to be made among these 20 people, formally or informally, and either individually or at group meetings.

Using this example of 20 people, the maximum number of ways they interact can be calculated theoretically as 190 (i.e. chose any 2 combinations from 20 which is: $^{20}C_2 = 20 \times 19 \div 2$). In other words there are 190 different ways of attempting to influence events in accordance with the wishes of each of the

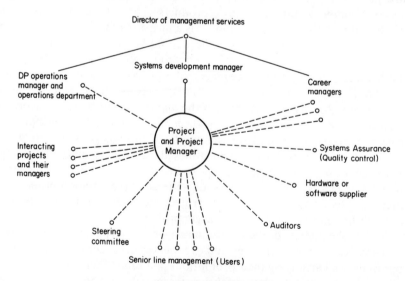

Figure 2.2   External project politics for a large installation
————Full line responsibility
- - - - -Indirect or dotted-line responsibiliy

20 people. In practice, some of these relationships are non-existent. For example, some people may be interested only in different aspects of the project, and, therefore, very rarely need constructive dialogues, or trade-offs of facilities other than directly with the project. Similarly, some of the 190 relationships are duplicated or eliminated if the head of management services, the data processing manager, the systems development manager, and some of the senior line managers form part of the steering committee. Some of these relationships also will be:

(a) strong or weak, depending on the person's functional relationship with respect to the project, and his responsibility in the organization
(b) junior or senior, depending on the relative status and grades of the individuals in question. Consequently, these 190 relationships can in practice be reduced by about 75%, to say 50 active political inter-relationships.

It is, therefore, apparent that no individual has overall power and influence over a corporate systems development project; certainly not the project manager or the systems development manager, even though they have been given full-line responsibility for the project's success. This political framework provides the necessary checks and balances, and ensures that the overall corporate views are reflected in each project. It is essential that senior management ensure that this process does not get out of hand and the project is left to proceed with minimum interference.

Small computer installations with non-integrated application systems obviously do not have this political problem or complex reporting structure, to the same extent as a large organization with integrated systems. As illustrated in Figure 2.3 a small project may be influenced by a total of 5 managers. This produces a theoretical maximum of 10 inter-reactions, but a practical number

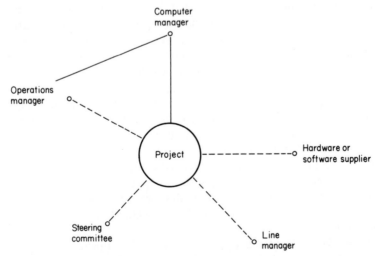

Figure 2.3   External project politics for a small installation (Key lines as in Figure 2.2)

of 8 relationships. Even this relatively high figure is important to bear in mind in order to ensure success in a smaller computer system.

The dangers of control by the line users

In a system development project set up at a corporate level, involving line user departments and senior line management, and probably operating in a political framework similar to that just illustrated, it is apparent that the computer department and the DP specialists easily can become squeezed out from the management of the project. This must be avoided at all costs, as it usually is to the detriment of the organization and can demotivate the DP specialists and DP managers. Expensive and slow development of unwieldy systems (with many uneconomical facilities) are often a result of too much line control. The cause of excessive line control can stem from a combination of weak managers in the computer department and disillusionment by the users with error prone, late, or inappropriate systems previously implemented by the computer department. The solution is self-evident, but is easier said than done in some installations, with credibility needing to be re-established over a period of years. It also may help if the head of the computer department is also chairman of the steering committee, thereby restoring the balance in favour of the DP point of view.

An example of the dangers of control by the line users
A director was made responsible for DP in a medium sized IBM installation. This was possibly because his division was becoming the main computer user, but more probably because he was always sniping at the head of management services, holding him responsible for the late, poor systems which did not use the latest techniques. This demoted head of management services was probably adequate, even though he was appointed three years earlier, when the company was using a computer service bureau. However, he did not have sufficient DP experience of an installation of the current size. His main problem was being politically weak, as he was always in a fire-fighting situation. Owing to a history of 'bitty' systems development, and the nature of rapid changes in the company's business, it required significant resources and many months to change systems for introducing new products or for new legislation, let alone coping with the usual system improvements that form part of system maintenance. The demoted head of management services could not defend himself convincingly against charges of blunting the company's marketing efforts, and of making the company's head office administration appear inefficient in the eyes of the sales force and in the industry as a whole. Also he did not possess a strategic development plan that could lead to quick demonstrable improvements.

Soon the head of management services left the organization and was replaced by the newly-appointed director for DP, who himself, in a previous organization, had DP responsibility for a very small installation in the first few months of obtaining its own computer. This director genuinely felt that he was qualified, and it was in his role, as a leader, to formulate and show the rest of the organization a strategic development plan. Not only did he design systems, he and his user colleagues also defined files and dictated which development techniques were to be used.

Over a year later, and with little improvement in the company's DP, a re-organization took place whereby the director of DP was promoted to become head of another division of the company. The management services department then became responsible to another director, and the pendulum swung the other way with the existing operations manager being appointed as head of management services, and the new director taking little involvement in DP.

In retrospect, too much user control put back this installation two years and caused severe demotivation of DP staff. Just possessing a sound development strategy may have saved the original head of management services. He would, more probably, have survived if he had split up his system development into about four basic projects, each with its own reporting framework. However, a deep understanding of the inter-company politics was essential. If he had used one department's needs to help him against another department, and one project's priorities against anothers, he may well have succeeded in obtaining a corporate freezing of requests for change, and have bought time to finish off essential maintenance work, establish a project to form a basis for future corporate systems development, and thereby steer his installation from being event driven.

HIGH LEVEL MANAGEMENT OF PROJECTS

Having set up a project, how does senior management control it? This section recommends a practical corporate control process, and makes a start in providing a methodology for identifying most matters that require senior management's attention during the course of a project.

Corporate control over the project manager's function

The project manager has been charged by the organization to control all the manpower, resources, and activities that constitute the development of a computer application system. At the end of the day, the organization must rely heavily on the ability of two people; the project manager himself, and his boss, who is usually the systems development manager.

These two people should have the necessary expertise to manage the development process, and form a focal point for the corporate control of projects. All the other managers involved in the complex process of corporate control, cannot implement successfully a new system by themselves or by using their own resources. They can only frustrate or facilitate the development process. Consequently, this book places much emphasis on the responsibilities of the project manager and the systems development manager.

Innovation

Pioneering a computerized application is obviously fraught with management problems, and a formal management methodology could, in this type of project, soon become *ad hoc*. In all projects there is usually a degree of original-ity that defies total reliance on previous experience. The greater the amount of innovation, the greater are the risk factors and the planning problems. In some projects, innovation predominates, e.g. in an Apollo-type project sending men to the moon. The same may be true when a project implements a new technology, though the product itself is conventional (for example, a new type of bridge). Experience shows that in business, most computer projects can be managed by the same methodology, even if the application itself or its technology is relatively new.

A point worth stressing is that a psychological balance may sometimes be necessary between a low risk approach using old techniques, and a higher risk approach involving an appreciable element of innovation. A tendency towards the latter may be necessary to stimulate and motivate the project manager and his staff to work on the project, instead of looking for alternative, more interesting tasks.

The general similarity of projects in all walks of life

A useful starting point is to examine projects in general, because there are many similarities between computer projects, and other types of projects (e.g. engineering projects). This analogy is reflected in the project management concepts in relation to computers. With notable exceptions, most projects never have to start from fundamentals; that is, one never has to build the very first ship, or the first office building, or the first bridge. Therefore, in planning any project, one can utilize the vast wealth of experience that has been gained on similar types of projects. For example, all projects start with a *concept* phase that defines the problems in broad terms, justifies the end-product and states how it will be built. It is then possible to *specify* the end-product's performance. This is followed by a *design* phase which may require the develop-ment of a prototype. The actual *production* of the end-product can now take place, culminating in the *operational* phase where the end-product is handed over to the client, and is in use. Finally, on-going *maintenance* is required, including changes and improvements.

The predictability of computer systems development projects

A similar argument applies to most computer systems development projects, which can now draw upon well over twenty years of accumulated experience in the DP industry. These projects are predictable, even before the end-product has been fully defined. Each new project will be developed in phases and will call for the allocation and scheduling of the manpower skills of systems analysts, programmers, O and M analysts, line users and clerical people. The projects will consume resources such as computer machine-time for testing, magnetic disc and tape files, and facilities for data-entry. Finally, computer systems development projects will require procedures that indicate what work needs to be carried out and to what standard. The framework for any project is known in advance, and it is up to the manager to plan and quantify the constituent parts of his particular project.

Many people working on development projects claim that as each project is unique, the planning and management methodologies of each project are also unique. In the main, the author does not subscribe to this view. It should become apparent whilst progressing through the text, that systems development projects can be predictable, and by following the framework presented in this book, a manager should be able to minimize the problem: 'Where do I start?'. By systematically working through these management planning facets, each with its known contents, management can select the components relevant to a specific project as it proceeds, gradually quantifying them and building them up. The process of controlling and continually revising these plans can then commence.

Project activities and project work streams

Having discussed the nature of a project from the outside, we can now peer inside and examine the constituent parts which make up a project. There are probably hundreds or even thousands of activities which define each project, and place a boundary around it. Ideally, these activities are planned at the beginning and are completed or become modified during the course of the project. It is necessary to clearly understand the nature of these project activities in order to appreciate some of the management concepts discussed later.

Conceptually, project activities can be considered as falling into certain types of streams, which are applicable for the entire duration of a project. These *project work streams* could relate to activities which are the responsibility of a particular department, e.g. a line department or the computer operations department. Alternatively, activities could be grouped because they relate to major logical areas where a manager is held responsible (e.g. the usage of computer hardware, or the data capture aspects and the associated clerical procedures). It is useful to consider the following main project work streams, and these originate from:

1. The user line-departments (either centralized or geographically distributed), whose requirements must be met by the project, and who are the raison d'être for the project.
2. Other computer projects which are also users: This situation arises in an

organization with an integrated computer system, where the system being developed by one project could provide both data and files for another project's use.

3. The systems development work. This is usually the focal activity in a project, because the systems analysts tend to co-ordinate work and gain agreement with people responsible for any of the other work-streams which may be involved.

4. Data capture and clerical procedures. Although these are associated with the systems design work, their importance, together with the fact that frequently O and M, or business analysts are involved (rather than systems analysts) warrants their treatment as a special activity.

5. Application software, produced by the programmers, to the analysts' (and users') specifications. This might also include software packages.

6. Computer DP operations, which should be involved in the design stages, as well as prior to running the live application systems. In particular, computer operations should advise on the optimum operational design of files and programs (for ease of running on the computer).

7. The usage of standard or acquired system software, which can be supplied by the hardware manufacturer or a software-house. This software does not refer to the application programs—it is the software necessary to make the computer hardware work. These activities include obtaining the best results from the standard software, as well as contingency planning for its lateness or deficiencies. The use of data base or file management software as a part of a larger project would be an example of this work-stream.

8. The usage of the actual computer hardware, which could include activities relating to the acquisition of hardware and terminals, optimizing through-put, or the requirements for the communications network.

Even in large projects, not all of these work-streams will be present explicitly, although they may be present implicitly. For example, a small project may not interact with other projects, and the application software, computer operations, software, and hardware usage may all be the responsibility of one person. Even so, it is usually easier to manage a project, if separate consideration is given to all of these work-streams.

Fully understanding these eight streams of project activities will assist in providing a systematic method of managing a project. Conceptually, the overall state of a project can be tracked by tracing the progress of each of these work-streams throughout the duration of the project. A delay in any one stream usually defers the whole project. It is important that all key personnel involved in each work-stream are both identified and brought together to resolve problems before proceeding further. These work-streams will be referred to in several future chapters.

Managing via system development phases

System development phases are a fundamental concept which apply to practically all system development projects. All managers in DP should comprehend them and educate senior line management regarding their significance. At this point, many readers may wish to omit this section, as they are already well-acquainted with the system development cycle. Perseverance is urged, because (a) the recommended treatment is not an academic analysis of how systems are developed but a *practical* method of *controlling* projects at the highest levels, (b) in practice, managers often do not adhere to these phases (often regretted later), and (c) the reader should simultaneously consider those projects in which he has been involved, which, in retrospect could have been better managed by working in the suggested sequence. For example, frequently some of the earlier stages of the development cycle are omitted, and the project's staff court disaster by building on unjustified foundations; or acceptance is not gained from all relevant parties at each phase of the cycle.

An example of the difficulties of adhering to the development cycle
A drug's manufacturer decided that a distribution system with a quick response to chemists' orders was vital. It was so obvious to senior management, that formal justification was not even contemplated. The senior analyst, assigned to the project, suggested he should start with the conventional feasibility study phase. Although apprehensive at first, he was soon convinced by senior management that a feasibility study was irrelevant, as this new system was vital to the company via a large centralized database.

Eighteen months later, with 20 project staff and £$1\frac{1}{2}$ million spent, it was proved conclusively that the project was not feasible; not using that centralized database DP approach anyway!

There are many different ways of dividing the systems development process into phases. The following steps are one method, having the advantage of being useful and having been proved to work in practice.

Initial Appraisal (pre-project business survey)
Feasibility Study
User Requirements (business data and process functional definition, systems
analysis, and logical system design)
System Design (technical design)
Program Specification
Programming (design, code, and program test)
Proving (system and user testing)
Installation
Post-project Evaluation (post-implementation review)
Maintenance

Common alternative names are given in brackets. Each phase is characterized by a set of limited clearly defined objectives; a time-scale short enough to be planned accurately; and measurable outputs which are reviewed before the project progresses. These phases, which are not necessarily sequential, and may overlap, are illustrated in Figure 2.4 which summarizes pictorially the sequence of development phases, and gives an indication of their relative duration. As it is virtually impossible to make all phase activities end on a

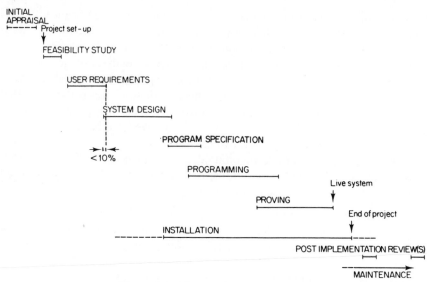

Figure 2.4   Phases of a 'typical' project

specific date, and obtain immediate senior management approval for the next phase, an overlap will occur between successive phases. Lax management should not allow this overlap to become more than about 10 per cent of the next phase's budget. (However, during the latter part of the project life cycle, a practical interpretation would be that, say programming for a specific program should not commence until its specification has been formally completed, documented, and received quality assurance approval, even though the program specification phase has not been completed for all programs.)

Each phase is subdivided into tasks, and each task into activities, which are manageable units of work usually requiring less than about 10 man days' effort. In general, tasks tend to evolve during the course of a project. Taking as an example a task 'conversion of files', this task, like most others during the earlier phases, mainly relates to identifying requirements and logical files. During the middle phases of a project, more detailed planning and physical design occurs. Towards the end of a project, more detailed schedules will be produced and the actual file conversion eventually will take place.

For those requiring more detail, Appendix 3 explains the special characteristics of each phase, and indicates the tasks and activities involved, the skills required, and who is responsible for completing them. However, it should be pointed out, that for some projects, the above traditional project life cycle, although providing tight management control, may be inappropriate, and may produce results too slowly. In these cases other life cycles may be adopted, such as one involving prototyping, the appropriateness of which is discussed in a later chapter. The main point being stressed here is that, from a corporate viewpoint, it is essential to have a standard methodology(s) which adopts systems development phases, otherwise managing the systems development process becomes virtually impossible.

The characteristics of phases and tasks can be combined with the earlier concept of project work streams. The latter should be thought of as defining and breaking down an entire project vertically, i.e. all its constituents; whilst phases and tasks define and break down an entire project horizontally i.e. the time span over the duration of the project. This two-dimensional conceptual representation can be usefully employed to define fully and manage practically all aspects of any development project.

The main benefits that management obtains by following the above phases, are that

1. the phases are the main chronological controlling mechanism for *all* levels of management
2. they are a well-tried and tested sequence of activities in the development process, and as such form a good basis of a project's development procedures manual
3. a project can be broken down into smaller, self-contained, more easily managed steps
4. each step should be taken separately and considered as a check-point, to enable agreement to be reached by all concerned, before starting the next step. It is essential that formal agreement is obtained from all those involved in respect of every phase. Formal agreement by all parties may seem obvious, but in fact business pressures often prevent it
5. practical milestones can be set and assessed in relation to these phases. The great importance of milestones will be apparent in project control
6. breaking up the project into these steps provides suitable reference points, a common terminology, and clear objectives. All can then clearly understand what the project is trying to achieve.
7. Senior line and DP managers can assess and report at each phase and justify the cost of moving on to the next one. The analogy here is with an inverted triangle. As the project works up the inverted triangle, larger and larger expenditures are committed and justified.

The consequences of a phased approach

It should be apparent that a phased project is a transient concept, unlike say, a fixed department within an organization. Each phase has varied problems, requiring different skills, staff members, organizational structure, and above all a different justification. Senior management has a built-in mechanism for reviewing progress and justifying further expenditure at the end of each phase. They should have sufficient information, and the formal means for abandoning a project at the end of any phase. The project manager, and all project staff should be fully aware of this situation. Ideally, the start of each phase should be the beginning of a new structure, with the project manager and team leaders producing firm estimates and schedules for the proposed work in the phase.

One of the practical difficulties in installing a new computerized system is that a project manager, or computer personnel in general, will rarely be involved in all the phases of any one project. Either their skills are inappropriate in some phases, or they will not see the project through from start to finish. This applies especially to long-lasting projects where computer staff appointments and responsibilities change. It is necessary to organize projects bearing this staff change over in mind. For example, good standards of documentation should be maintained. Projects are likely to benefit from this influx of new ideas and people, while computer staff gain experience in different aspects of project work.

The business review

Earlier in this chapter, an illustration was made of the requirement for, and the difficulty of, keeping to objectives. To avoid going astray, it is necessary to review both development progress and the eventual performance of the working system, against the original corporate purpose. Reviewing against objectives may appear obvious, necessary, and a trivial task. The author has found, however, that often these reviews do not occur, and the original purpose can easily become lost.

The task is not trivial because first, corporate objectives are best reviewed (and possibly subsequently amended) by 'independent detached corporate people'. This reviewing, plus the fact that large projects with considerable expenditure may be involved, necessitate the involvement of senior management. However, the expertise and motivation to review constantly must exist at this, the highest corporate level. It is then necessary to determine such criteria as who actually performs the reviews, when and how frequently they are carried out, how progress or performance is measured, and what information is used by senior management. Up to this point we have shown *when* senior management should review a project (i.e. at the end of each phase, or whenever major changes to plan occur) but not *how* they should review it.

One useful method is to have a steering committee made up of senior line managers, with at least two senior computing experts. It is preferable if one of the latter is not connected with the project under review, as he is more likely to take a detached critical review. If the organization does not have the expertise, it is suggested that the hardware supplier and/or a consultant be brought in.

The main source of historical information for senior management is from
(a) budgeting and manpower reports emanating from a project control system,
(b) management summaries of the documents describing the end-product which are issued during each phase, and
(c) plans for future work which are contained in a development plan, a document updated at the end of each phase. These documents (which are discussed in detail in later chapters) form the basis for justifying a project, and the measures by which management can control it.

The items on an agenda for a business review may well include:

A general review of progress.
The envisaged facilities for the end-product.
The schedule for going live and the staggering of facilities.
Trade-offs for optimizing alternative system features compared to development cost.
Historical costs and future projections.
Manpower and resource problems.
The effects on the user.
Anticipated problem areas.
The viability of the project in toto.
The viability of specific parts of the proposed system.

This section will be concluded by leaving DP management with the thought that they have an important contribution to make in educating senior management regarding the latter's reviewing responsibilities throughout the entire development process. Although this may smack of 'the tail wagging the dog', who else will educate senior management regarding sound information systems practice?

CHAPTER SUMMARY

The fundamental business purpose for an organization wishing to develop a computerized system is the natural starting point for discussing management actions relating to the development process, which may be via enhancements to existing systems or a new one, or even a combination of both. It is stressed that the development process is only a means to an end, which should result in improved line performance, and therefore improved corporate performance.

Methods have been suggested for identifying both corporate applications (i.e. those that fundamentally affect the whole organization), and local departmental applications. There are several categories of computer application systems, which hopefully bring improvements in performance, and the associated difficulties are discussed.

It is important to understand the political forces that form corporate objectives (which are compromises and not necessarily absolute). Senior information systems management need to influence these objectives and confirm that they are realistic—which is easier said then done! A possible conflict between benefits as seen by users, and benefits as seen by the DP department, together with the apparent ease of deviating from objectives during system development, leads to the need to establish high level corporate and individual user responsibility, involvement, and commitment to identifying and justifying potential applications and assigning priorities for their development. This responsibility should continue throughout the, sometimes, lengthy development process and involve continual reviewing of progress against the original business objectives, even though this task is shown to be difficult in practice.

The need for strategic planning is stressed from the highest corporate levels down to departments and projects. This is not only for sound business practice, but also as a significant method of improving motivation of staff. Several examples of the consequences of bad strategic planning are given for both of the above categories.

Having found a potential application system, and having completed sufficient work to justify the system in principal, senior management can formally set up a project to develop it. When they are deciding this they should ascertain via their computer department management, how far advanced technically is the proposed application system, and where it falls in the categories of complexities described. Senior management should be able to obtain, for each project, an appreciation of the originality and degree of complexity of their own projects relative to both the computer industry, and their own organization. This will enable risk factors to be assessed and the appropriate project manager, usually from within the computer department, to be appointed as early as possible, based on his past experience for that type of project.

After a project has been justified, and the project manager appointed, if terms of reference are to be drawn up, it is necessary that the senior line managers involved not only approve these terms of reference, but are active participants in their production. These terms of reference must be compatible with the project's objectives and anticipated benefits, and some general criteria for measuring success are given.

Projects in a large organization might report in different ways. These may well include:

1. the systems development manager, or equivalent
2. the specialist resource pool managers, or career managers
3. the relevant senior line managers whose departments will be the users of the system
4. the corporate data processing steering committee
5. the DP operations manager
6. other project managers
7. the hardware or software supplier or the turn-key management
8. the systems assurance department and internal auditors

Within these interested parties, up to as many as twenty managers may be involved directly. As some restraint is required, directorate should ensure that this complex reporting situation does not get out of hand, and that excessive control is not exercised by the users.

How does an organization control a project? Project staff often claim that their project is unique; however, this chapter demonstrates that the management methodology of most computer systems development projects is similar and, is analogous to projects in other walks of life.

The control of development projects at the highest levels, may be achieved by dissecting the development processes into a notional grid with (a) project work streams (the vertical axis) that span the duration of the project, and

(b) development phases (the horizontal axis) that break up the development process. It is necessary to ensure that the relevant main project work streams are represented, and have been assigned to each project. Confirmation should be obtained that these streams are making a positive contribution from the beginning—not just waiting until events dictate that it is their turn to participate.

Development phases, each of which can be managed and justified in isolation, affect all levels of the project's management and include chronological control mechanisms for abandoning or reorganizing, restaffing and replanning projects. Ideally, justification decisions based on the output of a phase should be taken before 10 per cent of the effort is expended on the next phase. Different project life cycles may be appropriate, with prototyping being included as an option.

Senior management should ensure that senior computing experts are present when reviewing progress at the end of each phase, and the development plan for the project should be used as one of the main sources of information.

Chapter 3

Projects and the computer department

THE COMPUTER DEPARTMENT, THE BUSINESS NEEDS, AND THE DEVELOPMENT PROCESS

We have examined the organization's business needs and seen how the organization justifies and controls a project to develop an application system. Effective organization of the computer department is now discussed, suggesting how it should interact with corporate projects, how best to facilitate the system development process, and how it incorporates ideas relating to joint line user and computer department projects. Ways of handling live production work and post live system maintenance are also covered.

Computer departments interacting with projects? At first sight this subject may appear strange; surely in many organizations a project just forms part of the computer department! However, we are emphasizing the need for *corporate* projects, and not departmental projects. As stated previously, a parochial, departmental approach to system development is usually not the most productive way an organization can invest its funds.

THE COMPUTER DEPARTMENT WITHIN THE ORGANIZATION

Before examining solutions to the project/department inter-relationship, a brief overview is appropriate as to how different organizations may concentrate their information systems expertise into departments (or divisions). Every computing department is different, and its functions and purpose could depend on such factors as:

(a) the size of the organization
(b) whether the department's chief role is to run production computer programs, or has the wider role of a management services division
(c) whether computing is within, say, the accounts or administration function, or a separate autonomous corporate division
(d) a decentralized or centralized requirement prevailing.

In addition to these corporate constraints, the actual reporting structure, job functions and job titles within a computer department could be determined further by:

(e) the size and type of hardware configuration
(f) a commercial or scientific orientated installation
(g) application systems run by a bureau or in-house
(h) the geographical distribution of computing within the organization
(i) the actual management personalities
(j) the experience of individual managers
(k) historical aspects and the inherited structure
(l) the types of computer application systems
(m) the length of time the organization has been involved with computing, etc.

In a large organization, the size of computer, together with the corporate responsibilities and functions it undertakes, could warrant not just a department, but an independent management services or information systems division within the organization, reporting direct to the board of directors (or the equivalent senior executives). This is often essential in order that the management services division works in an impartial and balanced way for all the line departments within the organization, and therefore, produces a coherent integrated set of computerized systems. At a level where annual budgets may be exceeding \$2–\$4 million, it may be worth considering converting the management services division into a corporate affiliated but separate limited company. In fact, the management problems within a large computer department are comparable to running a profit-conscious business with the inherent difficulties of controlling multi-skilled groups.

The advantages of a separate company are that it not only improves the authority and potential effectiveness of management services, but sharpens up the justification and budgetary considerations of projects; facilitating the implementation of a project management philosophy. In fact, the individual projects will acquire an additional shield for the protection and insulation of justified budgets. The main disadvantage of the separate company approach is that in the attempt to maximize the notional profit, the management services division may not necessarily adopt the most beneficial approach for the main organization. In addition, any profits may attract tax (which would not otherwise happen) and (in those industries and countries where it is relevant), the VAT considerations are an additional factor which may or may not be more advantageous.

An alternative to the above independent company is the management services division constructed not only as a cost centre but as a profit centre. In this case the division may advertise and tender for jobs, and the line user is free to go outside the organization for its computing requirement. On the other hand, the division might act as a services bureau selling off computer time, resources, expertise, system software and application software, etc., both inside and outside the organization. This approach may be appropriate in a parent company with numerous small autonomous subsidiary companies. Examples of projects in this case would be payrolls and similar self-contained application systems. The disadvantage of this type of financially constituted management services division is that it may be unsuitable for developing sophisticated corporate integrated systems.

With the advent of distributed processing, relatively cheap hardware may be sited at the (remote) user's premises. Responsibility for the actual creation, the processing, and the use of data in such systems also tends to move away from the centralized computer department and towards the periphery of the organization. Such organizations may wish to evolve, away from the conventional centralized management services division, towards one where the DP operations function is divorced from development; becoming a separate responsibility of the directors of the relevant line users. The system development and other information systems, or management services aspects can then be grouped into a separate division within the organization.

Whatever the organization, and irrespective of how its computing is structured, there is generally a need for the following functions. These are best performed by a centralized, corporate, computing department, where the necessary skills have traditionally resided.

(a) Providing a corporate computing utility.
(b) Responsibility for hardware evaluation and selection. This includes communications equipment, microcomputers, remote terminals, as well as the broad spectrum of information systems technologies.
(c) Responsibility for software evaluation and selection.
(d) Providing project management skills.
(e) Responsibility for the quality control of systems.
(f) Producing and enforcing standards for information systems, including the dissemination of lessons learned from past problem areas.
(g) Innovation, research and development for state-of-the-art technologies such as data-bases, communications, decision support software, etc.
(h) Providing a central corporate information service, both to and from the periphery of the organization, for all aspects of information systems. This might encompass a strategic planning role, a co-ordinating role, and an internal consultancy.

A SUMMARY OF ALTERNATIVE COMPUTER DEPARTMENT STRUCTURES

Conceptually there are three possible ways of organizing a DP department:

1. A simple hierarchy where, for example, junior programmers report to senior programmers, senior programmers to a programming manager, he to the DP manager who reports to a director. A similar situation occurs for systems analysts and operations staff. This is a rigid, people-oriented structure.
2. A pool structure where teams of people reporting to team leaders, are drawn from pools of skills and expertise. This is a temporary, fluid, flexible and work-orientated situation, where teams can relate to multi-skilled

projects, or, say, separate programming teams depending on the current work load.

3. A permanent multi-skill team structure, where the team leaders report direct to the DP Manager (or to the Systems Development Manager in larger organizations). These teams are dedicated to and specialize in specific areas of the organization and in special DP applications. Although this is a combined work and people environment, it still retains strongly rigid characteristics which may prove disadvantageous.

None of these alternatives are perfect, they all have pros and cons. Let us now examine some problem areas in DP work before recommending solutions.

SOME DIFFICULTIES RESULTING FROM CONVENTIONAL COMPUTER DEPARTMENT STRUCTURES

All but the smallest computer installations comprise many interdependent departments each with conflicting priorities. Often these conflicts are resolved at the expense of the development projects. For example, some of the functions for which a computer department is usually responsible include:

(a) The running of existing computerized systems (with response times and service levels often being of the essence) that enable the business benefits to be obtained and the organization to function efficiently.

(b) Maintaining and enhancing these existing systems which rapidly can become inadequate due to business changes or the emergence of latent errors.

(c) Planning new applications and the DP techniques, hardware, and software to run them.

(d) Providing the technical and management expertise actually to develop the system.

(e) Negotiating and gaining agreement and commitment from the rest of the organization affected by computerized systems.

(f) Introducing and enforcing standards on DP operations and the development process.

(g) Educating the user line departments, and potential users, about DP.

(h) Recruiting and training staff within the DP department to provide the necessary skills.

Although it is implied that a responsibility of the computer department is to achieve the development and implementation of applications, in practice this objective could be hampered by the pressures caused by the production and maintenance items (a), and (b) in particular, and (e), (f), (g), and (h) probably to a lesser extent. In other words, in order to resolve important current difficulties, development projects (with distant target dates) are often the easiest things to let slip.

Another problem is that over a period of time, the separate functions and departments within the computer installation tend to become more formal and independent. As viewed by the projects, the ensuing apparent red tape and difficult communication might cause frustration and delays.

An example of a programming pool
A small installation decided to pool all programmers for a variety of laudable reasons which included; to improve professionalism; to keep up good supervision and good standards; to improve career prospects in programming; and to maintain a constant work flow. The programmers were responsible for both system software, and application software maintenance and development. On average, each programmer could be working concurrently on three different systems. However, the system team leaders found the situation intolerable. Tasks they considered urgent could not be started because the relevant programmer had been given higher priority jobs by his programming manager. Systems development suffered and sufficient flexibility did not exist.

AN INTRODUCTION TO A PROJECT ORIENTATED STRUCTURE

What we must find then is the elusive combination that:

1. cares for people,
2. puts a strong emphasis on work,
3. ensures that this work is relevant,
4. encourages the development of expertise,
5. breaks down inter-company and inter-departmental barriers, and
6. improves the effectiveness of corporate jobs, i.e. the installations most important responsibilities.

This chapter proposes solutions based on an orientation of the information systems department towards projects. What then are the main elements of a project orientated structure? First, there is the need, as the project evolves, to provide as rapidly as possible, the correct numbers of people each with the correct skills which cover a wide spectrum of technical and supervisory experience. These usually include business analysts, systems designers, program designers, programmers, experts specializing in technical subjects such as communications, or data bases, as well as a host of other skills. Moreover, these skills need to be continually developed and updated both inside and outside project work.

Secondly, in practice, the computer department is not a simple hierarchical line structure, but needs to be considered in three dimensions. Two different structures (the departmental and the project) are superimposed conceptually at right-angles to each other. For ease of comprehension these aspects are treated separately within this chapter.

Thirdly, a case can be made for those people assigned to development projects to be separated, preferably with a different management structure, from the production and maintenance side of the computer department. (The pros and cons for this are discussed later).

General computer industry literature contains extensive ideas relating to computer department structures. The purpose of this chapter is not to repeat these ideas but to discuss how a computer department can be organized to facilitate the effectiveness of corporate computing projects. Obviously it is impossible to produce the 'best buy' in data processing structures. What has been attempted is to synthesize the best elements from numerous general commercial computer installations. It is intended that this should provide ideas for setting-up or, for the evolution of, computing departments. It should be stressed that existing individual personalities are a major influencing factor when attempting to re-organize the data processing structure. It may prove difficult to remove them or have their jobs changed, because their background or motivation may not fit in with the proposed revised functions.

AN EXAMPLE OF A LARGE COMPUTER DEPARTMENT

The type of department being illustrated

For this example of a project orientated information systems structure, a large organization is assumed because larger computer departments are usually structured explicitly into functional groups, covering a range of computing skills, with specialized responsibilities for such functions as; systems development, planning, the running of the actual computer, training and career development, administration, etc. Smaller departments could have all these tasks carried out by one person such as the data processing manager, making it more difficult to illustrate each function explicitly.

In the following example, a conventional centralized management services division is assumed, which is responsible for clerical procedures and systems as well as computing systems. The *principles* being illustrated could apply equally to any other installation, including a decentralized or distributed one. An installation where their computer configuration has, say, an upper capital value in the region of $800,000 has also been used in this example, as above this size the numbers of people may distract from the points being discussed and no new management ideas are necessarily added. Much below this level the organization may not have the breadth of resources, nor the brief, for management services, rather than just computing. The job titles and staff numbers quoted are only to illustrate concepts and give emphasis. In practice, one person may perform more than one function. The problems of smaller organizations will be analysed in a subsequent section.

A management services division structure

Figure 3.1 illustrates a proposed organizational structure of an information systems, or a management services division. It is noticeable that there are three

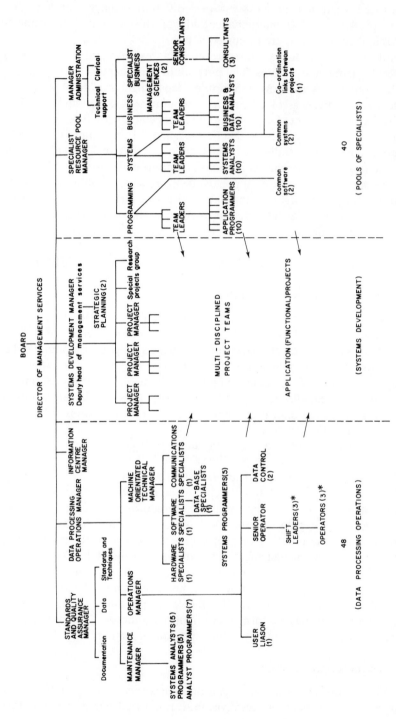

Figure 3.1 A structure for a management services division. The numbers in brackets refer to total staff. * 3 shift operation

main distinct groups which relate to (1) DP operations, (2) systems development projects, and (3) pools of specialist people. Reporting to the director of management services are six managers responsible for the following functions.

The specialist resource pool manager is responsible for career development; training; personnel and welfare problems; technical standards; allocation of staff to projects; and for creating centres of excellence. Under him are the technical specialist managers who are technical men managers (as opposed to project managers) and are responsible for the pools of specialists, which include systems analysts, programmers data analysts, and business/technical consultants. In practice these functions may be carried out by one or two people. Flexibility is improved if this group is also made responsible for common application software, common reference files, and business routines used by several projects.

The systems development manager has two main roles. As a strategic planner knowing where his organization and its industry are going, as well as the future of computer developments, he can continually devise and implement a co-ordinated information systems policy. He should also be a ruthless overseer of all the development projects and closely monitor the project managers. His strategic planning team initiates and evaluates new ideas for possible future applications. The different types of development project are incorporated in the systems development part of the computer department's structure. In other words, the complex, interactive, across-the-board projects can be run, just as effectively, as a more straightforward project. He may also have reporting to him (on a secondment basis) research groups that are examining for example, the applicability of communications based microcomputer systems within the organization.

The data processing operations manager, also reporting to the director of management services, has under his wing not only the usual operations people, but also is responsible for maintenance of live applications. The hardware, software, data base, and communications specialists, who report to the DP operations manager are involved in planning future operational requirements as well as advising on the use of the hardware and software by the projects. They deliberately have not been placed within systems development or the projects, as they should be orientated technically towards the computer as opposed to the line users. These specialists compliment the business/technical consultants, and again, this structure improves flexibility. The user liaison person shields the projects and operations from user queries and complaints and as such has a PR job. If results are consistently bad, no amount of PR will help—in fact it will only frustrate the line users.

The information centre manager is responsible for encouraging and overseeing end-user computing, be it microcomputer or mainframe terminal based. The administration manager is responsible for the wide range of technical support, training, recruiting, and clerical administration requirements within the division. Last, but not least, the standards and quality assurance manager serves an important function that does not exist, or is underrated in many installations. He is responsible for a wide range of quality assurance functions which may include: setting standards, policing adherence to standards, the quality of document- ation, the efficiency of programming, development methodologies, system development procedures, and system controls, etc. It is often a good idea to combine quality assurance and data administration, because in modern systems development methodologies the two tend to converge.

At least two experienced people (one covering for absences) are required to staff the data administration function. They are responsible for such areas as: naming standards, charting conventions, data analysis, entity relationships, data flow diagrams, the logical design of data-bases, data dictionary entries, etc. It is preferable if these people do not work in an ivory tower, but are actively supporting the development teams, in advance of events. To achieve this, they could be seconded to development teams, at appropriate times of the project life cycle, where they form a focal point for data analysis and design, and disseminate their expertise. In some installations this team may also become involved in measuring the accuracy of data on master files, and the accuracy of data being, passed between systems, etc.

If the installation has data-base systems, a data-base administration function is required. This is a technical role, responsible for such areas as: data-base control, physical data-base design, tuning the data-base, optimizing storage space requirements, security, recovery, technical data dictionary control, etc. As this is a technical job, it could come under the management responsible for systems programming, or a technical support team. In this example, it has been placed with data administration for two reasons. Firstly, there are advantages in keeping data orientated specialists together, especially if an information systems department is adopting a modern systems development methodology that places a great emphasis on data, and requires systems analysts to become data analysts. Secondly, it may be easier to arrange cover for the data-base administrator from within the data orientated team. If the data-base administr- ation function was elsewhere, extra staff may need to be employed to provide the necessary cover for this essential job.

The whole of the proposed management services division's structure main- tains the principle that any manager can only manage effectively about six staff directly. Above this number, he tends to lose personal contact and needs team leaders, etc.

However, the other extreme has been avoided where everyone is called manager for the sake of promotion and prestige. In the recommended organiza- tion of the management services division, an attempt has been made to call 'managers' only those people who are true managers; other people are called technical specialists, or team leaders, or supervisors.

The systems development manager is at the same level as the data processing operations manager and the specialist pool manager. This prevents a project from taking over completely, to the detriment of the division and of other projects. Similarly, this approach should counteract any tendency towards the bad use of the hardware and software by the projects for expediency. However, as the systems development manager is also deputy head of the management services division, he would use his position to ensure that projects are completed successfully to the satisfaction of line user departments as well as adhering to good standards. In practice, the systems development manager could also perform the career manager function for some or all of the specialist skills, especially in not so large installations.

Each project should include an appropriate representative from the data processing operations department. This is essential in order to plan and control testing, operating requirements and documentation, data control requirements, hand-over requirements, communication aspects, the clerical interface with the users when the system eventually goes live, user procedures, hardware, and software usage; in fact, everything relating to the interaction between the application system and the data processing operations department.

The project managers either can be reporting permanently to the systems development manager, or be assigned from any other part of the management services division or possibly from elsewhere within the organization. Most probably, the project manager is a systems man, but there is no reason why he cannot be a programmer, business analyst, or even a hardware or communications engineer for certain projects.

In most computer installations, it is found that however one structures the programmers, additional problems are created. In this suggested management services division, the programmers are in three separate camps; project work, maintenance, and systems software. This approach assumes differences in skills, experience and motivation are required for each type of programmer.

THE BENEFITS OF THE PROPOSED STRUCTURE

Benefits to the projects and the project managers

Although the day-to-day production work carried out by DP operations is probably the most important consideration, the projects are the most important aspect of the systems development objectives within the management services division. All of the suggested structure of the management services division reflects this objective, with the projects being supported from both sides, technically and operationally. They will draw their staff, as appropriate, from both these pools of specialist skills, which may be defined as groups of technically skilled specialists, based outside the projects, and possessing a high level of professional, but relevant experience, often developed specifically for the projects.

Removing the long-term staff career responsibility from the project manager, enables him to concentrate on his project, with a sound computing environment being created by an improved emphasis on target dates and achievement. Although some project managers welcome the removal of personnel aspects, others would treat this as a restriction and reduction in their authority. However, this is only an initial reaction relative to the current situation. The project manager should have specific short term objectives primarily aimed at achievement. He should justify his resources which in the larger projects may well comprise systems design, programming, and business team leaders, as well as substantial teams drawn from the pools.

Team leaders report full-time to the project manager and (by definition) will be responsible for leading a range of like skills (e.g. business analysts or application programmers) or leading a multi-skilled functional activity (e.g. designing interactive VDU screen layouts and prompts). The systems team leaders, by the nature of their jobs, will tend to schedule and monitor the other specialist streams. The team leader position should be treated as opportunities for training future project managers.

The projects in this environment should not have to contend with communications barriers caused by separate programming, O and M, and operations departments. For example, if a project wishes to make some test runs on the computer, it should do so directly, and not, as sometimes happens, via the programming department. (This latter concept does not exist in this example of a management services division). An illustration of just one advantage of the division's suggested structure is the comparison to a conventional project which relies on a programming department which in turn relies on an operations department. When attempting to perform systems or volume tests, prior to going live in this conventional case, some of the real life situations with which projects might have to contend, include: disc files allocated for testing purposes cannot be used for live data files; two or more connected programs written by separate programmers are unable to be run as one combined job; insufficient programmers' test time is available for testing a long simulated volume test run; insufficient disc space is available on the test discs for live file tests. If the job is complex and long, operations may not be able to cope, and they may be unable to produce the necessary job control language for running on the computer.

Benefits to computer department staff

A natural tendency is that specialist skills (programming, system design, business or specific technical expertise) as well as data processing standards, can become watered-down by project work, in the pressure to get things done. To counterbalance this tendency, centres of excellence are created by the career manager for the specialist skills. Both career development and standards are therefore, protected. By having career managers, there are improved chances of job rotation and obtaining different experience for the computer department's staff.

Job rotation and career development paths are an inherent part of the management services division's organization. For example, a trainee could start in the data processing stream within operations, move to the specialist resource pool as an application programmer, transfer into project work and then again into the business systems pool, followed by the technical systems pool. Although the combinations are obviously limitless and depend on the requirements of each individual, typical career development paths should be published enabling staff to see their way ahead. This is mainly applicable at the lower staff levels, but the principle still applies throughout the management tree.

Also inherent in the philosophy of the proposed structure are two principles:

(a) A technical consultant can have a higher status, grade and salary than the manager for whom he is working.
(b) A career development path for a manager has the possibility of alternating between the consultant and management roles.

The first provision ensures that good, non-managerial technical people can achieve both an appropriate and rewarding career, whilst the second policy enables managers to obtain technical experience without the pressures of daily management decisions.

The planning function

In many installations, the planning functions can tend to become an ivory tower and become politically weak within the division, especially with respect to the projects. This state of affairs is particularly noticeable if there are user-orientated project teams, or if the project managers are also involved in the planning of new systems or new facilities within existing systems. In these cases the planners are talking to the same users about the same subjects as the project's members, who are already in daily contact. It is probable that the project managers will line-up with the users leaving little work for the planners.

In the proposed structure, the strategic planning function is politically stronger and more effective for two reasons. First, as there are no permanent teams dedicated to a specific user(s), and as the project managers are only responsible for short term objectives, which relate to completing a project, the planning function staff will be discussing different topics with the user departments. They will also be considering a different time horizon, usually about two to five years in the future. Secondly, the strategic planning function should be staffed by people on a one-to-two-year secondment basis, preferably as a career development step. In this way, the people concerned with planning will not be too removed from practical experience nor from involvement in the latest techniques.

Maintenance

It is a rare installation that can precisely distinguish between 'maintenance', 'enhancements', and 'development' work. In principle, maintenance involves such work as fixing latent bugs, tuning the overall system, amending tax rates or other such data, catering for volume growth in the system, and accommodating for changes in the installation's use of hardware and system software. On this basis 'enhancements' refer to significant new business features added to existing application systems, whilst development refers to totally new systems. However, in mature installations a 'totally new system' may also require changes to existing programs, as well as writing new programs for existing systems. It is probably not worth attempting to give general guidelines as to what categories specific jobs fall in. Each case should be taken separately without too much concern over semantics. The important point is that for mature DP installations, as much as 60% of systems development effort could be expended on maintenance and enchancement work. This percentage is a growing figure, and much management effort needs to be expended to minimize this growth rate, otherwise the organization will have insufficient resources available to develop new vital systems. The broad principles covered here may help when assigning maintenance or development responsibilities.

In development projects a common reason for staff becoming demoralized is when they become involved in maintenance, rather than systems development. The easiest way to slow up any worthwhile and justified development work is for the computer staff involved to be distracted continually with maintenance priorities.

The suggested structure places maintenance outside the projects and in the data processing operations department, where the appropriate staff can be motivated to carry out maintenance as part of their job. An additional benefit is that it ensures the projects hand over an agreed, clean, well-documented system.

The other great benefit of placing maintenance outside systems development is that the data processing operations manager is held responsible for protecting the organization's computing investment, i.e., he will tend to build safely and steadily on the existing programs and systems. Systems development may, on the other hand, tend to be idealistic and destructive, wishing to start afresh rather than enhance existing systems; or to apply new, advanced and sophisticated techniques to solve the organization's requirements for application systems.

Placing the maintenance of all existing application systems in the data processing operations department is also logical, because after the system has gone live the project has finished. The data processing operations department is then responsible for running the system and is in (daily) contact with all the relevant users. It makes sense for the users to continue this established relationship by negotiating amendments, improvements, enhancements, and other aspects of maintenance to their system. Any changes costing more than say a few thousand dollars will have to be justified in a similar procedure to a project's own justification. This will require a proposal involving quantifiable benefits and a comprehensive planned budget that will have to be agreed by the data processing manager or the director of management services. Very large maintenance requests could well result in formal projects being set up.

Another benefit of maintenance being placed with the data processing operations department is that the organization's existing computer systems are better situated for improving their operational efficiency and their tuning. The appropriate skilled resources are at hand to improve the actual computer hardware and software utilization, increasing throughputs, reducing running costs to the users, and reducing the pressure for a larger computer configuration. It is very difficult for a system development project to tune a system in advance of going live, and many months of practical running experience are necessary. There may be less incentive for this to happen in other DP structures. Similarly, better application system facilities (e.g. revised sort sequences) and improved computer controls (e.g. for transaction data, or master file control records and reconciliations) are more easily introduced after the system has been in use for some time. If an operationally live system fails, owing to a latent systems defect, or because of program changes, the maintenance team are better placed to rectify the situation promptly.

In order to motivate the systems analysts and programmers who are working on unexciting maintenance, it may be necessary to make their jobs either for a fixed period, or as a specific assignment. This period spent working on maintenance should also be part of the training cycle. For example, it could be the training ground for team leaders, or programmers converting to systems, or users joining the management services division as trainees and gaining experience in all jobs.

Many information systems departments have a recruitment policy that restricts employment only to well-qualified high-fliers who obtain good gradings in aptitude tests. In large computer installations such well-intentioned strategies may be counter-productive. For many DP jobs, especially maintenance, such staff can be overqualified and become demotivated. With a more balanced longer term, personnel policy, an information systems department may be able to assign to maintenance work less ambitious, more mature and stable staff. Hopefully, such people will not be deterred by the low status, boring and unchallenging aspects associated with maintenance. The productivity of such people should not significantly drop due to these causes. However, it should be appreciated that, in general, the productivity of maintenance staff is lower than development staff. Old systems tend to be poorly documented, badly structured, and not written in the latest programming language. Consequently, the learning curve, and training duration for maintenance staff to understand an existing system, can become months rather than weeks. For the same reasons, fixing errors and making changes can become a slow, tedious, unpredictable exercise.

A disadvantage of placing maintenance outside of the systems development projects is that a relationship between a user department, and a special team responsible for that user's computing which understands that user's problems, can be broken at the end of a project. Although this may well be true, in practice staff change anyway and often do not wish to remain specialists in one area. Also, permanent user orientated teams can become too user influenced and implement a whole string of system features with little DP justification. This effort may well have been deployed to better corporate benefit.

Another problem with splitting maintenance from development is that, in certain installations, development staff and maintenance staff could be squabbling over the same program, with the latter having priority and holding up development. This may not only be an organizational problem, but could also be procedural. Some installations prefer to impress their users by treating maintenance as items on a shopping list: ideally, each week a new feature being made live. This approach may prove inefficient and error prone. It could well be superior DP practice to treat a large group of improvements as one development stage. Work can then be progressed through the normal development cycle; from the feasibility study to the proving and installation phases. This may allow improved justification of new features, less stepping on other peoples toes, improved control, programs to be opened up only once, and testing to be made more efficient.

However, a compromise is required between making improvements:
(a) in simple demonstrable steps, and
(b) in large complex jumps which increase risks and error rates.

An example of moving maintenance to a separate department
A DP Manager of an ICL 2960 installation had, about 18 months previously, made each project team responsible for all systems work for a specific user, thereby becoming experts within that users' application and improving rapport with the users. Although the users and DP staff were very happy with this arrangement, systems were developing in a piecemeal fashion. As each team was parochial and batch orientated, the installation was moving away from the mainstream of computing. On-line techniques, integrating systems, aiming towards a common database, distributed processing, etc. were being stifled. The DP Manager was also frustrated with system development work being held up by (vital) systems maintenance. So he appointed a systems development manager to concentrate on new corporate systems and on those systems with a development time horizon of over one year. All in-hand work of less than one year's duration would be made the responsibility of the DP operations manager.
Initially, staff were most reluctant to move over to post-live maintenance, especially those key staff working on important specific enhancements. However, after 6–9 months, concern about career development in maintenance, loss of status, not working on new techniques, etc., diminished. Maintenance targets were proving much easier to meet than the more nebulous system development targets; most promotions were in the maintenance department; supervisory experience was easier to obtain; and maintenance programmers gained systems experience earlier because the teams were much smaller and required less specialization. Not only was the system development manager able to plan and start implementing corporate systems (with the minimum hindrance from every day problems), but one maintenance team was able to implement for a user, a simple file interrogation system via VDU's. This was possible by the use of system software, and converting a magnetic tape master file to a direct access file, which was required eventually to effect the system development plan.

The information centre

The information centre concept has been in existence for several years as a method for promoting end-user computing, but still protecting and building on the corporate investment in DP. A large percentage of DP installations have accepted and implemented this concept. The intention is to avoid wasteful proliferation, and provide a focal point for the acquisition of end-user hardware, software, training, supplies, etc. Without such a function, users inexperienced in DP will not only have to learn in isolation important fundamentals of computing, but they could also introduce into the organization a multitude of incompatible computer suppliers. Such anarchy does not improve corporate productivity or effectiveness!

Information centre staff should encourage end-user computing, and actively market relevant DP resources throughout the organization. A controlled 'Do-It-Yourself' environment is created whereby users write their own programs and systems, either via mainframe terminals or personal computers. This may help to reduce the traditional systems development backlog for certain small, self-contained applications: thus avoiding the lumbering bureaucracy of traditional, detached, systems development work and its associated project management overheads.

It could prove beneficial not to use the information centre just as a peripheral activity, but as a strategic part of the organization's systems development effort. For example, users trained by the information centre's staff could use a fourth generation programming language, or a data-base query language to simulate their requirements, screen layouts, menus, etc. When the end users are clear as to their real needs they can pass over their accurate requirements to the appropriate systems development project team, and so improve the latter's productivity at the earlier phases of the systems development life cycle. Alternatively, under the supervision of the information centre, users can be given development tools such as downloaded mainframe files on the users' own personal computers, or a query language for accessing (copies of) corporate data-bases. The intention is to significantly relieve the development teams of producing management and other operational reports. Possibly 30% of a development project's effort is expended on producing numerous reports at the back end of a system. Similarly, a significant percentage of time-consuming maintenance work is taken up with changes to outputs. By giving users such tools as mentioned above, the information centre is enabling users to produce these types of reports and outputs themselves. This strategy helps to improve the productivity of systems developments teams, reduce the traditional backlog of outstanding systems development work that cannot be started due to lack of DP resources, and last but not least, involve the users more in their data and their systems.

The information centre should be staffed by systems analysts and end users already experienced in DP, acting as consultants to departments within the organization, who believe they can improve their department's effectiveness and productivity by using the relatively simple DP aids available to them.

Information centre staff co-ordinate both hardware and software being adopted by the users, ensuring that it is compatible, and adheres to the corporate short list of approved products. Links to the mainframe could also be handled via the information centre.

Training is also an important role of the information centre staff, as they can pass on their considerable relevant DP experience, and help the users avoid the DP mistakes they themselves made years ago. Advice is also required by the users on the optimum software tools available, and the degree of security required. Decision support tools are available for micros, as well as for mainframe solutions. Although, say, the same financial modelling package is available for both mainframe and micro, the former may, for the particular application in question, have additional features, and support a larger model. Apart from general training, users will require detailed advice as to how to use both hardware and software. As they cannot be expected to contact the original vendors for each small query, users need to refer to a central figure-head in the information centre for these normal day-to-day queries.

A basic project control function is also a desirable responsibility of the information centre. Someone needs to check that proper cost justifications for the application have been made, and that standards and quality have not been totally ignored. Under this heading comes good documentation, realistic recovery and security arrangements, and ensuring that the implementation of the user's system has no adverse effect on other parts of the organization (such as excessive usage of the mainframe's resources). Lastly, information centre staff may need to prod the user, reassure him, and keep him motivated during his own system development process. It is easy for a potentially good application system to become bogged down by the user's other corporate priorities, or the user becoming demoralized with a software package which is proving more difficult and time consuming to use for developing his system, than he originally envisaged.

QUALITY CONTROL

The purpose of quality control

The audit, or quality assurance function was briefly mentioned earlier, but its importance warrants a more detailed examination. It is instructive to set the scene by placing the subject of quality in the correct perspective.

To many hard-pressed analysts and programmers 'beavering away at the coal-face', the important goal is to meet a (tight) deadline. Obviously, their system or program is expected to 'work'. But what is meant by 'work'? If the system survives the first week, the information systems professional usually breathes a sigh of relief. The long-term view may be secondary. During the pressures of development or enhancement work, an individual is not usually preoccupied with what he is bequeathing to his successors.

In such an environment, the 'field of view' of development staff and managers may become very restricted and clouded by immediate pressures. Such aspects as documentation, thorough testing, programming efficiency and legibility, use of machine resources, performance, system controls, the accuracy of data within the system, the effects on other systems, in fact *quality* in general are not always uppermost in the analyst's, programmer's or even the project manager's mind. Consequently, the team(s) responsible for system development sometimes only obtain a blinkered, parochial, short-term view of the total system and its consequences. An individual analyst or programmer may not see his responsibility within the context of the corporate whole. It is possible that he does not appreciate that he is being funded by *corporate* money, and that he is being held responsible for developing or enhancing *corporate* assets.

'This is just a fact of life that must be lived with!', or 'Our installation has standards to overcome these problems!' may be the immediate reaction of many people in DP. This is a negative approach to quality that, as we shall see, is rather naïve. For example, obtaining a good set of *practical* standards is in itself a nebulous topic. It is one thing for a DP installation to have a set of standards. Ensuring that these standards are actually adhered to is a different problem, even if there is a desire by DP management to use them to produce systems of good quality. It is usually insufficient to rely on, say, the data processing manager or the systems manager merely to read through and approve a system specification. For a start, he probably has not the time nor the inclination to delve meticulously through documents, comparing them, section by section, to the installation's standards manual. Information systems management is often too pre-occupied with pressures of development schedules, a backlog of application systems work, and the latest technologies. In any event, there are numerous other activities to be performed within a computer department to ensure that high standards are maintained.

One solution to the problem is to accept that development staff and management are not realistically in a position to do justice to quality control, and to set up a separate specialist audit or quality control function which is not directly involved with development or maintenance work. It can thus take one step back, obtain a detached corporate view, and act accordingly to enforce good standards and improve the effectiveness of the installation. In DP, this audit function (which often does not exist or is underrated in many installations) is often termed system assurance of quality assurance, and performs the same role as the more readily acceptable quality control function in manufacturing industry.

Quality control is not something built into the end-product prior to its handover to the user. It should be applied continuously during production. Similarly, for systems development, quality control starts at the beginning of the development cycle and continues right through to on-going maintenance. The underlying philosophy is *not* to treat each system as being different, and requiring a once-off, unique method for managing it. On the contrary, commonalities should be accentuated in such things as development techniques, management methodologies, documentation, conventions adopted, etc. Where possible, the emphasis should be towards quickly developed, reliable, easily maintained systems, using well-tried, monitored, flow-line production techniques. The approach involves checking up on the work of the installation's programmers, analysts, and team leaders. A consequence is that, initially at any rate, these people may become antagonized; people do not like to have their hard work criticized. The quality controller may have to be prepared to lose more friends than he gains!

Before examining quality control solutions in detail, it is essential to ask 'Can the "good" quality of an end-product be defined?' For a computer system does it imply:

> reliability, maintainability, portability, flexibility, good documentation, accuracy with respect to meeting the user's expectation, solving the correct problem, cost-effectiveness, efficient interfacing with other systems, avoiding out-of-date technology, efficient use of the computer?

This list could continue indefinitely.

Although attempting to be objective is important, quality control is not something that can be defined in absolute terms. Attempting to achieve all the items on the above list may be a worthwhile goal, but is unrealistic in practice. Each organization has its own particular problems and each manager will probably have his own definition of 'good'. For example, while a software house, delivering a system to contract, might place great emphasis on the quality control of technical aspects of the end-product, a mature user installation might, initially, be more concerned with improving the quality of documentation in order to facilitate the burden of system maintenance work. The approach to implementing quality control should, therefore, be pragmatic, only attempting to achieve what is possible in practice.

The quality control department and its staffing

The computer department should be responsible for its own auditing and quality control. This requires a small, permanent, independent department which is led by a manager reporting directly to the head of the computer department. This top level reporting is virtually essential, because the quality control department has no executive responsibility. Its effectiveness is based solely on its persuasive powers, and on its recommendations being supported by senior DP management. To this end, summarized copies of all reports and reviews produced by this department should be sent to senior DP management, who need to follow them up. However well intentioned, negotiating at the lower levels of the computer department is not usually effective. Within a large project, a control team reporting to the project manager may perform many of the quality control functions discussed here, but the same principles apply.

As a rough guide, the number of staff in a quality control department should equal about 4% of the installation's systems and programming resources. If an installation has less than about 20 analysts and programmers, quality control may be a permanent function, but staffed part-time. Where possible, in larger installations, whilst staff are within this quality control department they should be on a dedicated, full-time basis. They should not be attempting to fit quality control work in between their development or other tasks. It may prove beneficial if staff are assigned to this quality control department on, say, a two-year basis. It should be a positive career move aimed at providing potential future managers with the chance to adopt the corporate view that is often impossible in the parochial environment of development work. The advantage of this approach is that the permanent department can gradually establish its authority, it allows continuity of reviews, and it enables a well defined professional job to be carried out. The two-year assignment for individuals allows sufficient time for them to learn their (possibly new) skills, but avoids them losing touch with the mainstream of DP. It similarly enables specialist knowledge and fresh skills to be added to the quality control department.

The quality control function needs to be staffed by experienced DP personnel, which means assigning systems analysts, systems designers, programmers, and consultants, the majority of whom should be at a senior level. Such staffing is essential, not only for the quality control department to be able to perform its job properly, but also to enable it to gain the respect of the development and maintenance teams being reviewed. As well as being experienced in DP, these individuals should preferably be tough, persuasive, objective, persistent self-starters, who are politically aware of the limitations and strengths of their status, and have the ability for good written and verbal communication.

It is preferable if the bulk of these people are transferred from within the installation, rather than recruited externally. In practice, although the development managers will object to losing their best staff, the quality control department may, in the short term at any rate, run smoother and be more effective if the staff intimately know the systems and personalities involved.

Responsibilities of the quality control department

The quality control department has many responsibilities, the first of which is to produce and maintain (or ensure that there is produced and maintained) a comprehensive set of standards for the installation. As is explained in the chapter on standards, there are many types of standards within an installation relating to systems and programming work, computer operations, clerical systems, etc. The connotation being put on the word 'standards' in this context is 'standardized', coupled with the multiple objectives of enabling a professional job to be done; improving communication both in the development process and in the installation; ensuring consistent systems are developed; making maintenance easier; and finally, providing an induction for new staff.

Apart from approving the installation's standards in general, and its development standards in particular, the quality control department has an educational role, and may be well advised to provide examples to illustrate these standards. A set of well-produced development documentation, that adheres to the standards should be chosen for this purpose, with improvements made where necessary.

This is more acceptable (and involves less work) than producing a theoretical sample document set, which will always be open to the criticism that it is academic rather than practical. These specimens may facilitate the job of educating development staff about the standards, and make it easier for development teams to produce good documentation by copying examples. A noted phychological benefit is that a borrower of a sample document may well want to produce a better document, that can in turn become the quality control example.

Moving on from the origination, co-ordination, approval, and production of standards, another responsibility of the quality control group is participating in the development or evaluation of development methodologies and techniques. This may involve a 'selling' exercise to information systems management and staff to obtain acceptance of a new technique, followed by an advisory and education service, during the early stages of its adoption. Associated with this aspect of the job is keeping the standards updated to reflect the use of new techniques/technologies. It is also necessary to evaluate the use of the standards in practice, and monitor areas where adherence to the standards is poor. Corrective action can be made after analysing whether the latter is caused by bad standards, insufficient education, or inappropriate techniques or technologies.

The other main responsibility of the quality control department relates to systems assurance, which is best achieved by basing the check points on the system development phases of each project. Examination of the documentation produced during each phase is probably the best way of ensuring that the method of development is sound, and that all the necessary tasks for each phase have been completed statisfactorily. In fact, a key element in quality control is this review of documentation (which also includes test plans and test run results). Apart from reviewing documentation, the quality assurer may also participate in design reviews, program walk-throughs, computer resource control, and in some organizations, error control and acceptance testing. The reviewer is attempting to achieve three things.

(a) Ascertain that the *end-product* will be sound, in respect of such aspects as overall performance, response times and controls.
(b) Ensure that the development *documentation* is sound in respect of such things as completeness; reasonableness; being readable and understandable by the prime intended recipients; having the correct format (e.g. pages numbered, dated, and author stated); and not being contradictory. It may be difficult for the system assurers to check on such things as processing rules or validation rules, which are, in this case, better checked by the users.
(c) Ensure that the development *plan*, which includes manpower estimates and schedules and realistic, and cost effective.

An extension of the responsibility for checking documentation applies to ensuring that program source code adheres to the installation's programming standards and conventions. All new programs or enhancements to existing ones should be inspected and approved, preferably prior to their going live. As maintenance work becomes a more significant part of a mature installation's work load, it is essential not only for the writer of a program to remember several months later how his program works, but, more likely, for other people to fully understand what was intended.

Another particular, and important ramification of the quality control of documentation relates to testing. Not only is it necessary to ensure that comprehensive test plans are produced, it is also essential to ensure that those test plans are executed thoroughly, with properly logged test runs. This documentation should link with the inevitable errors found, and the resultant error log should indicate when an error has been fixed and retested as being clean. This applies to both new systems, as well as to on-going test beds used for maintenance work on existing systems.

It may take a year or more for the majority of the installation's development staff to succumb to the pressure from quality control, and produce documents that adhere to standards. Personal preferences and idiosyncrasies, together with parochial viewpoints, die slowly. Eventually, the development staff should appreciate their own role in producing consistent, installation orientated documentation which is a contribution towards quality control. When this situation has evolved, the review of documentation becomes a less major aspect of quality control work: spot-checks being the norm, rather than detailed reviews of every document produced.

Another important function of the quality control department is to check the objectives of a system against those of the organization, including the system's cost/benefit value. This may be done during development (in conjunction with the review of documentation), but, as far as the quality control department is concerned, they come into their own when performing a Post Implementation Review. As previously explained, this should be carried out about six months after the system has gone live. In mature installations, the predominant maintenance and enhancement work can be treated exactly as the quality control of new systems. The same system development cycle applies. However, an additional check is necessary for on-going systems, to see, for example, whether the system and programming documentation has been kept updated over the years. A common failing is to accumulate notes of changes made to a system, but not documenting the entire revised system. This often makes it difficult to understand what is really happening within the system. The quality control department may base the timing of this type of review on a rating basis; for example, how long ago the system was last reviewed, its importance to the organization, the number of complaints or run failures noted, whether the system or certain programs in it are due for replacement in the near future, etc.

A general responsibility of the quality control department is that it may provide technical advice on any relevant DP matter, but this aspect depends on the skills and personalities within the department. Another important factor that affects the quality control department, is whether the organization's own internal audit function possesses significant DP expertise. If it does, duplication of the two functions needs to be avoided, possibly by the quality control department concentrating more on the quality of documentation, and becoming slightly less end-product orientated. This means leaving to the auditors such items as the accounting details, financial security implications, controls, and reconciliations.

The role adopted by the quality control department

In performing all of the above responsibilities, the quality control department may take either a passive or an active role. An illustration of a passive role might be waiting for reports or test plans to appear on a desk ready for review, or waiting until a system is about to go live and then signing it off. Experience suggests that most organizations are insufficiently disciplined for this to occur naturally. The quality controllers are not necessarily informed of everything that is happening. Human nature being what it is will attempt to push jobs through quickly, without the delays of formal quality assurance.

Even if documents and systems do turn up for review, the situation may not be improved. Say a user requirements definition has been produced and circulated by the development team to all its recipients. By the time the quality controllers have reviewed it and produced their comments, the project has probably moved on to system design. As far as the authors are concerned, they have no intention of putting their schedules in jeopardy by going back to make what they feel are academic changes to a document that has now become superseded. In other words, adopting this type of a passive role may place the quality control department in a politically weak situation, being too late to have any practical effect.

A similar situation may exist when the quality controllers, in a passive role, attempt to sign off the satisfactory completion of each development phase, or even the acceptance of a system prior to its going live. Such a formal sign-off procedure may become impractical for three reasons: it may be too late to expect any realistic impact, the project often cannot be delayed, and most importantly the situation is seldom black and white. Rarely is a document or development phase accomplished with 100% perfection. There is always something that could be improved. Furthermore, these suggested improvements by the quality controllers may be opinions, or of various degrees of severity. Who decides what is right and wrong? Who determines the trade-off for each particular system and situation? It cannot be the quality controller because he has no executive authority. It often cannot be senior DP management, because they may have been placed in an impossible or embarrassing position. They might interpret the situation as a late request by the quality controllers for more scarce resources to be deployed on a project, in order to rectify questionable deficiencies against standards, thereby causing unacceptable delays. In general, the answer is not to operate in this passive role.

In the active role being advocated, the quality control department is involved from the beginning of each project, development phase, and document.

The quality controllers must be aware of the installation's development plans and strategy, and possibly obtain feedback on the status of each current project from the project control system. By being forceful and pre-empting events, it is possible for the quality controllers to become actively involved from the start of each activity or document. Any contribution or recommendation they may make has time to be actioned or discussed.

This influential role can be further expanded when the quality control department perform post implementation reviews. It is usually easy to suggest improvements to both the user and DP aspects of a system, and these can be fed back to influence the organization's development plan and system development strategy for the future of that particular system. Similarly, when reviewing documentation for on-going systems, the quality of the documentation of each program can be classified, and used as a factor in determining whether programs are rewritten or amended for proposed maintenance or enhancement work. In these ways, the quality control department can improve its political leverage, and assume a positive and strategic role not only within the computer department but also within the organization as a whole.

How does one cost-justify quality control, and determine the optimum number of people assigned? The problem with a cost benefit analysis is that the costs and disadvantages of system assurance are all too apparent, while the benefits are unquantifiable and present a low profile. What organization is going to 'invest' money in an apparent cost overhead (especially in times of recession)?

To the people responsible for development work, quality control may mean an apparent increase in costs due to the slowing down of development and an increase in the volume of paperwork. Documents need to be produced for each phase of development as well as for on-going maintenance, and the thoroughness of testing usually requires additional planning, documenting and execution. Indeed the restrictions on the individual's freedom of action may be seen as an increase in bureaucracy, and to impair flexibility, with the net effect that deadlines are even harder to meet. In fact, none of the above need be true. One benefit of enforcing the adherence to standards is the resultant 'standardization'. Rather than slowing down development, it may allow fast production of (standard) documents, as well as improved estimating, based on consistent methods of phased development. Good standardized documentation also allows increased staff mobility, which is useful in a project environment and avoids the common problem of individuals becoming 'stuck' on one system, with the consequent demotivation.

One advantage of a quality assurance group is that although the quality of documentation will be improved, the actual quantity of paperwork will probably be reduced. More often than not, reviews will highlight that there is too much documentation to be maintained effectively, and suggestions may be made as to how it can be streamlined and automated. Similarly, a separate quality assurance group should have sufficient flexibility to treat each case on merit, and, for example, suggest that the documentation for smaller development projects can be a subset of the full standards, either by omitting or combining certain standard documents and sections. Development staff may well find that working within the confines imposed by the existence of quality control enables them to retain sufficient freedom, while directing them down clearer paths of development towards more accurate and easily attained schedules and deadlines.

In general, the problem with justifying quality assurance is that it is impossible to know what would have happened if the same development work was done with an improved emphasis on adherence to standards and quality control. Would there have been less aborts when the system became operational? Would there have been less call-outs at night for programmers to make urgent fixes (with less overtime costs)? Would the users have been more satisfied with their application? How much easier, faster and less expensive would it have been to maintain and enhance the live system?

It all boils down to an act of faith. Confidence can be gained by obtaining feedback from other successful installations, or by comparing the performance of 'good' and 'bad' projects in the same installation. Do the 'good' projects have better quality control and a better adherence to standards? Improvements are gradual and can only be measured over a period of years rather than weeks. No one is going to rewrite the documentation of a large system just for the sake of it. Improvements are more likely to be made in conjunction with maintenance and enhancement work. Similarly, development staff cannot be expected to understand the nuances and requirements after the introduction of a new set of standards and procedures. The quality control group is there to educate, cajole, persuade, and to act as the conscience of the development teams. It also acts as a double check to ensure that the 'optimum' is being achieved. Where possible, an attempt should be made at measuring the effects of quality assurance in terms of, say, the percentage time spent on maintenance work, or the number of errors found after a system goes live. The ultimate proof that assurance is beneficial is when a team leader acknowledges that he could not have completed a development so quickly with so few problems, without good adherence to standards.

In conclusion it is necessary to put the subject of quality assurance into perspective, in that it is mentioned in a total of about eight pages out of four hundred. This is probably about the right emphasis. The intention is not to stifle creativity by setting up a police state. Quality control does not produce systems; it is only one of the many management techniques for improving the effectiveness of systems development work.

AN EXAMPLE OF A SMALLER COMPUTER DEPARTMENT

Smaller computer departments have greatly reduced manpower, which consequently require fewer levels of management. In fact, only two levels of supervision may separate, say, the programmers from the manager of the computer department. By comparison, large departments may have 4 or 5 management and supervisory levels separating the computer department manager from the programmers. The functionalized structure shown in Figure 3.1 will be

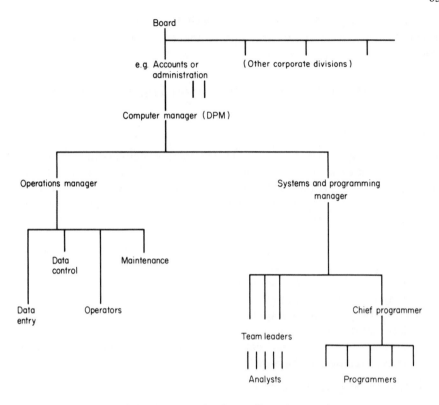

Figure 3.2   An example of a smaller computer department

management top-heavy in a smaller department, with the functions of, say, maintenance manager, machine-orientated technical manager, and specialist career managers being part of an operations manager or a systems and programming manager's job. Figure 3.2 illustrates an overall structure applicable to a smaller computer department.

All the functions and problems mentioned in relation to a large department apply to the smaller departments, but usually to a lesser degree. The majority of management functions in the smaller departments may be performed by only three people—the computer department manager, the systems and programming manager, and the operations manager. In addition, the main project management responsibilities may be carried out by the systems and programming manager, who will manage team leaders assigned to specific application systems. As there could be insufficient continual programming work to keep each programmer engaged full-time on one application system, a separate programming department, under a chief programmer, may be required; the chief programmer himself reporting to the systems and programming manager.

As the smaller computer departments have fewer staff and levels of management, a less complex or less formal control procedure may be required;

communication is often less of a problem, flexibility is improved, and scheduling usually becomes easier. A similar argument applies to the actual projects, which tend to become much less formal.

THE PROJECT WITHIN THE COMPUTER DEPARTMENT

Sources of conflict

Although an emphasis has been placed on projects, there are numerous other essential activities within a computer department. There are many conflicts of interest between (1) these other activities and the projects, and (2) between the different projects. These conflicts are best itemized to illustrate the problems so that compromises can be reached.

(1) Project/non-project activity conflicts are caused by:

    non agreement over standards
    non acceptance of common software
    disagreements over common links
    utility programs are not quite suitable
    data dictionary maintenance
    hardware, software and communications specialists have different ideas in relation to the projects.

(2) Project/project conflicts are caused by:

    chasing the same technical resources
    priorities for computer testing time
    requiring different file structures
    requiring different data contents for similar files
    the non acceptability of the quality of received data
    the non acceptability of schedules

A delicate balance has to be set up between the line users, the project managers, the system development manager, the technical specialist managers (or career managers) as well as the operations specialists. The suggested management services division structure should assist in keeping those potentially conflicting situations to a minimum. The main criterion, when resolving a conflict, is that a decision must be made for the organization's benefit rather than for any of the individual parties. This is rarely uppermost during the heat of the moment.

Staffing projects

Having established the position of projects within the computer department, the actual staffing of these projects can now be discussed. Many more concepts need to be covered before quantifying the numbers of staff and their skills, handling the user contingent, and structuring staff within a project. Here we just outline the broad principals leaving the detail till later.

Appointing a project manager is the initial requirement. It is common for one project manager to be responsible for several projects. This often results in him having a difficult job in scheduling priorities and resources across his projects. This practice, wherever possible, should be discouraged except for, say, a functional set of similar projects, each with independent resources. An example of this, is a project manager responsible for several accounting systems projects, where the assumption is made that all the main users are in the same division of the organization. In times of conflict, that division's management can resolve its own priorities.

Having appointed the appropriate project manager it is then necessary to staff the project with appropriate technically qualified people. Using the previous example of the management services division, the project's staffing may be negotiated via the career managers and the project manager, who is responsible for the day-to-day deployment of staff. A sensible project manager should bear in mind longer term psychological interests and preferences of his personnel. In other computer departments, project staff could be negotiated between the project manager and the systems development manager or the systems and programming manager, who are often responsible for both staff careers as well as technical management. The main concept being stressed here is akin to a grid structure, whereby the projects' staffing can be visualized as being superimposed on the computer departments.

CHAPTER SUMMARY

The main ideas in this chapter are relevant to the head of the computer department, but the recommendations may also be of more general interest in organizations deliberating on having a centralized computer department, and whether this should be a cost centre, a profit centre, or possibly a separate company. Alternatively the organization may be evolving to a distributed computer department where systems development may be separated from user control of DP operations.

For larger companies, the main criteria in setting up an information systems, or a management services division is that it should be balanced and impartial, so it may equally serve all parts of the organization. It is recommended that, where possible, in larger organizations a management services division (rather than just a department) is established, preferably as an independent profit centre, and accordingly a director should be appointed as head of the division. This director could be primarily a computer professional but, of course, he must be business-orientated.

It is obviously the responsibility of the head of the installation to define his department's/division's structure and make the necessary appointments or changes. Whilst doing this he should bear in mind some of the difficulties relevant to his organization associated with conventional computer department structures, and compare these to the possible benefits of a project orientated structure, along the lines outlined, together with the suggested method of staffing the projects.

The computer department manager in smaller companies should be allowed to define his department's structure. A similar project structure may not be possible and the small management team within the computer department may be responsible for very many functions, including writing and running programs. Senior management should appreciate that this department should also be impartial.

Quality control is obviously an important subject which is usually best tackled at the top levels of the computer department, rather than outside at a corporate level, or inside at a lower level. Establishing a separate systems assurance group is one method whereby the computer department can check on the quality of work being produced by the development projects. Staffed by experienced DP professionals, this quality control group should adopt an active role, and keep one step ahead of the development teams when reviewing their work.

Chapter 4

Costs, benefits, and budgets

INTRODUCTION

This chapter on budgets distinguishes between the corporate budget, the computer department's budget, the DP operations budget and the budget of an individual project. A comprehensive method of budgeting is detailed that could form a basis for justifying the project, and for its subsequent financial control. The financial and budgetary aspects of the computer department and its projects are probably one of the most influential considerations of all. The expression 'he who pays the piper calls the tune', applies to computing as elsewhere.

A CONVENTIONAL APPROACH TO A COMPUTER DEPARTMENT'S BUDGET

The overall departmental budget

A convenient starting point for this discussion is to examine the total budget for a management services division organized along conventional lines. In most organizations the budget is agreed annually, and usually is negotiated at a given percentage greater or less than that in the previous year's budget. This will actually depend on the economic climate, the organization's financial position, and on balancing and bargaining with the other corporate departments. Future project commitments also will be taken into account.

Having reached a compromise and established an (arbitrary) annual budget for the computer department, its head can distribute the budget between the various managers and teams within his department. This obviously entails the usual politics and lobbying by the interested parties. A budget for systems development work is one heading usually agreed upon. Directives on manpower establishment figures and corporate policy will restrict how the actual budgets are spent by each manager, as these directives will place restrictions on such things as accommodation and head-counts. Further restraints on approved hardware and associated expenditure are often an additional factor, complicated because delivery lead times are often greater than one financial year.

The system development budget

It is appropriate to consider in further detail the systems development budget, because in reality, it is often the amount of money left after deducting all fixed costs for hardware, communication lines, supplies, operational costs, software, and other known overheads and expenses. Traditionally, the systems development manager or his equivalent, has to allocate this remaining amount of money (adhering to establishment and other constraints) between all the current and proposed projects. In this way, systems development costs become treated as a departmental budget which is characterized by rigidity and a fixed time span for review—usually annually and monthly.

The project budget

Unlike the project budgeting philosophy, shortly to be recommended in this chapter, these conventional project budgets usually only include the salaries of systems analysts, programmers, and clerical staff plus the notional money spent on testing programs on the computer. Manpower supplied by the user departments, other interacting projects, and numerous other items of expenditure may be omitted. Often actual cost benefits resulting from the proposed system are not fully weighed against the projects' budgeted expenditure. These projects' budgets may be given to project managers as their responsibility to control, even though these budgets are only figures on paper, and do not tell the whole story.

The next step in the chain of events is that, throughout the duration of each project, changes in circumstances will produce variances in project budgets. Classically, a management services division seeks to tie up continually the global budget for the division with the budgets of individual projects. It even attempts to control projects by measuring their total weekly (or monthly) expenditure against these planned budgets. It is akin to chasing a rapidly moving target.

A RECOMMENDED APPROACH TO PROJECT BUDGETING

The above approach to the budgeting of projects and of the computer department has several conceptional flaws.

First, the plans, justifications, cost benefits, and all-embracing budgets for each corporate project cannot be directly tied to the total systems development budget, which is only a *departmental* budget. Projects transcend the system development and computer department's budget because they are not only influenced by outside corporate factors, but are also dependent on system development phases not monthly or yearly time slots. Additionally, a consequence of the project concept is that many people from different departments are really part of the project, and should be part of the project's budget. For if a project cuts across the organization's formal line structure, so must the project's budget.

If an organization is attempting to introduce a proper project management philosophy, it should ensure that projects have their own independent budgets, and that all of the many users, within each project, are included in that project's budget. This will include contributions from the groups within management services; from other projects involved; and from the line user itself; as well as all the hardware costs, computer running costs, and all additional overheads. For some larger projects, it may be appropriate to account for the accommodation used by the project, including that for the relevant line user staff. The appropriate rental should be included in the project's budget. In some cases, the capital costs for acquiring the computer configuration, or the equivalent rental payments to the suppliers, also should be reflected in the project's budget. For example, if one-third of the computer configuration is used by the project and its application system, both during development and after going live, then one-third of the computer rental should be reflected in the project's expenditure budget.

Another advantage of this approach to project budgeting is that it gives the project manager more authority over the people he does not directly control. It also means that he is given responsibility for controlling a substantial and more realistic budget, and is no longer just playing with figures on paper. Of course, a project's budget or justification is not fixed permanently, but can be changed and vary with the organization's fortunes and the economic climate.

As a result of this approach, the budgets for the management services division and for systems development are divorced from each project. In fact, the systems development budget should just include items such as the salary and other expenses of the systems development manager, the secretaries, the strategic planning function, and other beneficial activities not directly related to individual projects.

A further consequence of this project management approach to budgets is that it is very difficult for the management services division to overspend its budget. The budgets for the resource pools, the data processing operations, and the systems development groups are mainly fixed establishment figures covering staff, premises and computing hardware and software. The individual projects bear the brunt of variances and the consequence of bad planning or poor management.

Sophisticated budgeting is more likely to occur in management services divisions set up as profit centres or as corporate affiliated profit-conscious companies. By their very nature, they will encourage better budgeting systems, and they will facilitate the development of explicit project management techniques with comprehensive project budgets. Since these type of computer installations are measureably performance-orientated, the profit and loss element is brought into much sharper focus, in that projects are not only more carefully justified, but all the users back their belief in the proposed benefits by making revenue contributions from their own budgets.

The above recommendations are not simply black and white, and each organization will have its own established preferences and accounting methods.

It is common for large organizations with integrated systems to avoid the complexities of the above budgetary approach. This especially applies if a corporate systems approach is required for certain applications, where some intermediary systems may not be beneficial to (or require budgetary contributions from) a particular line department.

PROJECT/SYSTEM JUSTIFICATION

Overview

Before we proceed to consider detailed budgets and 'proper' cost justifications, let us stop a moment and take a philosophical interlude so that we may ponder and put things in perspective. A convincing case could be made for not examining the financial aspects of projects too closely, or not to plan in too much detail. Take at random, some of the world's significant projects such as going to the moon; or building the Sydney Opera House; or developing Concorde; or even building the Pyramids. It is a thought that probably none of these endeavours would have been started, let alone finished, if the people responsible for these projects knew in advance the total eventual cost. Nor if they had been aware of all of the problems that were going to occur, and what the eventual outcome, concensus judgement, or benefits would be. A similar situation has occurred with many computer systems—both state of the art and conventional. One could easily finish up never doing anything if projects were justified properly, and if emotionless accountants were the sole decision-makers. However, in the real world we do not often have the chance to spread the costs of a project over the population as a whole, nor do most of us work for a philanthropic organization. If the auditors, parent companies or share-holders are looking over one's shoulder, or if there is an economic recession, a take-over bid, or poor annual accounts, then there will not be any promotions from propounding the above philosophy on the advantages of finanical apathy! On the contrary, we require specific tasks related to cost benefit analysis. These should occur within each phase of development, and include the need to re-examine clerical alternatives. Documentation produced at the end of each phase of development should reflect and confirm this proper cost justification.

On-going cost justification

The cost justification of a computer application is not just a one-off exercise at the start of a project; it is a continuous process which occurs throughout the development of the system, with usually, the greatest emphasis being made during the earlier phases.

During the Initial Appraisal phase, the total system is cost justified from the overall business viewpoint. Using the limited information available, questions to be answered include:

. Is the system worth developing in the first place?

. Is a clerical system cheaper, or more effective than a computer system?
. Is a part-clerical, part-computer system the most viable option?

More information is available during the feasibility study phase, enabling the above questions to be re-stated and answered with a greater degree of certainty. Additional questions now need answering:

. Is a package the best alternative?
. Is the use of a bureau a viable option?
. Is a mainframe solution the best?

About this time, a decision has to be made whether the application is more cost effective if it is implemented by the enhancement of existing programs, or whether a new system needs to be developed. If a formal project is required (which usually means additional overheads with many multi-skilled resources), a cost justification of the project is now necessary.

Towards the end of the user requirements phase, a detailed development plan is drawn up enabling an in-depth cost justification to be made. Apart from reiterating the previous cost justification questions, the definition of user requirements should be scanned sub-system by sub-system, facility by facility, and report by report, to ensure that they each are best computerized.

. Are some better carried out clerically?
. Will the solutions to data capture problems be uneconomical?

By the end of the system design phase, the development plan is further updated as more detailed knowledge is available. Apart from all the previous cost justification considerations, the concept of trade-offs is introduced. It will cost so much, and take so long to produce a certain facility:

. Will it be better to dispense with that facility, or do it clerically?

Similarly, technical solutions and aspects of the system design can affect the profitability of the application.

During both the programming phase and the proving phase difficulties may arise or slippages occur. Further trade-offs may need to be considered to bring the project back to budget, or to bring the anticipated completion date forward. For example:

. Should certain system facilities be dropped or postponed to a later stage of development?

Even after the system has gone live its justification continues. One of the objectives of a post-project evaluation is to ensure that the system's anticipated benefits are being achieved. It should be apparent that cost justification is a continual exercise.

Initial cost/benefits

In general terms, for worthwhile applications, the initial cost justification should be obvious to senior management. If it is necessary to calculate the benefits in great detail and accurately, the overall justification may be marginal. In many cases, if the justification at this stage, depends solely on intangible benefits, the new system may not be worthwhile. The corollary to the last statement is that, if you cannot attach cost saving to intangible benefits, 'the intangibles' probably are not benefits anyway! There are, of course exceptions to this rule. For example, a new, sophisticated marketing system may be difficult to justify in terms of the increased sales information obtained from the system resulting in an improved market penetration by the organization, but obviously this information is required by the marketing director and his department. The benefits of this type of system may probably be tangible, but difficult to quantify.

Detailed cost/benefits

The above philosophy mainly applies to the initial stages of a potential project. A detailed costing of the project is necessary, at a later stage, covering every item of expenditure, and quantifying the benefits for the system option eventually adopted. Only then can the project in question be justified against the usual corporate criteria, and the project given the formal go-ahead.

In all cases, after the initial investigation has been completed, senior management must make a decision whether the application system should be implemented as maintenance of existing systems or via a new system, or whether it warrants a project being established, or whether no further action should be taken.

The project manager should prepare the comprehensive planned project budget and its cost justification, along the lines detailed later. These will include all the relevant items of expenditure as well as the quantifiable 'revenue' from the tangible and intangible benefits resulting from the implementation of the computerized business application. These financial details together with the user requirements, the detailed development plan, and any proposals on minimizing risk, can be handed over to the executive board, the relevant line management, and the computer department's managers to whom the project will report.

The corporate decision-making process can now impose tight and accurate justifications. Senior management should have all the information they require, in a form they can understand, to assess easily a potential computer project. Comparisons could be made with other corporate computer and non-computer projects; against the current fundamental corporate objectives and policy criteria, which should include the profitability, the cash flow requirements, the number of years for capital payback, the return on capital employed, risk factors, etc. Although the quantitative values of these corporate criteria will vary with the economic climate and the organization's financial fortunes, senior management should be able to treat computer projects as they treat any other corporate project or commercial proposal. In fact, computer projects should receive the go-ahead only after this detailed justification by the normal corporate decision-making process has been undertaken.

Marginal costing

In some organizations with their own computer installation, a different approach to justifying projects may be adopted. The argument is based on the fact that the computer and the computer room is there, paid for, and is not fully utilized. Similarly, there are operators, programmers, and analysts who are required anyway and cannot readily be laid off. Consequently there should be no need to charge fully for machine time either during development or for production running, nor charge fully for development manpower. If one adopts this attitude enhancements may become easily approved: the existing system is essential and has been paid for, why keep on justifying it? If an enhancement is considered in terms of the increases in unit cost for processing each transaction, its development cost may seem trivial. Coupled with this, the DP department, in looking for new applications, may for some systems, find benefits difficult to quantify and may find it easier, to be 'too thorough' and produce a long list of high development and running costs which make it difficult to justify new projects.

If the DP department is not set up as a profit centre, this approach is, if nothing else, pragmatic as it obviates the need to control machine time (which is very difficult to control effectively during system development), ducks the issue of apportioning costs among several users of an integrated system, and it allows some DP growth via new applications in an otherwise static installation (thereby improving morale amongst other things). However, at the end of the day can these organizations conscientiously claim to be putting capital to the best use? Could they obtain a better return on assets by investing elsewhere? Maybe they would be better off by just simply selling time profitably to outside users, or by acquiring a smaller computer in the first place?

Effects of inflation

If it is difficult for senior management to assess and justify computer projects in normal times, it is even more of a problem in an inflationary age. To appreciate fully the significance of this statement, it is first necessary to understand the main reasons for introducing a computer application system. These can be summarized as:

1. To counteract increasing labour costs and to reduce other costs.
2. To improve management control and decisions with more and better information, thereby improving sales and performance, and in general, increasing value.

Both these aspects are important because inflation not only increases the clerical (non-computer) costs for performing a function but it may also improve the cost/benefits of a proposed system at a *faster* rate. The rapidly falling price of hardware may accentuate this tendency. Each prospective system should be treated separately, and have the total budget and the cost benefits available in quantifiable detail. It may then be demonstrated that the benefits of the project's eventual computer system are increasing at a much faster rate than the escalation of the project's budgeted expenditure, of the prospective running costs, and of the existing function's clerical costs. Consequently, a project not justifiable a few years ago may be easily justifiable. Similarly, a project under review may be a more profitable proposition in, say, a year's time.

AN EXAMPLE OF DOCUMENTING COST BENEFIT ANALYSIS

It was hoped to present in this chapter a detailed example of an actual project's cost justification and its budget. The objective was to enable other projects to make comparisons and to obtain useful benchmark information on different labour costs, machine time costs, data capture costs, etc. During the course of preparation of this book the falling costs of hardware, and the rising costs of manpower have already made three attempts out of date. This section, therefore, does not give a quantified example, but recommends forms, checklists, and a procedure for carrying out a cost benefit analysis.

Time horizons and forms

The development time for the majority of DP projects rarely exceeds 3 years. It is doubtful if the useful life of a proposed system, after it has gone live, and when the benefits actually occur, is more than 4 to 5 years. After this time, major re-development is usually required for both technical DP and business reasons. Hence a 7 year time span is a practical maximum when examining the cash flow.

When determining future costs or benefits they should be based on realistic projections for:

(a) inflation
(b) business growth.

To focus attention on the costs and the benefits of a development project, three forms are advisable. Two of these forms facilitate the *detailing* of costs and benefits, whilst the other form conveniently *summarizes* them to facilitate management decisions. Even better is a spreadsheet model, based on the format of these forms, run and consolidated on a personal computer. These forms, or spreadsheets, should be updated and reviewed at the end of each phase of development.

Cost detail

The Cost Detail form (Figure 4.1) may be used for itemizing each of the following:

PROJECT/SYSTEM NAME	DEVELOPMENT PHASE	DATE
		VERSION
*DEVELOPMENT COSTS *DATA CAPTURE COSTS		PREPARED BY
*RUNNING COSTS *MAINTENANCE COSTS		
*EXISTING SYSTEM COSTS		

	YEAR 1 £,000	YEAR 2 £,000	YEAR 3 £,000	YEAR 4 £,000	YEAR 5 £,000	YEAR 6 £,000	YEAR 7 £,000	PROJECT TOTAL
MAN-POWER								
Salaries and overheads–DP								
SUB-TOTAL								
Salaries and overheads–User								
SUB-TOTAL								
External manpower								
SUB-TOTAL								
MANPOWER COSTS SUB-TOTAL								
EQUIPMENT								
Acquisition								
SUB-TOTAL								
Machine Time								
SUB-TOTAL								
EQUIPMENT COSTS SUB-TOTAL								
SOFTWARE								
SOFTWARE COSTS SUB-TOTAL								
SUPPLIES								
SUPPLIES COSTS SUB-TOTAL								
ADDITIONAL ITEMS								
ADDITIONAL COSTS SUB-TOTAL								
TOTAL COSTS								
Assumed rate of inflation % p.a.								

Figure 4.1   Cost Detail form

Development costs
Data capture costs
Running costs
Maintenance costs
Existing system/displaced costs.

It may prove easier if a separate form is completed for each of these independent categories, and the following five checklists should facilitate this.

ONE-TIME DEVELOPMENT COSTS (CHECKLIST)

MAN-POWER (including non-productive time i.e. payroll costs)
Salaries and overheads
  Systems analysts
  Programmers
  Technical specialists
  Business systems analysts/O and M
  User staff assigned to the project
  Secretaries, non DP staff, administration
  Managers and team leaders
Manpower operating costs
  General cost of labour overheads
  Recruiting costs
  Training
  Travelling
  Accommodation costs
  Expenses, subsistence allowances, etc.
  Fringe benefits, etc.
  Incentive bonuses for achievement
External manpower
  Outside Consultants
  Other

EQUIPMENT
Acquisition
  Purchase of special hardware
  Rental of special hardware
  Communication facilities
  Maintenance of equipment
Computer Machine Time (in-house or bureau)
  Project planning, control, simulations, etc.
  Program and system testing

SOFTWARE
  Purchase or rental of special system software
  Purchase or rental of special application software
  Purchase or rental of special development aids
  Ongoing maintenance of software during project's life time

SUPPLIES
  Data entry for development and testing,
  Magnetic file storage for development and testing,
  Input forms
  Printer stationery
  Cabinets etc.

ADDITIONAL COSTS
Sub-contracting costs
Installation, pilot or parallel running (DP & user)
Additional accommodation and storage, (DP & user) not included above
Printing, stationery, photo-copying
Publicity and marketing costs
Other (specify)

ONE-TIME DATA CAPTURE, CORRECTION, AND CONVERSION COSTS (CHECKLIST)

MAN-POWER (including non-productive time, i.e. payroll costs, plus a general cost of labour overhead)
Data capture manpower—users
Temporary staff, checkers, data coders, data correction

MACHINE TIME
Data capture, file creation
File updates (pre-live running)

SOFTWARE
Cost of developing and testing special once-off conversion programs

SUPPLIES
Data entry for data capture
Magnetic file storage for data capture
Stationery
Cabinets, etc.

ADDITIONAL COSTS
Data capture by bureau
Administration
Additional accommodation/storage space
Other (specify)

ON-GOING RUNNING COSTS (CHECKLIST)

MAN-POWER (including non-productive time, i.e. payroll costs, plus a general cost of labour overhead)
User clerical
User management and supervisory

EQUIPMENT
DP
Computer machine time (which includes an allowance for DP operations staff, rental, maintenance and building)
Printed lines output (which includes an allowance for printer stationery etc.)
Communication lines
User
Equipment (typewriters, calculators etc.)

Maintenance of equipment

SOFTWARE
Rental of special software package(s)

SUPPLIES
DP

Data entry (for production runs)
Magnetic file storage

User

Input forms
Special printer stationery
Filing cabinets etc.

ADDITIONAL COSTS
Other recurring expenses
Additional accommodation/storage space

ON-GOING MAINTENANCE COSTS (CHECKLIST)

MANPOWER
Systems analysts
Programmers
Users

EQUIPMENT
Machine time for testing

SOFTWARE
Maintenance payments to software supplier

SUPPLIES
Data entry
Magnetic file storage

ADDITIONAL COSTS
Administration
Other

DISPLACED COSTS OF EXISTING SYSTEM (CHECKLIST)

(N.B. The existing system may already be computerized; being run in-house or on a bureau basis)

MANPOWER
DP
User clerical
Supervisors

EQUIPMENT
DP
User
Maintenance of equipment

SOFTWARE
    Rental of special packages

SUPPLIES
    DP
    Clerical

ADDITIONAL COSTS
    Bureau costs
    Communication line charges
    Data capture
    Accommodation/storage space
    Other

Benefit detail

The measurable benefits to be derived from the proposed system can be itemized on the Benefit Detail form (Figure 4.2). It should be self-evident how to complete this form, with the user(s) supplying most of the information. Identifying and quantifying benefits are probably more difficult than assigning costs. To facilitate this, the checklist below may be used. In practice, benefits do not neatly fit into these precise categories, but this should not detract from the use of this checklist.

Intangible benefits, such as improved turn-round, improved service, or improved control, must have some cash benefit to even merit consideration, e.g. in terms of the retention of more or less business. For intangibles, therefore, minimum acceptable values should be assigned.

MEASURABLE BENEFITS (CHECKLIST)

REDUCED MANPOWER
    Reduced clerical staff
    Reduced supervisory staff
    Reduced typing and filing
    Less DP staff (for existing DP systems)
    Less overtime
    Improved productivity

REDUCED EQUIPMENT
    Typewriters
    Calculators
    Cabinets, filing etc.
    Less computer machine time (for existing DP systems)

REDUCED SUPPLIES
    Stationary
    Less magnetic storage (for existing DP systems)

NO ALTERNATIVE

Coping with increased volumes
Requiring faster response
Covering large geographical areas rapidly
Coping with peak-load processing

INCREASED CONTROL

Management statistics/information previously unobtainable

PROJECT/SYSTEM NAME	DEVELOPMENT PHASE	DATE
		VERSION
		PREPARED BY

	YEAR 1 £,000	YEAR 2 £,000	YEAR 3 £,000	YEAR 4 £,000	YEAR 5 £,000	YEAR 6 £,000	YEAR 7 £,000	PROJECT TOTAL
REDUCED MANPOWER								
SUB-TOTAL								
REDUCED EQUIPMENT								
REDUCED SUPPLIES								
SUB-TOTAL								
NO ALTERNATIVE								
SUB-TOTAL								
INCREASED CONTROL								
SUB-TOTAL								
VALUE OF EXTRA BUSINESS GENERATED								
SUB-TOTAL								
IMPROVED USE OF CORPORATE FUNDS								
SUB-TOTAL								
ADDITIONAL ITEMS								
SCRAP VALUE								
SUB-TOTAL								
TOTAL								

| Assumed rate of inflation % p.a. | | | | | | | | |
| Assumed rate of business growth % p.a. | | | | | | | | |

Figure 4.2   Benefit Detail form

Greater accuracy, consistency, reduced errors in data
Better cost control
Less lost customers

VALUE OF EXTRA BUSINESS GENERATED

Less stock-outs
Prompt dispatch of goods
Prompt handling of queries
Better service to clients and/or agents
New products introduced and administered easily

IMPROVED USE OF CORPORATE FUNDS

Reduced distribution costs
Eliminating bureau costs by conversion to in-house
Improved cash flows
Faster use of money received
Increased stock turnover
Reduced inventory, and work-in-progress
Less accommodation/storage space required
Reduced administration costs

SCRAP VALUE

Value of proposed system at the end of its life.

Cost benefit evaluation

In order to summarize costs and benefits, evaluate them and present them concisely to senior management, the Cost Benefit Evaluation form (Figure 4.3) may be used. The total costs from the bottom lines of the 5 Cost Detail forms, are transposed to complete the entries for

Development
Data capture
Running
Maintenance
Existing system/displaced costs.

The total benefits from the bottom line of the Benefit Detail form, are similarly transposed to complete the entry for measurable benefits.
The calculation of the following are self-evident:

Total returns
Net cost or saving
Cumulative net
Maximum negative cash flow p.a.
Pay-off period
Present value
Cumulative present value
Rate of return

PROJECT/SYSTEM NAME	DEVELOPMENT PHASE	DATE
		VERSION
		PREPARED BY

	YEAR 1	YEAR 2	YEAR 3	YEAR 4	YEAR 5	YEAR 6	YEAR 7	TOTAL	PREV. TOTAL
COSTS OF PROPOSED SYSTEM	£,000	£,000	£,000	£,000	£,000	£,000	£,000	£,000	£,000
Development Data Capture Running Maintenance									
TOTAL COSTS (A)									

Costs as % of turnover or budget

BENEFITS

Displaced costs-existing system Measureable benefits									
TOTAL RETURNS (B)									

NET RESULT

Net cost or saving (B-A)									
Cumulative net									

Maximum negative cash flow p.a.   −£

Pay-off period   years.

DCF

Present value factors @ %									
Present value									
Cumulative Present value									

Rate of return   %

| Assumed rate of inflation % p.a. | | | | | | | | | |

Figure 4.3   Cost Benefit Evaluation form

PROJECTS AND FINANCIAL CONTROL

Having set up a project, justified it, and agreed a planned budget, the relevant senior management will wish to maintain firm financial control and monitor actual and forecast expenditure and revenue (or benefits) throughout the duration of the project. However, in some installations much confusion exists between such terms as: financial control, budgetary control, and project control. So an explanation may help to clarify these fundamentally different concepts.

Project orientated financial control

Project planning and control revolves around tasks and *development phases*, with financial performance (amongst many other things) being reviewed at the *phase end*. This control is exercised via a *business review*, which characteristically *cuts across line structures*. Relevant financial topics at these reviews include:

(1) Estimated costs for all future phases of development, as well as the cost of the current phase and the total cost to-date. Although the latter are sunken costs (i.e. the money has been irretrievably spent and it is too late to do anything about it), it is probably sensible not to ignore them, as some people advocate, but to interpret them so that good money is not wasted on bad. In other words, the total costs expended to-date and the trends should be reviewed and compared against the original estimated costs per phase, thereby deducing a degree of confidence in the estimates of costs being made for the future phases.

(2) Anticipated tangible and intangible benefits based on the current expectations of the end-product's performance. Once again, trends between successive business reviews should be interpreted to enable a judgement to be made as to whether the final value of the system's benefits are worth pursuing. If problems occur and the project deviates significantly from the original plan, senior management should require the whole process of project justification to be repeated, but with updated information. This applies to the project's budget and proposed benefits, as well as the development plan and other supporting documentation.

Budgetary control

As opposed to the above project orientated financial control, budgetary planning and control are usually associated with *cost centres* and *departments*, whose financial performance are generally reviewed *monthly* and *annually*. This control is usually exercised within the appropriate line structure, by the *immediate manager* responsible for overseeing the cost centre. As is apparent, all of these factors differ from the project orientated control as explained above. One reason for confusion regarding the financial control of projects may occur in organizations having an unclear approach to project management, or having a corporate budgeting system, which is being used for two different purposes: monitoring departmental costs as well as project costs.

Financial recording and control

Organizations operating projects on, say, fixed price contracts, or computer departments which are profit centres, are more likely to place a greater emphasis on the financial control of projects. They may run a specific (computerized) budgeting system orientated towards projects, where all project costs are captured automatically. Items posted against relevant headings should preferably include a separation into user and DP costs (or internal and recoverable costs) for charging out purposes. Distinguishing between development and production costs may also be desirable. One has to record meticulously for every member of staff, who complete a weekly time and expense sheet, the number of hours a week spent on each activity. This can be costed and added to the computer running costs and other sub-contracting costs, etc.

Senior user management, the project manager, and the computer department managers can be provided with a weekly, but more probably, monthly project budget situation. Variances from the planned budget can be included as a feature of this system, to highlight potential problem areas.

Benefits of financial control

The benefit of financial control is that *certain* conditions can be highlighted such as detecting any misuses of the organization's or project's resources (e.g. photo-copying, telephones, etc.), or highlighting major incompetence or problem areas such as an individual using too much machine time for testing his programs. The ultimate control is that the manpower overheads do not warrant the achievement to-date.

In addition to promoting a true project management philosophy and a sophisticated project justification, this total financial reporting system could have further benefits. For example, the project manager will readily be able to prove and bring to his supervisor's attention the fact that insufficient resources are being applied to his project. This may relate mainly to user or computer specialists who are not working full-time on the project. The effects of pressures from other jobs can be seen, and if possible, rectified.

Another benefit of recording total project expenditure is that at the end of a project, accurate historical information is available for general use in planning, especially in the initial stages of other projects when making overall cost comparisons. This may prove useful for ascertaining similarities and giving confidence when justifying projects or amending their plans. Having a well-recorded history of expenditure may enable more meaningful extrapolations to be made. If this is to be the main benefit, the cost recording system should be as simple as possible, and require little work from the project staff, who may not be interested or motivated to fill in complex time sheets accurately, in order to accumulate weekly hours and costs. If a corporate computerized budgeting system is in operation, this may alleviate the recording and accumulation processes.

The project manager's spending authority

A brief comment is appropriate regarding the actual spending mechanism for the project budget. The project manager, up to specified limits, will have the authority over expenditure of all the items in his project's budget. Obviously, the systems development management, or the DPM, will check and review large items of expenditure. However, most of these (such as salaries, hardware, special software, sub-contractors, and accommodation) will be authorized automatically *for* the project manager, (and not by him) between the start of the project and its justification by the corporate decision-making process. In other words, there is only a limited amount of financial control that the project manager can exercise directly. To a certain extent, financially, he is a prisoner of circumstances and the rest of the organization. This may not be as bad as it seems because here is yet another example of checks and balances and corporate control over the project.

Actions resulting from financial control

What can result from tight financial control? A budget variance is likely to motivate management into one or more of the appropriate actions. At the highest level:

(a) The project can be cancelled.
(b) If possible, people and resources can be exchanged from a more profitable project to a less profitable one.
(c) Where appropriate, cheaper manpower and/or resources may be found.

At the lowest level a project manager:

(d) Can either reprimand or replace an offending person.
(e) May endeavour to regain financial target by undertaking certain tasks himself, becoming an appropriate skilled resource.
(f) Can cut corners and omit some contingency work (which may possibly increase risk).
(g) Can monitor more closely those problem areas that have produced the financial variances.
(h) In the last resort, can re-negotiate his budget on the grounds of poor planning or new factors having arisen.

Limitations of financial control

On the other hand financial control by itself, may have some limitations. If a project is behind schedule or is spending too much on, say, program testing, the damage is already done, and the budgets:

(a) may indicate variances to the project manager a month too late.
(b) may not pinpoint the cause of the problem, only the general area (i.e. programming).
(c) may not necessarily put the project back on the correct course.
(d) may not show how much actual progress has been made, but only the resources expended.
(e) may show that manpower is assigned, but not if it is productively employed.
(f) the budget may be on target, but no real progress may have been achieved.

The practical result of using financial control by itself is that the project manager may have overspent by the year's end (and lose face), or target dates may have to be put back, or the system under development may have to comprise less facilities: all of which are usually an automatic consequence of problem areas.

Differences between financial control and project control

The above illustrative list of limitations serves as an example of distinguishing between financial control and project control, and their applicability. From the point of view of the project and its project manager, the above types of problems should become apparent before financial control highlights them. Consequently project staff may feel this approach to project control is a myth. In practice they may see financial control as only a measure of 'how much petrol there is in the tank' and not of the amount of progress made. In this type of financial monitoring the vital concept of milestones may be missing, and even if they are introduced into the budget, and the cost measured for each one, the situation has not improved, becaused a milestone is known to have been met or not long before the costs indicate. Another problem with this recording technique is that most budgets are prepared at the earlier planning phases and tend to be out of date in later phases, even if they are updated weekly or monthly. In effect the response time with budgeting is usually too slow for controlling a project, even though budgets obviously need to be monitored.

To summarize, in developing information systems, financial control involves reporting against budget. It is mainly relevant to senior line management who should use the information, which is usually updated weekly or monthly, as a back stop to detailed project control. This project control relates to different things, and is carried out daily by the project manager and his team leaders when they continually optimize the development and effectiveness of manpower and resources. Senior management need not become involved too deeply with this aspect of project control, which is an extensive topic in itself, and is discussed in a subsequent chapter.

CORPORATE DATA PROCESSING BUDGETS

Up to this point, examples of budgets have related to single projects. This section discusses the total corporate expenditure on its data processing which, conceptually, is the total cost of all the organization's projects plus all the running costs for live production work, as well as all other items within the computer department's cost centres.

Hardware costs compared to software

Irrespective of the size of an organization's computer installation, the breakdown of expenditure is, in general, very similar. For example, staff salaries for computer specialists and other people employed by the computer department absorb about 50% to 55% of the total budget (which is a rapidly increasing percentage as labour costs increase and hardware prices decrease). This figure incorporates training, expenses, and other costs of labour overheads.

About 30% to 40% of the computer department's budget may be expended on hardware and its maintenance. It may be of interest to note that in general, the 30% figure or less applies to small installations whilst the 40% to large installations.

In other words, in deciding to acquire a small business machine, the smaller organization may well finish up paying three or four times the annual equipment costs for its total DP costs. How many such installations are aware of this fact in advance? In addition, this percentage expended on hardware is reducing each year as hardware becomes a relatively cheaper item of expenditure.

An additional 7% to 10% is required for stationery, magnetic discs, magnetic tapes, and other supplies necessary for the running of a computer installation. The remaining 3% to 5% of the budget relates to all other costs, which include communication lines; bought-in software; consultants; and microfilming, etc.

The DP operations department within the computer department is often responsible for the majority of the above expenditure. Between a quarter and a half of the above 50% to 55% labour costs is for the personnel in the DP operations department, together with the above 30% to 40% and the 7% to 10% relating to hardware and supplies.

DP expenditure compared to turnover

A useful exercise is to equate the total data processing expenditure with the size of the organization. A rule of thumb is that the data processing budget is approximately 1.5% of the organization's turnover. However, in some organizations or government applications, the 'turnover' is not easily defined and it may be more appropriate to talk in terms of total expenditure. Although an average figure of 1.5% is found, the range of the data processing budget percentage to the total turnover can vary from about 0.25% to about 3% for different industries or organizations. In a few highly mechanized organizations this ratio could even reach 6%. In practice, a precise figure quoted in isolation is not important because an objective of the exercise is to make comparisons of DP expenditure with other organizations in the same industry, and then bring to management's attention, significant variances from the norm. These comparisons can be examined to find the *reason* for variance, which may, or may not turn out to be an important factor in the organizations future well-being.

CHAPTER SUMMARY

On examining a conventional approach to a computer department's budget, it was shown how funds for system development may become squeezed out, and how, for expediency, the budget for a project may ignore some of the contributing manpower and resources.

The recommended approach advocates that in conjunction with the drawing up of the development plan for a corporate project, it is possible to produce a detailed budget, and predict how costs will be expended throughout the duration of the project.

The total costs are usually derived from several sources of planning. For example, the development effort and manpower requirements will give the labour costs; the resources and the operations requirements will give hardware, DP supplies and communication line costs; the testing plan will give machine time costs; and the training and support plan will be included in other costs.

Two financial aspects must be considered at the overall project level:

1. Costs and benefits associated with a project's justification (which can usually be defined on standard forms) need to be examined on a *calendar* basis, with up to a seven year time horizon. They should include development costs, running costs of the existing system, running costs of the proposed system, calculable and intangible benefits.

This justification, which examines the profitability of an investment of capital in the project, forms the control against which the project's actual expenditure and the system's actual performance are gauged over the period of development. Likewise, control may be exercised over any changes to plan which require amendments to costs or to anticipated benefits. This justification process should be repeated, at least, at the end of the business survey, the feasibility study, the user requirement, and the system design phases. The possibly advantageous effects of inflation are also illustrated.

2. Costs associated with project expenditure during development should be planned and controlled on a *phase* basis for each phase of development. Data required includes: actual costs of completed phases; firm estimated costs for current phases; provisional costs of future phases. Usually, costs are broken down into: manpower salaries, manpower expenses and overheads, machine time, equipment and supplies, data capture.

It is recommended that these budgets for each corporate project should have separate identities within the organization, and not be part of departmental budgets associated with the computer department and its system development function. Similarly, it is stressed that a separate system is required for project control as opposed to departmental budgetary planning and control. Departmental planning receives input from project planning but also data from other sources. For example, individual project plans provide details of machine time they each require. When these plans are consolidated they may form the departmental budget for machine time. Additionally, departmental budgets need to be built-up for stationery, office accommodation, expenses, etc.

To ensure that an organization does not become over-committed to its computing (or possibly not making a sufficient investment in DP), it is necessary to examine the business to DP ratio, i.e., the DP expenditure as a percentage of business turnover. Comparisons with other similar organizations, at possibly both an application and total DP level, are a useful exercise when determining a DP strategy or when estimating departmental or project budgets.

Chapter 5

The management of developing different types of systems

The next level of management responsibility for the system development process is now explained. Advice is given on defining in quantifiable terms, the relative sizes, complexities and risk factors of projects, for use when justifying them, and in the recommended project planning and control process. Consideration is also given to the project's end-product in conceptual terms which relate to other application systems within the computer industry, and to the technologies planned to be employed. These discussions form the basis for strategic decisions that must be made by the system development management function.

THE PURPOSE OF MACRO ESTIMATES AND THE BENEFITS OF QUANTIFYING PROJECTS

An example of the consequences of not estimating all factors

A combined marketing and ordering system for a greetings card distributor was only barely justifiable with £100,000 being the projected total cost of all systems development work including programming and testing. This figure was more or less achieved by the time the system went live. However, as no standard estimating methodology existed, the data capture elements were not fully considered: they were treated as the user's concern! To enable this system to go live, a demand history covering 30,000 customer and product items over a period of several years was required. The additional cost to capture this data and keep it updated before going live, eventually turned out to be nearly £200,000. Although this activity was not considered difficult at the time, nor were the (dispersed) costs noticeable, this figure only came to light during the project's post-implementation review, when the clerical costs, programming costs, data preparation costs, and machine time costs were analysed.

If the original development cost of £100,000 was only marginal, the £300,000 eventual cost was certainly not. Using a sound methodology to consider all factors before embarking on systems development may well have stopped this project at a very early stage. More probably though, the pattern of demand history would have been made less stringent. It would have been established during the first few months of live running, starting with estimated base figures.

The purpose of this section is to highlight major factors that contribute to a project's size, complexity and degree of difficulty. Methods of measuring the factors involved are suggested, and an attempt is made to quantify projects in relation to typical computer industry norms.

Senior line management, and senior computer department managers, as well as project managers should find this quantified approach and associated information useful when they are involved with several different types of strategic considerations. Examples of these considerations might include:

(a) Ensuring (when justifying the project, or at business reviews) that the *logistics of the project* make sense at the macro level (i.e. the overall highest level). It is helpful to have starting values to hand (to facilitate the problem of 'where do I start') and it is reassuring to compare pro rata, other projects against overall estimates for total costs, man days effort, number of staff, elapsed times, computer machine time requirements, other resources, the total number of program statements produced for the end-product, etc. If these total estimates for a project do not tie up and relate to general experience, it is highly probable that the more detailed planning is also wrong.

(b) Assessing the overall *risk*, after having quantified the complexity and therefore the degree of difficulty anticipated when attempting to implement the proposed development project.

(c) Preparing *provisional estimates* of future development phases, which is the responsibility of the project manager at the end of each development phase.

(d) Measuring the size of a project to assess the calibre of project manager required to implement successfully the project. The confidence of senior management, when appointing a project manager, depends on the latter's 'track record'. If a project manager has completed successfully several projects of a certain grade or complexity, he can demonstrate his qualifications for the new appointment in question.

(e) Grading projects to enable the computer department and the personnel department to set project managers' salaries and promotions according to experience. A relationship should be found to exist between market rates; the project complexity; and the individual project manager's grade and salary.

(f) Quantifying projects in order to assist when interviewing potential recruits. Difficulty sometimes arises in determining the size and complexity of the projects on which interviewees have worked, and in which aspects of project work they have had experience. The factors, quantified in this chapter might assist in both asking the right questions and in assessing the relevance of the answers when enquiring about experience related to project size and complexity.

(g) When acting as a consultant, or when trouble shooting, it is often possible within a few minutes of starting an assignment, to pin-point potential trouble spots, after asking a few strategic questions relating to macro estimates for the project. For example, a programming manager's estimate of the total number of program statements may not correlate with the figure produced by the systems analyst for the development effort and the total costs. The latter could have been accepted, without question by senior management.

Before proceeding, two words of warning are necessary. First, although an organization can make useful comparisons against other projects by referring to the following relative scales, if taken too far, this exercise can become academic. Secondly, in the computer industry, large complex projects are sometimes considered as status symbols. Often it is better strategic management to divide a large project into smaller and more manageable ones. This improves control, minimizes problems, and facilitates implementation. Alternatively, a very large project can be a series of phased projects each reviewable by the previous one. In other words, although the estimates and characteristics of a very large project appear to tie-up at the macro level, this is not a justification for proceeding along these lines. The proposed very large project may not be the best approach.

INDEPENDENCE OF THE END-PRODUCT AT THE MACRO LEVEL

How often is the objection heard 'each project is different, and it is pointless making comparisons to other projects!' This may be true at the detailed technical level, but time and again it can be shown that there are significant similarities in the management methodology associated with most system development projects, and this applies at all levels of an organization. This argument applies at the macro level where it is assumed that the project is, to a significant extent, independent of the *nature* of its end-product (which includes the technology used, and the system being developed). However, as will become apparent, the *magnitude* of the end-product bears a strong relationship to the project's size.

For the practical use of the grading of projects and for macro estimating, it is convenient to consider the following typical sizes of project:

Small
Small to medium
Medium
Medium large
Large
Very large

Although these may seem somewhat arbitrary, they are defined and quantified below, and are useful for reference purposes and during inter departmental communications enabling people to talk the same language. If a specific project falls between, say, the above small to medium and the medium grades, it can simply be compared pro rata to the values of these two project sizes.

THE FACTORS INVOLVED

1. Relative total costs

One of the major factors to consider in grading a project is its total cost, which as we have seen, could involve the accumulated costs for: all the relevant hardware; all the software; the systems and programming development costs (mainly salaries); the computer time used for program and system testing; all the clerical, data capture, and file-creation costs; the data preparation; the relevant line department's resources; and other costs which might include sub-contractors. These figures should be obtained from the budget, and development plan for the project.

As a rough guide, the table below gives a classification of projects by their total development costs (at the time of writing).

Project size	Total development cost
Small	£45,000
Small to medium	£120,000
Medium	£330,000
Medium large	£825,000
Large	£2,550,000
Very large	£7,500,000 +

This lower limit of £45,000 may seem relatively high to a very small installation, but this figure may be spread over one year and includes user manpower and resources which are not part of the computer department's budget. It is felt that the cost to an organization wishing to adopt a project management approach in order to develop a significant application system, has a realistic lower limit of about £45,000. It is necessary to stress that the relatively small £45,000 project may be very difficult and complex for a small, inexperienced company, and that the categories of size are in relation to the computer industry as a whole.

At first sight it may seem that the project's total cost is the prime measure of its size and complexity. However, in itself this total value of a project may not be a significant measure, or give the total picture. For example, a project which is orientated towards an application development (as opposed to pure hardware implementation) might tend to have a relatively low value, especially if this project does not have a dedicated computer configuration assigned to it, but uses an existing machine within the organization. Theoretically, if one of these low value development projects is to use a proportion of an existing (under utilized) computer configuration, that equivalent proportion of the capital cost of the computer should be assigned to the project. This rarely happens in practice, but is a simple way of equating different types of projects. Several of the other cost areas mentioned in the previous paragraph, will also not be included in a research orientated project.

Alternatively, a project as measured by a hardware supplier, could apparently have a high cost value even though it is a straightforward implementation. The hardware manufacturer, in this case, could grade the value of the project as the liability to himself if the project falters and he incurs penalty clauses as well as lost sales. The project as seen by the manufacturer, then, may have added to its cost, not only the hardware and the site preparation costs, but also the total development costs to be borne by their customer. Obviously, the latter values can become very high, especially if there is a communication system with hundreds of visual display units located around the country.

The message here is that cost by itself is an insufficient measure, and it needs to be augmented by more of the following factors.

2. Man years' effort

The next factor for the grading of projects is the number of man years effort required, which is obtained from the development plan, and includes all the overheads normally associated with systems; programming; and user resources. A guide of project size classified by the total manpower effort required for development is given in the table below.

Project size	Total development effort (in man years)
Small	2
Small to medium	6
Medium	19
Medium large	50
Large	164
Very large	540

3. Duration

Linked with the above factor of man years is the actual duration of the project. Obviously it is more difficult to complete a 10 man year project in one year, than to use less staff and take, say, five years. Although the classical management approach is to accept a linear relationship between the number of man days of a project and the number of people, this does not always work in practice. Pouring more than the optimum number of people into a project could make it more inefficient and difficult to control.

In general, very few significantly profitable corporate projects can be completed in under nine months. The following table gives typical timescales, if optimum resources are used.

Project size	Total duration (in months)
Small	8
Small to medium	12
Medium	20
Medium large	30
Large	48
Very large	72

A practical example of the use of this table was a proposed project which had many of the characteristics of a large project as defined by the other factors. However, either because of pressures from the users, or from poor estimating of the duration by DP staff, the project was planned to last only 2 years. Senior line and computer management, (some of whom were emotionally detached from the project), were persuaded by a consultant to re-examine the proposals to ascertain why a more reasonable figure of 4 years was not being quoted. In fact, a more detailed development plan drawn up by the independent consultants showed that an end date nearer 4 years than 2 years was more probable. Senior management then realized that their original objectives were too ambitious, and brought the development time back to 2 years by omitting certain facilities until a later stage. The cost of the project was increased though—by the amount of the consultants fees!

4. Nodes of interaction

A very important measure of project complexity is the *number of nodes* of *interaction* (or parties involved) being managed within a project. In the author's experience, non-comprehension of system complexity is an important factor in some mismanaged projects, or in some projects where significant under-estimates have been made. If one ignores the elements of complexity caused by system 'newness', or by state-of-the-art technology, or by having a large number of project staff, complexity can be considered as comprising two sources: in terms of the number of interactions within the *system* and within the *development* process.

1. System complexity may arise from the number of transaction types, the number of different departments inputting transactions; the number of fields on input data; the number of files being accessed; the number of fields referenced; the number of outputs; the number of processing rules and their complexity of logic, etc.
2. Development complexity may be the cumulative effect of interactions originating from having several companies involved in the project; various user line departments; some other interacting corporate projects; sub-contractors; hardware suppliers; software suppliers; more than one department within a management services division; numerous existing systems

and files required by a project but being maintained by a separate maintenance group—in fact, any group or individual not directly responsible to the project manager.

When grading a particular project, it is necessary to think carefully through the system and its development process and list all of the interactions. A high number of nodes might be an indication that the project manager should be a forceful, diplomatic negotiator. Any project dealing with five departments outside the direct control of the project manager can be considered as difficult. It is possible to have a small project, as measured by all other factors, having as many as 18 nodal points with which the project manager interacts, and which he influences diplomatically. It is equally possible that this project will slip or even fail because senior management will expect a quick implementation with few resources as it appears to them to be a small straightforward project. These types of projects should, with foresight, be avoided. If the project is necessary, a special management structure should be given to it to ameliorate the interaction problem.

The complexity of the system being developed increases as the square of the number of nodes of interactions, not just proportionately. For example, the simplest system could have only one user and one computer department to develop and run the system. This project would have two nodes and only one possible interaction. A project with two users, interfacing with an existing system, and, sub-contracted programming would have four nodes and six possible interactions. A fairly complex project could involve four separate user departments, interface with three existing systems, require negotiations with a mainframe supplier for delivery and facilities, require data communication lines to be negotiated and installed, and give its programming work to the computer department's programming pool. Theoretically, these ten nodes could form forty-five interactions. The dramatic increase in system complexity should be apparent.

It is sometimes thought that large projects are easy to manage: 'they are the same as small projects only the volumes are bigger'. However, even an expansion in volume tends to increase interactions between data fields (e.g. the interactions between salesmen, products, and customers will be much greater for a large customer file than for a system which handles a small product range and customer base). As a general rule, larger projects mean more interactions, requiring more staff to analyse, develop and test them, which in turn requires a management hierarchy for control, who then require even more sophisticated management techniques and support overheads. Very large projects, could have over 50 per cent of the manpower costs expended on internal project communication, support activities, and management. The end-product is built with the other 50 per cent of manpower costs!

5. Number of people

Another factor for project grading is the number of people directly reporting to the project manager, which is obviously linked to the duration of the project and its number of man years. This factor is worth considering in strongly people-orientated situations, where there is a low hardware cost project with minimal interactions, or a manpower intensive project with a short duration. This could mean that the project manager should be a specially qualified man.

In general terms, this factor is difficult to apply because the number of people on a project is not constant but reaches a peak before going live. It is not always easy to define who is actually involved on a project *and* reporting directly to the project manager. This applies even more so for integrated systems and interacting projects.

Some guide-lines of peak and average manpower is given in the following table for the standard projects.

Project size	Staff numbers	
	(at their peak)	(average)
Small	5	3.4
Small to medium	9	6
Medium	17	11
Medium large	30	20
Large	60	41
Very large	135	90

6. Number of program statements

A well-established and useful measure of the size of an application system is its total number of program statements. The benefit of using this measure is that a project is graded by the absolute size of the product it is developing. This yardstick is helpful for comparisons to other projects, as well as for determining performance ratios relating to the cost; man days effort; machine time; etc.; required to produce say 1,000 statements. However, as we shall see later, this figure needs heavy qualification together with a comprehensive definition in order to make it precise.

A guide to the total number of proven, deliverable end-product cobol statements, including the total number of written support program statements is given in the table below.

Project size	Number of program statements
Small	5,500
Small to medium	15,000
Medium	40,000
Medium large	100,000
Large	300,000
Very large	900,000

7. Project resources

Apart from the obvious main project requirement for manpower, the other resources required are the machine time for program and system testing and the resources for data entry (which is necessary for input to the computer of bulk programs, test data, and the capture of live data). The table below gives an indication of the total consumption of these resources by each category of project.

Project size	Total computer time (370/145 CPU hours) equivalent	Total data entry (man hours)
Small	22	88
Small to medium	66	240
Medium	200	640
Medium large	550	1,600
Large	1,800	4,800
Very large	6,000	14,000

For installations employing on-line program development techniques the middle column increases in value whilst the values in the right hand column decrease.

The previous set of seven factors can be measured in a precisely defined manner (e.g. £s, people, or program statements can all be identified and counted), but the remaining factors, although relevant, are more subjective.

8. Number of activities

A factor worthy of consideration is the total number of activities in a project, as well as the number of relevant, significant, and precise milestones. Although activities have been defined in general terms, it is not possible to stipulate what is an activity, because theoretically any activity can be sub-divided into smaller activities. In practice, people preparing a PERT network, or an activity schedule, tend to divide activities down to a similar psychological level of about 2–3 weeks duration, or about 10 to 30 man days effort, thereby making comparisons possible. A rough guide is that a large project may have over 1,500 separately identifiable and substantial activities; that a medium-size project may have about 300 to 800 substantial activities; and a small project may have about 40–100 activities.

9. Number of programs

Other less tangible and unquantifiable measures include the number of programs generated by the system, and the overall processing logic of the system. However, these are not very reliable measures as one very large complex program can be much more difficult to implement than say 15 much smaller, simpler programs. In fact, this could be a major factor in influencing the design strategy.

Although this measure is not very significant, it may be of interest to know that the total number of programs produced (including support programs) may range from about 250 for a very large project; 100 for a large project; 30 for a medium large project; 12 for a medium project; 5 for a small to medium project; and about 2–3 for a small project.

10. Data capture

The difficulties associated with data capture should not be ignored or under-estimated, especially when assessing the viability of a project or when quantifying the manpower and costs required. The author is aware of several projects where the (unexpected) data capture costs have exceeded the rest of the projects' costs. Although in some cases it may be possible to avoid the clerical capture of data by converting files from the old system to the new, it is often necessary to create additional data from clerical files. Whilst a very large project might need millions of records, a large project could be associated with a half a million or more master records, a medium project could well have over 40,000 complex records, and a small project could be fortunate to only take on 5,000 to 10,000 records.

11. Other factors

Additional factors for grading a project's complexity and risk could include the percentage of new or non-standard hardware or software; the novelty of the system; any geographical spread of the project; and finally a measure of the organization's own competence, as apparent from the success or failure of previous computer projects.

TYPES OF COMPUTERIZED APPLICATIONS AND THEIR COMPLEXITY

The above methodology dissects a development project quantitatively, at a high level and independently of the end-product. We now take the discussions down one more level but still relate to the system development management function within an organization, (which in smaller installations would be just one aspect of the data processing manager's responsibilities). This section considers those strategic decisions a development manager must make regarding a project's end-product. A fundamental starting point for any sound planning methodology.

The type of system and its complexity is usually determined early on, during the pre-project business survey or by the end of the feasibility study. The information set out below may assist in gauging this complexity, which is a useful additional factor to consider when authorizing the project to proceed, and when assessing the overall risk, especially at the early justification stage. The project manager may find it helpful to use this information to survey the project he has inherited, and to gauge what estimating factors he should use in his planning.

As organizations become more experienced in their computing, there is a tendency to evolve more complex systems. (However, the reverse is not true—organizations experienced in DP may sensibly implement simple systems). The projects responsible for developing such systems also tend to become more sophisticated and in turn can be regarded as requiring more formal management. Each type of project has its own particular problems, and its own risk factors; each requires its own special management skills. Detailed below are examples of development work occuring in DP and these can be classified into four broad classes of project.

Application orientated projects

In this type of project the emphasis is on the development of an application system implemented on an existing computer utilizing established system software: there is little regard for installing hardware or purchasing software. In general terms, the following different types of application systems require development:

(a) A 'straightforward' but possibly substantial, application system related to a specific function in the organization; for example, a payroll, or basic stock recording application. This type of system is self-contained, with its own files and flow of data between the computer and the user.

The system does not depend to any great extent on other computer systems or other user departments. Any interface with other systems is mainly of a clerical nature rather than computer orientated.

The management of projects developing this type of system is relatively easy, be it on a mainframe or microcomputer.

(b) The next level of development project is the one that implements a functional application system spanning the whole organization. These projects require a higher level of management skill than type (a) above, mainly because of the increased number of interactions.

A simple example of this type is a non-integrated order sales system. In this case, the following departments could be involved:

Sales, accounts, stock control, purchasing, and despatch.

This system is 'simple' because it is still self-contained. It probably creates its own files and data, even though it involves many line departments, but it need not use data and files created by other computer systems.

(c) An extension of system type (b) is a computerized application that not only spans many line departments, but also relies heavily on the data and files of other computer systems. As the number of systems and diplomatic interactions have increased, so too have the management skills required for development.

Examples of systems not using their own files or data are

(1) valuations of an organization's stocks and/or assets; or

(2) some accounting systems.

In the latter case, a customer invoicing system may use computer customer files *created and updated* by several line departments that are responsible only for customer servicing and production, and that are not concerned with accounting. The accounting department responsible for collecting payments will have minimal control over the data in the files, and could, in fact, just read them.

In an application system for paying the salesman commission on receipts, the development complexity is taken one stage further. Conceptually, the commissions system will only read data relating to receipts from the customer invoicing project which has, in turn, solely read data from basic customer detail records.

The management of this type of project has an element of 'remote control', and requires even more diplomatic skill than the previous type of project.

(d) The fourth type of development project is the 'across-the-board' system, which is a further evolutionary step from (c) above, because it assumes the existence of type (a), (b), or (c) systems. An example of this type is a management information system (MIS) in which there is no functional line department, as in (a), (b), and (c). The management information could come from any existing computer file produced by other projects; or this MIS project could require modification to the files of these other projects, or even create new files.

Other examples of across-the-board projects are a system that uses management sciences to develop linear programming techniques for use in the day-to-day running of an oil company (where tankers, products, markets, etc., are continually changing), or an animal feed-stuff manufacturer (where the least cost-mix of the constituents will minimize production and purchasing costs, and keep the output quality to specification).

These types of systems are generally more complex than those previously defined, and might require a more experienced project manager.

Projects that install hardware

This type of project is the implementation of a computer configuration, and usually would include all the host of associated tasks, e.g. site preparation, and acceptance tests of the standard hardware and software. It could consist of converting from one computer system to another, or introducing a computer system for the first time using established software. It is hardware orientated, and may or may not be for a dedicated application (e.g. a computer configuration dealing with solely an on-line seat reservation system). Even smaller computer configurations (after taking account of *all* the people involved on the project) could require several man-years of effort for their installation.

A computer hardware supplier usually refers to a hardware implementation project as a 'project'. This type of project is relatively easy to manage, unless it involves early delivery of a new range of hardware (and system software).

Software implementation projects

The difference between an application development project and a large software implementation type of project is not always clear-cut. Included in this category could be for example, an organization wanting to introduce a new file structure for future applications, or for a management information system. Conceptually a software implementation project is a means to an end rather than the end itself. Originating or implementing software packages, or operating systems, also could be included in this category.

In general, the management difficulty in dealing with software implementation projects relates to the end product itself, and this aspect is covered later in this chapter.

Combination projects

These projects could be any combination of the above three, e.g. a project could be responsible for installing a larger new computer configuration (supplied by a different manufacturer) and developing a greatly enhanced customer file interrogation system, using proprietary software.

END-PRODUCT TECHNOLOGY

This section examines alternative means of achieving the aim of the project, i.e. the exact type of computer system the user receives to run his application. Is a centralized or decentralized system appropriate? Is a batch or on-line system required? Should the mainframe be used or should one jump onto the microcomputer bandwagon? Is local and/or geographically remote access necessary? Is a data-base approach viable? Would a package be suitable? Or can the application be given to a computer bureau to run? These are the types of problems referred to under the category of 'end-product technology', and within this section comments are to be made regarding the difficulty and risk that management can expect when implementing such systems. Decisions on the choice of technology are usually determined very early in the system development cycle, either during the business survey phase or the feasibility study phase.

A new system or enhancements to the old one

In a mature installation one is often faced with having to make significant improvements to existing applications. An early decision is required whether to develop a new system from scratch, or to enhance the existing one.

The lack of flexibility, the possible frustrations with, or the limitation of an inadequate current system, coupled with the allure of the latest technology and the desire of the DP staff to adopt it so that their job interest may be improved, often causes an installation to plump for developing a totally new system. This should be resisted, especially for the reasons just stated. The main criteria for adopting a new approach should be market related. For example, if competitors are handling enquiries and orders over the telephone for the same day dispatch, it may be fairly obvious that continuing a batch system will not exactly be the best method of increasing market share. On the other hand, the payroll, monthly accounts, daily consolidation of branch office returns, or some statistics might benefit from remaining in a conventional batch mode. This does not necessarily mean to say that the same approach would be adopted if one was starting now.

Generally, it involves far less risk to enhance existing proven systems than to leap into the unknown. This advice is similar to the cliche advocating 'evolution rather than revolution'. It is also making better use of an organization's assets, is less expensive and of shorter duration. The documentation of enhancements is also usually easier: it may safely be less stringent because the users and the development team already know the basic system. A word of warning though, when producing a development plan, amending or deleting existing code and then testing it is far slower (as measured in lines of code written per day) than writing and testing completely new code. The ramifications of each change need careful checking out.

Centralized or decentralized system

To a certain extent, the very nature of the organization and its business dictate whether a centralized or decentralized system is appropriate. For an organization with a single head office, with few processing requirements at its branches, a centralized system would seem appropriate. At the other extreme, an organization with many subsidiary companies, several factory sites and warehouses, many sales offices, numerous servicing locations, or concern about controls and security, may well prefer decentralized systems, especially if the inter-company/departmental politics favour more autonomy from head office.

A current tendency is away from very large centralized systems, including those on a national or even international basis: examples exist of some large heavily criticized installations. This is because sometimes, it is difficult to make large monolithic systems work. Development time may be too long and expensive; or communication difficulties between people at many locations cause a low productivity; or it may be inappropriate for a parent head office to impose systems on their national or overseas subsidiaries. The latter point may equally apply to central government systems. Higher risk factors are associated with large centralized systems; hardware or software failure, sabotage, fire, or strikes may have less impact on an organization adopting many small decentralized systems. A further factor in the swing away from large centralized systems and towards distributed computer processing, is the impact of micro and mini computers, and the decreasing cost of hardware.

Mainframe, mini, or micro

Currently, some DP managers and systems development managers may have the same technical management decision to make as say, a manager responsible for transport had to make, when mechanized vehicles were replacing the horse and cart, i.e. the eternal problem of coping with new technology. In this case there is an additional political factor adding piquancy to the decision. Does he protect his organization's investment in their mainframe by loading new jobs onto it, (and thereby also protecting his central empire)? Or does he allow a proliferation of minis, small business systems, and microcomputers to be used for each separate application (and possibly lose his authority)? In many cases, it is difficult to tell the difference between a mainframe, a mini, a small business system or a micro. In the context of this chapter, this confusion is irrelevant and can be dismissed as a semantics problem. There is no need here to consider the background, the historical reasons for the development of these computers, or the different methods of marketing them. We shall illustrate the arguments by concentrating on the pros and cons of either extreme.

The increasing use of terminals and VDUs in particular is in the mainstream of DP. For many years now, the cost of adding terminals to a mainframe has been, and still is, relatively expensive: especially for the first few. The sales patter claims (quite correctly if taken literally) that it may only cost a few tens of dollars per month to acquire a terminal. At that price everyone should have one! However, the figure, in practice, may work out at nearer hundreds or thousands of dollars per month if the cost includes:

(a) connecting the terminal up to the mainframe. i.e. including lines, modems, multiplexors, network controllers etc.
(b) the additional CPU hardware (e.g. memory) and system software necessary to service the terminal(s).

Once over the initial hurdle of installing the first few terminals, it is difficult to quantify the above costs for extra terminals for new applications. There is also not much motivation in some DP departments to worry about detailed cost justification of these terminals.

For many years, the traditional cost justification of data processing favoured large mainframes. However, it is no longer true that large computer hardware is cheaper per instruction, than microcomputers. A mass-produced hardware industry currently creates billions of dollars of microcomputer sales per annum. Similarly, as software is now mass-produced, personal computer software is relatively cheap (hundreds of dollars per package, rather than tens of thousands of dollars for a mainframe equivalent) and is a growth industry.

What then, can the progressive DPM, or system development manager of a mainframe installation do, when confronted with new applications? Starting with the heart of the matter: the actual application, some situations resolve themselves. The DP manager of an installation processing a Membership File which comprises over 3 million names, addresses, and financial details, may have his options limited. So too does the installation, primarily, with number crunching applications.

Mainframes can, in these obvious extremes, form the basis of a strong case in their favour. Likewise, a very small business wishing to run ledgers, payrolls, stock recording etc., with low volumes to process could, with several reservations, purchase a microcomputer and use proprietory software packages. His needs may be well satisfied with a system giving him direct data entry with batch post processing, or even interactive data processing where files are updated as data is keyed in. Many more options exist though, in the vast area between these two ends of the hardware spectrum, especially where subsidiary companies exist or where certain departments or even specific business functions are off the main-stream of the organization's computing. An example of the latter is a property assets register and rent collection system for a national food retailer owning many of its properties. The system solution may equally well be via a mainframe or a micro; although the latter may well have the upper edge. In deciding which way to turn, let us briefly examine the information systems manager's predicament: first the political aspects and then the technical ones.

Heading up a large central computer department backed by an appreciable asset in the form of a mainframe, which nobody outside the department can understand, is obviously a strong position in which to be. However, this strength and empire protection, can gradually become eroded when users object to paying so much for their applications, and being required to wait a long time for their systems to be developed. Comparisons will eventually be made with other organizations who, for some applications systems, appear more successful with micros than with mainframes. The computer department can also come under attack for carrying high overheads that include a large operating system, and having many introvert specialists engaged in fine tuning the system rather than talking to users, understanding their needs, and solving their problems.

Alternatively, if the DP manager 'swims with the tide', he may *imagine* that he will lose his big mainframe in its big, expensively serviced room, and have it replaced by a powerful mini in a small room which processes corporate data and consolidates divisional operating performance figures. Other minis and micros 'owned' locally throughout the organization may be linked together by another mini controlling a network, enabling different locations to communicate with each other, or access the corporate data base held by the computer at head office. In practice though, it is highly unlikely that his mainframe will become displaced: it most likely, will carry on growing. In this scenario, the computer manager places his political strength, not via his hardware assets giving him a large budget, but on a broader corporate strategic and consulting type of role where he takes the initiative, advises the users based on his proven experience of information systems, minis and micros, influences their decisions, and co-ordinates how the local micros are used and, if necessary, linked. He can also have significant influence throughout the organization on such topics as viewdata, communications, standards, quality assurance, recovery and project control.

In this enlightened environment, the information systems manager expands his influence because of the certainty that the organization needs a corporate strategy for its microcomputers, if it wishes to achieve long-term corporate benefits, as opposed to short-term parochial and departmental benefits. Personal computers are by no means personal. They can fundamentally effect the corporate use of telephones, typewriters, telex and couriers. Office automation, in general, is also affected, as is the impact of microcomputer applications accessing central mainframes and minis. Who but the experienced, professional DP manager is capable of taking on this strategic and co-ordinating corporate role, whereby he can improve service, reduce costs, and improve productivity? He can initiate, gain commitment, and implement the use of personal computers to improve the organization's competitiveness in such key areas as:

(a) salesmen giving quotations and taking orders
(b) investment portfolio accounting, performance analysis, and graphical display of results
(c) home retailing
(d) home banking

In this environment, the DP manager accepts his inevitable central co-ordination role, and encourages users to introduce personal computers with their local operation. In return, the information systems department provides a central computing utility, with a structure, and acts as a catalyst to achieve corporate improvements in productivity and effectiveness. With personal computers on-line to mainframe corporate data, or talking to each other (even by swapping floppy discs), the information systems management must adopt a strong co-ordinating role, imposing the need to standardize, and even produce a preferred list of one or two vendors for each item of hardware and software.

The dyed in the wool DP manager who has been brought up on mainframes at possibly various organizations during his career, may be warmed towards this prospect and be pleasantly surprised after seeing his first live mini or micro installation. Admiration and incredulity is a natural reaction to witnessing user clerks performing, with apparent ease, their own transaction processing and accessing a data base. The reaction is even stronger if the observer is used to batch systems requiring card or paper tape input, having had problems recruiting and employing punch operators, and especially if he has suffered from users complaining to him about errors in data that must have been caused by their original coding and poor checking.

This scenario looks too easy. What are the technical snags that lead to the inevitable compromises? Lack of central control may tend to result in lower standards in general. With a proliferation of machines, each tends to have its own operating system, its own language(s), or its own subset of a standard language i.e., different compilers are required for the same language. Apart from the lack of portability, programmers need training in these differences, and this reduces their mobility and the flexibility of the organization's DP manpower. Similarly, interface problems can exist between the minis, the micros, and the mainframe. This may complicate direct communications or necessitate files to be re-formated.

Improved response times are possible on minis compared to the equivalent system on a mainframe which has many different types of user. However, mini computer users with many terminals may too have to wait, or even be allocated fixed time slots in order to obtain reasonable response times.

As the price of a microcomputer or small mini may be so much less than a mainframe, it is easier for users to push through the approval of purchase requisitions: there is a smaller capital investment, and costing becomes lax. In fact, many of the inevitable costs may be unforeseen at the time of purchase including sufficient allowance for depreciation and maintenance. To obtain the maximum output from the organization's investment, the performance of mainframes tend to be carefully monitored, and multiple shift working is common. This does not occur in many non mainframe installations, although a large number of on-line minicomputer systems do more batch processing in the evenings, than on-line work during office hours.

Last, but by no means least, the experienced mainframe programmer or systems analyst may be appalled by the lack of quantity or quality of basic system software on some micros or small business systems. In fact, they may have a feeling of *déjà vu*, especially if they were working on mainframes 10 to 15 years ago. With some micros, the application's user needs to be a programmer to operate the system! Very cheap hardware also requires very cheap application software, but obviously the latter cannot always contain:

. all the facilities of an expensive mainframe equivalent
. the same level of user, operational, programmer, and system documentation
. the same level of vendor support
. source code to enable easy customization (possibly due to fear of re-sale)

Distributed data processing

Distributed data processing continues the above theme and enables the power of the computer to be placed where it is most needed—at the business end, which may be, for instance, a warehouse, a cash point, a sales office, a remote depot, a subsidiary company, a government department, or even with brokers. In many circumstances this has a wide range of potential advantages. To the user, his computing facilities can be treated as another piece of business equipment, such as typewriters and filing cabinets. Apart from the obvious saving of transportation costs and the improvements in the speed of handling data, remote sites may be able to communicate without the need to go via the mainframe. Distributed processing allows further reductions of the load on the mainframe which should have less input and validation programs, less on-line control functions, and less program code (and clerical systems) for handling and rejecting errors. In fact, one shot data capture may produce significant systems advantages to the users, in terms of simplicity, accuracy and speed.

Improvements in flexibility may allow, for example, local client-orientated validity checks, or changes in input formats, but still retain the same format of files suitable for input to common programs. It may be possible to make less changes to standard software packages which are to be run on the mainframe. Another important advantage is that system security may be improved not only by the fragmentation of a centralized system to a distributed database, but also because, with local access and local files, restrictions to accessing the organization's total database are easier to implement.

The system development manager should treat distributed processing as an extension to his responsibilities not as a replacement. In fact, he has the potential to install better (smaller) systems, faster with less risk. The main problem is keeping a grip on related development and installation work at many remote locations, especially if each has different types of hardware. The obvious precautions should be taken to ensure that the system software exists and works in the proposed environment. Technical systems analysts and programmers are an installation's greatest asset. Distributing them around the organization on ever trivial tasks and without any overall career development paths is another aspect of distributed computing that should not be allowed to get out of hand.

Micro–mainframe link

Linking microcomputers to a mainframe is, potentially, a powerful technique that can create many corporate benefits. The assumption is that there is more to 'Personal Computers' than personal computing. Using microcomputers in isolation denies the benefits of accessing and sharing corporate or public data. Such data could be of strategic importance or merely operational: in either case, one avoids costly, error-prone re-keying of data. There is a wide scope in designing applications that require accessing mainframe data and programs, and then intelligently processing that data locally, off-line, using a personal computer. As far as the technology is concerned, the necessary hardware is, conceptually, reasonably clear-cut (comprising plug in PC boards, modems, controllers, and communication lines). Unfortunately, the software requirements are more complex and confusing.

Three categories of application systems can be implemented using this micromainframe technology. By far the simplest is terminal emulation, whereby the microcomputer is simulating a classical dumb terminal linked to a mainframe. This is an expensive way to provide merely a terminal, if it is not used for any other purpose. (A fully configured microcomputer with the necessary hardware and software, could be 2–3 times the cost of a terminal.) However, assuming personal computers are already in the organization for traditional uses, this could be a cheap way of gaining access to a mainframe. The disadvantages of this simplest link is that the microcomputer operator will need to master the complexities of the mainframe operating system, and he cannot use the micro's applications on the mainframe data-base.

The second category of application involves calling down, and storing on local discs, subsets of data from mainframe files or data-bases. Local processing and printing of such data can then take place using, for example, standard personal computer spreadsheets and word processing software. However, manipulation of data is required to make the mainframe files compatible with the microcomputer. An additional advantage of this approach is that (unlike the dumb terminal, or its emulation) all the local processing is off-line to the mainframe. This will, therefore, reduce the central processor's load, improve response times, and, depending on the communication lines in use, reduce line costs.

The micro–mainframe link just described can be further developed to provide a two-way file transfer: the micro sending data to the mainframe, as well as receiving it. The following is an example of such an application. A corporate financial controller extracts last year's budgets from the corporate ledger, and sends the relevant subset to each division or cost centre in a format suitable for a personal computer spreadsheet. Each division then updates the spreadsheet locally for the next financial year's budgets, and after obtaining local management approval, the spreadsheet is uploaded to the mainframe. After obtaining corporate approval for each cost centre's budget, the individual budgets are consolidated and fed into the corporate mainframe ledgers. These in turn can be downloaded again for local divisional notification, enquiry and control via personal computers.

The third main category of micro–mainframe link, is a much more generalized and user-friendly version of the previously described applications. The personal computer should be able to be used as a data entry, uploading, and downloading device. It should be capable of accessing, processing, and manipulating mainframe data locally. Data may be transferred both ways, either over-night or on-line. To achieve this, compatible communications software, resident on both micro and mainframe is required at each end of the link. However, at the time of writing, this ideal generalized solution is some way off. Currently, there are problems and deficiencies in both hardware and software, with few successful examples of micro–mainframe links. With over 150 relevant products on the market, there is much press hype, but the packages are relatively expensive, have few features and are not easy to use. The lack of user friendliness has several causes, one of which relates to the different environments and attitudes between the typical personal computer user and the typical mainframe user. A rigid, controlled, secure, complex operating system dominated environment is associated with a mainframe installation. The personal computer user, on the other hand, has not necessarily grown up with this traditional DP background, and he adopts a more casual approach, with less concern over security or standards, and uses a different, much smaller and incompatible operating system. Currently, it is not easy to use an interface to the mainframe data-base, and the micro user needs to master the mainframe's operating system. In addition, there is no automatic communication between mainframe data and micro application software. What is required is a simple selection, manipulation, and reformatting mechanism involving generalized software. At present, for each application, the DP department must write the specific software, with the inevitable long lead times. This is not the quick and relatively simple solution the micro user expects!

Having described above some of the basic hardware and software limitations, it is appropriate to examine some application orientated problems that may need to be addressed to achieve effective micro–mainframe links. In general, as the data capacity of floppy discs is far smaller then mainframe files, it is necessary to limit the selection criteria for downloading mainframe data held as large volume master files. Having successfully downloaded the required data, it will probably need reformatting for use by the personal computer's software. There is then a serious corporate security problem as floppy discs can easily be removed from the premises, and the data used for unauthorized purposes. This problem does not arise with dumb terminals linked to a mainframe. Not only must data be viewed at the terminal, but a complex, hierarchical identification code is required for the user to gain access to that particular set of data. With the casual personal computer environment, such essential corporate control is more difficult to organize automatically by hardware and software checks. An inbuilt restriction must be placed on what subset of data each micro can access and download from the mainframe. This must be enforced by physical controls locally.

Similar application control problem occur when attempting to upload data from a micro to a mainframe. Authorized persons only must be allowed to make specific authorized updates to master files held on the mainframe. Updating master files and data-bases in an uncontrolled manner is unthinkable on a mainframe. Apart from the above controls, it is necessary that a data validation program checks on every record uploaded from personal computers. As will be apparent, the benefits of micro–mainframe links need to be tempered by the practical problems involved. A gradual, step-by-step approach would seem more appropriate than attempting to rush into a full-blown system.

Batch systems

Batch systems are the traditional method of implementing computerized applications and are consequently well known, well tested and reliable. System controls and security aspects within batch systems are, in general, easier to apply than for non-batch systems.

With regard to difficulty and management risk, magnetic tape systems may occasionally be easier to implement than systems using disc files, because tape systems have been in existence longer than discs (but this is becoming much less important). However, there is a choice of file structure and processing methods for discs which may add to the development time, and some disc processing techniques can cause difficulty, requiring non standard software.

The easiest disc processing method is serial processing with carry forward and brought forward files, as opposed to the much more difficult system of up-dating files in place. Superimposed on these two approaches is the choice of disc access method which, in ascending order of difficulty, is serial, sequential with keys, index sequential, skip/selective sequential, and random. These are well covered in existing literature.

Remote job entry

Local processing, where the computer is in close proximity to the user and the sources of data, is easier to implement than a situation where data originates nationally, and the computer is not close to the user. The easiest sub-set of remote processing is remote job entry (RJE), where batch systems still apply, but input data is fed into a remote terminal (connected by telephone lines to a computer) and output reports are produced by the terminal. This minimizes delays (from carriers or by post) and allows errors to be corrected earlier, further improving throughput of the batch system.

Conventional remote batch working is becoming less attractive because of the cost of off-line data preparation. A refinement in RJE is to have intelligent terminals which allow local validation and processing. It is also possible to replace the need for an intermediary data medium (e.g. cards, paper tape, etc.) with direct data entry by the user on to say, a floppy disc. Batches of clean data on the disc can then be sent by RJE. A further degree of complexity is to replace the terminal by a minicomputer. The limitations of RJE is the eventual build up of input and output queues if too many jobs are being run, and the restrictions of line capacity on the remote printing of large jobs.

On-line systems

The next level of management difficulty is on-line systems, which tend to be more expensive than their batch counterparts. For example, a typical real time system could be available to its users for 8 hours per day, whilst an equivalent batch system might take less than 1 hour of computer time. There is also the overhead of terminals, modems and lines. To reduce the effects of a failure, on-line systems usually include an element of duplication and redundancy, which result in additional costs for extra hardware and software, as well as for fall-back facilities. Further complications arise from the need for a teleprocessing monitor, which in turn requires additional hardware and software overheads, as well as a management decision on which package to purchase (or whether to write one's own). Lastly, as all data must be readily accessible, additional hardware and software is required to handle the (usually significant) increase in on-line file storage.

Although on-line systems are in general, more difficult to implement than batch and RJE systems, there are several levels of difficulty. On-line enquiries, via a terminal, are relatively the easiest and less complex to implement. Relatively more difficult both technically and to manage, are data collection systems on-line to a mainframe, where data entry media (e.g. cards) are replaced. When data arises it is entered direct via a terminal. It is possible to validate and correct errors as they are entered, and replace conventional batch control, validation, and error control programs. Local, on-line, transaction orientated systems implemented on some minis or small business systems with relevant powerful operating systems, make this more and more an attractive low risk approach. But beware, because the lack of problems during development may be transferred to a different set of problems which occur during post live implementation. For example, there may be problems involved in tuning the system, so that several different users and the programmers can all access the computer when they need to, and obtain a decent response time.

The system that presents the next highest degree of difficulty to management and technical staff is the main file updating system on-line. This is a true 'real time' system and apart from traditionally being difficult to develop on a mainframe, tends to be very costly, in proportion to the required response times, up-times, file security and recovery.

Data-base

The data-base concept has been in existence for many years, and has attracted much intellectual attention and research. This has benefited its development to a sophisticated level, and has produced many useful spin-offs. Generally accepted principals now exist for understanding data, such as entities, data structures, and relationship charts. These are relevant to DP work, irrespective of data-bases. Similarly, many useful techniques have become adopted with such buzz words as canonical synthesis, third normal form, or relational tables of data. Systems development work in general has benefited from the growth of data-base originated techniques, even if the computer installation or project does not need a data-base. In particular, numerous development methodologies on the market are based on techniques developed for data-base work. In fact, such methodologies lead to automation of the system development process, irrespective of whether data-bases are adopted or not.

Conceptually, a data-base is data stored on a computer, not just as independent 'flat' files but in an interlinked and structured fashion. This data should not only be relevant to the organization's day-to-day operation, but should provide the source of information for management control and planning activities. Because of the complex software problems, and hardware overheads associated with data-bases, it is generally a better management decision not to write one's own software, but to acquire a proprietary 'data-base management system'. This is a software product used to define, store, maintain, allow access to, and control the corporate data-base. Proprietary data-base management systems usually have associated software that provides general facilities for accessing data-bases, and for obtaining the best benefits from them. Important examples of these are data-base enquiry languages and associated fourth generation languages.

Different structured data-bases are possible, but the market is currently moving from hierarchical towards relational data-bases. The latter is a method of storing data in the form of tables so that it is more meaningful in the business environment, rather than in the traditional fashion, which is highly optimized for computer systems to process. However, for high volume, fast response, operational systems, the hierarchical data-base may give a better performance, but this may be less important in the future as hardware costs become cheaper. For information centre requirements involving *ad hoc*, complex enquiries, relational data-bases may be preferable.

Many benefits are associated with adopting a (relational) data-base approach, but sound management judgement is necessary to disentangle whether the claimed benefits are really associated with the data-base. On closer inspection, the benefits could be derived from using the associated fourth generation language for faster programming or for prototyping. Alternatively, installing a data-base might (unwittingly) coincide with the adoption of a better development methodology which is based on a data orientation. Installing a data-base system necessitates moving from a passive to an active data dictionary. This ensures that all relevant documentation and cross-references are together, accurate, complete, and reflect reality. Maintenance work is therefore greatly facilitated. Giving users a data-base query language for producing their own outputs, or involving them with data analysis and entity relationships may relieve the system development teams of much effort. A spin-off from all the above techniques is that a saving can be made on the amount of documentation that needs to be produced and maintained, such as program specifications. These factors, not the data-base itself, may be considered as providing the major benefits in productivity and maintenance.

In general, the reasons for adopting a relational data-base approach include the need for flexibility in the system's design so that an easier and faster DP response can be made to market and statutory requirements. (Traditionally designed systems are notoriously difficult to amend for new products and features.) To improve flexibility of the data-base design, and to improve the chances of simplifying future systems changes, it should prove beneficial to map the original business orientated entity diagrams to the relational tables comprising the final data-base design. This confirms that the business requirements have been covered and are reflected in the final design. Another advantage of a data-base is the ease of taking different views of data, so that traditional sorts, and input/output problems are reduced, as are multiple file passes. In fact, because of these latter factors, the performance of an old system converted to a data-base may not necessarily be worse. This flexibility, coupled with the above ancillary benefits could improve system maintenance and enhancement productivity by 10% to 20%. The other major benefit is to improve the accessibility and usefulness of the organization's data, thereby assisting the management decision making process.

Summarizing this section, it could be claimed that most of the stated benefits could be obtained without data-bases. However, introducing a proprietory data-base management system seems to act as a catalyst in adopting, simultaneously, many of the beneficial techniques outlined above. A sound management approach could, therefore, be to move as many existing systems as possible over to data-bases, and so reap the associated and coincidental benefits as quickly as possible. The next (possibly less beneficial step) could be to tune and rationalize these new data-bases, and then worry if duplication of data, consistency of data between data-bases, and other purist considerations can add much in further improvements to the gains already realized.

The need for a data-base approach to systems is currently in vogue, with much sales activity by suppliers of software, consultancy, and training. Advantages claimed for the adoption of data-bases include a reduction in data redundancy; the ability to produce reports from information previously unrelated; a greater availability of information; reduced development lead times with improved system and programmer productivity; and last but not least, a significant reduction in maintenance costs, when fields are amended or added.

There is a school of thought whereby the data-base approach of projects organizing files independently of applications is largely disregarded in favour of traditional projects whereby applications and their files are developed together. In practice, many application orientated data-bases may be required, but only one data-base management system (DBMS) is necessary to support these data-bases. The management and technical problems that are experienced when introducing a data-base should not be underestimated, as they can be expensive in terms of additional hardware (more storage, faster processing), software (purchasing and implementing a proprietary package) and manpower requirements (including data correction, and conversion). Consequently, both development effort, and the application's processing time could be increased. Additional complications might also arise from the necessity to update in place (more sophisticated and more complex security), and concurrent functional processes may not be appropriate if the system requires serial processes to be performed. In some cases concurrent functional runs would not automatically give faster processing, as the multi-programming factor would increase. Additionally, there would be almost simultaneous requests for the same record which would introduce an element of serial processing.

Does the application warrant the effort expended on a data-base? In general, it is advantageous if a data-base approach is combined with teleprocessing, and if the system has many varied transaction types and enquiries. Batch systems, on the other hand, generally present a more limited use for a data-base, and may be difficult to cost justify. A management trade-off has to be made, in the short term between:

(a) implementing a conventional (batch) system as quickly as possible to obtain the business benefits as early as possible; or

(b) waiting for the data-base to be implemented and delaying the business benefits.

In the longer term, a justification based on a five to seven year view has to be made by management. The cost of avoiding duplication of data and associated accessing programs (as well as missing out on other data-base benefits), has to be compared to the cost of identifying, collecting, verifying, and converting data, and then setting up a data-base.

A management approach, that is often valid, is both a compromise between the above two alternatives, as well as an evolutionary stepping-stone towards data-base systems. This entails an intermediary data dictionary stage, where all systems, programs, modules, files, records and fields are held on computer (using a proprietary software package). A flexible cross-referencing system enables enquiries to be made of the 'where used?' nature, and items can be amended during the development or maintenance phases. However, a very disciplined information systems department is required. Development staff will be reluctant to keep a data dictionary up to date in a non data-base environment. There may be little benefit for the individuals concerned in using a free-standing proprietary data dictionary, which, in general, is not very user friendly.

Data-base administration is a difficult but important full-time function (particularly data privacy and ownership). There is no short cut, it is a slow, tedious, time-consuming exercise collating and agreeing items of data.

Viewdata

Viewdata is a generic term for transmitting, at relatively low cost, text and images to a wide audience, over national communications networks. Extensive participation is possible as the technology involves simply plugging into telephone sockets. Either the public telephone system is used directly, or a connection is made to proprietary networks, some of which may be industry orientated. The attraction of the system is that a host of relatively cheap, relevant equipment already exists in, say, the home, or branch office. Such examples could be remote terminals, TV adaptors, or microcomputers that only require, say, a modem, communications board or a colour board.

Although a basic passive system may be useful, with the audience just being able to receive pages of information (e.g. passive sales information of prices, availability, delivery), the real advantages accrue when a viewdata system is connected to a corporate information systems network. This, for example, would allow an active enquiry or quotation system to be established. A possible technique is to use a mini or microcomputer to interface the corporate mainframe to the public network. The minicomputer acts as a front end and converts a viewdata page to look like a mainframe network screen and vice versa. Telephone line costs need not be high, as local charge rates often apply, and pages of information may be quickly stored locally, for subsequent off-line use. An obvious problem to overcome is the restriction of access. Each user logging-on must be authorized, and restricted to particular records that he may view or amend (e.g. a salesman's own clients).

In conclusion, viewdata technology may be worth exploring, because in certain industries (for example, motor cars, insurance), it may provide a strategic marketing and sales aid. Benefits could be improvements in the productivity of salesmen, in the corporate image, and in customer servicing.

Packages

A valid approach to implementing a system could be to introduce a package supplied by a computer manufacturer, software house or even another installation, and where appropriate, appreciable reductions in time and cost may be made. Sensibly, the installation does not wish to 're-invent the wheel' or employ the necessary expertise. Packages may be technically computer orientated system software, or application orientated. The latter category includes systems such as stock control, ledgers, payroll, production control, etc., and general 'tools' such as linear programming or report generators.

Although initially a package approach may appear appealing; deficiencies and a lack of flexibility are often found during evaluation or implementation. Attempting to modify a package is not always easy, even if there is good documentation. The management decision to go ahead should assume it is more difficult to modify code, or add code, than write the equivalent amount of code from scratch. The machine time for testing such modifications is appreciably more (a factor of 10 has been known) than testing the equivalent amount of original code.

Bureau/software house

The management effort and risk could be minimized, in some cases, by using a computer bureau, which could run the application system (reducing hardware and site problems), or even by allowing them or a software house to develop the system (reducing in-house manpower and development problems). In some situations, a subsidiary company, or government body could use the group computer as a bureau, or use the group's centralized DP resources for development as well. Communication based systems, with the user having his own local terminals can make this option very attractive, and is an example of resource sharing.

A bureau approach may be valid for many applications of a specialized nature when local expertise is not available (e.g. investment portfolio analysis), or in some common business systems, when resources could be spent more profitably (e.g. payroll or bought ledger), or sometimes where the organization's own computer is too small for infrequent jobs (e.g. a large linear programming application), or when an organization cannot justify investment in its own computer.

In general, within a few years when problems arise, management in larger companies often lose the short term advantages of this method because of relatively expensive running costs, lack of flexibility to accommodate changes in business needs, and the difficulty in integrating with other systems, especially when the organization acquires its own computer.

In making the decision to subcontract development of a system and reduce management resources, it must be clearly established that the organization's management is not also abdicating its responsibilities.

CHAPTER SUMMARY

This chapter is relevant to the system development management function (or its equivalent), and covers the fundamentals of sizing a project and its end-product.

Macro-estimates of projects can be of use in several situations, including business reviews; preparing development phase estimates; appointing project managers; before formally justifying a project, and prior to a large expense being incurred. The quantified information given, may be used to confirm that the overall planned costs, man days effort, resources, product size, etc., are consistent with the pro rata tables of values for different sized projects. If there are significant differences, senior management should be made aware of the reasons for them.

It must be emphasized that the objective of this project-sizing exercise primarily is not to label a project 'small', 'medium', or 'large', but to determine if any of the measurable factors deviate significantly from the norm. For example, the estimated total project cost may appear too low for the number of program statements being produced; or the estimated machine time for testing is incompatible with the number of statements; or the number of staff is significantly disproportionate because of a high risk data capture problem; or a high number of interactions for a small project could indicate future problems.

Senior management, together with the computer department management, could decide whether the project is too large, and if it would be beneficial to replace it by smaller phased projects. After this decision has been taken, and the project graded, it should be possible to appoint the appropriate grade of project manager. It must be appreciated that the sizing of a project (and the appointment of the project manager) should be carried out as early as possible in the system development cycle.

The computer department and the personnel department could produce salary grades and promotional paths for project managers that tie up with these project sizes. In this way, the better project managers could be attracted, retained, and kept fully motivated. However, this mainly relates to large organizations.

Having attempted to assess the 'management difficulty' by quantifying the development project in overall terms, we take a more detailed look at the application system and ways of implementing it. This leads to a systematic method for the development manager to make strategic decisions. Consideration of the project's end-product is the starting point in any management methodology, and an important consideration is the complexity of the system, and the significance of interactions is stressed. Comparisons may be made between the end-product under review, and the complexity of different types of computerized systems. This information may prove useful when estimating development effort, producing schedules, or when justifying the project.

A further aspect of the end-product is its proposed technology, of which various types are available, each with its own advantages and disadvantages, and each requiring different levels of management competence.

Chapter 6

The particular end-product

INTRODUCTION AND THE DIFFICULTY OF DEFINING THE END-PRODUCT

The previous chapter considered the end-product of a project in conceptual terms. This chapter takes the discussion one stage further by examining the more important practical features of the end-product. The text moves from generalities to specifics and defines the planning methodology and tasks required for a particular end-product. This is important because the end-product is often difficult to define in black and white terms, and in large integrated systems may become amoeba-like, being difficult to keep within continual grasp and under complete control.

The topics covered relate mainly to the project manager's responsibilities, while the senior management in the information systems department exercises an important reviewing role.

An example of the difficulty in defining an end-product

The original schedule for a public utility's customer enquiry system plainly stated that the go-live date was 1st August. During June, the project control system was still confirming this date, and testing was going well. A public announcement was made that the system would go live in August. However, a few weeks later, just before conversion and installation, senior DP and line management took stock, and it gradually dawned on them that the end-product was not something that was black and white and went live on a specific day. In effect it included:

(a) A reference file in a new format which had to be live for at least one month with six other systems using it, before the main enquiry system could go live using this reference file.
(b) A set of tested programs which provided conversion information.
(c) Five feeder systems which had to be modified so that they provided basic data for the enquiry system.
(d) One month's information to provide base data for set-up.
(c) A further one month's running of a daily system to provide accumulated data.
(f) A monthly suite of programs.
(g) The main enquiry programs (which were to give a response within 3 seconds).

(h) A phased conversion of geographic areas.

Because of system, volume, and conversion considerations, a go-live date of 1st August actually meant that customer's enquiries (the main purpose of the system and the development project) would not be handled until the end of October at the earliest—and then only for a few areas. Because the project's end-product was not fully defined early on, senior user management ultimately were extremely annoyed, feeling that they had been deceived.

END-PRODUCT CLARIFICATION AND SIZING

The main purpose of a project is to deliver the end-product! Consequently, it is necessary for the systems manager or project manager to define this as early in the project as possible, as it forms an important practical basis for his subsequent strategic and tactical planning. For convenience, the end-product plan can be considered as comprising the following constituents, which are better treated as explicit and separate items:

(a) the delivery plan (the application's program code and documentation)
(b) the non-deliverable program code (especially written support software)
(c) the non-deliverable non-program generating work (numerous supporting activities)
(d) the data-capture requirements
(e) the conversion.

The delivery plan states what is being handed over to the line users as an operational system. It should spell out the programs that make up the system, and should contain estimates of their sizes in terms of, say, program statements and the expected degree of difficulty. Other factors which comprise the end-product are the documents relating to the specifications and user procedure manuals, together with application system training. Apart from some historical performance statistics and data, useful for planning future projects, these constituents of the end-product are the only tangible remains when a project has been completed.

An important reason for underestimating product size is failure to allow for non-deliverable programs that are necessary for support or are required for one-off use. Examples of these are programs to facilitate testing, or programs to convert files. Typically these non-deliverable programs could amount to an additional 20–30 per cent of the deliverable programs. It is sometimes unbelievable how this amount of one-off code builds up throughout the duration of the project. Even the development team may be surprised when, at the end of a project they learn the total number of lines of program code actually written.

Support code consideration during the earliest planning activity is essential. The supporting activities necessary to achieve the above program code are discussed in a later chapter in greater detail.

One of the most important influences on the size of the end-product is exercised by data capture, and/or conversion. As we have seen, it has been known for data capture to cost more than the rest of the development effort. This can occur when there are many poorly maintained, complex clerical files requiring conversion to the computer system. These topics are covered in more detail later in this chapter.

We have illustrated that the end-product comprises deliverable and non-deliverable components, program generating and non-program generating activities, and data-capture and conversion considerations. These will form the basis for management's planning methodology, and as such it is sensible to treat each separately. It should be appreciated that defining the end-product in this manner and sizing it is not a one-off exercise. This end-product plan needs continual updating throughout every development phase (from feasibility to installation). For example, at the earliest parts of the feasibility study, the known end-product could just be an overall 'guestimate' of the number of program statements to be written, with an allowance of plus 30% for support programs; whilst at the program design phase the end-product can be precisely defined in terms of the size and complexity of each program or module. The details of program sizes are particularly useful when estimating and producing the development plan.

SCHEDULE FOR THE DELIVERY OF THE END-PRODUCT IN STAGES

Having broadly defined the total end-product it is often a practical necessity for it to now be broken down into chronological *stages* of delivery. This has no connection with the system development phases discussed earlier, which always apply to each stage. Stages reflect the probable need to break down the implementation of larger systems into smaller business functions. Each period over which one of these business functions is developed and implemented may be termed a stage. This method not only improves control, but gives the user a working system much sooner than attempting to implement all facilities at one time. Scheduling stages will depend on many constraints, the most significant of which are:

(a) the practical business limitations imposed by conversion to the new system of customers, products, geographical areas, etc.
(b) business priorities which dictate those facilities required first
(c) the actual development time
(d) budgetary limitations, where attempting to bring forward a delivery date would increase staff and resource costs above annual limits
(e) the difficulty of obtaining experienced staff
(f) the delivery of hardware or software.

It must be appreciated that the publication of a schedule cannot be accomplished in isolation, nor based solely on considerations of the end-product which is itself influenced by a host of technical and development restrictions and compromises. The final end-product is what can be built in the time, with given resources, with available technology and with cost justifiable features. Detailed planning of the entire development process is required before target dates can be mentioned to either users or project staff—it would be naive to do otherwise. Illustrated here is basically a method of crystallizing and formulating the shape of the end-product, so that users and DP staff alike understand the staged nature of it. Any dates quoted at this time are *provisional*. The only dates to be relied upon are firm ones which relate solely to the *current* phase of development, and which have relatively short time-horizons.

Assuming the preliminary planning work has been done and having identified at an early date the main stages of making live each feature of the system, the project manager should draw up and publish a list with headings as shown in the example below (which related to an integrated reservation, ledger and marketing system for a hotel).

Description of system facilities available to user	User business functions affected	Provisional live dates
1. Cash book part of standard ledgers package.	Local accounts departments.	January
2. Profit and loss, and balance sheet.	Corporate financial control.	June
3. Reservations and bookings control	Local reception staff. Local cleaning staff. Corporate administration department.	March
4. Reservations and booking control with accounting.	Local reception staff. Local accounts department.	April
5. As 4 above plus automatic input to ledger package as in 1 above.	Corporate financial control.	May
6. Analysis of booking statistics.	Corporate marketing department.	May

A complementary bar-chart could also be drawn up to illustrate the schedule for delivery. Publishing this schedule may appear to place the project manager's head on a block, but this is not a practical problem because (a) changes in requirements often occur and this may provide an excuse for amending the delivery commitments by trading off quality and/or facilities against development time, and (b) the project manager should benefit from improved co-operation resulting from the project's clearer objectives.

MINIMIZING RISK IN THE DESIGN OF THE END-PRODUCT

Technical concepts for minimizing risks in the end-product may be incorporated in an application system, particularly while it is still in the design phase. The effects of ignoring some of these basic design aims may manifest themselves only after the application system has gone live, and in several cases, many months after going live. The overall basic objective then, is for the project to provide the line users with an application system they will be able to control, that is error free, watertight, accurate and reflects their changing business requirements, without latent defects or reduced facilities.

User transparency (and flexible systems design)

The project staff should attempt to build into the end-product, the philosophy of user transparency, i.e. the functional activities carried out by the user department ideally should be independent of the computer system; the computer files and their structure; the programs; the processing methods of the files; and independent of the user department's organization. Obviously this is easier said than done, because it means designing a system that accommodates, for example, new products being introduced, changes to line printer or VDU screen outputs, and alterations to the logic or processing rules. At best, this user transparency concept requires strategic thinking about future developments and their possible computing consequences. At least, the computer system should be designed flexibly, with data structures reflecting the business needs, so that it is easy to incorporate future changes in the line users' requirements.

One common practical method of producing this user transparency is to hold all variable information (e.g. validation rules, credit limits, processing rules for different products) on separate general reference files, which can be updated easily and separately from the rest of the system. However, having *too many* tables can be counter-productive. Excessive accesses to these tables may result in poor response times, or poor throughput. Additionally, keeping many (interdependent) tables in step whilst updating them, may become problematical.

Intelligent processing

In some cases, a system could be made more sophisticated if it intelligently interpreted certain errors, say, in transaction data. After making the necessary corrections, the system could continue to process an error transaction, and appropriately account for it, easing the load on the user.

The handling of standing order payments received daily on magnetic tape files from the clearing banks or the Giro system provides a simple, but very effective example of the intelligent interpretation of error data. Each record on these tape files needs to contain the individual customer's account number as devised by the organization receiving the tapes as input. This obviously facilitates accounting for each payment. However, this number has to be entered by the banks or Giro from the original standing order authority. Apart from the banks not requiring to get this code number correct for running their system, they need to cater for the maximum sized code used by any one of their customers. For the majority of systems this code is usually much smaller

(a) HOW AN ERROR CAN ARISE

0048261F	—	the actual customer number
becomes		
004 8/261F	—	errors after coding and data entry

(b) HOW ERRORS CAN BE EDITED CORRECTLY

	Errors		Correctly edited
Bank			
	0048261F..	becomes	0048261F
	0091505 E–	becomes	0091505E
Giro			
	6I/03755D	becomes	6103755D
	S6 08038K	becomes	5608038K
	82479F	becomes	0082479F

(c) EXAMPLES OF ERROR REDUCTION RATES

	Error rate before	Error rate after
Giro	33%	4%
Bank	24%	5%

Figure 6.1. An example of intelligent error processing

than the total number of spaces provided. Figure 6.1 (a) illustrates how some errors can be caused; in this case by data entry staff attempting to fill up all the boxes on a transaction coding form.

Figure 6.1 (b) indicates how a computer payments system using simple logic rules can intelligently edit out spaces, other erroneous characters and mis-alignments on these transaction receipts.

Some actual reductions in error rates for live runs are shown in Figure 6.1 (c). Even greater improvements could have been made with automatically generating and testing check digits, and also matching suspect code numbers to the master file and checking on additional data.

In conjunction with a suspense/reject concept, this example of intelligent processing might avoid the computer system being marred by data errors outside its control, and avoids the line user having to employ an extensive clerical team to resolve the problems. This approach has the psychological benefit of not passing on to the user too many limitations of computer systems.

Clean source data

It is necessary to have clean source data, but sometimes the source department is not directly involved in the system or in its development. This problem of error data may manifest itself most alarmingly in the more integrated or larger computer systems, where data could be created and coded in one part of the organization, and used in another part.

The usual solution to this problem is to place comprehensive validity checks within each program at the point of data input, as well as at the file update stage.

However, this approach does not tackle the *cause* of the problem. It is insufficient to design the system mainly with the user (s) who benefits from the outputs in mind. The psychological solution is to provide the originators of the data with sufficient benefits so that they are motivated to ensure that all their data is clean. The system should be controlled and operated by the user, and designed so that failure to correct the system will inhibit the efficient functioning of the user department. Adoption of this approach may be a good way to minimize risks from poor data.

Integrated data

In spite of incorporating the above design features, no assumptions should be made about the quality of data being received as input from another system. Also no system should be 'dumb' and accept the data it receives without question. This means that all such input data although theoretically correct should be validity checked for logical combinations, completeness and ranges of values. In practice, one method whereby 'impossible' errors may find their way onto master files is during conversion or data capture, possibly before the system goes live. What may happen is that the conversion programs are less stringent, or errors in the existing system are dormant and may not be appreciated. Possibly the earlier versions of programs used to set up the system are later found to be suspect but it is too late to assess the ramifications on the master file. Each program and system in an integrated set-up should have independent controls at every input and output interface. This is desirable because it helps to prevent some problems from arising, and if they eventually do arise, it is easier to find out what is causing the trouble.

Suspense/reject of error data

One way of controlling transaction data may possibly be via the introduction of a suspense/reject file. The idea is for the computer to 'remember' all errors, and periodically 'remind' the users to make the necessary corrections. This may be a good method of controlling line user staff responsibility, especially when there are many diffuse users submitting transactions. Two words of warning are appropriate. In the first few months of a system going live, errors in both existing data and new transactions could cause the suspense file to grow at a rate that negates the benefits. Secondly, this suspense system could become complex and expensive to develop. The solution is not to attempt to do too much automatic remembering, nor to have too severe validation on minor fields. Dating items that may have been on the suspense file over a certain period of time may also help.

Operational controls

Operation controls could include an automatic system to ensure that the correct files always are mounted and used in the correct sequence. Error recovery should be accounted for automatically, and in any dispute with the user regarding the accuracy of data, a DP operations department should be able to prove that the correct transactions, files, and programs were used. In addition, check point restart should be employed for lengthy batch runs, and graceful degradation built into on-line systems, enabling an easy and controlled recovery after computer failures.

Audit of dormant data

A common problem in data processing systems design is the treatment of master file records that have no transactions associated with them for a long period of time. The questions to be resolved include:

(a) Are there serious errors in the system whereby customers' outstanding orders or debts are not being collected?
(b) Are the records in question really dead? This is not always easy to establish. For example, a stock item or product part may be obsolete, but is still required as a spares part. Another example is when an order has not been received from a customer or broker for say 1 year. This may not mean that no orders will be forthcoming in the future.
(c) Can these dormant records even be detected? This is not as obvious as it seems, as many systems do not have a built-in search facility, nor is it possible to know when a master record was last accessed.
(d) Is valuable disk storage being wasted?
(e) Is the processing time increased excessively, because of the continual necessity to read a high proportion of out-of-date or terminated information?
(f) Is the response time similarly affected?
(g) Is it operationally cheaper to ensure that dormant records are regularly removed and placed in an archive file? Or is it better to leave them as they are?

It is apparent that the problems are not clear-cut. A possible solution might be to design the application system so that the last transaction date for each record is stored as part of that record on the master file. An independent audit program could read the master file monthly, searching for, and printing-out details of records, where no movements have taken place for, say, the last 3 months. The line user department could then investigate the records on this print-out. In addition, this audit program after say, a 13 month dormant period, might remove the records in question; account for them; and copy them to a magnetic tape archive file, after updating an index of records held on that file. The line users must check the print-out produced, and ensure that system errors do not exist, and that the correct records were archived. Finally, if a record is required to become reinstated some time in the future, the archive index will enable it to be returned to the live master file.

Fragility analysis (for more robust systems)

Another technique for minimizing risk, mainly useful during the proving, installation, or maintenance phases, is to carry out a fragility analysis. This basically is a brain-storming session involving the systems analysts, programmers, DP operations staff, and relevant users of the system. The idea here is to go through the system, step-by-step, and think of every possibility that can go wrong from any cause. Participants at this session, all of whom should be intimate with the system, should use a good, well-annotated system flowchart as a systematic guide, and be led by the project manager, who should ensure that all ideas are considered and not only the preconceived notions of the noisiest members.

Data quality measurement

Yet another useful way of minimizing risks prior to an application system going live, is to measure the accuracy of the system in advance by the use of a pilot study, which takes scientific statistical samples of both file data and transaction data. The system can be test-run and the results compared against manual or other records. Before deciding to go live, an error rate can then be established which may or may not be acceptable. This technique can, for example, be used for testing direct data entry or a coding form. In this case, the keying errors, coding, or transcription errors, or the interpretation of the coding procedures manual, can all be separately measured, and the acceptability of the input procedures can be assessed.

A further use of this measurement technique might apply to a system that relies on data passed to it from other systems. The reliability of these other systems can be ascertained, allowing the project manager to assess the risk of going live with his project, when its success depends on different projects or systems.

SECURITY AND PRIVACY

It is a sign of the times that discussions regarding computer systems are incomplete without a reference to the growing problem areas of security and privacy. In essence, security relates to the protection of computer based assets such as money, hardware, software, or data. Privacy involves restricting access to sensitive information such as personal data, salaries, etc. which are held on computer systems.

- The greater use of, and reliance on computers in general, is one such reason why these twin concerns of security and privacy are of increasing importance. As computers become simpler to use, unauthorized access also becomes easier. This can be contrasted to tradtional, centralized, batch processing which is becoming an ever decreasing component of application systems. By its very nature, batch processing provides limited access, as separate departments are usually responsible for systems work, programming, data input, and operation. Some degree of collusion is therefore needed to tamper with such systems. Replacing batch systems are distributed and decentralized information systems involving public communication lines, private switchboards, local area networks, and terminals, as well as the mushrooming use of personal computers. These systems are all designed for ever-improving user friendliness: the opposite requirement for tightening security and privacy. For example, copying sensitive data onto floppy discs is usually very easy, or someone whose terminal is part of a network may be provided with automatic log-on facilities.

Another reason for the increasing importance of security and privacy is a greater computer awareness by the general public, not only from the information systems training received at work, but from the media in general, with greater publicity for fraud, etc. In addition, law makers are catching up with the information systems age, making criminal offences of many previously questionable practices and abuses of computer systems. Particular examples are the data protection laws being introduced in many countries. Management are becoming personally liable legally for breaches of security and privacy.

Before information systems managers can plan preventative measures and recovery, it may first prove useful to list the main types of security and privacy threats. It is sobering to realize that, in practice, should any of the following occur, then losses to the organization are usually discovered by accident (rather than by audit or automatic control mechanisms).

Unintentional errors

Forgetting to produce back-up copies of main files
Controls within an application system that are missing
Accidental over-writing of master data
Erroneous update of fields of data

Accidental damage

Physical damage to hardware, software, and data caused by accidents such as fire, storm, flood

Unethical practices

Gaining unauthorized access to files
Passing on confidential information (such as mailing lists)
Using corporate computers for noncorporate uses
Eavesdropping over communication lines
Unauthorized copying of data

Criminal Actions

Theft of equipment
Theft of information stored on computer files, (such as customer lists)
Illegal copying of software (corporate or proprietary) which is protected by copyright.

Creating fictitious records

Falsifying records

Sabotage by bomb, arson, or the deliberate physical destruction of hardware, software, data, communication lines, etc.

Sabotage by nonphysical means, such as delayed logic errors in software (program code that self destructs on a certain date, or tests for a certain condition)

In practice, about 75% of losses occur within the above two categories of unintentional errors and accidental damage. Poor procedures and management oversights are the main causes for these failures. Deliberate criminal actions are by no means the major consideration for management preventative measures.

Who is responsible for breaches in security and privacy? In general, there is great reluctance for organizations to report such incidences, or to prosecute. Consequently, only a fraction of a per cent of culprits are convicted, making a mockery of the old adage 'crime does not pay'. Internal employees are the greatest cause of error, but historically, solutions to security problems have been aimed at external causes, such as hackers perpetrating break-ins to networks. Dishonest, or disgruntled employees are the least likely reported offenders. Male offenders outnumber females by about four to one, with a higher instance of abuses emanating from management and supervisory levels, rather than from the workforce.

Having briefly covered the problem areas, it is appropriate to examine some of the solutions to security and privacy, that can be introduced by information systems management. First, it is preferable to identify those assets which are at risk. Convenient headings might be money, data, hardware, and software. For each asset and risk, it is necessary to draw up a catastrophe plan that details the method of recovery, and the practical consequences of the time delay to effect that recovery. (For example, the plan will probably include the necessary advance arrangements that need to be made for stand-by hardware, and the time and manpower effort required to recover from a physical disaster.) Similarly, the catastrophe plan must allow for recovery of lost or corrupted data. It is also advisable to itemize insurable losses, and make the necessary provisions.

Catastrophe plans are the worst case, which hopefully should never be required, if sufficient preventative counter-measures are introduced by management. An awareness campaign within the organization is a good starting point, so that all management and staff appreciate the problem areas, and that accidents and mistakes are the most frequent cause of losses. Education is required on avoiding common errors and on the need for better system controls–both clerical and automatic. A decentralized security policy could be appropriate so that users are given explicit responsibility in specific areas. A central security officer could be appointed to formulate ideas, and to ensure policy is adhered to. The organization should have a policy of continuous security improvement, that includes an immediate start at making small improvements. In fact, employees could even be asked to sign to the effect that they have seen a copy of the organization's policy and procedures relating to security and privacy.

Within the information systems department itself, risks assessment should be at least an annual consideration, resulting in specific technical counter-measures being introduced. Restricting access to terminals and personal computers is a common approach. Switching on terminals or personal computers via keys may have some benefit (assuming the key is not left in the lock by an absent user). Not so common is the introduction of a special security procedure for issuing, initializing, and formatting floppy disks. Passwords for logging-on to networks, or to sensitive application systems, are almost universal. Ideally, each individual should be restricted to specific physical terminals, application systems, files, and items of data. Between six to ten characters are the optimum size of passwords, which could be set centrally, by the users, or a combination of both. In the latter cases, users should have some instruction in setting sound passwords. The advantage of a central element in the password is that a security log of transactions can be used to identify who input a specific transaction. This may be invaluable during an audit. Passwords should be changed monthly, even if this is rather a chore, especially as most people have several passwords for different applications, and remembering the current versions is not always easy. This leads to the counter-productive tendency of leaving a note of the password by the terminal.

Not only should the security system restrict the number of log-on failures to, say, four, it should also maintain an audit trail of unsuccessful attempts at access, and slow down the log-on procedure to foil hackers attempting diffferent combinations at high speed. For a similar reason, modem numbers should be different from the organization's telephone numbers, and together with passwords, they should not be published, especially not by means of bulletin boards. Similarly, help screens should not be provided before a user is logged on, and users not logging-off correctly should be disconnected. In certain circumstances it may be possible to disconnect users whilst they log-on and phone back to their authorized telephone number. This may work if private lines do not incur the organization in additional expense, and if there are no intervening private exchanges.

Computer security and privacy is a vast subject in itself. This section is only intended to give a brief overview, and such topics as detecting remotely the electromagnetic radiation generated by visual display units, encryption (protecting stored or transmitted data from being accessed or modified), and security products (both hardware and software) are not covered here.

SYSTEM CONTROLS

Having made management decisions about the end-product's size, set relevant target dates, and determined its nature, it is appropriate to consider how the computerized system will control itself. The subject of system controls is very important to senior management, user managers, and computer management, because an application system without controls is an ineffective system. It is relatively simple to design an application system that works when everything goes well; it is, however, much more difficult to design the system for the same application, so that it caters for all contingencies when problems occur or queries arise.

The purpose of system controls is to make the total system measurably water-tight, with all loss or corruption of data eliminated from the handling of transaction data, and the subsequent processing of master files. This should ensure that the application system processes data, that represents the true state of the organization's business. Controls are one of the few areas in systems development where management has quantifiable and tangible measures of how the system is performing, especially regarding its accuracy in processing all items of data. In most organizations the internal auditors will have more than just a passing interest in this area of controls!

In general terms, the essential point to stress is that a computer application system always comprises a clerical as well as a computer component. Both are equally important, and the application's system controls should reflect both these components. All the clerical procedures associated with the input and output aspects of the computer system should include control totals, as well as control totals reflecting the actual processing by the programs. Ideally, these totals should tie up with the files going into and coming out of the computer operations department. It is, therefore, apparent that system controls are not an appendage to an application system, but are designed as an integral part from inception.

System controls commence with the data capture and file creation associated with the setting-up, prior to going live, of any new application system. These data could either be captured from a clerical system, or from computer files obtained from other application systems, or most probably, from a combination of both. Every aspect of this data capture must be controlled (including counting and valuing all items), so that there is no possibility of gaining or losing data, or even of capturing incorrect or incomplete data.

Within the live application system, controls should be included along the whole chain, the sequence of which starts with the continuous data capture of transactions by the line users. It is followed by the batching of these transactions (if appropriate), their input to the computer, the subsequent validity checks, the file updating, and the print-outs of the files. Automatic computer reconciliations of inputs with outputs, should be a feature of the control system, which also includes continuity of processing wherever possible, accounting for possible errors and error correction. In all cases, the overall philosophy is that an audit trail both forwards and backwards must be established. It is necessary to be able to answer the questions 'where did a specific record come from?' or 'where did a record go to?'. If management needs to query a record, or if the system controls indicate an error anywhere in the total system, it should be easy to track down the actual cause of that error. If necessary, the query or error should be able to be traced back to an actual source document.

In practice, the most critical area is the quality of the source data. Transcription of data from one document to another should be avoided, and preferably the communications channels between geographically spread branches, head office and the computer should be via the computer or even computer source documents, rather than memoranda or telephone calls.

Management should appreciate that it could require over 30 man days' systems, and programming effort, to incorporate within a simple application, basic system controls which include an audit trail and a recovery method to cover every conceivable computer and clerical error.

Integrated controls

This basic system controls section concludes with an introduction to the wider consideration of controls within an integrated system. The necessity for batch control totals of items and values is a well known method of controlling transaction data that is used to update a master file. The concept should be carried further by making these individual batch controls meaningful and using them to update the main control record held on the relevant files. The number of records that are affected in the file needs relating to the batch control totals, but probably more useful, is a specific value of money associated with that file. In this way, it is possible to control all clerical changes produced by the many user departments which affect the main files, and ensure that all of these changes are on the computer. It must not be possible for clerical transactions to 'slip between the cracks in the floorboards' and be omitted from the computer system, especially at the interface between systems.

Closed loop controls

The concept of a closed loop is useful as a method of obtaining feedback of data errors, and as a subsequent self-correcting control mechanism. A simple example of a closed loop may be a personnel file, in which weekly control figures for new, terminated or transferred staff is used by the computer system to provide monthly manpower establishment figures for each department. Input data is created by the personnel department, and outputs are independently checked by geographically different departments (e.g. sales branches). The loop is closed by the feedback of data from the independent recipients to the data creators. In this example, the sales branches will (if correctly motivated) inform the personnel department of discrepancies in their headcounts. This type of concept is very useful in an integrated system.

Figure 6.2 illustrates a more complex integrated control loop involving a substantial number of line departments in a company. There are very few companies with a sufficiently integrated system to need a closed loop control as large as illustrated in this figure, but the principle still applies. The whole business cycle is involved, including customers' orders generated by the sales force, their dispatch, invoicing, and the subsequent payment of sales commission on the receipts. The problem of salesmen receiving commission to which they are not entitled is, in principle, eliminated. On the other hand, any

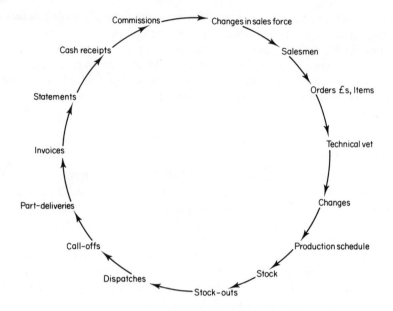

Figure 6.2 An example of closed-loop control. Control information
for each customer is quantified in *money terms*, and the *number* of items

delay in expected commission will soon cause a beneficial chase up round the
loop.

A system controls checklist

It is inappropriate to go into further detail on system controls as they are a
very large subject in themselves. However, the author has found that the
checklist in Appendix 4 may be very useful in practice when managers are
reviewing a system's controls.

CONVERSION AND IMPLEMENTATION

In some projects, the need for conversion from an existing system or the optimum method of installing the new one, might be a source of serious difficulty,
and might affect significantly the end-product and the schedule for its implementation.

An example of how conversion can affect system design

A project developing a purchasing system required major changes to an
existing, but basic, product file, so that the latter could be replaced by one
new common stock file. This decision necessitated the amendment of the
other systems that also used this product file, so that they too could access

the new stock file. The superceded product file could then be abandoned. To minimize changes and development effort, the system logic required converting the new stock file backwards to the exact format of the old product file. This was considered necessary if errors were found in the new purchasing system after going live, or if the other systems using the new stock file were not amended, converted and tested in time.

An important consequence of implementing this plan was that the data layout for the proposed stock file had to be changed significantly from that originally specified. Unfortunately this was discovered at a late stage. Particular examples of changes were that the proposed new product number could not be used (as it was mathematically impossible to calculate the old one), the number of characters for the new product description field could only be increased with difficulty, and the opportunity to use a new supplier code was not the expected success, because it meant that the old code had to be retained on the new file as well. Similarly, the intention of converting the suppliers' name and address from 3 lines to 4 lines plus post code, did not work in practice and required severe clerical intervention because the automatic conversion logic was inadequate for the poor quality of data.

Conversion is usually a self-contained system in its own right, with the systems and programming work spread over the same system development phases as required for new systems; the same need to define input, outputs, files, and processing rules; and the identical necessity to determine user requirements and a development strategy. The fact that conversion is only a once-off system does not detract from the fact that, like any other system development work, it must be done properly. In particular, the following is a check-list of tasks that may need completing.

Sample the accuracy of the current data.
Compare the proposed data to the current data.
Design the conversion method.
Determine the impact on the design of the proposed system.
Optimize the proposed system design and the conversion system design.
Design the system for the conversion of files.
Program the special conversion and/or data capture programs.
Prepare and execute the conversion test plan.
Determine the data capture and correction methods.
Identify user involvement in conversion.
Design the conversion procedures for both the user and DP operations.
Agree the involvement by DP operations.
Determine file maintenance methods to be employed (prior to the system going live).
Define the clerical and DP conversion controls to be applied.
Produce a schedule giving time scales for all of the above work.

MANAGEMENT BY EXCEPTION

The phrase 'management by exception' is a fairly common DP objective, but the introduction of the idea in practice might prove difficult, and frustrate attempts at professionalism. The basic problem could be that auditors and the line users may need convincing that for certain applications they only require exception reports out of the computer. They may have little confidence in this idea, as previous experience may tell them that computer systems are error prone, and accordingly, they may require frequent and detailed print-outs of everything. Consequently, mounds of computer print-outs will be produced, which no one can possibly wade through (although they may be used for reference if a query or emergency arises). A good expression that could be used when referring to this state of mind is 'management by the ton!'.

The user departments may need convincing about several potential problem areas, and working through the following checklist could be of assistance.

1. It has to be proved to the user departments that data is correct on existing or proposed files. Statistical data sampling may be appropriate.
2. All data needs to be captured and coded correctly. For integrated systems, the user may require to be convinced about the quality of data originating from the other feeder systems.
3. All internal computer processing should be demonstrated as accurate. This includes proper provisions for handling abnormal occurrences that frequently bug computer systems. Reconcilable controls are a major part of the answer.
4. A fool-proof total control system could be provided for all aspects of the system, which again gives confidence that the system is operating in a controlled manner.
5. It should be possible to demonstrate that the programs are actually selecting information in an 'intelligent' fashion. The management by exception reports may give the best 10%, the worst 10%, projections, or trends. The use of graphical output is a useful way of suppressing requests for large print-outs. However, these reports may initially require proof that they are correct, over and above normal system tests.
6. Another idea for convincing the users of the benefit of management by exception, is to design the system so that they have a quick response. For example, if a line user department is dealing with written customer queries, a visual display unit may be the ultimate solution. However, it may not be cost justifiable, or the user may be concerned about breakdowns, So his immediate demand may be for a computer print-out of the entire customer file, once a week, which would be its main reference. It might be better if the system was designed using micro-film, or if possible, twice a day, say, the user department receives file details for only those customers with queries.

To conclude this section on management by exception, the key idea being suggested is that the computer line printer should be used as rarely as possible.

When it must be used, it preferably should not be used as a glorified typewriter or tabulator.

DECISION SUPPORT SOFTWARE

Although the term 'decision support software' is often used in the information systems industry, its meaning is rather vague as it can apply to several differing situations. In practice, the definition of decision support software has depended on the current state of computing technology. Originally, it could have referred to terminals and mainframe tools (such as financial modelling, or statistical analysis tools). The term was then used to apply to microcomputers and such software tools as spreadsheets. It then became extended to encompass microcomputer links to mainframes, so that relevant corporate data could be downloaded to a local microcomputer, where, say, it could be manipulated, analysed, and presented graphically. Recent usage of the term decision support software has related to products employing artificial intelligence techniques.

Irrespective of semantics and the technology adopted, the objective of decision support software is to make managers more productive and more effective. This is achieved by helping them make better decisions – both short-term tactical as well as long-term strategic. Typical management aids are required for forecasting, risk analysis, financial models, statistical analysis, profit analysis, graphical presentation to highlight significant trends, accessing and consolidating corporate data, report writing, etc. In meeting the information requirements of (senior) management, several factors need to be catered for, if the information systems department is attempting to provide decision support software for general use within the organization. Flexibility is paramount, to cater for requests, which by their very nature are *ad hoc*, unstructured, and could occur at any time of the day (or night if say, a take-over bid is being fought). Some applications require stand alone processing, and a personal computer would suffice with the choice of a wide selection of standard software packages, such as spreadsheets and data manipulation, to the more exotic sales or negotiating aids. Provided the necessary data is available, accurate, and entered correctly into the microcomputer, the packages can assist managers to formulate better business decisions.

The above applications require the clerical capture of data. Possibly a more powerful form of decision support software feeds off corporate data held on a mainframe. This may be achieved in two ways. Either a terminal facility can be provided (such as a data-base enquiry language, or a financial modelling package), or extracts of mainframe files can be transmitted to personal computers. In either case, users will probably have to work with the organization's information centre, as they need access to experienced DP business analysts to initiate and formulate ideas, as well as to advise them on the use of hardware and software. In addition, users do not usually understand the structure of data held on the mainframe, and technical DP staff may be required to provide software to access, manipulate, transmit, and reformat the relevant data for local use.

As should be apparent, decision support software, is a worthwhile computing application. The information systems department can increase its effectiveness and political clout within the organization, by initiating the use of such software, and actively seeking the corporate needs for such facilities.

EXPERT SYSTEMS

Expert systems (sometimes referred to as artificial intelligence) have moved from the academic world to being used in practical commercial applications. Although a universally acceptable definition of expert systems is difficult to agree, they are best considered as a form of decision support software involving expertise and knowledge in specific *narrow* areas of jobs and subjects. Moreover, expert systems are capable of handling the complex logic and uncertainty associated with real life decision making. Thus, expert systems help users to make decisions, and should instil confidence by giving the reasons for the system's derived conclusions.

Obviously, a significant aspect of developing an expert system is to build up a knowledge base, which can then be further expanded and refined. Knowledge can be represented by hundreds or thousands of rules (such as, *if* A is present *then* B happens), or by examples of actual cases (where the system itself works out the rules). The latter approach may be more appropriate in those situations where all the rules are not known in advance (such as in weather forecasting). Extracting the relevant complex information to form a knowledge base is no mean task, as it may entail key company staff disgorging their lifetime's accumulation of expertise. This naturally presents social barriers, as people do not willingly allow themselves to be replaced by machines.

Avoiding this conflict is often a more practical method of introducing an expert system. The following escalating phases are not only more acceptable to users, but also follow the evolution of the complexity and sophistication of the expert system itself. Initially, an expert system should be used by experts as an *assistant* to relieve them from the tedious studying of volumes of data. Having gained confidence in the expert system, they can be considered as a *colleague* that reaches a joint decision with the user. Having attained this level of confidence, the ultimate phase is to regard the expert systems as an *expert*. In other words, the user accepts the system's advice.

Numerous examples exist of expert systems being used in commercial, social and government organizations. In fact, new applications are reported each week. As expert systems are relatively new, and experience is very limited, stories are heard about disappointment within organizations introducing expert systems because they were oversold, or the problem was too big for the system to tackle. It is also often difficult to ascertain whether an application was successful, in practice, and what were its actual benefits and limitations. However, as many commercial applications give the involved organization a competitive edge, relevant information is often kept secret.

Owing to traditional ways of conceiving application systems, it may initially be difficult for a corporate information systems specialist to consider how expert systems may be relevant in his organization. It is necessary for the novice to overcome the multitude of buzz-words emanating from the academic background of artificial intelligence. As many of the best applications of expert systems are not immediately obvious, listed below are random examples of strategic uses of expert systems that are being, or have been implemented. Hopefully, the information systems professional can use this list to produce some lateral thinking that triggers his mind when proposing relevant applications for his organization.

Scientifically orientated applications include:

(a) Sifting volumes of geological survey data to detect small significant changes that the expert(s) should concentrate on in his search for oil or ore deposits.
(b) Medical diagnosis not only to determine a patient's illness, but for satisfying dietary objectives (salt, protein, calories, fats, etc.) and optimizing farming conditions (crops, soils, yields, fertilizers, etc.).
(c) Grappling with the many variables involved with weather forecasting.

Social administration applications include:

(d) Fathoming out the complex administration rules relevant to a person claiming social security benefits.
(e) Advising on the relevance of specific statutory laws and regulations.
(f) Determining the environmental laws relevant for the disposal of different toxic wastes.

In the information systems industry itself, expert systems are being considered for:

(g) Getting to grips with the numerous factors involved in project estimating.
(h) Automating parts of the system development process itself.

General commercial applications include:

(i) Increasing factory throughput significantly, by advising on the day-to-day running of a chemical processing plant, or on production line maintenance, or on simulating a factory floor so that the optimum manufacturing schedules may be planned.
(j) Configuring customers' orders for complex technical equipment.
(k) Equipment fault diagnostics for diesel engines, electronic equipment, etc.
(l) Various personnel and line management functions such as matching people to jobs.
(m) Training and consultation aids.
(n) Intricate financial analysis of investment projects, where the expert system ensures factors are not overlooked by asking and reporting on all relevant questions.

Some of the above applications are relatively straightforward, such as diagnosing engine faults. The engine starts or it does not! Financial management applications may, on the other hand, be more complex.

In the commercial world, expert systems do not replace conventional high volume transaction processing systems, nor corporate data-bases. Expert system products may be used to augment these applications by integrating with them. For example, an expert system may assist a clerk in intelligently handling input transactions and queries at the front-end of a conventional application system. An expert system may also be used as a natural language front end to data-base enquiries. Although big pay-offs are possible with the integrated use of expert systems, stand-alone applications may also be useful. Expert systems should not just be considered as products, but also as a technology capable of being incorporated into mainframe, mini or microcomputer software. In this way, the performance, functionality and user interface of the application, or system software is improved.

There are a wide range of products on the market relating to expert systems. At one extreme are compilers, interpreters, editors, etc. for special programming languages such as Lisp and Prologue. Further up-market, these languages are supplied with development environments that provide tools to facilitate the building of expert systems. These products may include facilities to represent knowledge in a format similar to natural language, or to provide effective user interfaces. Some development environments include special high resolution graphic work-stations, which in addition to the above, provide fourth generation development tools. The latter include the handling of graphical and textural material via windows, icons, and pointers, etc. Also available are separate general purpose utilities, useful for handling knowledge when building expert systems.

For the above type of products, it is necessary to employ highly skilled programmers with at least three months training in Lisp or Prologue. This may not appeal to an organization which is attempting to improve the productivity of its traditional systems development work by automating it, and by reducing the need for programmers. Another possible problem at this end of the market is that some organizations, already bristling with mainframe terminals, office autom- tion work-stations, and personal computers, may be loath to introduce incompatible work-stations necessary for the development of expert systems. Alternatively, expert systems may come as specific off-the-shelf ready to use application packages (containing their own relevant knowledge base for a specific area), or as generalized expert system shells. These shells (many of which are based on personal computers) provide reasoning tools that enable the user or developer to build his own system, avoiding the necessity of the system developer starting from scratch. The particular knowledge base has to be added to the shell by the user. Low cost shells may have limited functionality, which is further compounded by their generalized nature, and an emphasis on ease of use.

Conventional commercial languages are being used for parts of some expert systems. Also the marketability of expert systems is being improved, so that users can expect the same facilities (such as menu handling, report generation, editing) that they have grown accustomed to in more traditional commercial software. As with conventional application packages, most users prefer to buy a system that does not require programming expertise to adapt it before it can work in their environment. Ideally, commercial users would like to use an expert system package after about 15 hours of training by the vendor. However, it is interesting to compare the 2 to 3 days product training required at this end of the market, with the 2 to 3 months training required for an expert system development environment. However, as the vendors at the expensive end of the market point out, this order of magnitude in training reflects the relative increase in functionality and flexibility in their products.

It is recommended that the professional information systems manager intending to make a start in using expert systems, obtains background training from the various suppliers in the marketplace. Practical experience can possibly be gained relatively quickly using a personal computer expert system shell. The information systems manager can then select a simple application (containing about 200 rules), that is not trivial, and is well understood in the organization. The application should be a recognized problem that has quantifiable benefits, but has not been solved by conventional data processing. A co-operative expert person should also be available, and there should be minimal delay in keeping the knowledge base updated. As this application should be nonthreatening to staff, an assistant type of expert system should be selected, i.e. a system that helps users overcome tedious routine.

In practice the 'eighty twenty rule' applies, as in other situations. The expert system should initially be built to relieve the corporate expert of the 80% of the more mundane and simpler cases. He can then concentrate on the more rewarding 20%. After experience has been gained with shells, the more expensive end of the market can be evaluated with some confidence and a greater appreciation of the subject.

OFFICE AUTOMATION

Conceptually, large data processing systems have been justified on headcount reductions of clerical staff. Office automation is different. It does not replace people, but it compliments and enhances their performance especially at the professional and managerial levels. Office automation conjures up various interpretations to different people. Some suppliers market office automation in terms of hardware, local area networks, links to mainframes, paperless offices, electronic diaries, electronic mail, etc. Even technologies such as microfilm and microfiche have been included as office automation, but these are receiving less emphasis. In fact, there has been much publicity and discussion on the subject of office automation for many years. In practice however, office automation has been characterized by the proliferation of different networks, with the non-integration and incompatibility of systems standing out as a problem area. This has led to the need to build hardware and software bridges between different office automation systems. Added to this scenario, the personal computer has produced a significant impact, with attempts being made to incorporate it in the organization's office automation system.

Not surprisingly then, with the above sorts of problems, some organizations have been reluctant to adopt office automation systems. Alternatively, disenchantment with office automation has been experienced in some organizations where user's expectations have not been realized. Many users just require simple-to-use word processing, spreadsheet, and possibly data-base packages run on a personal computer. High quality print may be an additional requirement for, say, user departments dealing with clients and other external parties. These people may prefer to be in control of their own environment, and not feel frustrated when the mainframe or network is down, or have to rely on a printer, sited remotely from their offices, or have to suffer from poor response times caused by heavy use of centralized office automation equipment.

Even though one can sympathize with this parochial view, networked office automation has such advantages as a large capacity for data storage, good communications potential, many users being able to access a document or spreadsheet (assuming this is an application requirement), and the chore of recovery and making back-ups is usually taken care of centrally. For an organization to obtain optimum benefit, office automation should not be used as a substitute for conventional work patterns. It should be used to improve productivity, and for better management control. For example, word processing (especially stand-alone systems) has been one of the most popular office automation applications. However, 'traditional' word processing is being overtaken by internal electronic mail for the exchange of short documents and memoranda within an organization. This may significantly change corporate inter-communication, and may affect relationships between superiors and subordinates. Managers can improve the co-ordination and control of subordinates, and possibly be able to supervise more people. In particular, project management is facilitated by the easier communication across departmental boundaries, and to staff assigned to remote locations. Assuming participants check for incoming messages, and overcome the inertia of using new technology, the timeliness of information is improved; be it the distribution of agendas and short messages, the calling of meetings, the evaluation of products, or the monitoring of project activities and reporting back their status.

Another interesting potential change, obtained via elctronic interactions, is the improvement in democracy within the organization. It is more difficult to filter out communication being sent to higher levels of corporate management. Similarly, meek or reserved staff (who have difficulty winning points over the telephone, or in person-to-person situations) have equal status and electronic access facilities to communicate their ideas, within the relevant parts of the organization, as more aggressive members of staff.

In conclusion, it is suggested that the information systems professional should take the initiative in introducing corporate office automation techniques. In fact, the information systems division should set up a group to determine the organization's strategy for the introduction of office automation. This strategy may contain two threads, the first of which is to latch on to any emerging industry standards for office automation; the second relates to performing a strategic business study of the organization's data. Senior management may be surprised to discover their main problems are text processing and not data processing. In this case, office automation may assume a higher priority than it would have otherwise.

LIVE OPERATIONAL ENVIRONMENT

The last, but by no means least end-product consideration, is the operational environment of the computerized system. For each stage in the schedule for delivery (which was described earlier in this chapter) it is necessary to itemize: the hardware, the system software, the communication lines, and the terminals required to run the end-product.

This phased operational requirement for running the application is necessary to enable the data-processing operations department to plan for the entire installation. As the lead times for delivery of most items on this list can run into years rather than months, this aspect of the end-product should be considered as early as possible. A provisional assessment should be produced during the feasibility study, and the firm requirement issued by the end of the system design phase.

CHAPTER SUMMARY

The end-product of the project has to be examined in detail and is relevant to the responsibilities of the project manager and his supervision by a senior information systems department manager (e.g. the systems development manager).

The first thing the users wish to know is when they will receive their system and how the facilities will be phased. To produce this information, the project manager must first quantify his end-product in terms of program sizes, additional support programs, and necessary clerical activities.

Sensible end-product planning, incorporates concepts to minimize risk in the design of the application system. Several ideas are given to achieve this—a total and automatic people-proof system!

As organizations become more and more reliant on their computers, security and privacy assume an increasing importance, which the information systems manager cannot ignore. An analysis of many of the problem areas enables contingency plans to be made, so that recovery is possible from any disaster. A continuous programme of security improvements should be planned and implemented.

The end-product should contain system controls and audit trails to cater for all queries or to detect errors in processing. A checklist is provided to assist management in its efforts to ensure that the proposed system is watertight.

The conversion and implementation of the system, although only a transient part of the end-product, is often a significant source of difficulty, requiring many management decisions.

An end-product, that provides the user with management by exception is a desirable but difficult objective to attain. Ideas are given for providing an acceptable system.

Generalized facilities should include relevant decision support software (possibly including expert system shells) and office automation aids. These may be provided by the information systems division as a whole, or possibly as part of a specific development project.

Finally, as the end-product cannot be achieved without a computer, the necessary computer hardware, software, and operational environment must be defined, together with its build up over the implementation period of the project.

Chapter 7

How the end-product will be constructed and controlled

A feature of this book is the extensive treatment of the predictability of the components of a project which require planning, monitoring, and controlling (i.e. management in its widest sense). Having determined *what* the end-product is to be, this chapter elaborates on managing *how* the end-product (as defined previously) will be constructed and controlled, *how* changes in specification are kept in check, *how* the development process will be supported, and *how* the data requirement and the files are designed. In smaller installations, this responsibility could lie with the data processing manager who may also be acting as project manager. In larger installations, corporate control of this subject is placed in the hands of the systems development manager, but in very large projects the project manager himself could have total responsibility.

END-PRODUCT CONTROL

As we have seen, a computer application system is a difficult product to define. Considerations that must be taken into account include the technology to be used, the facilities to be provided and how these will be delivered in stages, and the anticipated cost benefits of the system. Consequently, to ensure that the end-product eventually turns out as a coherent and viable system, plans must be made for quality control in general. Particular areas of concern are controlling the trade-offs between user facilities and technical expediency, the continual technical vetting during the development of the system for its expected performance (in terms of say, program size, response times, running times, storage requirements, and accuracy of processing data) and for the technical co-ordination of all the skills involved. These aspects of the project constitute the control of the end-product. In many medium-sized or large projects, a separate control team, reporting to the project manager and responsible for the above areas, could be a valid solution.

CHANGE CONTROL

Coupled with the above difficulty of defining and controlling the end-product is the fact that the situation is an ever changing one. It must be realized from the outset that the product will change continually throughout the duration of the project (as well as after the project has been completed), and the consequences of this must be planned for. Only rarely does the computer system remain unchanged during its development. Either the line user will require new facilities, or change his mind about previously agreed facilities, or he will not have understood the system in the first place, or it was not explained to him fully by the project staff.

Although the users are blamed most frequently for not adhering to a freeze in their requirements, the systems analysts themselves often change their minds. The main causes for this are: cutting corners; inadequate consultations with the main project activity streams; not adhering to good analysis and design standards; changes caused by systems analysts not understanding fully the real requirements of the line users; the emergence of genuine new ideas, which could improve the end-product; the technology chosen is either too advanced, or out of data; the original estimates of manpower and resources have proved to be excessive or insufficient.

In practice, changes are continually imposed on the project, and it is difficult to control them. Change control is required to ensure that all amendments are controlled and cost-justified. It is also necessary for the documentation and library to be kept up to date, and for all the other ancillary plans to be updated. It is most important that a precise and agreed procedure is followed by senior responsible people, who will vet, justify and approve each proposed change to the facilities, to the technical system design, or to changes in any plans or estimates. The general need is to maintain a mutually agreed current reference from which to work.

To achieve this requires an expensive overhead. A useful procedure is to make a member of the project management team (i.e. one of the managers reporting direct to the project manager) responsible as a *change controller*. He would have a small team to assess the impact of changes, and would negotiate the acceptability of a change to all the project work streams. In some instances, it may be necessary to obtain final approval by an internal project committee or the organization's steering committee. A changes register formally notifies project staff and users of proposed changes and their status. This register might include a description of the proposed change, the originator of the change, the users' or the project's decision, the decision of the change control committee, and most important, the reference to the pages of documentation affected by acceptable changes. Any major or urgent change should be separated from the majority of routine changes, and thus draw it to the attention of the project manager speedily.

SUPPORT

In order to build the end-product, it is essential to utilize numerous, behind the scenes, support groups and activities. (These are analogous to scaffolding, templates, jigs, and tools in engineering.) They may take up about half the manpower and resources of a large project, and are, therefore, important. The mass of short-lived redundant information which is not delivered to users includes such items as test cases of transactions and main records; testing drivers; module simulators to assist in program testing; system simulators to assist in the design of the product; special programs to create files, reformat data, analyse files of data, capture and validate data, report errors, generate reports, provide a data dictionary, and convert data from one system to another. Lastly there are programs to generate data for program and system test purposes. All this creates many extra pages of documentation, requires additional clerical resources and a significant increase in the amount of programming. As these facets of a project are a predictable requirement, they need to be considered by management in a support plan. A useful checklist of project support functions is given in Figure 7.1.

Appropriate
Phases
(If not all)

TECHNICAL FUNCTIONS

Production of standards;	
Quality control;	
Operation of a project control system;	
Assistance in creating and updating the development plan;	
Longer-term planning, co-ordination, special tasks;	
Liaison with DP operations, controlling computer time, data entry, teleprocessing facilities;	
Arrangement of system simulators, pilot studies, and data sampling;	FS, UR
Software evaluation of say, report generators, data dictionaries, test harnesses;	UR, SD
Production of test cases of transactions and main records;	PS
Arrangement of testing drivers, data generators;	PS, P
Arrangement of module simulators;	PS, P
Programs to create files, reformat files, analyse files, capture data, validate data, convert data between systems;	SD, PS, P, PV
Set-up and maintenance of testing and program library.	SD, PS, P, PV

PERSONNEL FUNCTIONS

Recruitment;
Training: line, and DP;
  establish requirements, training material, courses, etc.,
  arrange individual bookings.

ADMINISTRATION FUNCTIONS

Maintain status and schedule of documentation;	
Maintain document library;	
Typing;	
General administration;	
Office moves and accommodation arrangements;	
Provide clerical resources, arrange temporary clerical staff;	PV, I
Supervise data coders.	PV, I

FS = Feasibility study.   UR = User requirements.   SD = System design.
PS = Program specification.   P = Programming.   PV = Proving.   I = Installation.

Figure 7.1 A checklist of support functions within a project

PROJECT ADMINISTRATION

Communication

Project administration is the responsibility of the project manager, who should capitalize on his 'honeymoon period' when the project is initially established in order to propagate the project concept, and produce a focal point for all people concerned with the project. The key word for achieving this is *communication*, which the project manager needs in order to:

1. Create an identity within the project for all involved.
2. Create unity with the many parties engaged in the project.
3. Create a sense of enthusiasm and therefore improve motivation—which is half the battle for success.
4. Minimize the formal barriers that will exist (because the project cuts across the accepted line structure of the organization) by continual social, as well as business dialogue.
5. Ensure the line users obtain what they expect! Although this may seem obvious, it is not so in practice. Normally, the users specify their requirements for the system, and it may take a year or more for the system to go live on the computer. Inevitably, by this time, requirements have changed, previously agreed ideas have been forgotten, and new people are involved. The outputs from the frozen computer specification may not be the same as the users are subconsciously expecting. It is essential that the project manager and some of the key staff not only have relevant sound business experience to understand and anticipate user problems, but also keep in continual contact with the users to restrain their expectancy.
6. Explain to the line why some user requirements cause more severe technical problems than others.
7. Above all, achieve the common purpose of both the user and computer personnel, so that they all are working to the same project objectives.
8. Create confidence at all levels—a project cannot succeed without it. Everyone must be aware of what has to be achieved in both the short and long term, including the strategy of overcoming all the potential problem areas. Confidence should follow.
9. Enable the analyst and user dialogue to flourish, so that the user defines reasonable facilities, and the systems analyst acts as a catalyst.

One of the most common ways a project can go sour is because of poor communication. This cannot be over-emphasized. A project manager should ensure that all members of the project staff, including users, are continuously and informally talking to each other. This could be a far superior method of communication than a whole library of relevant manuals, reports, memos, and specifications.

Regular presentations to relevant people should ensure that the users are satisfied and have no need to keep requesting information. These presentations should cover facilities and problems, as well as procedures and schedules, and should not be lengthy set-pieces, but where possible, incorporated as part of the continual informal discussions and activities with the users.

No surprises should be a key theme in dealing with the line users. All reports, manuals and documentation should be previously agreed with all the relevant parties and recipients before official distribution or circulation. In this way, not only will members of the project clarify their own thinking, and eliminate errors and misconceptions, but the users should be more confident that the project is achieving its objectives.

A further development of the previous idea is not to communicate via memoranda unless absolutely essential. One should only *confirm* by a memorandom or report. The time wasted in developing ideas or in conducting a dialogue via memoranda may be significant. Apart from this, misunderstandings may occur, coupled with an inevitable lack of depth in comprehending the problems involved, when using this form of communication. The personal approach usually achieves much greater success and one is more likely to obtain agreement.

One of the best ways to improve project communication is for a project manager and his staff actually to work in their user departments on a temporary basis (as opposed to just visiting them). Unless the DP individuals already have the relevant experience this may be for days rather than hours. Traditionally, lack of time usually rules out this exchange, but if a project has this activity planned from the beginning it has more chance of being included. The purpose of this is threefold. First, it improves mutual confidence between the line and computing specialists. Secondly, it is essential that the project members see the real problems at first hand, and obtain a deep understanding of how the computer will interact with the line departments. Thirdly, these visits will stimulate user interest in both the proposed application system and its development project.

More problems are caused within the project by the general lack of verbal communications of ideas than through staff leaving or being transferred. It is better to have people on a project sharing the same room and exchanging ideas, rather than put them in separate rooms in different locations and let them write memos to each other. This aspect of allocating office accommodation within a project is a vital factor in improving team communication; but can cause antagonism if not arranged tactfully. It may also be beneficial if the project is situated in the main user area. This especially applies in the early stages, but a presence should be kept throughout the duration of the project.

In addition, the project could benefit by producing a standard discussion report form. This should be used for all significant meetings, comments, telephone calls, queries, agendas, minutes, and discussions. The standard form should show the name of the project team and have pre-printed spaces for names of people attending the meetings, the subject matter, the objectives of the meeting and a margin for writing initials opposite any notes indicating any action to be taken. An example for a suitable form is given in Figure 7.2.

148

REGIONAL HOSPITALS' STOCK CONTROL PROJECT

DISCUSSION REPORT		
Date	Subject	
Attendance		
Objectives of meeting		
		Action by:
Any queries to be addressed to the author		Author:

Figure 7.2   An example of a Discussion Report Form

Meetings should be kept to a minimum; both in number and duration. Attendees generally may become bored and the topics may not be relevant, interesting, or helpful to specific individuals. A distinction should be made between the formal meetings referred to above, and the preferred method of communication via continual and informal discussions.

Improving users awareness of DP

There is no reason why experienced users, let alone new users should be experts in DP techniques, standards or even methods of working. This is often a cause of conflict because as a service unit, DP staff should, in general, react immediately and positively to reasonable user requests. What may appear as perfectly reasonable to the users, though, may be seen as impractical, unnecessary, or of low priority to DP staff. It is up to the DP management and staff to educate these particular users about computing, by gradually establishing what the user *needs*. Experience often shows this is not necessarily synonymous with what the user *thinks* he wants.

In general, a good way of improving user awareness of DP methods (and therefore gaining his co-operation) may be for project staff to take the initiative in arranging a computer education and training programme for the user personnel. This could include booking certain people on formal computer training courses (if necessary, paid out of the project's budget). However, in some circumstances this direct approach may, if not done tactfully, emphasize and add to the problem. In these cases, it may be better to work continually with the users but keeping a low-profile. Members of a project also could arrange, as part of the natural activity, informal computer presentations and lectures on certain relevant topics. This has the additional benefit of reducing certain users' apprehensiveness about computer personnel.

To ensure the smooth conduct of a project, the usual visits made by DP staff to the users should be two-way; the users should also be given an introduction to the computer department. These visits can include an insight into the functions of the computer and data control clerks as well as the less tangible jobs of systems analysts and programmers. The DP staff work can be explained by taking one or two relevant features, pertinent to the users' system under development, and showing how the total creative process eventually finds its way onto the computer, including all the blind alleys that have had to be dropped.

General administration techniques

A common approach is that the user(s), parts of the DP department, individual teams within a project, or possibly the DP operations department produce their own separate documents relating to the same system. This does not usually signify a sound state. By using subtle administration techniques, the project manager can dramatically improve cohesion across the project. For example, one aim could be for all personnel to produce and work from *project* documents (rather than personal ones) that are readily identifiable and are regarded as common property. This might apply to reports, plans, specifications, notes of meetings, terms of reference, or even memoranda. This creates an administrative focal point, improving communication, and furthering the project concept.

Taking this concept one stage further, the project manager should insist on central project filing, which not only allows him to review all documentation automatically, but avoids the usual practice of individuals (and constituent teams) privately filing their own working papers and essential documentation. In an emergency, no one can ever find the vital documents! The project's central filing should contain all working papers, all discussion reports, all project control documentation, and all reports with their master copies. In particular, if a data dictionary is not used, it is important to include in the central library all input, output and main file layouts, together with their program usage, so that all specifications produced by the project staff refer to this central library. The two advantages are, that if the data content of a file changes, it is easy to know what are the consequences, and the documentation still remains valid.

In an organization where all the departments involved in the development project are contributing towards the project budget, the project manager is assisted in obtaining commitment and improving communication, by the fact that all parties in the project are interested in how their contributions are progressing against target. Another administration technique to help create the project image is to review regularly progress with all key people present.

To conclude this section on general administration, it may prove advantageous for a project to have both a distinctive name and a symbol (often referred to as a logo). Preprinted project names and logo stickers can be used with great effect on all project documents and reports, and can assist in making all parties identify themselves with the actual project. A similar idea is for all people who work full time or are seconded to the project to have desk name plates which display the project name and logo. This is a small psychological technique that can improve the project manager's influence over staff who are not his full line responsibility.

Senior management should be able to see the effects of projects working with their user departments, and they should encourage the interchange of staff and ideas. This aspect of communication within the project is one of the most important means of securing success. Senior management should look for the project image and a project identity being created for good effect. To this end, a set of administration notices could be produced by the project manager, setting out all the above ideas on administration which initially may be instructive, and subsequently will be useful when inducting new members.

Public relations

A general mention is appropriate, of the public relations requirements applicable to certain projects. If the project's application system is novel, sophisticated, very large, or of a pioneering nature, not only will the relevant user departments be extremely interested in what is happening, but other departments, and other organizations within the industry or computer world also, may well wish to visit the project. If uncontrolled, this natural curiosity may cause friction. It is best to expect this, and from its inception, organize the project accordingly. It will be apparent that an appreciable overhead in wasted time and effort may be expended on:

1. Arranging visits, including the dates, times, and number of people, their level of seniority, their particular interests, refreshments, meals, accommodation, etc.
2. Preparing presentations, visual aids, and hand-outs.
3. Preparing demonstration programs (especially for interrogation systems).
4. Being invited as guest speakers at conferences, etc.

The project secretary and the administration team can be of great assistance on these occasions, but in general, the project manager and some of his team leaders will have to become involved.

FOURTH GENERATION PROGRAMMING LANGUAGES

As can be gauged by the following list of expressions used to describe products claiming to be fourth generation languages, some confusion exists as to what actually is a 'fourth generation language': application generators; report generators; data-base user languages; non-procedural languages; command level languages; and even graphics packages. A non-procedural language enables an emphasis to be made on what needs to be done, and on the business aspects of an application system. This can be compared to an earlier generation of procedural languages (such as COBOL) where a professional programmer must concentrate on the computer aspects of the application.

Typically, a fourth generation language is an interactive programming language, which although free standing, often links to a database management system. An analyst/programmer whilst sitting at a VDU can, for example, design screen layouts and data formats, create files, capture data, write programs and test them; all on-line. The main benefit of considering the use of fourth generation languages is to improve productivity and speed up the program development process. Typical claims are that by using a fourth generation language, the programming work can be completed up to 35 times faster than, say, using COBOL. Coding and testing may be significantly faster, but there may be little improvement in analysis and design. Programming work, typically, only covers about 30% of a system development project. Over the entire project life cycle productivity improvement of between 200% and 1000% have been quoted. Compared to other development techniques, so the sales literature claims, using fourth generation languages, not only is a quantum leap possible in improving development productivity, but also an attack is possible on the large back-log of development work.

Improved user involvement and satisfaction is also possible, as users can program some parts of the system. The user can directly contribute such items as input/output procedures, screen layouts, and screen dialogues. In addition, fourth generation languages are usually good for setting up menus, and calling in relevant programs from the menu response and selection. By employing such techniques, users may assist in the prototyping capabilities of the fourth generation language. Prototyping can impact a large part of the project life cycle, and produce results in hours (not the traditional days or weeks). It is arguable whether the productivity gains during systems development are due to prototyping (which does not necessarily require a fourth generation language) rather than from using the fourth generation language itself.

In spite of much vendor hype, fourth generation languages are not necessarily the best way to improve development productivity (automated development methodologies, or intelligent COBOL generators, for example, might be better general tools). In general, fourth generation languages require experienced DP staff–not users who would not comprehend the impact of a command on the network or the hardware and software resources. Typically, an experienced programmer may require two days training to convert to a fourth generation language. A user, inexperienced in DP, may well require several weeks training to become proficient in using a fourth generation language. In fact, some fourth generation languages are better for DP professionals, whilst others, such as a data-base query language, may be more appropriate for end users. Organizations, therefore, may need to acquire two different products, (possibly produced by different suppliers).

Fourth generation languages are not, therefore, necessarily a user friendly query language nor an end user aid, except for small stand-alone, simple applications such as one-off decision support tools, consulting corporate data-bases, or low volume personal systems. In such cases, a sound method of working is to adopt a step-by-step approach, gradually increasing the facilities and scope of the system. One only moves on to the next part of the system after the previous part has been working satisfactorily.

In general, large user developed systems will have the wrong structures and prove difficult to maintain. Although fourth generation languages provide an incentive to easily change systems, there is little incentive to document the changes. Documentation may, therefore, be poor. Claims that fourth generation languages are self documenting may be true for certain small systems, and may well apply to, say, file, screen, and report layouts, or in the context of reading system processing rules in the programs' source code. However, for documenting the feasibility and requirements of large systems which involve many development staff, the fourth generation language may be irrelevant. Similarly, claims that a fourth generation language significantly speeds up programming may be misleading because the programming phase is only a small part of the entire project life cycle. In fact, it could be argued that as maintenance is by far the longest phase of an application's life cycle, the fourth generation language should not be terse for quick programming, but verbose and English-like to improve the legibility of its self documentation ability. It may also prove difficult to interface neatly with existing non fourth generation software, particularly large, complex, on-line systems, which have been tailor made and built up over many years.

Another general problem with fourth generation languages (apart from the DP installation having to learn yet another language) is the possible drain on computing power for both development work and live systems. Typically, an application system developed with a fourth generation language might consume twice as much central processor resources compared to more traditional languages. Any productivity gains and speed-up of the development life cycle, could be offset by the additional hardware required to run the application system. Even worse, the particular fourth generation language may not be able to cope with large complex systems involving high volumes and quick response times.

As it is relatively easy to amend systems using fourth generation languages, and as users as well as information system staff may have easy access to the installation's fourth generation language, the associated security problems are important to resolve. For example, operational versions of systems should be separated from development versions, with access severely restricted. Control of passwords should be tight, with a master code required to change programs, and possibly users being limited to screen design only.

Ideally, a good fourth generation language should be capable of handling complex, integrated systems which are typical of large DP installations. Features should include an active (not a passive) data dictionary, which is central to the language. This dictionary should be used interactively for such things as names, validation rules and data item descriptions. Table driven data structures improve flexibility, and relational tables reflect the real world. The facilities described above, make it easier for the developers to alter data structures, files, data items, etc. In other words, the language should be flexible enough to change the system quickly, and so reflect the normal volatile business world. A fourth generation language that generates compiled COBOL hinders prototyping, whilst an interpretive product may prove to be slow at run time. It should be possible to access any data-base or file via the query language, and produce relatively simple interfaces to, say, COBOL code. Report and graphics generators should form an integral part of a fourth generation language, which should also possibly contain some decision support facilities such as statistical analysis, or a spreadsheet. Finally, a fourth generation language that runs on a personal computer, as well as a mainframe, is a bonus worth having.

Many managers of information systems departments have a natural tendency to dislike being locked into a proprietary software environment. If an installation's systems are written in a fourth generation language, the computer installation could be committed to that language and supplier for up to five years or more. The situation may be worse for a third party software developer using a fourth generation language. Every sale might necessitate a royalty being paid to the supplier of the fourth generation language, as well as the necessity of the purchasing organization also having the same fourth generation language installed to enable the software to run. To avoid this situation, package vendors will opt for a fourth generation language that generates stand-alone application code in a universal language such as COBOL. Admittedly, the COBOL will be proprietary, but this is usually more acceptable.

In conclusion, management should be open minded to changing the approach to system development work by the use of fourth generation languages. Users and experienced DP staff should be allowed access to a good product that meets the criteria discussed in this section. In a controlled manner, certain project teams and their users should experiment with the fourth generation language in differing small systems, and circumstances. One possibility may result, whereby using a fourth generation language, a working system is developed very quickly that soon shows up the deficiencies and problem areas. The scope of the system can be re-established, and the system can then be properly written in an efficient procedural language using more traditional methods. Alternatively, only parts of the application system may finish up being written in a fourth generation language.

Although examples are quoted of performance and other problems arising when information systems departments have converted to fourth generation languages, many other examples exist where fourth generation languages have become mandatory for all system development work (both batch and on-line). In these (usually well-managed) installations, performance has not proved to be a serious problem, and providing the issues in this section have been addressed, the benefits have outweighed any disadvantages.

FILE DESIGN

An important aspect of some larger computerized systems is the management approach to designing its new files. This is a fundamental consideration, the strategic importance of which is measured by the number of years that the organization's data processing will be 'locked into' this file design, and the great expense (and delay) involved if the file design subsequently requires changing. In practice, an organization may have to face the consequences of bad management at this stage for up to five years.

The problem could warrant a senior file design team to be established as early as possible. This team should include several competent business and technical specialists covering the interest of hardware, software, and the applications systems using the proposed files. The installation's data administration function will naturally become involved. This team will not only investigate the consequences of different data contents; file structures; and file processing; but will carry out simulations and measurements of data usage within the organization, both at present and in the future. Questions to be resolved could include whether, for example, a customer main file should be grouped or linked by such considerations as:

(a) Product types they purchase
(b) Salesman
(c) Subsidiary companies or their branches if the customer has autonomous purchasing
(d) Subsidiary companies or their branches if the customer has central purchasing and payments
(e) Geographical area
(f) Nearest distribution depot that services the customer, or
(g) Discounts a customer receives.

Each of these different kinds of file structure will, in general, be more beneficial to only one department or function within the organization.

After having examined the above questions, an optimum file design is required based on the frequency of usage and for supplying the necessary management information. As an example, the following types of functions or departments may all require access to the main customer file: marketing, product design, sales, invoicing, distribution, product pricing, despatch, factory, or depot siting. Each item of data will have different frequencies of usage: depot siting may only be required annually for one function, whilst data referring to salesmen may be required daily for several different functions.

This file design may take several months, and should be set up by the project manager or systems development manager (with the organization's maximum confidence) at the earliest stages of initiating a potential application system. The result of the file investigation will be required irrespective of the outcome of the subsequent project justification. An organization cannot go wrong if it understands its own data.

CHAPTER SUMMARY

Having determined the end-product it is necessary to consider how it will be constructed. Once again the management methodology is well established, and is the responsibility of the systems development manager and, for larger projects, the project manager.

Controlling the ever-changing end-product requires firm management, and a control team could be made responsible. Changes to the development plans occur throughout the duration of the project. A procedure is required to control these and to update current documentation as each change is approved.

Support functions are vital to a project, and can consume up to half of the manpower. A checklist is provided to assist in the planning and control of these support activities.

Project administration is an important method of both serving the users and extending the project manager's influence, as well as a good way of controlling a project. Sound administration is a good means of keeping open all channels of communication and senior management will readily detect any failures in it. Continual discussions at a personal level, with no surprises, is advocated as being superior to communicating via memoranda and reports. Tactful training of users regarding DP methods may also be appropriate, as is the need to give the users what they require, not necessarily what they requested. Possibly, the public relations requirement of a project may also need some consideration as part of administration.

The adoption of a fourth generation programming language for an entire system, or possibly for only a part of it, should be considered by the project manager, in conjunction, with his systems development manager. Little harm can result from using a fourth generation language (which has been well evaluated and recommended) in a controlled manner whilst, say, establishing user requirements or screen dialogues. Depending on performance measurements resulting from these trials, a decision can be made as to the eventual use of a fourth generation language in the application system's final end-product.

In larger projects, file design could be a major area of strategic importance. To control this aspect of developing the end-product, a methodology might be appropriate and a special team might be made responsible for file design.

Chapter 8

Standards and techniques

The topic of 'standards' causes many DP professionals to 'switch off'. This chapter continues the theme of how the end-product will be built, by taking a *practical* view of the minimum DP standards required, and couples them with useful techniques that facilitate systems development. For smaller projects, standards are usually defined for the entire computer department. Larger projects may well have to produce their own. Discussions regarding the thorny problem of documentation conclude this chapter.

THE NEED FOR STANDARDS

Standards may seem inappropriate to experienced analysts or programmers. Frequently they are seen as restricting, dry, and too heavy to read. So they get filed and are rarely referred to. In many cases, the imposition of sophisticated standards on a small or medium sized project could well be counter-productive and slow down the development process. The reasons for this might be too much form filling, over-documentation, or the creation of red tape which could sap the available productive manpower and its enthusiasm. However, even in small or medium-sized projects, basic standards are essential, even if they only act as a checklist to ensure that nothing is overlooked, (e.g. which reports? when? what content? and to whom should they be addressed?) and as an aid to communication.

For larger projects, the need for detailed standards becomes more necessary, because the many people involved will be unable to communicate effectively without them. Useful standards should improve quality and simplify testing. They could minimize programmers misinterpreting the program designer's aims, the system designer putting his own interpretation on the users' requirement, or the users' requirement document not reflecting the users' needs, etc. However, an excessive concern by an inexperienced manager on standards is sometimes a sign of a lack of confidence and knowledge, and he may be relying on standards to help him out. Standards should document experience, not be a substitute for it.

PRODUCING STANDARDS

Producing standards can be an expensive time-consuming exercise with which a new installation or a large project might be faced. Occasionally an organization sets up a larger than usual project, and finds that the procedures for smaller projects no longer apply. Development standards that work in practice are difficult to produce by a computer department (or a project) in isolation.

A recommended approach is either to use consultants to produce a set of standards, or adopt a set of development standards obtained from a similar sized installation (that is successful) and modify them where necessary. High calibre experienced staff are required for this. In larger installations, the standards and quality assurance department is responsible for producing standards and procedures. This department may well recommend the adoption of a sound proprietary methodology for systems development work.

TYPES OF STANDARDS

Within a computer department that has been established many years, a formidable volume of procedures and standards can evolve steadily. It is convenient to categorize them and think in terms of several types of standards which might relate to logically and physically separate volumes. The complete and compatible set of standards should comprise major *logical* volumes of standards, viz:

Systems development standards
Computer operations standards
Clerical systems standards
Administration standards, including references to company/organization
    procedures
Computer department procedures
Project control procedures
Back-up documents and library including hardware and software manuals

The *physical* volumes should be dictated primarily by their appropriateness to the individuals using them and by their actual size. The standards manuals should be supplemented as necessary by specific procedure manuals such as that for the project control system, and reference manuals for hardware or software. An overview of the suggested contents of each volume is as follows.

Computer operations standards

Computer operations standards, although mainly relevant to the operators, data controllers, etc., have an important impact on certain areas of system development work. Included should be procedures for data preparation (if applicable), data control, computer operating, job submission, testing, and for terminal usage. Comprehensive standards should also exist for the detailed documentation of systems prior to their live running, as well as standards for data coding and submission, for the design of printed output, and the design of names, codes, and messages. The production and update of these standards is usually the responsibility of the data processing operations department.

Clerical systems standards

Clerical system standards are mainly self-contained and relevant to O and M, or business analysts. However, some initial surveys may lead to computer system development and accordingly there is an impact on computer development. Standards for user procedure manuals, or clerical input and output controls, may also be relevant, if produced by the clerical systems team as opposed to the computer systems development team.

Administration standards

Administration procedures for the organization, and the DP department in general, should exist for recruitment, training, typing, expenses claims, the library, etc. A separate manual should exist for running the project control system containing forms, procedures, and job accounting, etc. Many administration procedures such as holiday notification may be more adequately conveyed to staff by memorandum.

Back-up documents and library

These include detailed hardware and software manuals, reference books, system utilities, etc. To reduce maintenance, a minimum number of copies should exist, which are regularly updated and held in a library. Reference may be made to these in the standards manuals.

Systems development standards

Development standards should follow the sequence of the 'Project Life Cycle' and cover most aspects of systems and programming work for systems development, enhancement, and maintenance activities. These may be supplemented by such documents as data standards (e.g. permissible formats), programming standards (e.g. coding conventions), testing guidelines (e.g. how to prepare a test plan), and standards for data communications (e.g. the network protocols). These standards may all be held as separate volumes.

STANDARDS FOR SYSTEMS DEVELOPMENT

Objectives and philosophy

This section is a comprehensive summary of the standards applicable to computer system development work, and the following overall philosophy could well be adopted, as it has worked well in several installations.

These standards should be aimed primarily at the analysts, programmers, and team managers responsible for developing, installing and maintaining application systems. As the majority of these readers should be experienced in DP, these standards should not 'talk-down' to them. It should not be a training manual, nor should it be an encyclopedia of DP which attempts to cover every possible topic. The content need only relate 'how to develop a system', and include both systems and programming tasks. It is recommended that to achieve these objectives the content should be primarily aimed at the quality assurance aspects of systems. Details of such things as 'timeliness' need not be covered here. Where appropriate, reference may be made to the project control procedures.

Confusion is often caused when a standards manual is a combination of different concepts such as: conventions, techniques, references, documentation, procedures, tasks, phases. Each of these should be treated separately, preferably as separate sections or manuals. To further improve comprehension, an attempt should be made to divorce standards (which should be regarded as generally accepted DP industry practice relating only to systems development work) from procedures and policy which relate to company requirements. Using this approach, standards should require little amendment. For example, the project life cycle, or what information is required in a system specification is mainly invariant. Procedures which could change more rapidly (e.g. job titles, circulation lists, how to complete time-sheets, arranging advertising and interviews for recruiting, or defining job accounting codes) should not be covered in this volume. They should be included in separate volumes to facilitate their more frequent updating.

In a further attempt to improve comprehension, the system standards should not only follow closely the sequence of the project life cycle, but could well be sectionalized to the job in hand. The purpose of development phases should be separated from the tasks to be carried out in each phase. These in turn should be separated from the documentation to be produced, from the standard forms to be used, and from the conventions and techniques to be adopted. The opportunity could be taken to clarify names by introducing unambiguous and easily understood titles of both documents and development phases. (e.g. avoiding the confusion caused by not being sure when to produce, or what is the difference between a system proposal, a system specification, or a system definition).

In keeping with the above concepts, the system development standards could be issued so that each person has their own personalized conveniently sized handbook— (*not* a tome relevant to all staff and to all functions within the computer department). A handbook of about 130, A5 sized pages, (i.e. 65 leaves) can contain most system development standards. In this vein, it is recommended that the format of the system development standards be kept brief and concise, in a concentrated note format (not long winded prose) but still being comprehensive, and comprising useful checklists. Checklists are useful on a daily basis. These ensure that all activities have been undertaken, that all documents are produced without omissions, and as a guideline in estimating and planning. Where appropriate, reference should be made to more detail in technical back-up documents, procedures manuals, as well as to other compatible standards such as those produced by computer operations department.

It is essential to differentiate between the full set of standards relevant to large projects developing a new system, and a sub-set of these standards which is applicable to: (a) maintenance jobs, (b) conversions of systems from bureaux, (c) small development projects, (d) implementing packages, or (e) enhancement to existing DP systems. Guidance should be given on these, e.g. when to combine or omit earlier phases or reports for expediency.

It is also necessary to distinguish between the evolutionary documentation required for developing a system and the documentation for an existing system which is required for on-going maintenance. For example, at the end of a typical system development project, transitory documentation such as the feasibility study, the development plan, the test error log, etc., are redundant, whilst after a system has gone live, system and program specifications are usually out of date and inadequate for maintenance purposes. When system testing is carried out it usually results in changes to both the users requirement document and the system design specification. A complete list of validation and error messages for each program is frequently only available from the programmers after they have made all the necessary changes to fix errors found during testing.

It is, therefore, necessary to revise the system and programming documentation. In making this revision it is sensible to take into account the new situation which exists now that the system has gone live, e.g. the availability of actual program listings with comments, or module hierarchy charts from the compiler, or actual print-outs resulting from testing. These can now form part of the documentation: they were not available when the original program and system specifications were written.

For ease of use, and to facilitate keeping it updated, the documentation for on-going maintenance should have one logical system document (for use by the analysts), and one logical program document (for use by the programmer(s)). The latter may well relate, physically, to each program. It is also more practical to adopt the philosophy that the documentation for enhancement and maintenance work can be less rigorous and less comprehensive than for new development work. One must assume that the reader(s):

(1) is a member of a team (and not one person who is likely to leave the organization)
(2) has a detailed knowledge of the system

Consequently there should be no need to have free standing documentation for, say, the user definition of enhancements to a current system.

The system development standards are intended to be very comprehensive and may not be appropriate in all circumstances. It may be necessary to omit or alter part of the standards in a controlled way for certain situations. For example, if a project only involves a merge of 2 existing DP systems which is transparent to the users, the user requirement phase is irrelevant, and the system design specification document may not require all the sections and headings appearing in the standards checklist. However, some standards relating to names, dates, conventions, or adherence to the project life cycle will always apply.

Where possible, the quality control of development work against the standards should be built into the standards. It is envisaged that as everyone will be working from the same handbook, adherence to the system development standards will come about by natural checks and balances within the department. For example by:

Managers reviewing and approving feasibility study or user requirement documents.
Senior programmers accepting system design specifications.
Programmers accepting a program or module specification.
Systems testers accepting linked programs.
Operations department accepting a documented and tested system.
Post-implementation review.

Also inherent in these standards is that the start and conclusion of each development phase is a self-contained checkpoint for management planning and control.

CONTENTS OF A DEVELOPMENT STANDARDS MANUAL

Phases

One of the first sections of the standards manual should be the definition and purpose of the system development phases (e.g. as in Figure 2.4 and Chapter 2 and Appendix 3). From these phases fan out the necessary tasks and documents and their sequence of production.

Tasks

The tasks to be completed in each phase of development can then be listed. These tasks should be broken down one further level into more measurable activities which can be described more fully in a checklist format. An example of tasks and activities within a phase is given in Figure 8.1. It is hoped that this example appears familiar. The intention here is not to introduce new ways of working, but literally to apply standard well-tried DP practices.

Documentation

Included in the standards manual should be a contents checklist for all major documents. The subject of documentation has wider psychological implications than standards, and is more extensively covered later in this chapter, under the section headed 'documentation'.

Phase	Tasks	Activities and particulars
Initial Appraisal	*Orientation/background reading*	Establish terms of reference, define problem areas, read standards.
	Management (planning and control)	Produce the estimates and schedules for the phase; update the project control system, and the associated reporting; allocate tasks.
	BROAD STUDY	Identify user departments involved. Discussions with user management. Identify business constraints. Consider existing deficiencies.
	REVIEW EXTERNAL INFLUENCES	Government; legal; economic; competition; company policy; corporate plans; unions.
	FORMULATE ALTERNATIVE DEVELOPMENTS	For each alternative approach make broad estimates of: development effort, implementation timetable, costs and benefits, advantages and disadvantages, clerical or computer solution.
	REVIEW FINDINGS	Within the computer department; with user(s) management
	REPORT PREPARATION	Produce the Initial Survey report. Publish, discuss, amend, and agree the final version.
Feasibility Study	*Orientation/background reading*	Read the Initial Survey report, any subsequent project initiation documents, and the phase standards.
	Management (planning and control)	Produce the estimates and schedules for the phase; update the project control system, and the associated reporting; set up team(s); allocate tasks.
	DATA GATHERING	Study the user departments, their business functions, and their existing systems. Prepare user organization and staffing charts. List premises and equipment used. Determine volumes. Identify security arrangements, and critical time-tables. Ascertain users expectations.
	ANALYSIS AND CONSOLIDATION	Summarize findings quantitatively. Identify shortcomings and design constraints.
	OUTLINE REQUIREMENTS AND FACILITIES	Define broadly the facilities required by the user and the basic DP elements.
	INVESTIGATE AND EVALUATE ALTERNATIVE SOLUTIONS	Clerical, computer; in-house, bureaux; centralized, decentralized; packages. Assess risks, technical and operational feasibility, interfaces with other systems.
	OUTLINE DESIGN OF PREFERRED SOLUTION	A feasible design based on the best alternative solution. Consequences on user's accommodation and resources.
	TECHNICAL CONSIDERATIONS	Effects on existing hardware, software, communication lines, terminals, response times, and through-puts. Upgrading required of current configuration, if applicable.
	COST/BENEFIT STUDY	Record the cost of the existing system. Estimate development and on-going running costs. Determine savings and benefits. Justify return on anticipated capital expenditure.
	DEVELOPMENT PLAN	Provide firm resource estimates for the user requirements phase, and provisional estimates and schedules for the remaining phases. Outline any contingency plans.
	FEASIBILITY REPORT PRODUCTION	Product the Feasibility Study report. Publish, discuss, amend, and agree the final version.
	Conclusion of the phase	Acceptance of the Feasibility Study report by senior management, and their authorization to proceed with the user requirements phase.

Figure 8.1   An example of a checklist of tasks and activities within each phase

Standard forms

The use of standard forms are an inevitable part of DP standards. Although a blank piece of white A4 paper may often be the best standard form (many different forms with many boxes to be completed can be counter-productive), a compromise is necessary to improve efficiency and communication. In general, forms should be kept to a minimum, they should be simple to use, and preferably form part of a compatible set (i.e. look alike and be similar to complete). Where possible, forms should (a) be designed for a word processor system, and an even greater bonus would be that they may be replaced by standard formats. (b) evolve in their usage, so that basic detail documented during systems analysis can be augmented during system design and program design without duplication or transcription of data. If these approaches are adopted then copies of the final (most detailed) standard formats may be used when writing the initial information prior to typing, but only those fields relevant to the work in hand are used. The word processing operator can call down the standard format, and only type the relevant headings and fields to produce custom made forms.

Useful items to consider under the heading of standard forms for facilitating systems development are those for:

The logical and physical layouts of outputs, inputs, files, and records.
Defining processes.
Print layout and VDU screen layout.
Output (printer or VDU) derivations (i.e. the origin of each field of output data).
Cross reference charts (for files, records, programs, modules, decision tables, test data, etc.).
Messages/user codes.

Also required are various administrative forms used for making changes to systems and programs, as well as for making systems and programs live.

There should be no need to give detailed procedures for the completion of these forms, as they should be simple. Either common sense will prevail or, where necessary, examples of both blank and completed forms/formats can be illustrated.

Methodologies and techniques

Development standards should not only state *what* should be done, but also give guidance on *how* the tasks should be performed. As development methodologies and techniques is a broad subject in itself, it too is covered later in this chapter.

Conventions

Conventions may be considered as the more local or parochial aspects of standards. They may apply to compulsory aspects of development, or simply reflect good working practices where commonality is advisable to ease the communications problem. The development standards should include conventions to be adopted, and a checklist of the more important headings is given below.

Operational standards	— console messages, error codes, restarts
Programming	— program design conventions, coding conventions, JCL usage
Naming conventions	— modules, programs, files, records, systems
Printing conventions	— start of reports, separators, headings, end of report, distribution lists, printing controls
Input conventions	— batching, transaction identification
Calendar date formats	— input, output, processing, and file formats
Structuring of codes	— record keys, transaction types, etc.
Microfilm	— conventions for production and retrieval
Testing	— guidelines and procedures for program, system and user testing

THE SEQUENCE OF THE CONTENTS OF A STANDARDS MANUAL

The above topics may be included in a development standards manual in one of two different sequences. The first method of sequencing could contain separate self-contained sections entitled:

(a) Definition of the system development phase
(b) Tasks to be completed in each phase of systems development projects
(c) Documentation required for each phase of development
(d) Standard forms to be used
(e) Program design and program coding conventions
(f) Other development techniques and conventions.

The advantage of this sequence is that the standards are logical and easy to understand, and are ergonomically designed for use by experienced readers. Any individual need only consider one section at any one time, and only a few pages are relevant at any point in time.

For example, if someone is assigned to carry out a feasibility study, at the start of the phase he may well ask, 'What tasks must I do during the feasibility phase?' He can then turn to the appropriate page (thumb indexes and section dividers help here), and refresh his mind as to all tasks to be completed. Alternatively, when, for example, a system design specification has to be written, this will occur near the end of the system design phase. He may well ask, 'What should I include in the system design specification document?' Turning to the documentation section will enable the appropriate check-list to be used for headings contents, and formats.

This accounts for the first three sections on phases, tasks and documentation. On the other hand, standard forms, techniques and conventions cross phase boundaries, and should be treated separately. For example, a designer may ask: 'How do I incorporate structured design?' or: 'How do I test systems?'.

The alternative sequence, which is more common, is to have the standards manual arranged as a section for each phase. The contents would then assume the form:

> *System design*
> Phase description
> Tasks
> Documentation
> Forms
> Techniques
> Conventions
> *Program design*
> Phase description
> Tasks
> Documentation
> Forms
> Techniques
> Conventions

This format will equally apply to the other phases. The advantages of this sequence is that the standards always relate to the job in hand, and have less cross-referencing, i.e. a person undertaking program design, need only open the manual at one section, but he may have many pages to thumb through.

With modern technology, a traditional printed standards manual is becoming dated. Apart from the slow lead time in printing amendments, publishing them, and physically updating the changed pages, readers of a standards manual may be unaware that relevant information exists in the standards to facilitate their work in hand. Alternative media, to printed paper, could be:

(a) floppy disc for microcomputer display and word processing update by the authorizing standards department
(b) mainframe based, with interrogation via screens
(c) laser video disc, with the appropriate viewing and updating equipment

In all cases, electronic display and search facilities enable the standards to become more usable.

METHODOLOGIES FOR SYSTEMS DEVELOPMENT

Recently, numerous methodologies and associated systems development work-benches have been appearing in the market-place. The impression gained is that everyone is jumping on the bandwagon! In general, a system development methodology is a collection of proven techniques that have originated or have relevance during different parts of the project life cycle, but have been made consistent by the particular vendor, so that they tie up as one moves through the systems development phases.

The majority of the better methodologies have several features in common. They use an efficient diagrammatic representation of data, functions, and relationships, which replaces much of the voluminous text traditionally adopted. This can be a significant advantage, as text is error prone, and usually incomplete. In addition, as people seem to find only parts of the text relevant to themselves, they do not comprehend the bulk of the document, and cannot be sure that they are aware of all the facts. Users understand and relate well to the diagrammatic build-up of their parts of the system under development.

Another common feature of modern methodologies is that systems development is driven by the analysis and design of data rather than totally on processes and functions. The theory is that the inherent stability of data (as opposed to functions) leads to systems becoming more stable, which makes maintenance easier. Thus, a typical methodology will require the system developers to commence work by producing such charts as data structures, entity models, information flows, data flows, events, and entity life histories. (These charts comprise boxes, connecting lines and symbols.) In the better methodologies, these pictorial concepts can be extended to the determination of a pre-project business strategy. The board of directors, under the guidance of the information systems management, and possibly outside consultants, determine their organization's information system requirements, and the priorities of systems development projects that need to be established to meet the corporate objectives. As intimate user involvement, at the highest level, is a feature of the better methodologies, an additional advantage is greater user commitment to a system and improved accuracy in defining it. This, coupled with the significant benefit of reduced maintenance and better strategic planning, is the main reasons for acquiring a (clerical) methodology. However, it should be stressed, that if an installation already has a sound project life cycle with effective standards down to the task level, a proprietary methodology will probably not reduce the elapsed time or man-power required for system development projects. In fact, after converting to a methodology, the intensive learning period will initially cause development projects to slow down, rather than speed up.

Up to now we have referred to clerical methodologies, where the 'technology' is based on pencil and paper, erasures and templates. The main long-term benefit of selecting and adopting a methodology is that the better ones have evolved and been recently refined so that they allow for automation of the system development process. This can provide the main means for quantum improvements in productivity and quality whilst developing information systems. Methodologies have been introduced which are based on proven computer aided design techniques emanating from the engineering industry. For example, personal computer based software is available to greatly facilitate drawing charts to represent data and processes. Such software may automatically update a data dictionary whilst the systems analyst adds descriptive text to annotate his screen drawn charts, and while he is drawing the lines and symbols which define relationships between the data represented as boxes. Using such an approach leads the way to automation of many analysis, design, and programming tasks. Either stand-alone packages exist for specific parts of the system development process (e.g. analysis), or all-embracing packages that cover the entire project life cycle are coming on the market that involve personal computers, mainframes, and teaching aids.

Productivity gains of 15% initially and 30% after two years have been achieved by early users of automated methodologies. In large DP installations, this would result in savings in excess of one million dollars per annum on the systems development budget. Because the potential savings are significant, and because the vendor's cost for developing and launching an automated methodology is so high (tens of millions of dollars), the cost to an organization contemplating the introduction of an automated methodology is also very high. Even the cost of introducing a clerical version of the methodology is relatively expensive. To use the methodology effectively, it is necessary to provide extensive classroom and on the job training, as well as practical consultancy for users, systems analysts and designers. Medium and small sized computer installations may, therefore, have difficulty in cost-justifying not only the automated development tools, but even the clerical methodology. With this in mind, the following section relates to well-established free-standing techniques for the many information systems departments that do have have, do not need, or cannot afford a total system development methodology.

TECHNIQUES TO FACILITATE DEVELOPMENT

There are many techniques currently being advocated within the computer industry, that claim to facilitate the system development process, or reduce development time and costs. Much sales activity emanating from computer manufacturers, consultants, software houses, training establishments, etc., purports to demonstrate the merits of particular techniques. However, techniques seem to come and then go out of fashion: they are found not to be the panacea that cures all ills! The cynic can enquire: 'If these techniques are so good why does not everyone use them?'

Also there is often much confusion over the words 'technique' and 'structured'. For example, the DP market is filled with buzz-words like 'structured analysis', 'structured design', or 'structured programming', which many people interpret as new techniques. In fact, many of these so called structured techniques are, in essence, formalized methods of working. The word 'structure' may become debased or used in a different context from normal, referring more to procedures, sequences of tasks, forms, or even 'carrying out the job in the normal accepted way'.

This section attempts to categorize some of these techniques, indicate in which development phases they are relevant, and comment (possibly conservatively) on their benefits in the author's experience. It is difficult to find one technique or methodology that is strong for all phases of the project life cycle.

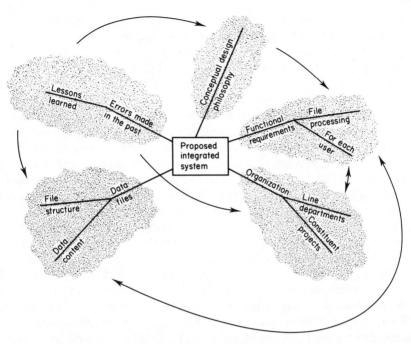

Figure 8.2 A technique for pictorially representing a system

For example, some are better for data analysis and dealing with user requirements, whilst others are better at, say, program design. A general observation is that

(a) the larger the project, the more necessary is the use of development techniques.
(b) although many techniques act as a systematic methodology, or a useful checklist, they can also be very restrictive, reduce the need for imaginative work, and may take the interest out of creative tasks.
(c) some techniques are useful for making less experienced staff more productive, faster than a conventional learning and training approach.

Techniques useful during the initial appraisal and feasibility study

Apart from the use of checklists in the standards, there are not many techniques applicable to the business survey or feasibility study phases. The main problem is that of cost and technical justification of alternative systems. Standard forms as used in the chapter on budgets could be of assistance.

When designing any new, highly interactive system and discussing it with other people, it may be very difficult to represent it other than pictorially. Not only have all the interactions with the line users to be considered and represented, but a file structure has to be depicted, and a file processing method determined. At the same time, past mistakes should be remembered (within both the organization or the industry in general), as well as necessary organizational changes to the line departments and computer projects, to enable the application to be developed and run successfully.

A suggested pictorial representation that will illustrate all these facets is shown in Figure 8.2. Ideas radiate logically from the centre, and similar concepts are grouped within boundaries. This technique was shown during an educational program on BBC Television which appeared several years ago. In fact, the logic and content for most of the chapters in this book was so prepared. (Accusations of illogical chapters can now be blamed on the technique!). In a matter of minutes, up to 30 pages of text can be represented on one page. This diagramatical form is useful not only for clarifying ideas, but sometimes it is superior to making pages and pages of notes, which by their linear nature cannot depict easily all the cross-references and interactions. The pictorial representation is easy to explain at senior management meetings, with the additional benefit of requiring only one sheet of paper (although sometimes a large sheet) as a hand-out at the end of the meeting.

This pictorial representation can be combined with the well-established charting techniques for entities, information flow, etc., and can be used for the conceptual design of very large or even corporate systems, and this approach allows the whole design philosophy of the new system to be open-ended to enable future developments by evolution, if it is necessary to add new facilities. However, to achieve this, a deep understanding is required of both computing, as well as the relevant industry for which this new system is designed.

Techniques useful when preparing the user requirements

This phase mainly relates to fact-finding and recording information. The most useful 'technique' is to spend most of the time with the user departments! Data analysis, data and process charts, decision tables, or cross-reference charts may be useful to facilitate analysis. During this phase there is a significant amount of conceptual system design required, and a useful technique is to have standard forms for systematically identifying and defining the total system. These forms relate to:

Logical Inputs	—	Each transaction type, its logic contents, and its characteristics
Logical Outputs	—	Each report, or screen layout, its logic contents, and its characteristics
Logical Files	—	Each file, its contents, and its characteristics
Logical Records	—	Each data field and its characteristics
The processing rules	—	Each logical process

Techniques relevant to design

Several techniques are claimed to assist in the system design process, but in the author's experience, they may be of limited use, or relate to conventional standards and procedures for carrying out systems design, or have more relevance to program design. In some installations it is difficult to separate system design from program design, as the same person is responsible for both. This section therefore deals with design in its widest sense but assumes that the logical sequence of working is:

High level system design.
Detailed system design.
Specifying what each program should do.
Designing how each program is constructed.

The basic technique for design then, is to approach the task in steps, with at least an overall design, followed by a review, and then a detailed system design. Starting with the forms produced above which appear in the user requirements document, and logically working through them, a system design usually presents itself, after the long tedious slog of timing out all possible alternative file structures and file access methods.

A useful design approach is to use a general parameter-driven system, in which a file holds all variables of both a business nature (e.g. number of days before reminder letters are sent, or required percentage service level), and of a DP nature (e.g. block sizes of files).

Modularizing or sectionalizing programs is a well-accepted approach and in many organizations is more a standard than a technique. The advantages of this approach include improved flexibility for assignment, scheduling and control of programming work; easier handling of errors; and hopefully, a reduction of duplication by collecting a library of common or re-useable modules. Additional advantages are that, as the system is subdivided into small manageable sections, estimating and the subsequent control are improved. The time taken to design, code, and test a standard-size module is relatively easily measured and may be refined as work progresses.

Traditionally, programs, especially for real-time applications, have been split into modules for the above and other technical benefits. The only problem is how large (or small) is a module? Some authorities have suggested module sizes of say 50–100 source statements; others claim a practical size is 1000–2000 statements. The range 150–350 statements seems convenient. This is a compromise between too many modules (to compile, test, document, schedule, and control, as well as creating significant machine-time overheads), and modules which are too large to gain the benefits of modularization.

For actually converting detailed systems and programs into modules, several techniques are currently in vogue (with magnificent sounding names!).
Some of these are:

Top down step-wise refinement: where the starting point is an elementary program that would complete the whole job.
Top down by functional decomposition: where the whole problem is broken into a number of pieces.

Bottom up: where the program is built and/or tested from its component parts.

Design based on data structures: where the program structure relates to the input and output files, i.e. matches exactly the structure of the user's problem.

Of these techniques, the latter is well liked and can produce consistent (if not optimized) modularization. It also has the advantage of producing one design (and so removes the necessity for deciding which alternative program structure to choose). A systematic method of program testing follows, especially when coupled with another technique which limits the logic within a program or module to three basic structures: sequence, iteration, and selection. It can be demonstrated that any logic can be expressed by these structures, which also have only one entry and one exit point. The disadvantage of basing program design on (parochial) input and output files is that the latter do not usually relate to the organization's business, or to the earlier phases of the system development life cycle. Consequently, a business change (a frequent reason for maintenance requests) requires a change to the input and output files, and thus to the program's structure. Significant savings in maintenance effort may not be possible, nor may it be easy to link a data change in the user requirements to the programs and modules affected.

A technique that replaces flowcharts for specifying modules is to use a design language which is a mixture of a basic vocabulary of English, and a high-level programming language. This technique, sometimes referred to as pseudo-code, or structured English, can help to reduce communication errors and improve program documentation.

'Structured programming' is a loosely defined but well-publicized collection of techniques which combines many of the previous concepts. It is useful not only to minimize risks in programming design, but also in the programming and testing phases of a project. It is beneficial in the maintenance of an application system, when the ease of modification is an important factor. One method of implementing structured programming requires the design process to be managed in a 'top down' approach, where the main or control modules could be specified and written at senior technical management or technical director level; the next level of modules by the project manager or programming manager level; and finally, via senior programmers to all the programmers.

The advantage of this approach is that the main business or technical strategy is planned and controlled by the responsible hierarchy of management, which can assign the next level of the problem, as well as specify the interfaces between the interlinking modules. Hundreds of modules present an interface, linking and scheduling problem, as opposed to a conventional program.

Secondly, while management or the technical specialists are designing each module, they are forced to concentrate their minds on only one problem at a time. They therefore tend to abstract the relevant information relating to the process performed by that module. They will also tend carefully to perfect the interfaces between modules. For these reasons, the quality of the specification is improved, as there should be less errors when the modules are eventually linked together. This supposes that a strong technical management environment exists.

A disadvantage is that structured programming usually requires a few key people with experience of the technique, otherwise serious errors at the early stages can have important repercussions.

Programming techniques

Two general types of techniques apply to programming, and these relate to writing code, and testing it subsequently. The subject of testing is discussed in the next chapter. If a design language or pseudo-code is adopted for program design, which is given to another programmer, then that programmer may become a coder and tend to follow the pseudo-code blindly, and not be too critical of the logic. This is to be avoided by involving the programmers in the design of their own programs.

If the module logic is restricted to basic structures, the coding should be similarly restricted and structured, and branch statements eliminated. The latter has become an infamous constraint advocated by many but achieved by few. In general, coding conventions and techniques are a large subject in themselves, and are found in most installation's standards manual. This area is well covered in other publications.

Proving techniques

Proving is one aspect of testing, and techniques relevant to the proving phase are discussed in the next chapter.

Implementation techniques

Apart from following a good set of phase tasks, there are not many useful techniques to assist work in the implementation phase.

General techniques

The previous techniques were mainly relevant to one development phase, but the following can be used during several phases.

Prototyping

Building a 'prototype' has long been associated with engineering development projects. In improving productivity and automating the system development process, ideas have been borrowed from the longer established engineering industry. Applied to information systems, prototyping can produce an end-product faster than a more traditional project life cycle, as many phases and much transient documentation is eliminated. Prototyping assumes that appropriate tools are available to build systems rapidly and interactively. Such tools include fourth generation languages, input/output generators, simulators, etc.

In the simplest prototype, the highest level screen is a menu. Each item selected from this menu calls either another menu or a program. A fourth generation language is useful to create the control logic for linking the screens and for simulating the ensuing processing. The lead analyst and user can walk-through the relevant part of the application system at the screen, agreeing to a practical compromise of improvements worth incorporating.

Permanent system documentation may also be simplified because some prototyping techniques are self documentary. Prototyping affects, and can benefit, most system development phases, unlike numerous other DP techniques, which usually only improve the effectiveness of one phase (e.g. aids to assist data analysis, or to facilitate testing). Improved communication is one key reason for the success of prototyping as a technique. Most users do not actually know what they want until they 'feel' and see their system in operation. With prototyping, they can actually see operational versions of such aspects as their system's inputs and outputs. Prototyping usually reveals omissions, inconsistencies, and misunderstandings. It is then relatively easy for the user to suggest improvements to the system under development, and rapidly assess the affects of the changes. Compared to the traditional method of communicating during system development (i.e. vast quantities of text produced and amended over relatively long periods of time) prototyping encourages the users to become better involved and committed to their system from the earliest phases of its development. Thus, the users are able to make a contribution they otherwise would have been unable to make.

Theoretically, the optimum benefit of prototyping is to refine speedily the prototype (using appropriate software development aids) into the live operational system. In practice, this ideal might only be achieved for small systems (or parts of systems) that involve few resources to control, such as one-off enquiries, or producing new reports from existing files. Large systems, with high volumes of transactions, involving complex updates, and requiring efficient use of many DP resources, can still use prototyping to resolve problems quickly and to determine the optimum screen dialogues and procedures. The prototype sub-systems can then be thrown away, with the final system rewritten using traditional DP methods and languages. In this way, prototyping may speed-up conventional systems development.

Users having seen a prototype up and running, usually imagine that the application is almost complete. They cannot comprehend that the information systems development project needs to expend much effort in adding the validation and editing routines, the error messages, the security aspects, the back-up and recovery features, etc. Consequently, users can become impatient waiting for their systems to become operational. To minimize this effect (as well as for better management control) it is preferable to have phased developments, with small projects implementing small parts of the total system.

For sound management control, prototyping can be poor, compared to the traditional system development life cylce. By its very nature, prototyping is an ill-disciplined technique allowing only infrequent management review. There may be too much iteration, with an open ended commitment by the information systems departments. Users can easily make uneconomical improvements, with the systems analyst/designers attempting to respond to every whim.

Not only may prototyping produce poor integration of systems (with an analyst taking a parochial view of his part of a system in hand), but prototyped systems may result in severe maintenance problems. One reason is that documentation of the system may be poor, as the development can jump from a prototype to a live implementation, with the documentation of the system analysis, data analysis, design, and testing all missing. Another reason for maintenance problems is that by definition, prototypes are 'lash-ups' built on the foundations of the previous 'lash-up'. Not only could there be difficulties in interfacing with existing systems, but this method of quick development may well produce inefficient systems. Much maintenance effort, and high levels of expertise may be required to tune the system so that it makes efficient use of the DP resources.

Walk throughs

'Walk throughs' are a brainstorming technique, the purpose of which is to improve the quality of systems and programming work by a group of reviewers. This might often be appropriate at the design and programming stages of an application system.

The basic philosophy is to produce a desire for open analysis, open systems design, open program design, and open program code. In essence, the system or module designer explains his system or program logic to a meeting of appropriate specialists, with the objective of finding errors in it. A brainstorming session develops, and as the objective is *not* to gain formal confirmation or commitment to the proposed logic, the atmosphere should be free and relaxed without any emphasis on the quality of the presentation, or any feeling of guilt if flaws are discovered. To assist this goal, usually it is better if people of the same level of management are present at a walk through.

A practical problem can arise, especially during the design of the system, programs, and modules, when management and staff tend to spend a significant amount of time attending other people's walk throughs. As their own work is interrupted, attendees of the walk throughs could tend to become demotivated, spend little time on preparation, with the session resulting in general disappointment. It therefore becomes difficult to get reviewers to attend when they have different projects and priorities.

Technical reviewers who are outside the project usually do not have the necessary business and systems background. In practice, business and time constraints are usually more important than technical problems. Often the technical arguments impact the user requirements. By the time of the technical walk through, it is usually too late to alter the user requirements, as they have already been agreed. Unless a long-term business, system, and technical strategy exists, together with a cost justification, and data and transaction volumes provided by the users, the finer technical improvements emanating from walk throughs often cannot be justified, or warrant the development time. In an installation with much political in-fighting, these sessions may well end in a 'blood bath', and in these cases this technique may be more relevant to the technical aspects of, for example, programming

Data dictionary

The use by members of a project, or preferably by an installation, of a 'data dictionary' can both reduce risk and improve staff productivity, compared to an alternative practice of clerically defining and filing data items. A data dictionary is basically a central library of all data fields used by every analyst or programmer. As this data dictionary is held on a computer file, it requires its own system for accessing and updating data. Obvious advantages include reduced coding by the programmers (by using a copy library facility), non-duplication of effort by the analysts and programmers, and accurate up-to-date (computer produced) documentation. The laborious and inaccurate alternative is to amend each program separately after every change is made. As the computer system can print out cross-reference lists of all the files and all the programs that use each data item, it is relatively easy to assess the impact of making changes to an application system, and ensure nothing is overlooked.

The main disadvantages of this technique are that it needs the basic computer system, which may have to be acquired or developed specially, and like all computer systems there are additional costs and formalities in setting up and running it. The rigidity of having to complete correctly a computer input document, learning how to use the system, coupled with the slow access (if not on-line) to computer held information (compared to a clerical file) can slow up system development.

In instances where the data dictionary is used passively (i.e. entries are *not* an *integral* part of development work, but an optional nicety), obtaining accurate information may be very difficult, and the dictionary can easily lose its credibility if it is not totally accurate. Reducing the scope of the dictionary to the barest minimum of what can be achieved practically is an important consideration. The initial use of a data dictionary is limited in the case of an installation inheriting, possibly, hundreds of independent programs which were written without a data dictionary. It is easier to start from scratch. Also, it is not always practical to use the dictionary at the lowest levels of data (e.g. programmers' data names or intermediary files that are only used between two programs). Overall though, the benefits usually outweigh the overheads, especially in installations with data-bases, or with well-disciplined systems development staff, or where the data dictionary procedures are user friendly and easier to use than more traditional methods. The optimum approach is an automated entity/data diagram charting aid (e.g. microcomputer based using CAD CAM software), where labelling and connecting data boxes automatically update the dictionary.

DOCUMENTATION

Types

Unlike the end-product of engineering projects, the only tangible output from a computer system development project is documentation, which is predictable, in that

(1) it must be relevant to each development phase;
(2) it must enable staff to have reference documents relevant to their skills and functions;
(3) it will comprise deliverable and non-deliverable items.

The documentation which may accompany the end-product includes the systems specification and the program documentation (for use in maintenance work), the operational procedures (which are for use by the data processing operations department), the user procedures manual (which is given to all relevant user departments), and the conversion or changeover procedures, (which are produced for both parties, but have a finite lifetime).

The non-deliverable documentation includes all the reports produced at each phase of development, the implementation plans, all the internal working papers and documents, weekly project control and scheduling documents, budgets, memos, discussion reports, progress reports from all personnel, the project log, changes documents, and the appropriate indexes and amendments registers.

In practice, all this output will fill several filing cabinets. Documentation will evolve during the course of the project, and should be part of the normal activity relating to the task in hand. To facilitate the production of good documentation, tasks should be made self-documenting where possible. It should not be considered as a nuisance, nor as an overhead to be completed at the end of the project's life. In fact, significant milestones should be set which require the signing-off of documentation during the course of the project.

Good documentation is essential to minimize risk. Key people falling 'under the proverbial bus' should only be a minor interruption in the project, and a replacement should be able to take over rapidly if the documentation is adequate. It is difficult to legislate for good documentation and standards, as people regard these as a chore giving them little personal benefit. As stated earlier, a thick, dry, departmental volume on standards for documentation is often ignored.

178

What is needed is a flexible format and approach by the project manager. Apart from attempting to gradually change attitudes of mind, the project manager or systems development manager should, either personally or via their quality assurance groups review all documentation, and ensure it is adequate. Any deficiencies should be treated diplomatically. It is advisable to insist on maintaining a central team file for all documentation and working papers.

Documentation plan

As all this documentation is predictable, management requires a documentation plan to define in advance all the documents that are required, to establish a standard format and typing conventions, to define the use of standard forms, to recommend documentation aids (e.g. auto flow-charts or networked word processing software on microcomputers), and specify project or department standards relating to the preparation, approval, distribution, and subsequent status of documents. It is also necessary to plan the location of the library, and to devise a method of updating it so that authorized, current versions are always available. Larger projects could require considerable clerical and typing resources.

Figure 8.3 summarizes all the essential documentation required for systems development and on-going maintenance and illustrates when it is produced. Each phase of development concludes with the publication of specific documents, which must receive management approval. It is recommended that

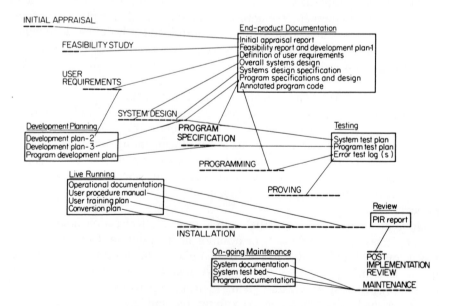

Figure 8.3 When documentation is produced

the systems development standards include, as a series of check-lists, the purpose, content and format of each of these documents, including their chapter and section headings. Figure 8.4 gives an example of such a checklist, which again should seem familiar.

The use of a check-list means that, in any document, it is necessary to mention all items on the list, even just to state explicitly that a certain topic has been considered but was deemed to be irrelevant. This procedure not only facilitates reviewing that a job has been done thoroughly, but also enables senior management to see how much change is involved and therefore assess the accuracy of estimates of development effort.

It could well be a standard, that prior to distribution, the contents of all documents or reports should have been agreed in advance with the relevant people. When a report is received, it should contain therefore 'no surprises' and merely confirm what the recipient knows and agrees. This theme has already been expounded under the general heading of 'communication'.

FEASIBILITY STUDY REPORT (sometimes termed a 'System Proposal')
The purpose of the Feasibility Study report is to present to senior management (both user and DP) a documented, cost justified, feasible proposal, that will enable them to decide on the merits of further development work.

MANAGEMENT SUMMARY
A brief summary of the following: Requirements of a new system and how they are met. Effect on the user departments' organization and structure. Effect on the computer department. Costs and benefits. Development plan. Alternatives considered. Main conclusions and recommendations.

INTRODUCTION
The reason for this report, who requested it, any special terms of reference, the scope of the investigation, the method of approach and any acknowledgements.

CURRENT BUSINESS PROBLEMS
A brief description of current problems, and any anticipated future ones. The effects, if any, on other departments.

EVALUATION OF ALTERNATIVES
For each possible alternative solution: the pros and cons; an outline description; the reasons for its rejection.

PROPOSED SYSTEM FEATURES
Business Functions
A concise description of the system for each of the *business* functions involved.
An outline flow diagram which shows the inputs, processing, and outputs.
The processing timetable for the users and the DP operations department.
The clerical interfaces with the proposed computer system.
Computer Functions
An overall system design for the best alternative(s), illustrating the *DP elements* involved (e.g. terminals, screens, hard copies, program functions, on-line storage).
Security, controls, stand-by, degradation.
Interfaces with other DP or clerical systems.
Limitations of the proposed system.
The effects, if any, on the network, throughput, response times, etc.

DEVELOPMENT PLAN
How the project should be managed, including its reporting structure.

Estimates of staffing levels, skills required, and other non-manpower resources.
Estimated completion dates for each development phase.
Contingency plans.
Suggested areas requiring specific examination in the user requirements phase.

EFFECTS OF THE DEVELOPMENT

Effect on the user(s)

Any changes in office space requirements, including that for any special equipment.
The necessary organizational changes, including regradings, staffing, training, etc.
The schedule for implementing any user changes.
How conversion to the proposed system will influence implementation.

Effect on other systems and projects

Any changes to existing systems and programs which are receiving or providing data.

Effect on the DP operations department

Machine time for testing and live running. Additional file storage, data entry, etc.
Lead time for ordering relevant hardware, software, communication lines, or premises.

COST/BENEFIT ANALYSIS

Benefits

Cost savings.
Extra business generated, improved service.
Increased asset value of proposed system.

Costs

Existing system.
Proposed system development costs for each phase of development.
Proposed system running costs including maintenance.

Justification of the proposed system

Cost/benefit assessment. Tangible and intangible benefits. Disadvantages.

CONCLUSIONS AND RECOMMENDATIONS

Figure 8.4   An example of a documentation checklist

General guidelines to formats

Useful items to consider under the heading of format might be that all published documents adhere to the following checklist:

* The use of a word processing system should be encouraged for producing documents. Ease of production, better quality of layout, and ease of amendment are some potential benefits. Addicts to the system need not only use it as a glorified typewriter, but possibly more akin to using a scratch-pad, where ideas, sections or chapters may be formulated and developed over several iterations to form the complete document.
* The title page should contain— the document's name
                                the author's name
                                the date published
                                the version number
                                (for larger projects) the project's name
                                (for larger projects) a unique project
                                    document number (also indexed in a
                                    central documents register).

* The circulation list should form part of the document.
* A contents page, which gives the page number of the beginning of each section should precede the text.
* The top of *each* page should state (or be pre-set on a word processor system):
    the system name
    the program or module name, if relevant
    the originator
    the date
    the version number
* All pages should be numbered (from the title page to the end of any appendices).
* A management summary should appear at the beginning of each document, which is essential for a rapid appreciation of the contents.
* Supporting information such as detailed tables should appear as appendixes.
* Each document should have a record of the total number of pages, or a last page indicator is required as reports tend to lose their last few pages!
* Changes in text should be indicated where practical, by a vertical mark to the right of the text.
* For sidewards pages, the top of forms should be on the left hand side.

Without intending to insult the intelligence of secretaries, and bearing in mind that the subject often crops up, useful items to consider under the heading of typing conventions are:

* Using one consistent type font, (i.e. all typewriters and printers within the installation should produce similar looking reports) so that the typing work load can be spread and corrections or changes easily handled.
* The headings for sub-sections within sections could start with capital letters underlined, followed at the next level by capital letters not underlined, followed by lower case underlined at the next level down.
* Whether subsections should or should not be indented.
* Using a paragraph numbering system which relates to the subsection headings and the indentations.

CHAPTER SUMMARY

To develop any worthwhile system, standards are required. The only debatable point relates to the level of detail that is appropriate for any one project, and how one acquires a good set of standards.

There are several different types of standards required in an installation and these are briefly described, but the main emphasis here is on the systems development standards. A detailed philosophy is given whereby a personalized handbook can be produced for distribution to all analysts and programmers, which contains practical standards relating to reality in DP, (not pious hope as is often the case). The suggested contents of such a standards manual are itemized together with alternative sequences and layouts.

In order to facilitate the development process, several development techniques are described, together with their relevance during each development phase. The adoption of an overall system development methodology is also discussed, as is the appropriateness of prototyping.

Documentation is the main tangible output from a project, and as it is an important communicating medium in larger projects, it must be considered as an important heading under standards. A checklist is provided detailing which items of technical and management-related documentation are produced in each phase, as well as advice on formats to be adopted.

Chapter 9

Testing

In this chapter an explanation is given as to why testing may take up half of a project's resources, and advice is offered in formulating a testing strategy, quantifying the number of errors anticipated, planning what steps should be taken in testing, and who should complete them. Techniques to facilitate testing are included as well as suggestions relating to which testing utilities and aids may be usefully employed.

THE IMPORTANCE OF TESTING

All the facets of the testing of a computerized system prior to it being allowed to go live, could well consume at least one half of the total project's expenditure. Consequently, testing is a very important subject in the management of the development of systems. At first sight, this high cost for testing may appear exaggerated, but its breakdown for a typical project is illustrated in Figure 9.1 which is explained as follows:

Manpower

During systems design, about 25% of the manpower for that phase should be considering systems testing and producing test data. This is equivalent to about 4% of the total project's manpower. During program design, about 25% of the manpower for that phase may be expended on planning for program and module testing, which is equivalent to about 2%–4% of the project's total manpower. Actual testing during the programming phase may consume up to 50% of that phase's manpower, which is equivalent to approximately 11%–17% of the project's total manpower. Eventually, for the proving phase, all manpower assigned to that phase is assigned to testing and this may account for about 24% of the project's total manpower (and may be well over 25% for large complex systems). Totalling the above, results in at least 40% of the project's total manpower being involved with testing. (In some installations, the adoption of top down testing techniques may give the apparent affect of less testing effort being required during the proving phase, and more during programming. Alternatively, less effort may be expended in test planning

Development phase	Approximate percentage of the phase's manpower	Percentage of the project's total manpower	Percentage of the project's total machine time
System design	25%	4%	—
Program design	25%	2%–4%	—
Programing	50%	11%–7%	30% +
Proving	100%	24% +	30% +
Total of project's resources devoted to testing		40% +	60% +
Percentage of project's total costs		25% +	25% +

Figure 9.1   The percentage of a project's resources devoted to testing

during system design, but this may be more than offset by increased effort being required during the proving phase. None of these factors affect the general argument).

Machine time

During the programming phase, about 30% of the project's machine time may be consumed, and another 30% may be required for the proving phase. (The remaining 40% of machine time could be required for such activities as system simulation, software evaluation, running a data dictionary, project control systems, data capture, and conversion). Accordingly, at least 60% of a typical project's machine time costs are used on testing, and if, for example, data capture is a small exercise, and a manual project control system used, nearly all of the machine time may be used for testing.

Total cost

The 40% of the project's total manpower accounts for about 25% of the project's total expenditure, whilst the 60% machine time accounts for another 25% of the project's cost. Accumulating the manpower and machine costs results in a conservative total of about 50% of the project's total costs being expended in testing, as stated at the start of this section. The background to these figures and their justification should become apparent during the course of this chapter.

TESTING STRATEGY

Problems to overcome during testing

In attempting to adopt a strategy for optimizing the testing effort and its cost, the manager must balance precariously between two extremes. On the one hand, reducing testing costs may give an early targeted live date, but equally might well create user dissatisfaction from an error-prone end-product. The latter will also incur the users and DP staff in much effort and extra cost during and after implementation. The error prone end-product may cause delays in the users receiving system benefits, and involve them in making alternative arrangements to run the system. In fact, the additional implementation costs (and implications) might outweigh the savings in testing. On the other hand, excessive expenditure on thorough testing might push up development costs and delay going live, without apparent benefits, because it is almost certain that errors will still be found after the system has gone live.

It is virtually impossible to test everything within a system (i.e. all the possibilities within all the modules, programs, sub-systems, clerical aspects, files, data, processing rules, etc.) because there are just too many combinations in even the smallest system. Both user and DP management should accept this situation as the norm, and plan to have appropriate manpower and other resources available for rectifying errors after the system has gone live.

An optimum strategy for testing

In the author's opinion, the optimum testing strategy should reduce to a minimum the manpower requirements which would have been devoted to testing. This may be achieved by redeploying resources (that otherwise would have been spent on attempting to find and test every condition) in an effort to reduce errors at source. Thorough tests (only requiring minimal effort) should still be performed to detect and rectify the fewer number of errors found. If DP management adopt this approach, effort is required in analysing why, how and where errors occur. For example, in larger projects an important source of errors is caused by communication misunderstandings, and the following formidable chain is typical:

—Users give their requirements to systems analysts (who may misunderstand).
—The documents produced by systems analysts (which could contain requirement errors) are used by the system designers (who could misconceive certain features).
—The system designers interpret the requirements and match them to the necessary hardware and software, (but misunderstanding may cause different aspects of the system to tie up incorrectly).

—The system designers may misinterpret DP operations requirements.

—The system testing team, the program designers, and possibly analysts in other projects might misapply the documents produced by the system designers (which may also contain specification errors).

—Data libraries might be set up by a person independent from the programmers using them.

—The program designer interprets his understanding of the optimum hardware and software usage.

—The program coder may misconstrue the module specification produced by the designer (which may also contain logic errors).

—Two different program coders producing modules of the same program, may incorrectly comprehend the method of linking their modules.

Adopting the first part of this recommended strategy for testing does not even involve testing! It requires building quality into the system from the start, not testing it in afterwards. Emphasis should be placed on eliminating the cause of errors by using good development standards, techniques, communication, and quality control. This is discussed elsewhere. The other part of the recommended strategy for proving requires thorough testing using, the steps, techniques, and planning discussed in this chapter. However, the effort and cost associated with the testing will be reduced because:

(a) There should be less errors to find, analyse, rectify and re-test,
(b) The amount of necessary test data will be minimized by not attempting to produce data for every condition, and
(c) The duplication of tests and test data by the several parties involved should be eliminated.

If those people who have just completed testing are asked how, with hindsight, they could have improved their effectiveness, almost without exception they would say that more time should have been devoted to test planning. This planning should occur during system design, when the system designer's mind is tuned to the actual conditions and data that are relevant to testing. One extra week of planning spent in the system design phase, may save several weeks in the proving phase. However, more often than not, people do not learn from their mistakes, and the necessary level of detailed planning does not occur. This failure may be due to pressures to meet the system design specification deadline, and pressures to keep the program designers and programmers busy.

Most standards relating to testing just state: 'Produce a test plan'. This is usually followed by the statement: 'Ensure all conditions are fully tested during system testing'. Advice is rarely offered as to how these tasks should be performed. It is hoped that this chapter will recommend useful and practical advice in order to speed up and improve the effectiveness of testing.

PLANNING FOR FINDING ERRORS

Errors are commonly referred to as bugs (which has a connotation of inevitability tinged with respect). They are never deliberately inserted into program code, and are scattered randomly throughout the entire system (including the clerical aspects) and its programs. As a guideline for planning purposes, there could well be between 14 and 20 errors per 1000 lines of written program code for a fairly complex system, comprising 30,000 or more written program statements. This may reduce to about 9 or 10 errors per 1000 lines for a simple system, or one comprising no more than 20,000 written program statements. Finding these errors is an equally random process. Not knowing in advance where the errors will occur, a systematic search must be conducted throughout the system. The rate of finding errors (i.e. the number of errors found per week) is a function of the man days effort expended per week in testing and searching for errors. Assuming that no more than optimum resources are deployed on testing (i.e. not too many people treading on each other's toes), the relationship between finding errors and elapsed time is approximately linear. For example, a non-scientific spot check on 4 different projects resulted in between 13 and 17 errors found per elapsed week. One would have instinctively thought that the last few errors would take longer to find than the first few errors. This is not necessarily so, and is illustrated in Figure 9.2, which is, for a large project, a graph of the accumulated queries raised during the entire period of testing. In this case, quality assurance and accuracy was paramount and the project was not time critical.

Two points of general interest also appear in the graph. First, having found errors throughout the proving phase, suddenly the errors ceased and the project team were surprised to find that they had finished. They had a completely clean run. All the planned test shots had been finished, and all known errors were cleared. The sharp cut-off at the end of testing is reflected in the graph. The other observation relates to the bump in the graph, the start of which

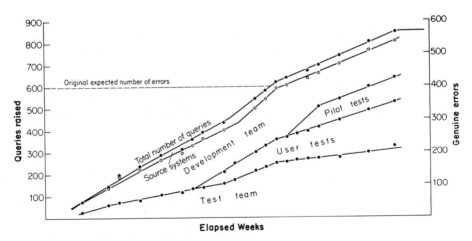

Figure 9.2   Accumulated queries raised during testing

coincided with the missing of the original dead-line for going live. Inevitable repercussions by senior DP and user management highly motivated the project staff (the numbers of which were not increased) to work harder for the next few weeks and they consequently found more errors per week. The project staff then returned to normal working!

This linearity seems to apply elsewhere in testing and managers may find the following yardsticks useful. These yardsticks, as well as those already quoted above are applicable to an average installation, where there are a range of staff: from experienced personnel to trainees, being meticulous to slipshod, some being DP orientated to recruits from user departments. Also included in this typical practical situation are possibly DP professionals new to the organization or possessing experience with other hardware or software.

(a) Testing cannot be rushed. Estimating at one elapsed week for the thorough system testing of each 1000 written statements of program code produces realistic results. Actual figures for several different project's proving phases have ranged between 0.7 and 1.2 weeks per 1000 statements; the lower figure relating to smaller or less complex systems.

(b) A generous estimate of the man days required for proving large systems is 16 man days per 1000 statements. As testing comes at the end of the development sequence, it is more often than not squeezed between users wanting an early delivery date, and the previous development phases being behind schedule. Whatever figure one offers as an estimate for the required testing effort will inevitably be challenged. Why not then start with a generous figure!

(c) As a cross-check just prior to system testing, the effort required for the proving phase may well be about double that already expended on the user requirements phase.

(d) During the proving phase, about 1 CPU hour of machine time (IBM 370/145 equivalent) is required per 1000 statements of end-product and support program code. (As mentioned earlier this may represent only 30% of the total projects' requirement of machine time).

(e) Modifying existing program code (e.g. for maintenance, enhancement, or adaption work) may well take more effort and machine time.

Bugs cannot always be classified in black and white terms as definite and unacceptable errors that necessitate correction to program code. In general, it depends on who is raising the queries, and the following categories are nearer the truth.

. Inaccurate test data or erroneous expected results
. Non-vital bugs, or restrictions found in the system which are acceptable and do not require program fixes
. Possible omissions or defects in the system (e.g. insufficient control totals) highlighted by testing
. Apparent errors being raised, when correct program changes do not become

reflected in a specification which may have been allowed to become obsolete
. Errors caused by changes to specifications not reflected in the programs
. Errors that are tolerable to enable the target live date to be met, but corrections are needed as post-live enhancements
. Users not receiving what they expected, but they may be prepared to accept these defects subject to negotiation.

In Figure 9.2, the two vertical axes reflect this difference between 'queries raised' by the numerous parties involved in testing, and those 'genuine errors' which actually resulted in changes to program code.

STEPS IN TESTING

As with many other complex tasks, a sound approach is to test computer systems in steps. Each step escalates the size and complexity under consideration. The project manager should ensure that the following steps have been considered, even if a few are discarded as being inappropriate.

Module testing

Module testing is the lowest level of testing, and typically involves only a few hundred lines of program code. The testing of a module, in itself is performed in several escalating steps, which are:

(a) Desk check

Prior to compilation, checking the coding of individual modules, and or program sections, preferably with another person. Most programmers will laugh at this, considering it as an impractical step. However, instances can be quoted of programs being desk checked and then compiled and followed by a clean run, in only one test shot.

(b) Compile

Using the compiler to check format and system errors of individual modules.

(c) Module test data

After a clean compilation has been obtained, modules, or even sections of modules, can be tested individually with extensive test data.

(d) Module linking

When individually tested modules are available, they can be linked and tested with data to demonstrate that adjacent module interfaces work correctly.

Program testing

Program testing involves several steps, the first of which is to test the program in isolation. Where appropriate, this may involve linking all the modules in a program. Having achieved a tested program, adjacent programs can be link tested, to highlight any interface errors (e.g. where one program mis-reads a file created by the previous program). Errors here would be mainly due to communication errors between program designers and the programmers.

The system now works as far as the programmers can tell, i.e. it meets the program specification.

Suite testing

Suite testing is a preliminary step to systems testing, and involves linking a group of programs which form a logical grouping, i.e. a suite. The purpose of this testing step is to ensure that there is a logical flow of data and its processing across several program interfaces. Thus the data need not prove all conditions, but only those that cause records to be passed through the system. Errors at this stage are mainly caused by communications errors between the systems designers and the programmers.

Sub-system testing

System testing should not commence until program testing is complete. For smaller systems, the suite and sub-system could be the same, but for larger systems it may be appropriate to link test all programs and files in a sub-system, in order to prove that the sub-system works independently (and performs no unspecified function). A sub-system could be a logical DP function (e.g. file handling, or suspense and error handling) or a business function (e.g. checking for stock availability during order processing, or a monthly processing requirement).

During sub-system testing, machine orientated factors are being considered. These might include the ability of the operating system to handle many terminals, the correctness of the transaction control software, the speed of the file management software, the suitability of the data communication aspects, the operability of the recovery procedures, the ability of batch and on-line sub-systems to work concurrently, etc.

System testing

The purpose of system testing is to ensure that sub-systems link correctly to form a complete system that performs as the system designers intended. The tests should be designed with the intention of trying to break the system. For totally integrated systems, it is essential to test the application system with all its interacting systems, either existing or under development. By the end of system testing it should be possible to ensure that the system performs in accordance with the system specification in all its aspects. However, to achieve this, several steps are required.

(a) Single run

Using the minimum amount of all-embracing test data, the system is run in its entirety as a single pass, until all errors have been detected and eliminated. Errors at this stage might be caused by poor communication, giving rise to incompatible data or wrong processing, or technical errors highlighting hardware deficiencies, software deficiencies, poor response times, degradation and restarts not operating correctly, or slow throughputs of data. It is also necessary to prove that the degraded and standby systems give the users a satisfactory service.

A further important testing stage is obtaining the approval of the data processing operations department.

(b) Cyclic tests

Having demonstrated that the system works once, it is necessary to prove that it works over several cycles. For example, to-day's run of the system should link correctly with yesterday's closing position after the necessary clerical actions have been taken. Several cycles are usually required to test the ability to correct invalid or rejected data, and to thoroughly test daily, weekly, monthly and annual runs of the system. Calendar dates relevant to the system are usually an important consideration in determining the number of test cycles.

(c) Volume tests

Up to this point, the *minimum* quantity of test data compatible with testing all conditions is used. It is necessary to perform volume tests with a large quantity of realistic data, in order to test how the system copes with overload conditions, multi-volume files, overflow of data on files, terminal response times, network capacity, re-starts after breakdowns, and lining up stationery changes on the printer. It is also necessary to prove that internal program counts, work areas, and file sizes, for example, are adequate.

(d) Clerical tests

Also at this stage, the man/machine interface is being tested. This includes user procedures, the use of controls, error correction in practice, and the distribution of computer output. In effect, all aspects of communication with the users are being tested including all input and output clerical procedures.

User acceptance tests

At this point of the testing sequence, the computer department has, to the best of its ability, tested the system. User testing should not commence until sufficient system testing has provided confidence that the system is reasonably clean; otherwise, the user(s) may be unnecessarily perturbed with the bad results, and their testing schedules will be thrown into disarray. As acceptance is required from all users of the system, it is essential for them to prove that the system works to their satisfaction. The users check the outputs primarily to prove the system against their definition of user requirements, the tests being designed to simulate the day-to-day running of the system.

It is important that the *entire* system is tested (i.e. both the computer part of the system as well as the associated clerical procedures), because the previously described system tests only affect a part of the total system (the DP elements). It is also essential that the *normal* system is tested, because it is often necessary, during system and program testing, to force error conditions. This necessitates the use of abnormal entries into programs, as well as adopting special utility programs to create transactions or master files. The normal system entails testing all the clerical processing, inputs, data entry, output distribution, the use of the outputs, as well as the use of the draft user procedure manual. As before, the users will need to carry out the cyclic and volume tests, and will usually request several iterations of the running of the system until they are satisfied that most errors are cleared.

Apart from proving that the system meets the users' needs, user acceptance tests are also a means for training the users, and forming a focal point of expertise prior to the users' full-time adoption of the system.

During this stage of system testing, the auditors should test the system to their satisfaction, preferably with their own test data. More probably, they would vet the test results and ensure they were thorough and met the audit requirements.

Pilot running tests

The final step is to test the changeover from an existing system to the new application system, and formal proof may be obtained by several methods that the new system is correct. One method, called parallel running, entails running the old and new systems side by side and comparing the outputs. As this stage usually lasts a month or more, it can be very difficult and expensive to carry out. If the computer system is performing a new function, comparison is not always possible as there is no old system against which to compare. In this case, extended pilot running is required.

It is now possible to perform live running of the system by the users.

Maintenance (or regression) tests

After the system has gone live, it will be constantly amended, and then require re-testing. A comprehensive test pack, based on all the test data used in the above steps of testing, should be handed over to the team responsible for maintenance after the project has been completed. This test pack will form the basis for future maintenance tests, which are sometimes referred to as regression tests, the objective being to prove that changes in the system have not unintentionally induced erroneous changes elsewhere.

In adopting this approach, management should be aware that much time and effort is required in keeping this test pack continually updated. For enhancement work, almost by definition, this test pack will be inappropriate, and the usual extensive test data must be prepared to test fully the enhanced features of the system. This theme will be expanded upon later.

TESTING TASKS WITHIN EACH PHASE

The overall testing sequence

Testing activities cut across several development phases, and Figure 9.3 overleaf illustrates the overall testing sequence, and indicates which type of activities are performed in each phase. To complete the picture, the relationship between development tasks and testing tasks are shown, together with the flow required to produce an accepted system. It is apparent that, whereas development is a simple linear sequence, the testing sequence is complex, iterative, and jumps over development phases.

In more detail, the testing tasks within each development phase are given below:

System design phase

Whilst the system logic is being developed during the system design phase, much planning for the actual testing in future development phases should be taking place, and this can be summarized under the following headings:

Checking systems logic

During the period that system test conditions and test data are being considered, the actual system design (as documented on flow-charts and in the system specification) should be automatically reviewed for correctness in its system logic.

Test planning for the proving phase involves the following types of activities

(a) Proving phase test plan
   A test plan is developed stating how the tests will be performed during the proving phase.
(b) System test data

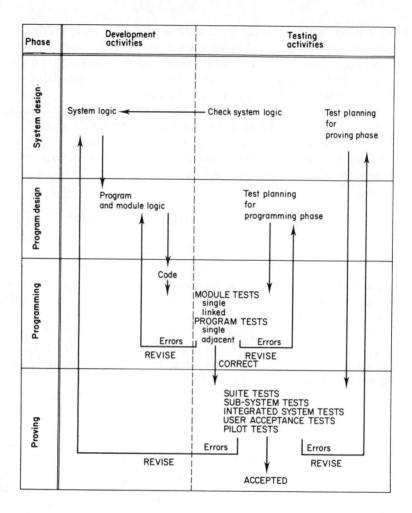

Figure 9.3   Overall testing sequence

In parallel with the above planning, exhaustive test conditions and test data should be determined, together with expected results.

(c) Acceptance criteria

Also in parallel with the above planning, the users' acceptance criteria should be established, together with their test conditions and test data. In addition, the testing requirements and acceptance criteria of the DP operations department should be obtained.

(d) Testing aids

To facilitate testing it is usually necessary (especially for larger systems) to employ utility programs, provide systematic testing techniques, and produce a set of testing procedures. To achieve these objectives, effort needs to be expended on evaluating existing programs, techniques, and procedures. Where deficiencies are found it is necessary to purchase, write, or amend programs.

(e) Preparation and environment for system tests

Before the proving phase can start, all the necessary files, test data, data preparation, JCL, and other operational aspects should be completed.

Program design phase

Whilst the programs are being designed, modularized, and the logic is being determined, the test planning for the programming phase should be taking place. This includes scheduling the production and the testing of each module; determining the programs' test conditions, test data, and expected results; and setting up all files, data, and JCL prior to the testing of complete programs in the programming phase.

Programming phase

Having coded and compiled modules they can now be tested with module test data also produced during this phase. When the modules have been linked, the completed programs can be tested using the plans produced during the program design phase. Errors detected may require that modifications be made to both the program design logic as well as the test plans.

Proving phase

Having produced individually tested programs, the test planning (produced in the system design phase) can now be implemented to perform the already described sequence of suite, sub-system, integrated system, user acceptance, and pilot running tests.

Although the start of systems testing requires adjacent programs to have been link tested (by the programmers), it should still be necessary to have a complete suite of programs to test the system's inputs and outputs. This requirement may be relaxed if intermediary test files and expected results have been set up between each program, or more probably, at key points in the suite and system. However, in all cases it is important to stress that as the requirements for the system testing sequence might affect the program development sequence, the latter should be agreed with the system testers.

With respect to the effort expended by DP staff during the proving phase, about 50% is involved with system tests (suite, sub-system, integrated system), about 30% on acceptance tests, and about 20% on simulated live running tests.

Implementation phase

A system can never be fully tested prior to live running, as errors will come to light weeks, months or even years after implementation has been completed.

Although it is not recommended as a method of testing, the data processing manager should plan for the rapid availability of appropriately skilled resources to correct these latent errors.

WHO IS RESPONSIBLE FOR TESTING TASKS?

In a very small project, one person, an analyst/programmer, may design, write, and test the entire system. However, the larger the project, the greater are the number of people involved. This usually means a greater number of different skills are available. This opens up the possibility of many different ways of people becoming involved in testing. The project manager might choose, for the reasons stated, one of the following organizations for his particular project.

The use of a testing team in general

The principal of different people being made responsible for writing, as opposed to testing a system, is sound, and is another example of checks and balances. In theory, it is necessary to test the compatibility of the system in the following areas:

the system design to the users' requirement,
the program design to the system design,
the programming to the program design.

In general, the work during the phases related to the users' requirements, the system design, the program design and the programming phase is carried out by teams of people with different skills. The corresponding testing will also require similar skills, probably arranged in teams. Either, completely different people are involved, or, more usually, the same people test different aspects to those they designed.

A general problem is that a test team may have different opinions to the development team with regard to what constitutes errors and defects. A procedure is required for resolving (a) possible omissions or defects in the system, (b) which errors are not vital to correct.

A general psychological problem with separate testing teams is that initially, they may be resented, and viewed as 'big brother'. They may not be taken seriously, and may not be given the latest versions of programs, documentation, or changes to specifications. Appropriate procedures may be required with the onus on the development team to notify other teams.

A testing team during the programming phase

During the programming phase it is conceivable to have a separate team (with programming skills) testing modules coded by other teams. Although this approach thoroughly tests modules and their documentation, it is, in general, not very productive. For many small modules there is an overhead whilst the tester learns what is happening, and there are additional difficulties associated with scheduling the arrival and the eventual fixing of modules.

It is probably more efficient (and more motivating) for the programmer to test his own code. The original program designer independently carries out linking tests at the program level. An exception to this generalization is in the case of a team of trainee coders, who are being closely supervised by a senior programmer. In this situation, it could be valid for the supervisor to test and link the modules as well as test completed programs.

A testing team during the proving phase

The systems testing during the proving phase could well be performed by the designers of the system. However, in larger projects, with more available staff, a testing team mainly comprising systems analysts/designers not involved with the original system design, would provide additional checks on the system logic. If this latter approach is preferred, the project manager should appoint this testing team during the system design phase, prior to the commencement of system test planning, and before producing system test data.

This team, although responsible for system proving tests, will be in existence

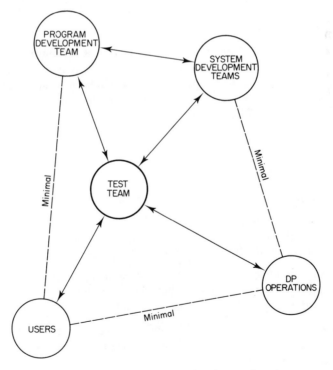

Figure 9.4 Testing interactions—during the proving phase

from the early part of the system design phase, during the program design and programming phases, as well as in the proving phase. A logical conclusion to this approach may be to make this team responsible for *all* testing procedures, even though they may not be directly involved with module and program testing.

If a decision is made to adopt a testing team approach, management should appreciate the complex interactions that might result from this decision. Figure 9.4 illustrates the interactions that may exist (during the proving phase only, in this example) between the testing team, the users, DP operations and possible separate systems and the programming development teams. Of the ten interactions possible only five are strong, and of these, four involve the test team directly. In other words, everything relating to testing goes through the test team; other dialogues will only exist to clarify and resolve errors.

Another potential interaction difficulty is that the development team (as opposed to the testing team) may be responsible for the production of the live environmental operating instructions and JCL. Not only will this tend to duplicate the work that the system testers must do, but also the development team will not have the system testing experience to test their operating environment. Consequently the test team will become involved in this joint activity with appropriately experienced people.

Testing by a combined group

A proving phase technique of testing by means of a combined group representing all relevant parties, is based on the arguments that testing involves many different types of skills and departments, and that corporate systems are being tested, not separate departments or functions. Consequently, proving should be carried out by a testing group allocated full-time, that comprises the following skills.

Systems
O and M/business analysts
Programmers
DP operations
Each user department
Internal auditors
(External auditors, if appropriate)

This team would then only need to test each input, program, output, etc., once and on completion sign off on behalf of the company.

The disadvantages of this approach are that:

(1) for many projects, the structure of the organization or computer department may not readily allow such a group to function smoothly (part-time let alone full-time)
(2) each representative will have different requirements

(3) forming a committee with many dissimilar requirements can only slow down testing, not speed it up

(4) systematic testing (by path or data structure etc.) may require inputs, programs, and reports to be tested several different times

(5) when the computerized system is eventually live, each department will normally operate as a separate unit, and a false system will be set up if testing is operated by a group.

A sub-set of this approach, where a combined user team represents departments within a division, could be advantageous when acceptance testing some stages of a project which only affect one division.

A testing co-ordinator

An alternative to the above method of organizing testing is to appoint a testing co-ordinator. This might be appropriate for medium or smaller projects where there are insufficient system skills to have teams of system designers and testers working in parallel during the system design phase. The functions of this testing co-ordinator would be to provide a testing service in order to improve the productivity of the rest of the project's systems and programming manpower. The type of tasks he would be responsible for might be to:

Write JCL
Allocate devices
Allocate files and labels
Maintain a centralized file of —test data
                                           —source programs
Control the latest versions of programs and modules
Provide a testing back-up service
Educate staff about using testing aids
Submit jobs for running
Keep records of the number of test shots and machine time used.

From the nature of this person's brief, he would need to be appointed about half-way through the system design phase.

Who does what during testing

Figure 9.5, summarizes pictorially the information covered to date on the subject of testing. In particular, it states, for each development phase:

(a) the tasks that relate to testing
(b) who performs those tasks
(c) which type of test is currently under consideration

During the system design phase the system designer, or system tester, who should have a high skill level, will produce the test plans and the test conditions,

Phase	Tasks relating to testing	Who performs tasks	Tests under consideration
SYSTEM DESIGN	. PROVING PHASE TEST PLAN . EVALUATE —utilities —aids —techniques . DETERMINE SYSTEM TESTS CONDITIONS . DETERMINE TEST DESCRIPTIONS	SYSTEM DESIGNER or SYSTEM TESTERS (i.e. systems analysis with a high skill level) USERS (for acceptance tests)	SUITE TESTING SUB SYSTEM TESTING INTEGRATED SYSTEM TESTING
	. SPECIFY TEST DATA . SYSTEM TEST PREPARATION . PROVIDE utilities and aids	Systems analysts and programmers with lower skill level. Users.	USER ACCEPT-ANCE TESTS PILOT TESTS
PROGRAM DESIGN	. PROGRAMMING PHASE TEST PLAN —programs —modules . DETERMINE PROGRAM TEST CONDITIONS	PROGRAM DESIGNER (high skill level)	MODULE TESTING AND MODULE LINKING SEQUENCE
	. PREPARE PROGRAM TEST DATA . PROGRAM TEST PREPARATION	Programmers with lower skill level	PROGRAM TESTING
PROGRAMMING	. MODULE/SECTION TEST DATA PREPARATION . DRY RUN MODULE . MODULE COMPILE AND TEST . MODULE LINKS	PROGRAMMER	MODULE TEST-ING (if applicable)
	. PROGRAM TESTS	PROGRAM DESIGNER	PROGRAM AND LINK TESTING ADJACENT PROGRAMS
PROVING	Implement plans produced during system design phase and perform proving tests	SYSTEM DESIGNER or SYSTEM TESTERS	SUITE TESTING SUB SYSTEM TESTING SYSTEM TESTING
		USER	USER ACCEPT-ANCE TESTS PILOT TESTS

Figure 9.5   Who does what during testing

as well as evaluate testing techniques and aids. This work might then be handed over to analysts and programmers with a lower skill level, or even temporarily employed clerks to actually produce test data, and testing aids. In parallel, the users will be planning their acceptance criteria and tests, monitored by the development team, who also provide technical assistance. Full details of user test run requirements should be made available to the development team by the users so that interface/reference files, etc. can be set up before user testing starts, and valid master files created. Users need to allow plenty of time to work out a test plan, prepare data, and to have their work vetted by DP staff.

During program design, the program designers, who should have a high skill level, will be producing the programming phase test plan, and program test conditions. Programmers with a lower skill level can then take over this work to prepare data and for actual program tests.

During the programming phase, each individual coder writes, complies, tests and links his modules with his own test data, possibly under the supervision of a senior programmer. The program designer can then perform the program tests.

Finally, during the proving phase, the plans produced during the system design phase are implemented and performed by the system designer, or system tester, and then by the user to complete the sequence of proving tests.

THE TEST PLAN(S)

The purpose of a test plan

So far we have examined, at a somewhat high level, who is responsible for the different aspects of testing, and what must be tested. This section details at the lower levels:

(a) how testing is planned (so that all conditions are systematically considered),
(b) how testing is actually carried out.
(c) how these two aspects are documented.

Although there is a difference philosophically, between planning a job, carrying it out, and documenting it, in practical testing the three are tackled together. Because of the volume of technical detail, especially relating to program testing, for those managers who are not close to testing, much of the detail and techniques involved with testing appear as a separate appendix, which is referred to in this section.

In its widest sense, the test plan is a series of decisions relating to every aspect covered in this chapter on testing, relevant to a particular project. In a limited sense, the test plan is documentation whose purpose is both to advise and commit all project work streams (systems, programmers, users, DP operations, testing team) to the proposed method of testing, and to the actual data being used for testing.

In practice, several documented test plans are required because of the differing requirements for testing during the programming phase and the proving phase. In addition, the test data for user, systems, program, and module tests are usually prepared by different people at various times (although sometimes it is possible to minimize duplication). For example, a system test plan is produced at the end of the system design phase. Its purpose is to provide an overall testing strategy, to facilitate the production of comprehensive test data, to measure subsequent testing against the plan, and to demonstrate that thorough testing is being contemplated. The documented test plan also serves to ensure that adequate manpower and machine resources are available, and to warn DP operations and other parts of the computer department of an imminent call on their resources. The user test plan, on the other hand, is a separate document, produced slightly later by the user, to a similar format but with a differing strategy.

The logical sequence of planning the tests and documenting them can be considered under the following headings:

(1) A management summary of the logistics: (manpower, machine time, resources, schedule).
(2) The strategic and tactical approach: (dividing the system into logical pieces, testing them in stages, and testing each stage in cycles).
(3) The test conditions: (the purpose of each test shot, what is being tested, inputs, expected results, the structure and content of test master files).
(4) The test data: (the creation of test records, and the compatibility between master files and inputs).
(5) Preparation, test runs and schedules: (assembling records into files for specific test cycles, scheduling run dates).
(6) Test control, fixing errors, and procedures: (evidence that all conditions have been tested, and that all errors have been fixed).

These are now briefly covered.

Management summary of the logistics

After some of the following detailed work has been completed, and after several iterations, the logistics of the proposed testing need to be summarized, with the estimates of total man days testing effort, the optimum number of people required, the machine time, and other resources required.

A schedule of the tests in calendar time is also usually necessary. To back up these estimates, a measure of the total program size (e.g. total number of statements) and the anticipated error rates (e.g. based on size and complexity) should be available. It is also advisable to state which types of testing are to be performed.

When the installation's own configuration is inadequate, or does not yet exist, it is advisable to include a statement of the computer system required for testing, its size, peripherals, communication lines, etc. System testing could well require different hardware to say module testing. A schedule therefore, may be required of hardware and software for each step in testing.

We also need to state precisely who is responsible for the many facets of testing, and in particular, who produces test conditions, test descriptions and test data, and who in the user departments is responsible for setting acceptance criteria, producing test data and vetting the results of tests. There is a need to define responsibility for actually submitting tests, logging their return and status, fixing errors, and for the subsequent re-testing. Finally, it should be essential to appoint a person responsible for keeping a program library updated, as well as all required testing documentation.

The strategic and tactical approach

The highest level of planning is to break testing down into escalating stages, based on the logic of the system itself, the anticipated availability of programs, and the proposed schedule of implementation. Within this breakdown it is advisable that the mainflow conditions are tested first, and the exceptional test data later, thus enabling the end of the system to be reached as soon as possible.

Each system has its own unique strategy, but in general a stage is:

(a) A system function which occurs in different periods of time e.g. a daily, monthly or year-end part of the system
(b) Conceptually, self-contained parts of the system or functional areas occurring concurrently e.g. Type A personnel and Type B personnel, or Type A products and Type B products
(c) Combinations of the above systems functions
(d) Non mainstream conditions and obscure tests.

For testing maintenance or enhancements to current systems, stages may reflect a practical sequence such as: testing current programs with existing data; testing modified programs with existing data; testing modified programs with new data relevant to the system changes; testing modified programs with new and old data combined.

Within each testing stage it should now be possible to plan which test-cycles check what, e.g. simulating successive and cumulative daily and monthly runs; or simulating input, set-up and updating a record.

Again, each system is unique, but examples of cycles might be:

(a) Successive daily runs each with different transaction types
(b) Successive daily runs, whereby the first sets up a record on a master file; the second re-inputs any corrections from batch control, validation or update errors; the third amends the master record; the fourth performs post update handling.

Set out in Appendix 5 is a selection of basic techniques that should facilitate the overall planning of system tests and ensure that all aspects of the system are considered systematically. On reading them through, testing by transaction type, and testing by report may be preferred for a given system, as this basic approach treats the system as a black box, and tests the correctness of inputs and outputs only.

Consideration is often required as to the degree of duplication between system and program testing. It is also necessary to determine whether system testing will involve (1) setting up all intermediary files within the system, or just a few strategic files, and (2) calculating the expected results from the system. Creating all intermediary files may seem an excellent idea but in practice will be a considerable overhead. Difficulties in maintaining this system may occur when file formats change or data has been incorrectly predicted. It will also require a considerable overhead in machine time to compare each file from each program. Rather than create all interface files, it may be more feasible to identify key points in the system and predict the data at those points. This would reduce both maintenance and machine time, as well as assist in locating errors and enable tests to continue or even start, before previous error programs are corrected.

The test conditions

Having planned a sound strategy it is now possible to formulate what *conditions* are to be tested, and the purpose of each test run, by working through the system design specification, possibly using a technique detailed in Appendix 5.2.

A systematic approach is to list all *correct* conditions relating to the flow of data through the system, e.g. under the following types of headings: batch control (if relevant); each transaction type on input; interfaces with other systems; reference files; validation, master file updates; post update processing, output files; each report; system controls. By use of another technique in Appendix 5.2, this list can be expanded by determining corresponding *error* conditions, and then *combinations* of conditions; the aim being to break the system. It is also advisable to work through the entire list of error messages that may be produced by each program, including all validation, update, console, or abortive end messages. This acts as a cross-check that all conditions have been considered.

It is now possible to write detailed descriptions of all the types of test data and inputs being contemplated, and these together with the high level expected results should be documented, possibly on a standard chart. At this time it is important to consider the structure and content of the test master files. Planned tests of the clerical parts of the system and at the user/computer interface should be stated at the same level of detail.

The test data

Creation of test records followed by actually coding test data is the next logical step, but a problem that should not be underestimated is achieving compatibility between test data on master and reference files, the conditions to be tested, and test data for input. This is amplified in Appendix 5.2, together with arguments about the desirability of producing, in advance, *detailed* expected results. In most cases the latter is impractical. An approach based on inspection of the results and working backwards is usually quite sound for larger or complex systems, provided the checkers have the right level of skill, together with an eye for detail.

Whilst setting up test files, an ideal to aim at is that one record only should relate to one test condition. This avoids errors being disguised or hidden. Multiple conditions should preferably be tested after each condition has been checked separately. Another useful idea relates to those numerous occasions during proving when new conditions emerge which require testing. One should avoid changing existing test-data, but add new records or files to test these new conditions. The potential difficulties of the alternative is to corrupt or lose existing conditions, the original test plan documentation becoming invalid and requiring difficult correction.

Preparation, test runs, and schedules

By this stage a database of test records should have been created for master, reference, and, possibly, intermediate files, as well as for compatible input transaction data. These test records can now be assembled into test files for use in a specific sequence of test cycles. This forms a test run plan, so that for each stage and test cycle there is not only a schedule of when each test will run, but it is apparent which records were input, the results expected, and which files were used.

The above method of producing test data is mainly applicable to system testing. Short cuts can be used for acceptance tests or pilot tests when extracts of historical or live data can be used.

Test control, fixing errors, and procedures

The discussions up to this point have mainly related to the planning work which is necessary prior to the proving phase. A project should now stop playing at testing and actually become immersed in the frustrations of forcing an erroneous system to run on an unsympathetic computer. Appendix 5.3 and 5.4 may provide some useful ideas on running test shots, this section concentrates on providing evidence that all conditions have been tested, and that all known errors have been fixed.

After a few weeks of testing, without a comprehensive logging system, it may become difficult to match errors to print-outs, or to runs, test shots, and cycle numbers. A definition of some of these terms may prove helpful. The test cycle numbers are at a high level as defined earlier in the test plan. The test run, the next level down, is a unique incremental number that may be associated (for convenience and ease of reference) to a specific part of the system, i.e. a specific stage and cycle of testing. The test shot is a unique incremental number allocated to *every* job submitted, and at the lowest level, is equivalent to an attempt to carry out that run. For example, at the earlier stages of testing, run number 3 may refer to testing 'day 3'. To successfully test 'day 3', ten test shots may be required. Towards the end of testing, 400 test shots may have been required, and run number 129 may refer to testing the entire system, after all important errors have been fixed. In practice, it is difficult to maintain a correlation between the test runs conceived whilst test planning, and those required whilst executing the tests when new ideas and problems occur. It is recommended that the run number is written on all test outputs as the prime reference number.

The following system and forms (which tie up with the test run plan discussed earlier) help to reduce the problem of controlling test runs and errors.

Run logs

During sub-system, integrated system, user acceptance, and pilot run testing, a chronological run log should be kept by the testers that controls the submission of each job, and its outcome. This is analogous to a user's batch register, and will enable the test team to ensure that all jobs have been run.

The log might contain:

. job name
. test shot number
. test run number
. submission date
. version number of test data input (optional)
. version number of files (optional)
. version number of programs (optional)
. version number of expected test results (optional)
. brief description of the test
. summary of result (e.g. successful, failed, abort)

Error log/fixing control

Whenever an error is found, the system testers need to:

(a) accurately refer to an error (the same or similar error may arise from several different types of tests)
(b) reproduce the exact conditions, if it is necessary to re-create it to obtain further information and reports
(c) record and control the hand-over of an error to a programmer for fixing and
(d) to re-test a fixed error sometime in the future.

The format of an error log containing the minimum detail to achieve the above, might contain:

. the unique error number

. a record key or identifier
. the name of the file or report in error
. the stage and test cycle
. the test run number
. the program (if the error is applicable to only 1 program)
. a brief description of the error
. the action to be taken
. the date and run number when the error was fixed and re-tested as clean.

For control purposes, it may prove beneficial to keep a separate set of control figures which relate to the state of testing. The table in Figure 9.6 illustrates a comprehensive method of control.

	b/f Totals	Reported on this log	c/f Totals
Errors fixed to date and re-tested as now clean	15	+ 54	69
Non-vital errors and acceptable restrictions	17	+ 3	20
Oustanding queries/errors requiring resolution	60	− 36	
Possible omissions or defects in the system specifications			23
Queries/errors compared to the system specifications			1
Apparent errors caused by changes to specifications	53	− 26	27
Apparent errors found to be in the test data	5	+ 10	15
Total testing queries/errors reported to date	150	+ 5	155

Figure 9.6   Consolidated status of test results

TESTING ON-GOING SYSTEMS

A fair proportion of proving work in a mature installation revolves around the testing of enhancements to, and maintenance of, existing systems. Within this environment, new system development work may also impinge upon existing systems, which will result in their modification and in the need for their subsequent testing. In these contexts, the objectives for proving are different to a situation in which one is testing a new system in isolation. An emphasis is placed on ensuring that changes to any part of the system do not unintentionally, affect:

(a) some other part of the same system.

(b) another, but interacting system, which may either be receiving data from, or supplying data to, the amended system.

In conjunction with these objectives, which are of paramount importance, there is the normal requirement of performing the separate system and user testing of the new features under development. These require the same proving techniques and procedures as for any new system.

The actual method and sequence of testing should reflect these multiple objectives. In principle, there should be available a maintenance test pack to confirm that there have been no unforeseen changes. Ideally this test pack may be automated using program utilities and with screen simulations for transactions, that are normally input by VDUs. The enhancements/new features should be tested using separate, very detailed test-packs. This should entail the usual systems tests followed by the users' tests. After the enhancement has been made live, the original maintenance test pack needs merging with the new systems, (and possibly the users' new) test data which was required to test the new features. In this manner an updated test-pack is produced for future on-going testing. Unfortunately, there are no short cuts to this procedure and, it is difficult to carry out. Merging, and keeping the test pack updated is laborious.

On the brighter side, testing in this environment has some advantages. As proven systems are running, it is relatively simple to use these existing programs, (or more probably, for security reasons, copies of them) to set up test files, and expected results files. This luxury is not normally available when preparing files of test data for testing new systems. (Special one-off programs may be required). Likewise, it may be easier in this maintenance environment to validate thoroughly test data, and produce logically correct master files. A further significant benefit is that the live system ensures that compatibility is auto-matically achieved between records and fields on master files or reference files. This compatibility may be further extended so that it exists between records on these files, and input transaction data that is intended to access them.

Who should be responsible for the above testing? Some installations have an acceptance/quality control team to check out current systems. This team often reports within the DP operations department, although it may be respons-ible to the systems development manager or even the DPM. Unfortunately, there is no clear-cut solution, or preference as to the way it operates. Giving the responsibility of testing to an acceptance team, often means that they are not au fait with the latest nuances of the system. This may result in an inefficient and ineffective method of testing. Especially if they wait passively for the development team to hand over a system to test. Even worse, the testing may not be carried out thoroughly, because there may be insufficient time between the development team handing over the enhanced system for final acceptance, and the immovable date for going live, which has been promised to the users (by the development team). In other words, the acceptance team may be in a politically weak position to carry out a proper job.

One recommendation, although by no means perfect, that has been previously advocated in this book, is that the team liable for maintenance of the system, (who preferably should be within the DP operations department) should also be responsible for its acceptance tests. The project development team produces the new test data and proves that the enhancements are correct. The testing activities of both the maintenance team and of the development team should be under the guidance and approval of the installation's quality control group. As with all control or assurance teams, they should actively become involved with the development teams, *prior* to the production of a document or a test plan. After the enhanced system has gone live, it should be the mandate of the maintenance team to keep the test pack updated, including merging it with the new system's (and possibly users') test data.

TESTING UTILITIES AND AIDS

Introduction to the benefits and problems

To assist in the testing of modules, programs, and systems, several utility programs might be employed. These utilities may save manpower, reduce the clerical effort required for testing, form an essential part in setting up the actual tests, or may reduce the computer time required for testing.

It is difficult to produce generalized utility programs that cater for all testing requirements, and all types of files. For each system, the project manager, his team leaders, the support manager, or the testing co-ordinator has to decide:

(1) which utilities are to be used,
(2) which of the existing utilities within the installation are relevant,
(3) which utilities can be purchased (e.g. from other installations, software houses, etc.),
(4) which utilities can be specified and written by the project or within the installation itself.

An example of a project developing its own testing utilities

The manager responsible for testing a fairly large system was initially so overawed by the task ahead, that he insisted that the project write its own utilities to facilitate system testing. Nothing on the market was sufficiently sophisticated, and in particular, he required a program to create test data, and another to print any type of file.

Several months later, these programs were written and tested by an analyst/ programmer who eventually left to work overseas. No one else knew how to use these programs, nor could they understand the documentation. In the few cases where test data was created by using this program, inter-record fields were not set up with compatible data (highlighting a severe practical limitation is using the utility for testing).

Eventually, project staff ignored these (expensive) utility programs and used a well-known (less ambitious) proprietary package, which was obtained by the computer operations department, and which was continually maintained, well documented, had support offered and included training courses. Testing then proceeded uneventfully.

Using utilities is often essential. The lesson learned in this installation is to think twice before writing one's own.

The following is a list of useful utilities, with brief comments aimed at assisting a management decision relating to their adoption. In general terms, as the cost of providing each of the following utilities is measured in thousands of dollars, the larger the project, the more easily is it to justify the use and/or the acquisition of these utilities. However, the overheads in using program aids should not be under-estimated. Apart from the cost and time for acquisition, significant time may be expended in learning how to use them and appreciating their idiosyncrasies, in overcoming software faults or in the generation of invalid data because of, say, the difficulty of specifying inter-field logic.

Test harness

If bottom up testing is the planned method of testing modules and programs, the following features are a consequence:

(1) Modules must be able to be tested individually, exhaustively, and in any order regardless of the availability of other modules in the same program
(2) It is necessary to emulate missing modules which call, or are called by the module(s) being tested
(3) Various files of test data must be accepted
(4) It is preferable to override program errors which would have caused the program to terminate to enable it to continue to its logical end
(5) Similarly, it is desirable to have automatic recovery from errors caused by invalid test data
(6) It is also preferable to allow several tests within a run using varying input data and parameters
(7) It may be essential to handle VUD's on-line, and interact with the system software.

Although it is possible to test modules in random sequence using in-house routines developed for each program, this method is not always desirable since few of the above features required of a test harness are usually available. The time and cost considerations usually make it not feasible either to write an installation's own test harness, or, for larger projects, to attempt testing without a harness.

Consequently, a valid management decision might be to purchase a test harness utility for bottom up testing larger systems. However, for smaller projects either top down testing will be carried out or the management may decide to make do without a test harness.

Library maintenance

Programs are required which set up libraries of a) system software; b) source, object and linked modules; and c) test data files. Each of these elements, should be updated, especially as testing proceeds. Most of these functions have to be provided by the installation or project itself by a combination of standard software, standard JCL procedures, and by writing one's own simple programs.

Generation of test data

In larger projects there may be considerable clerical effort required to create test data, and in particular test data relating to setting up very large and complex main, reference and sometimes intermediary files for testing purposes. Because each file is different, a separate program needs to be written (or generated) for each file. This program requires the record layout details, together with parameters of fields, valid values, maximum and minimum values, and increment values between adjacent records.

An approximate management yardstick is that this program(s) is worth producing if the fairly low skill level of clerical effort to produce the necessary test data is greater than one man-year.

Selection of data from files

One method of creating test data, especially for volume or acceptance tests, is to select data from existing files. A program(s) is required with the ability to feed in the required logic, to select precise fields within particularized ranges from specified records.

Reformating files

The format of a file occasionally needs to be converted (e.g. changing to packed decimal a character field produced by the previously described selection process) into a format suitable for the testing purposes. Once again simple files do not present a problem as standard programs are usually available.

Creating test files

If data is produced clerically, it is essential to have a program to create the appropriate file. Apart from the simplest file structures, special programs usually need to be written for each file. It is a good idea to be able to create files via a data dictionary or its equivalent, not only to reduce development effort, but the program can be easily updated if the file layout changes. Ideally, each record should be allocated a test cycle identifier and a sequence number. Once loaded, it is essential to be able to amend or delete records, including the addition of new records to an existing, or to a new, cycle. Correcting test data is a common occurrence.

Intelligent comparison of test files

To avoid the time-consuming clerical chore of checking print-outs, a program could be used which compares two files: one of the actual results and the other of the expected results. It is then necessary to list all discrepancies. To be of practical use, this program must cater for most common file types and compare them intelligently. This means, for example, that: missing records and unmatched records must be recognized, the record's key requires identification, a partial comparison of only some fields may be required, the two files may be organized differently due to overflow, error fields, and records should not affect the program, files on different devices may be compared, the files may have a different block size, or have a different sequence of fields.

A further feature of this program should be its ability to work in conjunction with a print utility which should print discrepancies between the two files side by side. Blanks for missing or unmatched records should be left to indicate which fields are in error, and only print those records in error.

Particular uses of this utility might be to compare the before and after state of master files when they have been updated, or compare the latest test results with the previous. In both cases, detecting that only expected changes have occurred is simplified.

A very useful feature would be the ability to compare automatically a printed report to the expected results. Theoretically this may be achieved by comparing the spooled print file to a specially created file of expected results. In practice though, this is not usually so. Apart from a possible inability to access the operating system's print files, or to specify a key for each print line, it is very difficult to know in advance the *exact* layout of complex reports, the precise spacing, or even the specific wording. Perfectly legible reports tend to be completely rejected for trivial reason, e.g. the presence of one extra space character.

It is apparent that this utility program is complex and difficult to write, and a management decision to acquire such a program is probably safer than attempting to write one's own.

Printing test file contents

In order to ascertain the state of files after a test (or even before), a generalized print utility is required. This assumes that, in most cases, the system itself, does not automatically provide a print out, or if it does, the appropriate program is not ready for use during testing. To be practical, this print utility must relate to many file structures, cope with different record types within a file, convert some data fields into printable formats, and selectively print some records, or certain fields within a file. This utility should preferably access a print layout library to obtain the appropriate format, which for simpler jobs could be tabular, with headed columns and one line per record, but for more complex jobs would have to print each field and its name with the record spread over several lines.

Taking back-up copies of files

The need to reproduce files often occurs. In general, the requirement exists to copy any file format to the same or a different format, as well as to an alternative storage medium. Most installations have such utilities.

Automated systems testing—disadvantages and advantages

Many managers consider that one comprehensive test pack can be set up relatively easily, in a standard manner to test thoroughly any system, preferably automated via utilities. The intention of setting up and using an automated testing system is that one text pack is available to test an entire system, with the expected results (both files and reports) held on backing store. Utilities can automatically compare that actual results with those expected. In practice, this approach is difficult to attain.

A problem of automating testing by use of utility programs is that during testing, errors and amendments to both the system itself and to the test data will occur. This necessitates changes to the test packs, and the expected results, as well as changes to all the test results files including, possibly, intermediary files. This is very time consuming.

This technique will have only limited use during the early stages of system testing because testing will take place in systematic steps, each requiring different tests. There is not much commonality or repetition. However, towards the end of integrated systems tests, acceptance tests, and pilot tests, the consequence of fixing one error, (in for example the last program in an 18 program system) needs to be tested against all previous 17 programs. As testing 18 programs 'manually' can become tedious after fixing each error, an automated testing system may become essential. This system test pack will then form the basis of regression tests by the system maintenance group.

CHAPTER SUMMARY

One of the chief consumers of resources, manpower and costs in a systems development project is the testing of the end-project. Consequently, management should attach great importance to producing an optimum strategic and tactical testing plan, part of which should relate to the sound management of system development prior to testing, to reduce the tedium of finding and correcting errors. To effect this, it is important to appreciate the theory of why errors occur, how they are detected, and how different categories of errors arise.

Escalating steps are required in the testing of the end-product, and they should be scheduled and linked correctly. Briefly, the total logical sequence requires each module to be tested separately; systematically testing each module with its interacting modules; testing the whole group of modules to form a program; testing the programs together to form a complete system; and testing the system's integration with other systems. Finally, the total system has to be tested by the line users, computer operations department, and possibly the auditors or a quality assurance group and their formal acceptance has to be obtained.

To achieve the above logical testing sequence, there are well defined tasks to be performed during the relevant development phases. Planning and preparation activities should occur during the system design and program design phases, while the actual tests themselves are run during the programming and proving phases.

It is sometimes preferable to have new people responsible for testing programs and systems, i.e. not the original people who designed and wrote the programs. Several options exist and responsibilities can fall on several different groups.

To ensure that all conditions are considered and to improve the chances of carrying out thorough testing, various techniques are available, and they should be adopted in the appropriate development phase. A documented test plan is necessary that sets out the potentially very difficult planning, scheduling, and linking problems. It should also contain the detailed test conditions, test data and expected result.

It is also sensible to detail the tools that are available for the various facets of testing, together with the procedures that should be adopted, and the responsibilities of people involved in the testing. Planning should also include any extensive support requirements, and the procedures necessary for reporting on errors and bugs found, together with the methods of correcting and re-testing them.

Computerized testing aids are usually essential to enable testing to be performed efficiently. Some general purpose utilities are required which include a file create program; a generalized file print program; as well as an intelligent compare program. The idealized approach is to aim at a generalized test-bed that is totally automatic and carried out by the computer. The principle is that all the expected results (i.e. all file changes and outputs) should be stored on the computer. Whenever a program or the system is being tested or amended, the generalized test-bed can be run and the results produced compared, again by the computer, against the file of expected results, and any discrepancies printed out. In theory, therefore, the computer will automatically highlight what has gone, or will go wrong. In practice though, a compromise with this ideal situation should be reached, probably with a strong *ad hoc* element.

Thorough and efficient testing is an essential part of systems development. The key elements for success include strict adherence to: detailed planning, a systematic evolving approach, detailed preparation of test conditions, careful coding of test data, detailed checking of test results, and error logging and control.

Chapter 10

Project planning and re-planning

This chapter on project planning starts by defining the purpose and extent of planning, but warns of its limitations. Detail is given of a systematic approach to planning, when it should occur, and how *practical* plans are both iterative and evolving. Finally, an examination is made of the consequences of the (parochial) project's planning on the rest of the DP department and the organization as a whole.

THE PURPOSE OF PLANNING

Why plan?

Some people express a dislike for planning, or a disbelief in its usefulness in practice. Smaller projects involving only 3 people may reach a successful conclusion without too much planning, but even then, reliable costs and end dates require prediction from the outset. Without a considerable amount of planning (and subsequent re-planning) a larger project will have considerable difficulty in meeting its objectives (assuming, of course, that quantified objectives can even be set without detailed planning). One reason for this difficulty is that larger projects require tens or even hundreds of people and other costly resources. An efficient interaction between these people (and the resources they require) is highly unlikely without extensive planning, which usually needs to be at the task level of each individual.

What requires to be planned?

As previously discussed, to manage the development of a system, a whole spectrum of planning is required. Concepts range from determining project phases, their appropriate tasks and the sequence of these tasks, through a host of macro-estimates and budgets, to the consideration of end-product planning, technologies, techniques, standards, and testing. Not least of management's planning considerations are the 'people aspects' covering such things as organization, structure, support functions, administration, etc. All these facets of planning form the project's development plan, which sets out how the deliverable end-product will be built.

215

This chapter limits the scope of planning work to providing basic quantified data in four main areas, which relate to:

(1) the man days development effort required to complete the project, which allows
(2) the determination of manpower requirements in terms of staff numbers, their skills and availability.

It is now possible to think in terms of

(3) elapsed time, target dates, schedules and viable completion dates.

Finally

(4) the resource requirements of computer machine time, supplies, data capture, etc. need to be ascertained.

The uses of these plans

Having produced the above quantified information, it can be used for several purposes, one of the most important of which is to calculate (or re-calculate) project development costs and the subsequent system's running costs. It will be recalled that the system development manager and project manager provide these figures. Senior management can then confirm that the proposed cost benefits are (still) sufficient to justify the project. If so corroborated, they can set firm budgets for the next phase of development.

A second use of these plans is that they can be referenced by all levels of management for controlling the project, and subsequent progress can be monitored against them. These plans could also provide the data to develop further intentions relating to staff recruitment and training, as well as to decide upon the proposed organization and structure necessary to manage efficiently all the proposed people. It is also possible to assess the impact of the project on the line users, the hardware, software, and operational requirements, as well as the rest of the computer department. Last but by no means least, these formally documented plans often form a useful basis when changes occur, or when an alteration is proposed. It is necessary to establish and assess the impact of either the changed end-product or an alternative method of development.

Large and small projects

Although these planning considerations apply to most projects, there is a great difference between large and small projects. As larger projects tend to have specific people assigned to particular functions, detailed explicit plans need to be produced for such things as: the project's structure, staff training, project control, documentation, hardware and software, testing, etc. One person may be performing several functions in a smaller project, and these documented plans are inappropriate. For example, very small projects, or an organization with a small DP installation, probably will condense all planning into one document possibly called an implementation plan, which includes an associated budget. In medium sized projects, organizational plans may become implicit rather than explicit; training plans may only apply to a few people; the project control plan may be inherited from the rest of the computer department; the documentation plan is probably *ad hoc*, with documents being produced as required; and the operations plan, resources plan and testing plan tend to be omitted. This does not mean that these projects need not consider each explicit problem area in this planning framework. It means that the correct management approach is to consider each facet, but handling and documenting it appropriately.

PROBLEMS IN PLANNING

Changes

A good plan is one that lasts longer, without changes, than a bad one! Any plan will have to be changed eventually, and as the title suggests, re-planning is an inherent part of the original plan. Any practical scheme must reflect these continual modifications, and as any manager knows, this is easier said than done.

Management targets

One unfortunately common problem in project planning is for senior users and/or DP management to set target dates and deadlines which might be motivated practically or politically. These dates may relate to company activities which reflect important business, legislative, or corporate events and problem areas. The actual plans eventually created, to justify these end dates, are often produced by working backwards. It is therefore, not surprising that they may prove unrealistic, although they may initially appear feasible. This type of approach often gives planning a poor image, with demotivated staff not being consulted or committed. The more junior members of staff can easily become cynical about the value of planning and with management's attempts at planning.

Mis-use of techniques

Another traditional planning method is to draw a maze of bar-charts relating to such (vague) items as programming or systems design. Often, a long time horizon is taken, and firm end dates are quoted. After the project has been approved, it may be found that for each month, if the project falls behind in schedule, the bar-lines become longer! This is an example of the mis-use of a good technique. A similar comment may apply to the use of PERT networks which are often useful for *clarification* of large, complex projects with many interacting and dependent activities. As with bar-charts, the pictorial representation enables management, at the planning or re-planning stage, to assess rapidly an overall situation, pin-point bottlenecks, and determine the critical path. However, a cynic could claim that a network could give senior management a false sense of security by 'proving' that an impossible target date will be met. Unwittingly omitting vital activities or under-estimating durations of known tasks, or even over-looking important dependencies, can soon produce poor plans.

SUMMARY OF AN APPROACH TO PLANNING

We have mentioned a few of the problems, so what are the answers? This section serves as an introduction to a solution for sound planning. The proposed method of planning allows for changes, and assumes the necessity for continuous updating. To overcome the problem of senior management imposing their own arbitrary targets, the proposed planning methodology is readily demonstrable to them, and confidence in it can gradually be instilled. Techniques to be advocated not only reflect favourable practical experience, but relate to the progress made by a development project and consequently the level of detail required at that instant of time.

In general, the systems development manager, or the project manager likes to know what and when to plan. It is desirable to work within a basic framework and from a checklist, which is augmented by performance statistics based on previous experience, preferably relating to the current installation. The following approach to planning has been well proven, is based on the known predictability of projects, and is formally structured.

WHEN SHOULD PLANNING OCCUR?

The first consideration relates to the set times for planning to occur and when appropriate resources should be assigned to the planning tasks. The system development life cycle provides the basic 'alarm clock' for management's planning and control. At first sight it may be thought that management's planning starts during the pre-project business survey and continues during each phase of a project right through to its completion. However, it is preferable if planning is not a continuous process spread evenly throughout the project's duration, but is structured chronologically to occur at the time of three types of events.

These are, the end of a phase, the start of the next phase, and thirdly on an *ad hoc* basis at any time when major changes or difficulties occur which necessitate the revision of previous plans. A manager should aim to concentrate his planning (and his appropriate manpower responsible for planning) into the few weeks (or days for smaller projects) at the start and end of each development phase. It should be remembered that planning tends to reach a peak by the end of system design, prior to the last major justification by senior management and the line department users, for the continuation of the project. Maximum planning resources should be made available at this time.

The advantage of restricting planning to these specific periods of time is that the process becomes more definable and meaningful, as the plans will relate to the relevant requirements and the specific areas of interest at the start and end of a development phase. These are occasions for major reviews: project staff are psychologically geared to taking stock.

THE EVOLUTION OF PLANS

Planning should not be an activity that occurs once in isolation, but should be treated as an evolutionary process that each time builds on previous less precise plans. The initial ideas are very general and the subsequent ones become more refined and detailed. This evolutionary aspect manifests itself in several ways.

Iterative steps

During each planning occurrence, for whatever reason, an iterative process is usually necessary. This means that the work undertaken for the first attempt at a plan, must be repeated by going round a loop several times, in order that the separate threads tie together. Examples of the causes of this might be because the initial attempt is 'shot down' by a reviewer detecting a false assumption, or impractical end dates are predicted, or unrealistic numbers of staff are required. It is more often than not impossible to know in advance if a plan is going to be viable, or even which premises should be used. For example, the total development cost of a project depends upon a numerous number of independent factors. Only a fortunate planner would produce at his first attempt, an optimum cost benefit plan, without having had several attempts each time using alternative restrictions and basic assumptions.

Provisional estimates—when and why

As previously discussed, one occasion for planning is at the *end* of development phases, when the planning should relate to the problems at hand. An important consideration at the end of each phase (or when a major change is proposed) is that of the business review by senior management who re-examine the end-product, the proposed method for implementing it, and the major milestones for its development. Within this objective, provisional estimates and plans are required to enable this review of the entire project to be achieved professionally. The plans should relate to *all* subsequent development phases, and estimates should quantify the development effort, numbers of people, elapsed time, non-manpower resources, and costs for each successive phase. This objective for provisional estimates is also compatible with the need for a strategic overview of the entire project, which is required for senior management's justification.

Only when these strategic provisional figures for the whole project have been produced and agreed, can tactical firm estimates be made which relate to current specific areas of the project. Looking at it another way, provisional estimates take the whole project and break it into phases. Firm estimates start with detailed lists of tasks and activities and build them up into development phases. The beauty of this approach to planning is that provisional estimates help to overcome the errors caused by oversights and omitting to consider all detailed tasks. This is a high probability when carrying out the apparently more accurate firm estimates based on the consideration of each individual task. How to tackle provisional planning is dealt with later.

Firm estimates—when and why

Provisional estimates relate to the requirements at the end of a phase. The other major planning occasion is at the *start* of a phase when, hopefully, the project has just been re-justified by senior management. The pre-occupation now, is with a possible re-organization of staff, the introduction of more staff, the allocation of tasks, and the detailed tactical planning of activities in the coming phase. The situation calls for detailed firm estimates that only relate to the *current phase*. At this point in time, no one (not even the project manager, DP manager, users or senior management) is interested in future phases. They were concerned a few weeks ago, but not now.

Firm estimates are produced by a completely different technique to that adopted for provisional estimates. Here the approach is to itemize every conceivable task requiring completion during the current phase. The summation of this list provides the firm estimate for that development phase. A crucial point is the comparison between this firm estimate and the previously produced provisional estimate for the phase in question. A significant discrepancy is usual (with the firm estimates lower). This discrepancy should be investigated by re-working the two iteratively, until a satisfactory reason for the difference can be explained; often the reason is over/underestimated or missing items. These agreed itemized figures should then be used by all levels of management to monitor progress during the phase. This is the other main purpose of providing firm estimates.

Planning techniques reflecting the project's progress

At each different planning occurrence, the project has evolved. More and more detail is known enabling greater accuracy of plans to be made not only from utilizing the increased level of knowledge, but also, from the use of different techniques that can digest this information. For example, at the start of systems analysis work, the state of knowledge relates to the business and DP functions that are required to be built into the end-product. Estimates at this point of time must be based on management's skill in calculating the effort required to develop these functions. However, at the end of program design, detail is available of the function and complexity of each module, program and even possibly of the experience of the programmer who is going to write a particular

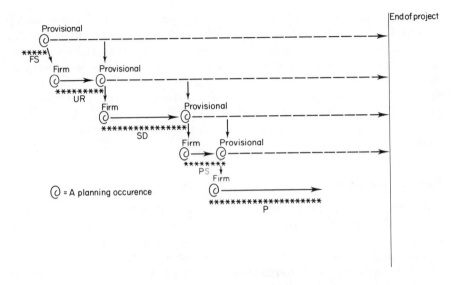

Figure 10.1 An illustration of the planning sequence

module. Consequently, estimates at this point of time might employ sophisticated formulae for calculating the programming effort required for each module.

A bird's-eye view of the phase based planning sequence, described so far is illustrated in Figure 10.1. The iterative and evolutionary process is depicted, together with the high to low level planning cycle as provided by the provisional and firm estimates. Each phase starts with a firm estimate (a cyclic event in itself) which takes input from the previous provisional estimates, and produces output relating to the current phase only. At the end of each development phase, provisional estimating (also a cyclic event) takes place. Input is obtained from both the previous set of provisional estimates, as well as from the actual performance achieved during the phase now coming to a close. The outputs relate to the end of the project.

HOW TO PRODUCE PROVISIONAL ESTIMATES

This section expands the planning techniques mentioned above and suggests a range of complementary practical methods of actually producing provisional estimates. In doing this, many of the concepts elaborated in previous chapters are brought together and utilized, including the end-product plan, the support plan, and the macro-estimates in particular.

Using macro estimates

At the earliest stages of a project, there is little quantified information available that enables development effort and resources to be determined. One method that gives a 'feel' for the magnitude of a development project is by using macro-estimates and in particular the tables given in Chapter 5. As explained there, the procedure is to work down through the ten factors considered and to match each one to the project in question using a combination of experience and the knowledge available at the time. This may appear arbitrary and hapha-zard, but in practice it works. It is possible to arrive at a mutually agreed size of project with corresponding values of program statements, development effort, and project resources, which are, at this point in time, to a sufficient level of accuracy.

Using the end-product plan

If the project has been in existence for a short while, e.g. it has nearly reached the end of the feasibility study phase, a more tangible recommended method for carrying out provisional estimates is to start with the end-product plan as explained in Chapter 6, and the support plan as explained in Chapter 7. This enables estimates of program sizes to be made which can then be used to calculate the necessary development effort. To minimize oversights, it may be found convenient to build up lines of program code and development effort under three headings.

(a) *Program code for the realization of the end-product*

Starting with the end-product delivery plan (which basically is a list of all the systems and programs that will eventually give the user his live operational system), one obtains figures of the total number of lines of program code. Depending on how far the project is along the system development life cycle, these estimates of the number of program statements on the end-product plan may relate to systems, sub-system, functions, programs, or modules.

(b) *Support Software*

Support software may include a range of programs required for assisting the development process, and for converting an existing system to the new one. The details of these should be obtained from the support plan. Deve-lopment effort can be assessed from the anticipated number of support software statements that it is necessary to write, and from the estimates of purchased software to be modified and/or tested.

(c) *Support Activities*

Those non-program producing support activities specifically required by the project need consideration at this time. Examples of these, which might include planning, control, standards, data capture, etc., have been discussed in Chapter 7 in relation to the support plan. Estimates may now be made for the effort required to complete these tasks.

An attempt has been made to *quantify* what the project is actually trying to achieve, (i.e. its end-product and supportive tasks). Using, as a basis, these global measures, several complementary techniques can be employed to arrive at realistic quantified estimates of development effort.

Estimating development effort from the end-product's size

Having some idea of the total end-product's size, it is possible to produce estimates of the development effort. Two yardsticks are useful based on 'typical DP industry projects' and assuming the usual mix of staff skills, background, and experience within an installation. These ignore such obvious variables as the experience levels of individual staff, or the complexity of the system, etc.

(a) For each 1000 lines of end-product, about 67 to 75 man days are required to develop it. This refers to all DP staff (systems and programming) and to all the system development phases that comprise the total project from start to end.
(b) For programming work only, about 15 to 20 man days are required to program design, code, and test each 1000 lines of actually written code. This assumes normal conventions on spacing out program statements and comments. These yardsticks apply to both conventional programming and so called structured programming. As the latter necessitates more design work and optimization, the 20 man-days figure may be nearer the mark.

  A practical example
  A company wished to convert from a bureau system and bring it in-house. As part of the feasibility study, estimates relating to programming were required. From comparisons to the existing program sizes on the bureau's machine, and making allowances for the installation's smaller machine from a different manufacturer, an estimate of 10,000 lines of code was obtained. To this was added 2,000 lines of support software required for conversion, plus 3,000 lines for some additional reports and system enhancements. This made a total, on the end-product plan, of about 15,000 lines of program code.
  How much programming effort is required?
  As an emphasis was to be made on good program design and testing based on data structures, the 20 man days per 1000 lines yardstick was used to give $20 \times 15 = 300$ man-days programming effort.

DP industry inter-phase relationships

If the development effort for the total project is known, or an estimate for the development effort for the programming work is available, what effort is required for each development phase? These are known as inter-phase relationships. Once again a typical DP industry project is used, and in the author's experience two phases, proving and programming, seem to give the most consistent figures for different projects. The proving phase nearly always seems to consume between 23% to 25% of the project's total DP manpower, whilst the programming and program design phases taken together usually account for about 30% of the project's total manpower. The other phases are a bit less predictable but the table below may give a useful starting point.

Development phase	%Effort
Feasibility study	6%
User requirements	12%
System design	15%–17%
Program specification	7%–16%
Programming	23%–14%
Proving	25%–23%
Implementation	12%
Total project	100%

In practice, the above interphase relationship figures vary with project size. Large projects, because of the complexity of their interactions, require more emphasis on user requirements, system design and proving. Consequently, the percentage effort expended on these phases will be relatively higher, whilst the other phases (and in particular, programming) will be proportionately lower, compared to smaller projects.

Another influencing factor is that mature DP installations tend not to rush in and start programming, but prefer to spend a greater percentage of their projects' effort on sound feasibility studies and user requirements. This trend is further re-inforced if a project is adopting a modern system development methodology. In these instances, a great emphasis is placed on data analysis, process analysis and the production of charts depicting the interaction of these two aspects. Users are deeply involved ensuring that the foundations of the system are sound. The net effect of this approach is that proportionately more of the project's development effort is expended in the early phases of the project life cycle.

A practical example
A marketing agency intended to develop their own new system for the control and analysis of different marketing techniques and for the use of different media for advertising. From:
(a) examining the sizes of unsuitable but similar software packages,
(b) comparisons, via the hardware suppliers, of the sizes of systems run by competitors,
(c) the use of the macro-estimate tables (e.g. as per Chapter 5), it was felt that the development effort would result somewhere between a small-to-medium and medium sized project i.e. about 25,000 program statements.

The very first attempt at a development plan, produced by interpolation of the macro estimate tables, looked something like the table below.

Cost	£200,000
Total development effort	10 man years
Duration	15 months
Maximum number of staff	8

Assuming the above figure of 10 man years, and using the above inter-phase relationship table, the development effort was apportioned over the system development phases as shown in the next table.

Development phase	Man years effort
Feasibility study	0.6
User requirements	1.2
System design	1.5
Program specification	0.7
Programming	2.3
Proving	2.5
Implementation	1.2
Total	10

Interphase relationships based on performance to date

Once a project has passed the feasibility phase and the user requirements phase, an opportunity arises to use another technique for provisional estimating. Based on information collected (e.g. by a project control system) on the project's performance to date, a completely independent cross-check can be made. A technique involving the inter-phase relationships may be used, but in this case starting with known data relating to completed phases.

A practical example
A large banking system was about to start system design. It had taken about 10 man years to carry out the initial appraisal and feasibility study and about 19 man years to complete the user requirements. Senior management wished to know how much total effort would be required, and, in particular, how much effort for the next phase—system design.

Assuming the feasibility study took 6% of the total manpower, and the user requirements took another 12% of the total, the 18% (6% + 12%) of the total manpower would be equivalent to 29 man years (10 man years + 19 man years).

(a) The total manpower is therefore $29 \times 100 \div 18 =$ about 160 man years.

(b) If system design consumes 15% of the total manpower, then it will require $15/100 \times 160 =$ about 24 man years effort.

Departmental performance comparisons

All of the above techniques for producing provisional estimates assume industry norms. It is preferable to use the equivalent performance statistics, for one's own installation. The results from using local statistics can be compared to the industry figures as produced above. Unfortunately, many organizations do not keep this information, or retain it in an unusable or inconsistent manner; or the computing department has not been in existence long enough for reliable records to be assessed.

Elapsed time

Having estimated the required development effort, the number of people and the elapsed time for the project can be considered. Theoretically, the project manager can simply convert the man day totals into a provisional estimate of elapsed time, if he knows the average staff numbers for the coming phase. This might prove difficult as there usually is a net increase in staff during the first half of the project and a net decrease during the latter parts of implementation. Nevertheless, it is relatively easy to take an average of staff numbers for the phase and compare this figure with a practical estimate of the available people. These figures should be increased to include all contingency planning and associated activities, which hopefully should prove redundant.

To this raw figure, in total man years, should be added an overhead for unscheduled project work, non-project work, other company work, personnel absences and other usual diversions. It is unrealistic to expect all of an employee's working time to be spent on productive or scheduled work. The net practical effect of the above is that of a possible 260 elapsed days per year (52 weeks of 5 days each), it is rare for an average project member to exceed 170 man days of *scheduled relevent project* work. For some very large projects this figure may approach 130 days, owing to interaction overheads (meetings, reviewing other people's work, start ups, general communication problems, and additional supervisory overheads).

Ratio of analysts to programmers

When project planning, it is usually necessary to break-down estimates of manpower into systems and programming skills. The table below illustrates that due to the complexity of larger system development projects, a greater proportion of systems analysts and systems design skills are required compared to programmers.

	Small projects (%)	Medium projects (%)	Large projects (%)	Very large projects(%)
Programmer	76	65	52	49
Analyst/designer	24	35	48	51
	100	100	100	100

Non-manpower resources

Non-manpower resources can now be estimated using a similar approach to that employed for development effort above, i.e. a combination of macro estimates and departmental statistics, to which can be added the relevant figures from Chapter 9 on testing. Finally, costs can be calculated to produce a provisional development plan.

HOW TO PRODUCE FIRM ESTIMATES

As with provisional computations, the logical method of producing firm estimates is to start with the end-product, then determine the development effort, assign people, establish completion dates and finally consider non-manpower resources. However, a completely different approach is advocated, because the firm estimates in hand relate only to *specific* tasks and activities in the *current* development phase. Although some people recommend using firm estimates of all tasks for the entire project (e.g. when setting up a PERT network) the accuracy of the tasks with long time horizons are apt to be unreliable, and, more importantly, irrelevant to the current work.

Current phase activities and standards

The first predictable management task is to list in great depth all the activities that must be completed by every individual in order to complete the current development phase. These should be spelt out in detail and written down explicitly (as opposed to just implicitly). A good set of system development standards should provide a useful cheeklist of activities to be considered, as well as their expected measures for completion to a good quality. One should work from first principles assuming that everybody else may misunderstand the meaning of these activities. An objective way to formulate and group these activities is to think in terms of major milestones and lesser events in time, and then list all the tasks that have to be completed to reach that point in time. Major milestones may be the completion of a phase, or the publication and agreement of a user requirement document signed off by all relevant user management. Events may be agreement of the format of a report, or completion of test data preparation.

When actually carrying out this work, it may prove beneficial to think, as before, in terms of deliverable, non-deliverable, and support-orientated tasks. If necessary, a further breakdown of events and tasks by functional teams within the project should be employed.

Estimating the effort and skills required

Having produced this list, each activity can now be 'sized'. The techniques for this are described later in this chapter, but the idea is to write down against each elementary activity the number of man days' effort required to complete it. At this stage, the actual elapsed time is irrelevant, and should not even be considered. In assessing the man days' effort required, the project manager should assume, initially, that the activity is being carried out by an optimum number of standard men. At a later stage in the planning process, when actual people have been appointed, these standard man days can be adjusted to account for the experience of each individual, as well as any increase in effort caused by too many people assigned to a crash project. The choronological sequence of tasks should be taken into account, as well as their interdependence. For a large project and an experienced manager, it could take several weeks to draw up this detailed list of activities and the estimated resources. It will entail several visits and discussions with all relevant parties.

At the end of this step, a list of every activity should have been produced with a firm estimate of man days effort to complete it, in accordance with known standards, and the manpower skills required. This list of activities and effort may be drawn up on a form similar to that illustrated in Figure 10.2. (The manpower man days, indicated (e) is used later, in chapter 13, on project control.)

Trade-offs and elapsed time

As part of the iterative planning process, the next step is negotiating trade-offs and finalizing elapsed time. This takes place in conjunction with assigning and scheduling people. Initially, the man days effort for all activities can be totalled, but as already explained, these man day figures are theoretical and do not allow for holidays, sickness, training and other project and non-project overheads. A quick estimate of a feasible end date can be made using the technique already outlined in the section on provisional estimates. The next step is to convert this quick estimate into a more accurate estimate of the total elapsed time. This requires examining the interactions of all activities, the scheduling of individuals, any consequential delays, and sometimes the analysis of the critical path. For larger projects, these steps might be best achieved using a pictorial representation, e.g. bar-charts, or a PERT network.

If the first important planning difficulty, when preparing firm estimates, was thinking of every significant activity, the next major problem is assigning start and end dates to each activity to achieve an acceptable live date. The

Items being estimated

Project
Development Phase

Task, or Program	Description and estimating criteria	Skill	Manpower (Man days) (e)	Machine
		Totals		

Comments, dependencies

Authorized by_____ Date_____

Prepared by_____ Date_____

Figure 10.2 Activities and effort

former planning difficulty requires a broad and deep technical experience, but the latter problem requires an ability for managerial trade-off negotiations, because the project will be constrained mainly by one of the following major factors:

(1) Time is of the essence
(2) Costs are to be kept to the absolute minimum
(3) Negative cash flows are not to exceed certain limits each year
(4) Resources are scarce (e.g. there is great difficulty in obtaining analysts or programmers with the required skills)
(5) Suppliers' delivery dates (e.g. hardware or software has a long delivery date or will be late).

Usually a combination of several of these constraints exists, but if all apply, then the project manager and the organization should re-assess their objectives.

The theoretical and idealistic approach is for the project manager to plan out the elapsed time schedule, and apply optimum resources to each activity to achieve a logical end date. Obviously, this luxury does not apply in practice, and some of the above political factors must take precedence. Scheduling by the project manager has to take place within this framework. With respect to the time critical projects, if one must accept the end dates set by senior line management, it means attempting to pour in the appropriate amount of people to meet the deadlines. However, this will not necessarily achieve the desired result, as many problems require optimum resources and a minimum elapsed time. Alternatively, one may have to start from an imposed project's annual budget and the project manager will have a maximum amount available per annum, and can apply resources at that rate to meet the (amended) deadlines. In all cases, the process is once again, very iterative with the necessity of going round the loop several times. A combination of several approaches is usually required, and the project manager may prove that neither the original budget, nor the end target date is feasible! Consequently, the schedule will be re-arranged and an acceptable compromise agreed, between senior management, the line users, the computer department, and the project's staff.

Planning and scheduling

It is important to separate (conceptually) planning from *scheduling*, although in practice, they are connected. The plan of what needs to be done, and the effort required to achieve it, can be developed, or amended, without recourse (in the first instance) to a schedule of how the plan will be attained over a period in time, and where the manpower and resources will be allocated.

Assigning and scheduling people

It is now possible to negotiate and determine the number of people needed for the project, the type of skills, and when they are required. This is done by assigning all the activities as the responsibility of actual available people, or to the additional manpower still to be acquired for the project. (Recruitment may be necessary, or transference of people from other projects). Now that the actual people have been assigned, it is possible to schedule each activity, week by week and person by person using a scheduling chart similar to Figure 10.3

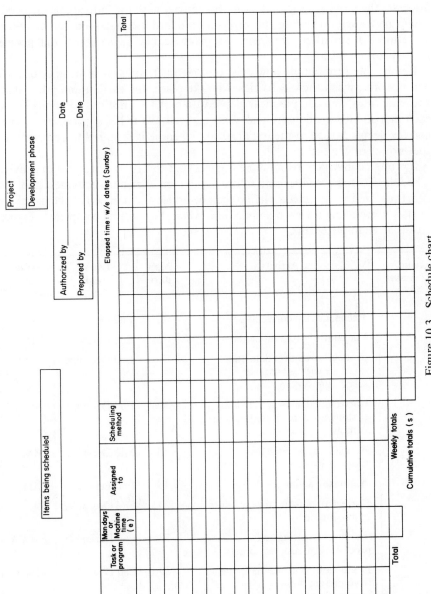

Figure 10.3   Schedule chart

which may be preferable and more flexible than the often used block diagrams. It should be mentioned that in the whole of this process so far outlined, a key idea of *no surprises* should be adhered to. It is assumed that the project manager discusses the number of man days for an activity with the individuals involved, where necessary amending the original standard estimates on the activities and effort list, and after agreement, assigns these man days to the actual people in the plan.

Reasonable firm details now exist of which activities each member of staff will perform, when these activities will take place, the earliest and latest start and end dates, and the practical elapsed time. Allowance has to be made for each individual's availability and skills, as well as for his unproductive time, and for delays caused in the initial period when he is required to comprehend the project or the task.

It is often convenient to combine Figures 10.2 and 10.3 to produce an activity schedule. To the activities and effort list (which shows all activities, and the effort required for their completion) can be added the name(s) of the members of staff responsible for each activity and when they will be completed. Figure 10.4 is an example of this.

Item Number	Activity	Man days	Latest finish	Action by
1	Reconciliation corrections	12	End October	FA
2	File control program module	15	End October	FH
3	Production control data and interface with subsequent scheduling system	50	End December	RK/FH
4	Correcting details of individual customer orders, in conjunction with users, prior to take-on	30(o)	End December	HH/BG
5	Action lists, overdue lists, progress lists	15	End December	MM
6	Automatic action for delays	15	End February	MM
7	Correct all outstanding customer billing problems	20	End December	RK
8	'Intelligent' vetting and processing of customer orders	30	End December	FH/FA
9	Production control enhancements from present files	30	End December	MM/FA
10	Redirection of correspondence to sales force	15	End November	RK

(o) Open-ended estimates

Figure 10.4 Activity schedule

To finalize the phase plan, it is necessary in conjunction with the above, to transcribe the activities for each individual to another list to produce a personal schedule. The purpose of this schedule is to allow each person to see what he is supposed to be doing, cross-check unproductive time and absences, ensure that all the allocated jobs are simultaneously feasible, clarify activities requiring several people, and to ensure that each man's percentage utilization is as high as possible. This is not always possible with the schedule chart produced earlier, because it was then more activity orientated than people orientated. A further concept at this stage is that one should plan to schedule actual people—not activities, departments or teams. An example of a Personal Schedule is shown in Figure 10.5. Some computerized project control packages (both mainframe and personal computer) are available on the market that will relieve the manager of some of this repetitive chore.

	MAN UTILIZATION (Man days)						
Days available	15	21	15	20	20	Total available 91	
People	Oct	Nov	Dec	Jan	Feb	Each activity	Total
MM		Item 5			6		30	50
	Item 9					20	
RK	7					20	50
	10					15	
	3					15	
FH	2					15	45
		3				15	
		8				15	
HH		4				30	30
FA	1					12	37
		8				15	
		9				10	
AP project (2 analysts)		3				10	20
		3				10	
PC project (2 programmers)	1-10					25	50
						25	
AP project (1 programmer)		3				25	25

Figure 10.5 Personal schedule

Non-manpower resources

Having planned the development effort, management's attention should be turned to non-manpower resources. An appropriate computer together with available machine time is the main resource required for testing. Often, one or both of these factors are missing. Early estimates of machine time are essential because there may be delay in acquiring a suitable computer. Chapter 9 on Testing contained some yardsticks for estimating machine time.

Additional ancillary resources include special input and output stationery, as well as reserved magnetic disks or tape files, together with data entry resources. The latter may not only be necessary for programs, programming amendments, and test data, but also for the capture of existing data that are associated with most commercial systems. Departmental statistics may be available to refine data entry figures. Other equipment and supplies (e.g. filing cabinets, etc.) can also be considered under this heading of resources. Common sense, based on a small degree of experience and a check-list is a sufficient guide to estimating most non-manpower resources. This topic of resources is covered in more detail in a following section in this chapter which looks at the requirements in relation to DP operations.

PERFORMING SIZING AND ESTIMATING

What is sizing?

It may be useful to elaborate on what has been termed sizing, and suggest appropriate techniques for carrying it out. Basically, the idea is to tease out in advance all the problems involved with an activity, and cover everything that can possibly go wrong with the necessary contingency plans. Having obtained a feel for the situation, the number of man-days' effort required to complete each activity can be estimated. This is necessary for both the original plan, as well as any subsequent re-planning when the unexpected has happened. To a certain extent, the process is indefinable, as it is based on experience. As in all planning, it is a mixture of 'gut-feel' and comparison with similar completed projects, extrapolating as necessary. However, refined estimating yardsticks usually help.

Estimating criteria

Up to now, various estimating yardsticks have been considered in several chapters, but with minimal qualification. To avoid accusations of presenting a slovenly treatment, the limitations of these, and any other yardsticks should be heavily stressed. Many figures have been quoted by various sources to assist in estimating, but generally they are difficult to apply, unless a manager has practical experience of their use, or the figures relate to measurements made in his own installation. One problem in using these figures is comprehending to what they relate. Consider the programming yardstick '20 days per 1000 program statements', as an illustration of the predicament. By itself, the statement is meaningless! Are the days elapsed days or man days? What is the complexity of the job? How experienced is the programmer? Even specifying the number of statements needs to be more precise, because the following should be stated:

(a) the programming language,
(b) whether procedure or total statements are involved,
(c) whether statements are lines actually written or a count of the number of verbs,
(d) whether all of the total number of statements in the end-product have actually been written, or whether they include repeated modules or file descriptions copied from a data dictionary,
(e) if lines of comment are included.
(f) if new code is being written, or existing code is being amended as part of maintenance.

It is apparent that a book may be needed to explain all the variables and qualifiers and what is included in any one estimating yardstick. Using yardstick figures for estimating may defer the problem slightly, as it is necessary to know in advance the number of pages, or the size of the program, which in itself can be even more of an estimating difficulty.

So what is the answer? The first rule is only to use generally published figures, if nothing else is available. As soon as possible, these figures should be monitored and refined so that they relate to the installation's own environment. The next most important rule is to make any estimating yardsticks tie up precisely with the installation's information systems development standards. It is then relatively easy to know what is included in each figure used. When using yardsticks relating to the end-product program code, it may be of interest to note that more consistent results seem to be obtained if the figures refer to lines actually written.

Estimating rules should be made relevant. For example, a commonly quoted figure is that a programmer should complete 20 coding sheets per day. This is not very helpful, because a programmer does not sit solidly coding all day; there are many more activities for him to cover in the whole programming job. Likewise, it is essential not to confuse performance monitoring with planning and estimating. People do not like being treated as machines. Not only is their co-operation required when having to confirm estimates, but if alienated they will press for easy target dates.

Who and how?

It is probably better if the manager responsible for planning, works in conjunction with other people. These could include a special planning or scheduling group, team leaders, consultants, technical specialists, representatives of the hardware or software suppliers, or the line users. In fact the manager should obtain feedback from anybody assigned to specific tasks or who is even remotely concerned with the project or application under review. The process applies both to the initial project planning and the subsequent re-planning, after variances have been detected.

A proven way of sizing the list of activities is using the standard 'brain storming technique', which has been described elsewhere in a different context. A group of relevant people can be gathered round a flip-chart or black board, to assess each item in a controlled manner. The project manager controls the session and draws out all ideas, and balances the contribution from all the participants. As each problem is usually complex and interactive, it is best to use a pictorial representation. Each activity or problem should be assessed down every logical path; minimum risk established; contingencies accounted for; and all consequences can be assessed and agreed by the group. Eventually the flip charts or blackboards are a pictorial mess. To conclude this brainstorming session, the outcome should be summarised by the manager who sifts through the ideas, and clearly sets out the points agreed.

THE CONSEQUENCES OF THE PROJECT'S PLANNING ON THE REST OF THE ORGANIZATION

The final level of the planning structure is to consider how the project's own plans affect the rest of the organization, which in turn affect and place restraints on the project's original attempt to produce a plan in isolation. The implementation of all the above planning could have an effect on (and be affected by): DP operations, the line user, other systems and projects, and the computer department itself. These are now considered in turn.

The effect on DP operations

The DP operations department (or its equivalent) needs considerable relevant information, usually in much more detail than is required for the project's own internal needs. Planners (comprising the project's staff, DP operations staff and any co-ordinating departmental staff) are therefore required to prepare an operational plan which is basically in two parts that cover the requirements of DP operations

(a) during development
(b) during live running.

(a) During development

All the equipment, software and special aids that are requisite to develop the overall systems should be identified, and schedules for its acquisition and installation need to be drawn up. Coupled with this should be estimates of the DP operations resources needed over the period of development. In particular, the following check-list may be useful.

(1) Machine requirements in terms of CPU time, CPU store, elapsed time, disks, tapes, peripherals, terminals. This is for general project use, but in particular for programming, proving, and implementation. For some complex projects a chart of machine utilization per calendar month as well as for each development phase, may be useful.

(2) Data entry loads for   — programming (if not on-line)
                                — testing
                                — file creation/data capture

(3) Supplies   — cards/paper tape (if applicable)
                                — stationery
                                — file storage

(4) Communications, and   — facilities
telephone line   — volumes
requirements   — scheduled usage

(b) Live production running

All equipment, software and special aids necessary for live running, should be identified with schedules for acquisition and installation. This could be phased, if applicable, and kept in step with a protracted installation phase. Estimates of DP operations resources required for live running should be given and the following check-list may help:

(1) CPU requirements   — daily volumes/transactions to be processed
                                        — daily run times/on-line times

(2) CPU store, disks, tapes, and peripheral requirements

(3) Data entry   — daily volumes, peak loads

(4) Additional equipment.

(5) Communications requirements — lines, modems, terminals

(6) Details involved with preparing the site to receive the computer or additional equipment.

(7) The date when each piece of hardware is to be delivered, and then installed, and the various pieces of software needed with the respective dates of their use.

(8) The correct sequencing, run dates, and timing of each program and job for live production running.

(9) Details for handling file creation and file conversion.

(10) Data control between user(s) and DP operations department.

(11) Operational procedures.

(12) The formal hand-over requirements by the project to the operations department.

In addition, this operations plan states who is responsible for each activity in order that the hardware, software, communications lines and ancillary equipment can be operated satisfactorily and to schedule. Included in these responsibilities is the provision for communication lines, and for a reduced operational service during breakdown, to users dependent upon the application system, at geographically separated locations.

The above operations plan may include a provision for training in DP operations; this might consist of training operators and data control staff about exceptions to, as well as the contents of, operating manuals relating to the application system.

This operations plan, which is technically orientated, complements the user-orientated schedule for delivery.

The effect on the line users

The line user can be affected in the following ways, and consequently plans need to be drawn up to meet his needs.

(a) The numbers and types of line staff required for the development and live running of a project should be considered, together with details of redeployment, if any, and the training program. The schedule and responsibility for the production of user manuals should also be defined.
(b) The proposed line user organization and responsibilities of each section during live running need outlining.
(c) Any special premises and equipment required for the system should be described with details of completion and delivery dates.

The effect on other systems and projects

All interfacing systems and dependencies need identification and plans made in conjunction with each party of the clerical or computer systems changes required. This in turn, may create the need for the planning of development effort in other projects along the lines discussed in this chapter.

The effect on the rest of the computer department

As a result of the consolidation of each project plan, data is available for inclusion in the departmental planning process. For example, three projects may be under development each calling for extra staff with specialized skills, at particular times. These shortages are then included in the departmental forward planning process so that staff can be provided in a co-ordinated manner.

Similarly, different hardware and software facilities may be needed by each project. These can only be identified by the project, but should be consolidated at the departmental level. The results form input to the DP operations forward planning process for resources.

In general, the following check-list may prove helpful when planning the project's interface with the computer department.

(1) Manpower
   —the effect of manpower into and out of the project during its duration, including specialist skill requirements for use with other computer projects.
(2) Personnel functions
   —the effect on the computer department of requirements on training, recruitment, redeployment, career development and personnel functions in general.
(3) Administration
   —the project's call on the computer department for administration, clerical, typing, secretarial, stationery, support, etc.
(4) Accommodation
   —the call on the computer department for desks, furniture, premises etc., to support the project.

CONTINGENCY AND MINIMIZING RISK

One of the reasons for setting up a project is that there is an element of risk associated with the development of a proposed application system. So far, a plan has been suggested for the development of a system, but no plan is complete without detailed consideration of the possible risks, and the ways of minimizing them with contingency plans during the implementation of the project.

One of the key factors which makes for a successful project is having the correct attitude of mind, that enables one to be aware of the necessity to adopt a minimum risk approach. This does not mean just a simple, reliable implementation of the project, or allowing a half day per person per week for contingency. A minimum risk approach demands more long-sighted, comprehensive objectives. It is necessary to minimize risk throughout the project's development strategy (relating to how the system will be built). This entails ensuring that during the development process the correct techniques are employed within the project's strategy. This should enable the project team to produce and implement the application system as rapidly and accurately as possible, without too many pitfalls. Some of the concepts associated with these objectives of minimizing risk are now discussed.

Total in-depth planning is recommended for any project. 'Total' means anybody and everybody who could influence the project; they should all be accounted for and planned for. 'In-depth' means sufficient detail should be planned to avoid delays and problems during development, as well as to avoid misconceptions by all individuals involved. Good planning has a high element of contingency. The consequences of each individual activity being late or going wrong should be carefully considered in advance. Alternatives, fallbacks, and possible degradation of users' facilities should be well thought out.

It is important not to get into a box situation creating unnecessary and impossible problems. An example of this is when an application system must go live prior to the launch of a new product. A recommended approach, if possible, is for the new product to be processed clerically or by existing systems (and if necessary, converted later). This avoids any delay in the project's progress causing intolerable strains on the launch.

For some projects it may be worthwhile to have one or more full-time members of the project team working solely on the alternatives. Of course, if all goes well, all this work will be completely redundant. Even for the very largest and most complex projects, the right contingency plan should always give an application system, even if the hardware or software does not work to specification, or has not been delivered in time. In this case, the project should have had built into its plans, the ability for the application system to use alternative older, tried and tested, machines and operating systems.

A minimum risk grid

In considering planning for minimizing risk and all contingencies, it is useful for the project manager systematically to work through the relevant main project work streams, and then chronologically through each system development phase of the project. This is best shown in the form of a grid and Figure 10.6 illustrates what is involved. To simplify this example, only three phases are represented, and comments have been included to illustrate only some of the minimum risk considerations. When drawing up these minimum risk grids it must be emphasized that a preferred way to achieve a successful project and a sound application system is to:

(a) Think out every step in the total system.
(b) Think out the consequences of every correct or incorrect situation.

Worrying about the future

One purpose of planning is to affect what the project does now, and not academically to look into the future. This is an important concept and enables a project manager to make today's decisions with greater certainty. Earlier discussions on firm estimates were based on this premise. In other words the project manager should mainly worry about short term problems, as the long term difficulties may change by being superseded. This, of course, is the opposite to the system development manager's function relating to planning and implementing strategic systems.

A simple example of this may be a file interrogation application which is planned to use visual display units going live within 18 months. If the initial interim phase is to produce a printer output with similar data, it could prove possible, if additional effort is not required, to structure this initial output format, the system, and the interim program with visual displays in mind, thus minimizing the transition in 18 months' time. It is irrelevant in respect of today's decision, if for any reason the visual display system is cancelled sub-

Main project work streams	Chronological development phases		
	System design	Programming	Installation
1. USER LINE DEPARTMENT	Keep users advised whilst specifying the system and agreeing the optimum facilities.	Avoid user dissatisfaction caused by delays in programming, lack of contact, and intangible progress.	Ensure user procedures are produced jointly. Arrange user training.
2. OTHER INTER-ACTING PROJECTS	Inability to agree on data interfaces to be avoided by early meetings.	If programming manpower is scarce, ensure co-operation even if other projects do not benefit directly.	Ensure other projects understand conversion.
3. SYSTEMS DEVELOPMENT	Ensure correct justification, and signing off by senior line management, for the more exotic screen outputs.	Ensure agreement with all other work streams prior to commencement of programming.	
4. CLERICAL PROCEDURES	Ensure interactive and evolutionary design of ergonomic clerical and coding procedures with O and M staff and users.		O and M staff to train users and monitor data coding problems and errors.
5. APPLICATION SOFTWARE	Ensure programmers understand the systems specifications and agree the computing consequences.	Build in numerous milestones for every program and each programmer.	Ensure DP operations department signs off and accepts maintenance for live application.
6. COMPUTER DP OPERATIONS	Obtain agreement on the proposed file handling methods.	Produce contingency procedure, if other systems cannot be modified in time, to read newly created or converted file.	Avoid user dissatisfaction caused by poor operations standards, slow turn round and insufficient data control.
7. SYSTEM SOFTWARE USAGE	Ensure with supplier that the best use is being made of the operating system.	Write contingency system software.	Arrange for the supplier's specialists to be available.
8. HARDWARE USAGE	Investigate the credibility of the manufacturer's schedule for delivery; examine alternatives for future stand-by.	Arrange suitable computer for program testing.	Arrange for alternative hardware, if late delivery. Chase up leased telephone lines.

(NB In practice, there will be *numerous* activities in each box)

Figure 10.6   A systematic minimum risk grid

sequently, or as in most likely, the hardware and software technologies change, as will the system requirements and the screen lay-outs. In other words, by all means think about the future, but do not waste excessive time on it, otherwise today's targets will never be met, and the future will not be reached!

Staff independence

Staff independence is vital to the organization of a project, the principle being, if a person is away sick, or on holiday, or even leaves, somebody is available to take over without much difficulty. In practice, for the more critical activities, it may be better to have two people working on an activity, in a complimentary fashion, rather than just one person. This may sound inefficient or a luxury, but remember we are referring to results orientated projects and minimizing their risks; with the consequences reflected in their cost justification and budget.

The extension of this principle is that the project manager should appoint his own deputy to lessen the impact of unforeseen absence, which also will assist the deputy's career devolopment.

The consequences of a minimum risk approach

In summing up this section on minimizing risk, it is apparent that extra effort is required to carry out all these additional activities, which in turn will lead to later target dates. Where appropriate, it is essential for the organization, through their project managers, to plan for all this extra effort in the original project justification. All these additional resources, activities, and costs should be included in the approved budget. As part of a minimum risk implementation, the line users must be persuaded to freeze their requirements as early as possible. Changes requested by line users can often be incorporated as maintenance after the system goes live. Sometimes a possible approach is to treat the first three months of the system specification as tentative.

All projects contain an element of innovation and research. For example, new hardware or new unproven software might well affect performance or delivery; or the application system has features that previously have not been implemented; or a new development technique may be employed, or suitable staff may not be easy to find. All projects should have a contingency plan, which will minimize the risk that the projects may not proceed as planned. Each activity or anticipated event that is very likely to cause trouble should be highlighted independently and an alternative method planned. All major dependencies should be similarly assessed, together with the effect of slippage.

In the case of projects with a high element of research, a 'research diagram technique' could be used, which charts every consequence and alternative as in a flowchart. Each alternative path is given an assessment of its probability of success, and the likelihood of achieving an end result through the various paths can then be assessed.

THE CONSOLIDATION AND FINALIZATION OF PLANS

Having produced the basic phase plan, its implementation milestones and manpower requirements, the project manager should gain agreement and commitment from all parties involved, preferably in writing. He can now consolidate and go round the planning loop one more time, to finalize the actual schedule for each item; re-assess the critical path; and negotiate actual start and end dates with every individual department or sub-contractor associated with the project. The project manager can complete his budget, together with the other final plans for such things as the organization of this manpower.

As with the provisional estimates produced initially, these final plans and budgets should be compared against recorded data for similar but already concluded projects. Obviously, adjustments will have to be made for differences, but it is reassuring to have confirmation that the total costs and time estimates are in the same order of magnitude. It is probably easier to make this comparison with other projects at the end of this planning stage, rather than assessing individual activities earlier.

The results of project planning, as described in this chapter, should be consolidated, summarized, documented and published in a development plan. The purpose of this plan is to inform all relevant parties and senior management on *how* the system will be built, and how the manpower and resources will be managed. Following this advocated planning methodology, the embryo of a development plan should appear in the report emanating from the feasibility phase. A detailed development plan is then produced at the end of the user requirements phase. This is updated at the end of the system design phase, and possibly again at the end of program design.

THE ROLE OF SENIOR MANAGEMENT

The project manager, or his equivalent, is the person mainly involved in the topics discussed, as he will be the key person responsible for planning a project and replanning the consequences if anything goes wrong during the course of the project. However, senior management and the line users require to understand the plans for their justification of the project, or for authorizing changes to the project, if problems arise.

Senior management will probably treat with natural caution, the presence of impressive-looking PERT networks and bar-charts, because, as they are probably well aware, these charts can prove that the project will work, just as easily as they prove that the project is impossible!

Senior management and the line user(s) should be provided with a list of the project milestones, which they should readily understand. They should ensure that the plans have been created by *all* parties involved with the project, including the relevant main project work streams. At the same time, senior management would probably wish to enquire how activities have been sized, and how the plans have been produced, in order to obtain their own independent assessment of the quality and reliability of the plans they are about to authorize.

Senior management should appreciate that it is not always possible to set critical target dates for a project by pouring in the appropriate resources. Most problems are constrained by a minimum elapsed time, and it may be more appropriate for the line users to negotiate for the optimum number of people for the earliest reliable date for the system to go live.

Finally, in all project planning and re-planning, senior management and the line users should assist the project manager and the computer department to negotiate 'trade-offs' for practical live dates, part of which is the substitution of resources, costs, or time for the reduction in facilities, response times, reliability, resilience, or controls. An alternative option could be the phasing of facilities in the system with the ensuing phasing of the benefits.

CHAPTER SUMMARY

Having defined in some detail the concepts relating to the construction of the end-product, it is now appropriate to use this information to quantify such items as development tasks and the man days' effort they require; staff numbers, their skills and availability; elapsed times and completion dates; computer machine time for testing, and other non-manpower resources necessary to complete the project. Usually the responsibility for this area of management is entirely with the project manager (or the equivalent). It is stressed that much planning is usually required in order that a large project meets its objectives.

Ideas have been presented in this chapter to assist in producing these numerated plans, which then can be used for four purposes. First, to determine costs and budgets which can be used to re-affirm positive cost benefits of the project. Secondly, these plans should be used for control purposes and for monitoring subsequent progress. Thirdly, for devising plans relating to staff training, organization of manpower, as well as for the administrative side of the project; and fourthly, these quantified plans form a basis for assessing the impact of any proposed changes to the end-product that may occur during its development.

Common difficulties (that sometimes give planning a poor image, especially at the less-senior staff levels) are management setting tight unsubstantiated target dates first which necessitate planning backwards, or the misuse of such techniques as bar-charts or PERT giving a false sense of security. Traditionally, difficulties have arisen (and always will?) over changes to plans, and so a practical approach is necessary that bears this in mind.

In general, the recommended solution to planning is to use a structured approach, the highest levels of which relate to:

(1) time, i.e. *when* a manager should plan, and assign resources to planning
(2) iterations, i.e. not only necessitating several attempts to refine a plan on each of those occasions, but also building on the last plan produced

(3) Macro then micro i.e. formally preparing a high level plan before starting a low level plan and then ensuring their compatibility

(4) *evolution* i.e. as the project proceeds, utilizing the more detailed information that is available, as well as adopting more appropriate planning techniques to assimilate the information

(5) procedure i.e. *how* a manager carries out all the steps necessary for a good plan and its associated estimates

(6) people i.e. *who* are the people involved in the planning and estimating process

(7) interactions, i.e. *consolidating* the many separate plans and examining the *consequences* of the project's (parochial) planning on the rest of the organization.

Having first split the planning process into these self-contained concepts, each one can be examined in more detail.

Planning should preferably not be a continuous process spread throughout the duration of a project. It should be structured chronologically to occur at the time of three types of events. These are at the end of a phase, the start of the next phase, and *ad hoc* when major changes occur. Maximum planning effort is often reached towards the end of systems design.

On each occasion when carrying out planning, an iterative process is usually necessary to ensure that all aspects tie up. A similar concept relates to the suggested planning structure of separating in time, provisional estimates from firm estimates, the latter only being attempted after the former have been demonstrated as reasonable at a macro estimates level. Advice is given on ways of carrying out provisional and firm estimates. Another aspect of the evolutionary theme is that, as the project proceeds, more and more detail (in both breadth and depth) is available, to the planner. Consequently, the estimating techniques used, say, at the start of analysis should differ from those employed at the end of program design when every module of every program has been fully specified.

The procedure used on each planning occasion should start with the end-product: the final end-product for provisional estimates; and the development phase end-product for firm estimates. If the end-product is to be made live in a staggered fashion, completely separate plans should relate to each stage in which a major systems feature occurs. Each provisional plan should then relate to all the development phases, whilst a subsequent firm plan focuses the mind on the tasks, activities, and standards necessary to complete the current phase. Estimates of man-days development effort and the necessary skills to complete these activities can be followed by considering actual and required people and their day-to-day schedules. Advice is given on actually performing sizing and on the people involved. Also discussed is the role of senior management in the planning process.

Practical trade-offs can take place to establish realistic milestones, but these cannot be confirmed until resources (machine time, data entry, supplies, etc.)

have been considered, and all plans have been consolidated so that the net effect of them on the rest of the organization has been assessed.

Having produced detailed plans, it is now necessary to refine them further, in order to prevent them becoming invalidated by the unexpected. A contingency plan is required, the purpose of which is that the project always should be able to produce a viable application system irrespective of mishaps.

Chapter 11

Project organization and structure

Up to now, the discussions have had a task orientation emphasis and a start towards a people orientation is now overdue. Having planned out the tasks required for a project, and determined the manpower requirements, how is this manpower best organized and structured? This chapter starts by identifying the staffing and skills mix that are the constituents of a project. As the personnel and skills required usually differ from those people that are actually available, a manpower plan needs to be drawn up as a means of bridging the difference. It is then necessary to comprehend the special method whereby a project manager gains authority over his staff, and how different management styles affect the important practical considerations of personal relationships and the resulting political situations that arise when implementing a system. The discussions conclude with information on how projects are organized and structured, with examples of how these change as the project evolves during the different phases of development.

THE COMPOSITION OF PROJECT STAFF

It is now opportune to take up and expand upon a theme which was started in the second chapter, dealing with the constituents of the staff requiring to be managed within a project. Conventionally, an organization (via its department responsible for computing), may appoint a project leader chargeable for the successful implementation of a substantial application system. Other people appointed to staff the project may include systems analysts, programmers, business analysts, and possibly other data processing orientated people. Users, in many installations, are treated as 'a them and us' situation. Either they are not fully consulted and involved, or complaints are heard that they have too much influence over the project. However, experience suggests that restricting the project to the DP specialists, often limits the project's chances of success. The users, i.e. all those key people who will directly or indirectly use the computer application being developed, should ideally be involved as an integral part of the project. The effect of these non DP people may possibly become more significant as the organization becomes larger, or as the system becomes more complex. In a substantial integrated system, these people might include numerous skills and functions from the rest of the organization, any of whom could delay a project, affect the requirements for the system, or frustrate the project's implementation.

It will be apparent that, for the duration of any project, project staffing should include all the users (in the widest possible sense), as well as the usual systems analysts, programmers, operators, data coders, business analysts, the hardware suppliers, any special software suppliers, and any general sub-contractors. In fact, *all* these people should be represented within the main project work streams; preferably explicitly. How this amorphous group of individuals is blended into a coherent purposeful team has been referred to previously in several different sections, but is further expounded during this chapter.

SKILLS REQUIRED IN PROJECT WORK

What expertise and skills are required by project staff? In general they need to be versatile. This requirement means that they should not be merely transfer-able between teams, but also be able to apply different skills as required through-out the project. Ideally, each person should possess the necessary skills re-quired during analysis, definition, design, programming, proving, installation, etc. This ideal is not always possible, although, in smaller installations, comput-ing specialists may need to have this broad range of skills.

Separately identifiable experience and skills required in computer system development projects may include:

Systems analysis
O and M and clerical analysis and design
Overall and detailed system design (batch or on-line)
Overall and detailed program design (batch or on-line)
Program coding
Program testing
System testing
Installation
Conversion of systems
Planning and estimating
Cost justification
Negotiating trade-offs
Business expertise
Hardware expertise (mainframe, mini, communications equipment, etc.)
Software expertise
Technical expertise (e.g. system software)
Data capture, data correction, and data coding
Supervising juniors
Leading teams

For ease of planning, it should be appreciated that, in practice, staff obtain DP experience in similar circumstances. The above skills can, therefore, be grouped into four broad categories, which are:

Analysis (business orientated with minimal detailed programming and technical machine experience)

Analysis and design (experience in technical system design and/or programming

Design and programming (programming background leading to program and system design experience)

Programming (coding and module design, with minimal detailed experience in overall program or system design).

A MANPOWER PLAN

It will be a lucky management services manager, let alone a project manager, who can claim to have the right numbers and levels of the above skills. From the basic data contained in the project's development plan, and using the above list of skills, it is possible to develop a manpower plan. This should indicate all the people that are required; whether or not they can be identified; when they will be involved; the necessary skills; the necessary levels of experience; the total number employed permanently as opposed to temporary contract hire; shortages; redeployment; terminations; and whether staff will need to be recruited internally or externally. User resources should also be identified and incorporated in this manpower plan. For larger projects, it may be advantageous to plan for the eventual maintenance and enhancement of the live system, and identify the relevant manpower numbers, skills and time schedules. This is often necessary towards the end of a project, as people may prefer working on a different system, and when planning for maintenance it is a good time to consider appropriate career advancements.

An ideal golden rule is that any individual, at any one time, should not be shared between projects and project managers. Always a time will arise when there is an impossible conflict of priorities. If a person has to undertake more than one job, it only should be for one project manager. This is particularly relevant in smaller installations on the occasions when there is an insufficient work load in one project for a particular person's skills. In addition, the longer-term career development of staff should be considered and balanced against the short-term requirements of the actual project.

This manpower plan interacts with the development effort plan (explained in Chapter 10 on planning) where the man days effort required for an activity depends on the experience and the skill of the man appointed to that activity. Similarly, the development effort plan will provide the total man days' effort required, and the manpower plan will state (or restrict) how many people are available. Only when these two plans are harmonized can the total elapsed time be determined.

Training project staff

A project's training plan should result from the matching of project activities and requirements against the manpower plan, and highlighting any deficiencies.

Existing or recruited staff may require to be trained in the latest techniques, in new hardware and software products, or in new technologies. This training plan is only part of the career development plan of an employee and is probably short term. The training plan itself could consist of job rotation, courses, seminars, and practical experience. Line user staff may be involved in this training, but, in this context, their training is confined to a general computer appreciation, and to project management techniques. This training plan also covers the induction of new project members, and where necessary, some staff in other interacting projects who require knowledge of the project's methods and systems.

THE PROJECT'S REPORTING STRUCTURE IN GENERAL

In practice, a project manager has a unique problem in establishing his authority over the staff in his project. This can be illustrated by examining how project staffing is traditionally organized. In general, the majority of people associated with a conventional, technically-staffed project are under the direct control of someone whom we shall call the project leader. He accepts a full-line reporting responsibility for his analysts and programmers. This reporting structure is clear-cut for career development, man-management, and project control. Also conventionally, all the other people associated with a project are not represented within the project, and are only consulted when appropriate, to a greater or lesser extent. There is not necessarily a tangible involvement or commitment to the project by these other people.

The essential point that should now be apparent is that the majority of people associated with many successful projects are outside the *direct* control of the person leading the project. Theoretically, it is easier if the project leader has everyone reporting to him direct (with a full-line responsibility). In practice, he probably does not even have a dotted-line responsibility for the majority of people required for the successful implementation of his project.

It is apparent that any person leading a worthwhile project has to manipulate skilfully a host of individuals, some of whom report to him with a full-line responsibility; fewer still for whom he has only dotted-line responsibility; and the majority 'reporting' to him without authority. For this reason, the person leading a project, as defined in this book, has been referred to as a *project manager* and *not* a project leader, in order to differentiate between the two concepts.

The staffing of larger projects may, by the necessity of requiring several levels of supervision, be further grouped into teams. For the sake of clarity, we shall define a team as either:

(1) a group of people having similar skills and working on a similar activity (e.g. the bought ledger parts of the accounts department involved in the project; or a team of programmers working on the communications software; or a team of business systems analysts defining the users requirements for an application system), or

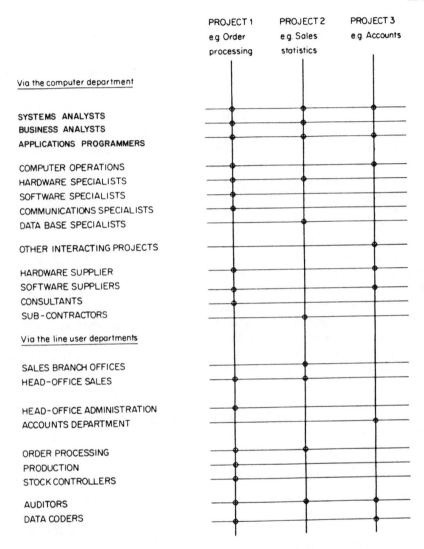

Figure 11.1 A grid representation of project staffing

(2) a group of people with dissimilar skills, but responsible for a specific function (e.g. a sub-system; or a file design team).

By definition these teams are led by team leaders.

The project manager will, therefore, be controlling teams of people, as well as individuals working on the project's activities. In larger projects, the project manager will be in direct contact with a few key people who will either be team leaders, or be technically orientated individuals who are not managers.

A well set-up project *cuts across the organization's formal line structure*. It can be visualized as a grid with the vertical lines representing computer projects and the horizontal lines, the normal organization line structure. Figure 11.1, illustrates this principle, and indicates that not all functions will be involved in every project, nor necessarily will they be separate departments, functions or people. For example, in a smaller project the hardware, software, and operations work streams could be the responsibility of just one person, the DP operations manager.

The project manager can attempt to persuade the organization's DP and line management who are involved, to assign to him (with a full or dotted-line responsibility) all the key people. However, this rarely improves the project manager's control. The crux of the problem is that the project manager *cannot legislate* for his position and authority. He must be able to *persuade diplomatically* all the individual people, companies, departments, and sub-contractors that affect his project, to carry out all their planned activities to schedule.

It may help unification if the staff assigned to a project are able to reside with the project, not in their own department. Office space should be allocated to projects, and senior management need persuasion to assist in making this space available.

In any organization there are usually many projects, and this tenuous, ill-defined project-staffing concept should be accepted by the line users and the computer department as a permanent way of life. However, the actual composition of any project is transient. In the course of time, members of projects come and go, in accordance with the planned schedule of activities, all of which are under the control of the project manager. If a project is to advance successfully, the project manager in conjunction with the systems development manager has to work at disseminating this staffing concept throughout the rest of the organization.

MANAGEMENT STYLES AND THE POLITICS WITHIN A PROJECT

Consideration should now be given to a further and important factor which affects the way a project is both structured and organized and therefore managed. This factor relates to using alternative management styles and the ensuing politics within the project.

Creative tasks as opposed to repetitive or mechanical tasks

Before discussing management styles, it is necessary to examine two types of work that occur in systems development projects. These are, in the extreme, creative tasks, and 'hard slog' tasks. Each is discussed in turn.

Examples of 'hard slog' tasks occur during analysis, coding, testing, etc., with these activities possibly taking up to about 80% of the total development effort. Correspondingly, many staff are required for these activities, with the consequential need for teams, team leaders, and a management hierarchy. Management of these activities is facilitated by control against (well established) data processing standards adopted by the installation or project. Examples of this type of control could be pre-defined formats of say, the user requirements document, or ensuring adherence to defined programming standards.

The other type of project work (in this context) relates to creative tasks which occur, for example, in parts of the feasibility study, or during parts of system design and program design, or when originating a testing strategy, etc. These creative tasks probably involve no more than 20% of the development effort, but, as they affect the fundamentals of the project, these creative tasks could affect up to 80% of the consequences. Relatively few staff are required for this creative work and, as their output is so vital, it may prove beneficial if they report directly to the project manager, or his deputy.

Alternative management styles

Having examined these two types of work, the appropriate organization and structure necessary to reflect the management of these types of work should be pondered. It is suggested that projects (or line departments) can be managed by two separate and opposing styles, and these may result in two dissimilar methods of personal interaction (or internal politics). These two extremes are:

(a) using groups, committees and/or a democratic approach to decision making and to 'getting things done', and/or adopting a consultative management approach.
(b) giving individuals the responsibility for decisions and developing areas of work, and/or adopting an autocratic approach to management.

The culture of an organization, i.e. the particular management style reflected in the above two extremes, which has evolved over its history, may or may not motivate employees, depending on their personal preferences, and similarly may or may not attract prospective recruits.

A democratic approach to management

The committee or democratic approach assumes that a group of people will perform better than an individual. Hopefully, the committee will take the prime suggestions from the best people, and build on these ideas; removing faults detected by all members of the group. This is termed synergy.

This approach could be appropriate when management is not sure what to do concerning, for example, a novel research type project. On the other hand, this policy could indicate weak or new inexperienced management. As mentioned when discussing the benefits of project management, committees are a helpful method of relieving the political pressure on the computer department caused by many forceful user departments, parent companies, auditors, etc. It is easier to blame a committee than an individual, and likewise it is more difficult for an outsider to get something done when confronted by a committee.

A major problem with this approach (apart from the well-known slow reaction time, difficulty of getting things done, and the insensitivity of committees) is the political problems caused by the inevitable consequence of the personal interactions within a committee. For example, good communication skills and the ability to argue and persuade are required in this environment. In practice, the person who has these natural skills, shouts the loudest and strongest, and has the firmest political base, usually wins. Technical ability is not necessarily the most important aspect, because the individual with the greatest political leverage may not be DP-orientated. Consequently, democratic groups may not always pick up the prime ideas and build on them, but the group may tend to drag discussions down to lower levels, with the technically experienced people becoming demotivated. In practice, synergy may be difficult to achieve.

On the other hand, the group approach may improve self-criticism and might produce an open attitude for project staff to know what is being developed and provide opportunities to improve the work being produced. In particular, all output documents might be reviewed by the group with open invitations for the feedback of any comments. This policy may be useful to improve the performance of people working on repetitive tasks. In a large project developing an integrated system this approach is often necessary in order to detect and minimize errors, and reduce communication misunderstandings or difficulties.

An autocratic approach to management

Having discussed the group or democratic approach, it is appropriate to examine the other extreme; the individual and/or the autocratic approach. This basic philosophy states that democracy is not appropriate to a thrusting business environment, which requires benevolent autocrats and an emphasis on individualism. The argument continues by pointing out that, in the history of mankind's achievement, an individual person, or a complimentary pair, have been responsible for producing the acknowledged masterpieces in music, literature, art, science, architecture, etc., etc. It could be argued that as great symphonies were not written by committees, the heights of good ideas and innovation in a development project should also not be given to a committee, but entrusted to appropriate individuals. It is important however, that as in most walks of life, these key individuals have proven experience with an established credibility in their areas of responsibility.

This environment may be more motivating to the individuals, but is more difficult to co-ordinate and control. A strong dictatorial approach is required by the project manager to ensure work is completed correctly. However, even with this state, a compromise with the committee approach is possible, as the rest of the project can still comment on output and work undertaken. Similarly, individuals wishing to further themselves will be open to self-criticism and review, as in the case of the group scheme.

Summarizing the conclusions of this individualistic approach; at the lower staff levels, people can be given individual areas of responsibility (possibly on a medium to long term basis) where they can develop their ideas and work by themselves or in complimentary natural pairs. These people will need to be tightly controlled and co-ordinated by the responsible management. At the higher staff levels, the key innovative people should report to the project manager (or his deputy), as their work could affect 80% of the effectiveness of the project.

INTRODUCTION TO THE CHANGING STRUCTURE OF A PROJECT

Team structure

Having considered the general manpower aspects of project management, the next predictable consideration for management is to decide how the project will be organized. The organization plan (which tends to evolve) indicates how the project will be structured, the function and responsibilities of each person or team, to whom they will report, and whether the functional reporting will differ from the line reporting. For example, like skills could either be kept as one team, or dispersed amongst several teams. In the latter case, they would have to report to their functional manager (e.g. the manager who may be reponsible for the conversion sub-system), or their career manager (who is usually outside the project), as well as to their team manager (e.g. the programming supervisor within the conversion sub-system). Conflicts of interest of this nature should be set out in the organizational plan.

Project organization compared to departmental organization

Organization of projects vary greatly from that of departments. Projects place different demands upon their personnel. Usually, when a department is created or reorganized, the intention is that it should last for a comparatively long time and be capable of handling a reasonable variation in its workload. A project has two different characteristics; namely, it has a finite lifespan known from its initiation, and it progresses through definite and distinct phases. Each phase requires its own mix of skills and organization. Thus, project personnel must expect to be reorganized fairly frequently. Project teams are created, expanded, contracted, and disbanded. All positions within the project are temporary ones.

Changing problems, needs, skills, and structure

The organizational plan should show significant changes of structure as the project evolves. For example, staff involved at the early phases of a project might be mainly systems analysts with very few programmers. In the middle of the project, there might well be many more programmers than systems

256

analysts. Similarly, a program testing function might be required at the middle of a project, but not at the beginning of a project. Consequently, the management and reporting structure must be planned together with the location of personnel.

The remainder of this chapter elaborates on the ideas required to be set out in an organizational plan, and illustrates practically how the project's structure changes with its evolution. In general terms, as the project follows the development cycle, the problems, functions, required skills and staff numbers change. Management's considerations and emphasis should continually keep in step.

EXAMPLES OF PROJECT STRUCTURES AT DIFFERENT PHASES OF DEVELOPMENT

To illustrate the above cumulative effect of management's changing emphasis on a project's structure, Figures 11.3 to 11.9 inclusive, are snapshots at seven distinct points of time relevant to a medium-to-large project. Figure 11.2 illustrates when these snapshots are taken in relation to the system development phases. It is assumed that the project in question does not have its own dedicated computer, but relies on the DP operations department for its machine-time. A project environment is assumed, as opposed to distinct departments of skills (e.g. O and M or programming departments). The benefits of this approach

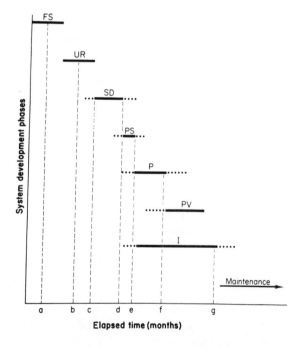

Figure 11.2   Project structure and development phase

are to minimize the number of interactions; improve communication and decrease the incidence of dotted line reporting, thereby improving control. In the following structure charts, functions should not be confused with people. Normally, one person is responsible for several functions. The objective, here is to illustrate what needs to be done at specific points in time, and how staff may be organized to achieve this.

Mid-feasibility study phase (a)

It is assumed that the project manager has already been appointed. As illustrated in Figure 11.3, three distinct groups are reporting to him, and they would be working mainly towards producing a feasibility study document.

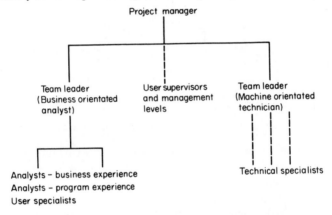

Figure 11.3 Mid-feasibility study phase (a)

It is possible that only the systems and business analysts have a full line reporting responsibility to the project manager, which may be via a business orientated team leader. The line user specialists assigned to the project may only be part-time, and at this stage, might only need to be at the supervisory and management levels. The project manager would have minimal reporting authority over these specialists. A technical machine orientated team leader could report directly to the project manager, but the specialists under him probably also may be on a part-time secondment.

Mid-user requirements phase (b)

The project has successfully completed the feasibility study, and has received senior management justification for the user requirement phase. At the mid-point of this phase, the preoccupation is in agreeing and documenting the users' requirements in terms of their inputs, outputs, data, and processing rules. Assessing methods of converting from existing systems might also be an important consideration. A structure to reflect these needs is illustrated in Figure 11.4.

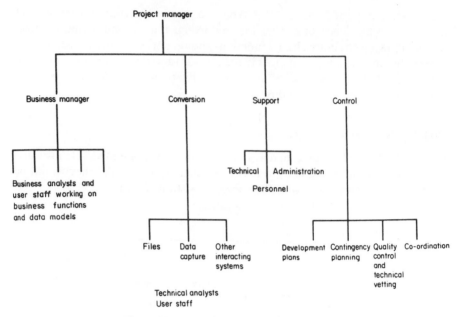

Figure 11.4   Mid user requirements phase (b)

A business manager leads the group responsible for negotiating and documenting the users' requirements. This group might well consist of systems analysts who have either a business or a computer programming background, O and M analysts, and user staff.

The contemplated conversion difficulties might warrant a team of both technical analysts and user staff, led by a team leader, which would be examining existing systems and files, current and additional data required to be captured, as well as other systems interacting with the proposed system under development.

In this example, the project is large enough to require its own support section which may be responsible for personnel, technical, and administrative project activities. Relevant technical support functions during this phase may relate to such items as systems simulations, software evaluation, data administration, or data sampling. Personnel functions might relate to recruitment and training. Administration function might include word processing services, office accommodation, the administrative aspects of running a project control system, and maintaining the project's library.

If the project is fairly large (say over 30 technical staff at its peak), a separate control team may be essential. Staffed by senior and experienced DP people, this team might be made responsible for planning (and in particular, producing the project's development plans), for contingency planning (especially if much innovation is involved), for quality control of the end-product's design, and for the technical vetting of the working papers, user requirements, and other outputs from the teams in the project. Ideally, the small number of specialists in this project management team should all report direct to the project manager. The elimination of a hierarchy within this team improves their responsiveness.

Early system design (overall design) (c)

The users' requirements, together with the associated development plans, have been agreed and justified by senior management. The project is now involved in producing the optimum logical design which will ensure that all future development work knits neatly together. Figure 11.5 illustrates a structure that assists in this objective.

The project's growth in staff may include consultants and technical advisers from the hardware manufacturer and a full-time project secretary all reporting to the project manager.

The business manager (sometimes referred to as a functional requirement manager), may find his team reduced in numbers compared to the previous user requirement phase. However, his group of business and technical analysts have the important dual responsibility of keeping up-to-date a published base-line of business and data definitions which includes changes to the users'

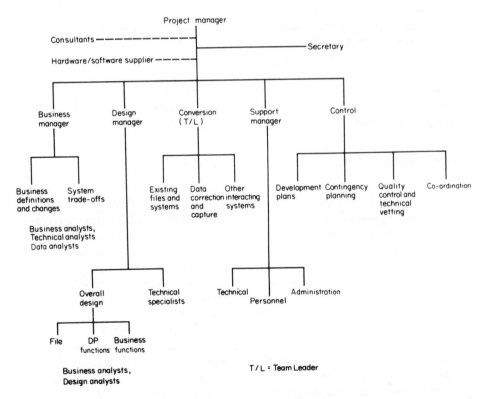

Figure 11.5 Early system design (overall design) (c)

requirements, as well as negotiating system trade-offs. The latter are the frequently required compromises between the users' idealized system requirements on the one side, and the technical difficulties or uneconomic costs arising from the systems design and conversion teams on the other, who are attempting to meet the users' requirements.

The newly-appointed design manager becomes the nucleus for the detailed technical systems and program design activities. His team at this time, might consist of business analysts, analysts with programming experience, and other technical computer specialists, such as communications experts. They could well be deciding which files are required and their structures, how each business function will be incorporated into the total system, and what special DP functions are required to be developed to, say, access the files, print numerous reports, or to control transactions being sent via a communications network. This unit, working from a user requirement document produced by another team, is an example of built-in cross-checks within the project.

The conversion team, possibly with a few additional people included, might still have a similar function as described previously. They should, by now, have completed documenting existing files and systems and be in the course of producing an optimum method of converting these files and systems to the proposed new system, together with ideas about the necessary programs. The complexity of the conversion process may necessitate a specially developed conversion system. Usually, the new system and its main files will require more data than existing computer files. This conversion team should, therefore, be identifying all additional and missing fields, assessing the amount of error in existing data, and producing practical plans of how all this data will be captured.

The functions of both the support team, and the control team will still remain as previously described.

Late system design and the start of program design (d)

Having completed the finishing touches to the system design specification document, with, probably, a start being made to program specification and design, the project is poised for a rapid growth in staff numbers, mainly programmers, and Figure 11.6 represents a possible structure. A project secretary is engaged as before, together possibly, with consultants and supplier representatives. Similarly, the business team and the support team have unchanged functions, save for the former team having its staff numbers reduced and the latter team requiring greater numbers of staff. The business team may also be starting to think about planning user acceptance testing.

The control team continues its responsibility for quality control and contingency planning, as well as assisting the project manager in his usual strategic and tactical planning. Some additional control functions are required and these relate to controlling changes to the system (from any source), monitoring progress, and in this example, planning all aspects of testing.

A technical manager might be made responsible for all machine-orientated

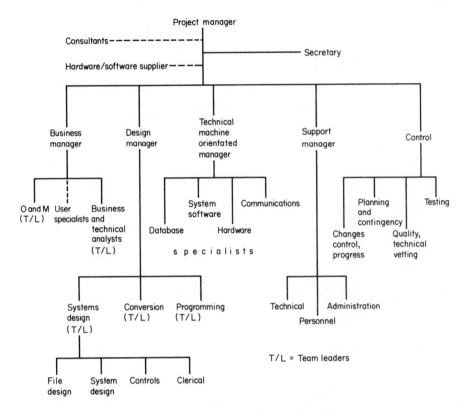

Figure 11.6 Late system design phase (d)

development work, and accordingly has the appropriate hardware, software, database, or communications specialists reporting to him.

The main thrust comes from the design manager, whose teams could be functional and contain the appropriate skills. For example, there could be team leaders responsible for file design, conversion, system controls, clerical systems, overall program specification etc. The previous separate conversion team might now become devolved in other teams. Putting overall program design under the design manager is a conscious attempt to prevent coding from starting too early.

Late program design and early programming phases (e)

The number of people assigned to the project probably is reaching its maximum, and programming should be under way. Figure 11.7 illustrates a suggested structure that is a compromise between functional teams and teams of similar skills.

As programming is the main production task, the design manager's function and his team can be dissolved. It could be appropriate to place the majority

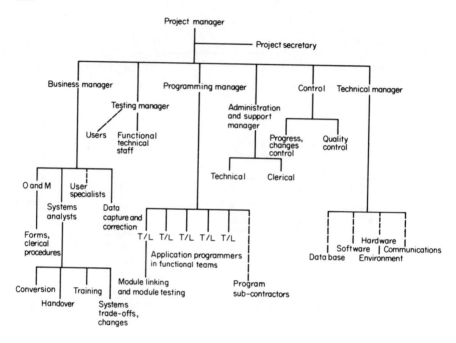

Figure 11.7 Late program design and early programming phase (e)

of the application programmers under a professional programming manager, who would be responsible for the functional programmer teams, as well as any sub-contracted programming. This group, producing program and module designs, and programming from other people's specifications, is another example of checks and balances within a project. This principle might be extended still further, in this example, if under the programming manager there is a team of program designers made responsible for linking modules, or testing programs. The individual programmers having planned, coded, and tested each individual module, now hand them over to this linking team, who build up the modules into programs. If this approach is adopted, the problems of this team are relatively complex, as they must acquire the necessary support software and simulators to enable them to carry out their tests, plan, and schedule the overall testing, ensure that modules arrive as required, or that simulated modules can be used for a test, evaluate results, and fix bugs.

While the programming is taking place, the business analysts and user teams could be divided functionally and be concentrating on installation tasks such as data capture, conversion, file creation, user training, and user/operational procedures. The other major problem area for the business application manager is to continue negotiating any changes in the user requirements, system design specification, or program specifications, according to the changes control plan. These amendments usually occur, and to minimize disruption and distraction of the project's staff, a small team should have responsibility for examining the feasibility, consequences, and resource overhead for each requested alteration. The support and control team would be involved in this function, and assist the business manager and project manager in optimizing and negotiating the necessary trade-offs.

To accommodate the increased staff numbers, the administration and support group will have grown, and be led by a manager responsible for tasks that require both technical and clerical skills. The technical support tasks might involve at this time, controlling computer time (i.e. acting as a link between the computer operations department and the project teams); arranging bulk data entry; updating the standards manuals; providing training material and courses, and possibly ad hoc technically skilled tasks for any team within the project. The administration tasks may include setting up and updating the library; physically distributing and updating the major project document-ation; ensuring that status and scheduling documentation is produced to plan; and providing general word processing and secretarial support. As project staff numbers are probably peaking about now, the personnel support aspects of recruiting, training and assimilating staff will be greatly reduced.

The technical manager has a similar role as in the previous phase, but his teams are probably placing more emphasis on the environment for the hard-ware, and making the necessary arrangements for communications lines and terminals. (With possibly long lead times of telephone lines this may need to be tackled much earlier). In addition, this technical team could be starting to test, or acquaint themselves with, any standard or non-standard system software.

A major function responsible for testing, might have been established. This group could accept programs (where the module testing and linking have already been completed by the responsible programmers), and carry out the system tests; the integration tests; and the acceptance tests. Unlike the module linkage testers, this group may only be interested in the inputs and outputs of the application system and how it conforms to the user requirements. At this snap-shot in time, the test group might prepare a test plan, determine the expected results; prepare realistic test data; arrange appropriate machine time; develop or acquire special programs for testing, etc. This group, verifying other people's work, is another example of checks and balances.

Mid-programming, early proving, and implementation phases (f)

The main problems at the early proving and implementation phases are to find and fix errors; start delivering the end-product; create the files; train the users in the product's use; and obtain the technical facilities, e.g. communication lines. Figure 11.8 illustrates how these areas may be reflected in the project's structure.

The testing team continues to take responsibility for systems, integration and acceptance tests, and eventually liaises with the business manager and user group, who usually carry out the conversion and any trial running. The latter also will be responsible for producing user procedures, the data capture,

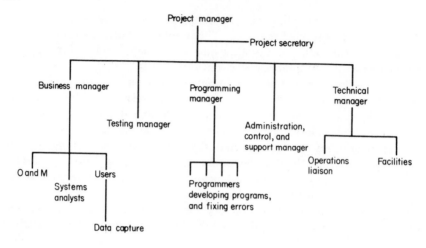

Figure 11.8 Mid programming, early proving, and implementation phases (f)

and training aspects; in fact, completing the activities assigned to them when discussing Figure 11.7.

If all is proceeding well, plans can be laid so that the programming manager's teams can start to be reduced, with the intention that eventually a programming team leader could be brought in to replace the programming manager, and control the declining numbers of programmers working on the final programs, changes, and fixes. If many changes occur, or many errors are found, the opposite might occur, with more people being assigned to the retained programming manager.

The technical manager will be ensuring that all the operational facilities are provided according to the facilities plan. He should be liaising with the computer operations department with respect to the operational plan and the hand-over requirements.

Also at this time, any consultants, or representatives from the hardware, or software supplier, may adopt a less strategic role and, in theory, need no longer report directly to the project manager. If matters are proceeding smoothly, the previous control team may now be devolved as, in this example, the testing has been taken over by a separate team, and quality control is automatically carried out during testing and proving. Similarly there should be little strategic planning and contingency required and this together with changes control and progress measurement could be combined with the support manager's role. This organizational approach can be contemplated after all design work has been completed and the project is felt to be on its down-hill path. The main advantage for the project's *central* intelligence, previously held within the project management team, to be devolved to separate functions within the project, is that it avoids project management by remote control. Tighter control is thus exercised during the main production and implementation phases, when project control systems for measuring progress can become very unreliable.

If things are not going well, or if control of the technical design of the end-product is a problem with the possibility of, for example, response times of the screens being too long, the centralized control team needs strengthening not devolving.

The administration, control, and support functions are, as in the previous structure, under one manager. At this time, they might be responsible for measuring progress, scheduling work between teams, and predicting end-dates. Administrative tasks may include publishing user manuals or clerical checking of system inputs and outputs. Technical responsibilities might involve program library maintenance.

Late implementation phase (g)

The project should be completed shortly, with the application system handed over to the data processing operations department for live running. The project should, by now, be mainly concerned with the remaining users converting to the application system, and in making final changes and amendments held back by the freeze to the system design. Figure 11.9 illustrates how a project's structure might reflect the tasks in hand.

A user liaison function might be the main channel for user queries in order to shield the other project staff from these constant distractions. The technical specialists need no longer be a part of the project on a full-time basis, but should be available for the occasional query. The analysts and programmers probably can become less specialized and replaced by programmer/analysts. At about this stage, a project manager is no longer required and may soon be superseded by a team leader. This small team may be ready for a protracted take-on of new geographic areas, or new products, as well as for maintenance. The responsibility for the application system may probably have now been handed over to the DP operations manager. This last step is another example of checks and balances, where the DP operations department has to vet and accept the project's end-product.

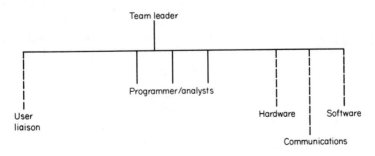

Figure 11.9   Late implementation phase (g)

SMALLER PROJECTS

The previous example assumes a fairly large project, where hierarchies of functionalized people are a necessity for management's control. This luxury does not apply at the other extreme, where the smallest projects may merge into the computer department itself, and, as an example, a small installation, or distributed processing outpost can be run effectively by only three people:

(a) The computer manager, who carries out all management planning, scheduling, and control functions for both the development and operational aspects, as well as some systems analysis and design.

(b) A programmer analyst, who as a technical specialist, also carries out analysis and design work, but programs as well as undertaking some computer operating.

(c) An operator/trainee programmer, who deals with most of the data entry, operating, data control, and some programming.

In general though, a typical small installation could well have a project whose structure, during its programming phase peak, is depicted in Figure 11.10.

The administration and support function could have insufficient work for a full-time team, and the project would have to share the computer department's administration and support group as well as secretarial assistance. For a similar reason, the project could share the programmers, who are grouped in a programming department and who might report to a programming manager. The same argument could apply to the use of O and M analysts, but the majority of the systems analysts probably would be reporting full-time to the project manager via a team leader. If data capture is a problem, a small full-time team of coders could be established, and augmented by temporary clerks.

User management could report ad hoc to the project manager, as could the technical specialists from DP operations; but the line user specialists could report via the systems team leader.

As will be apparent, the majority of reporting is dotted line, and this will

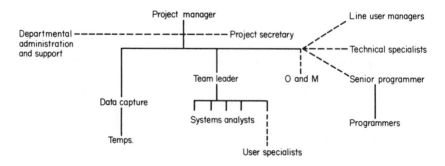

Figure 11.10   A smaller project's structure during the programming phase

cause the project manager much frustration whilst attempting diplomatically to control resources in several different departments. The large and the very small projects tend to have less of this handicap.

Although this structure is more tenuous than the previous very small project, or the earlier medium-to-large example, all these projects still have to consider the same facets of project planning; the same development cycle; the same constituents to the project work streams, and the same principles of management.

The smaller projects, having less staff and fewer levels of management, do not require formal procedures or a complex reporting and project control system. Similarly, they frequently have less internal and user interactions, which improves communication, and could facilitate significantly the systems analysts job by reducing the number of negotiations and agreements, both during the design and testing stages.

Unlike larger projects, the staff in smaller projects will each perform several functions, and this can cause its own problems. For example, the data processing manager could be responsible for all the planning, estimating, and control as a part of his responsibilities. Consequently, these aspects of a smaller project could become not as thorough, less professional, and more error-prone. Also, as there are less checks and balances, and fewer people available to comment on plans and produce them, there is a greater risk of errors or omissions in the project's planning. A further factor affecting estimating is that fewer people make it much more difficult to average out variances in individual performance yardsticks, with the consequent lower probability of the total projected figures being accurate.

The project manager of a smaller project has the psychological problem to overcome that, as his project is small, he has less apparent excuse for failure, and his organization expects success. This section illustrates that small projects or small minicomputer or microcomputer out-stations within a distributed network, have their own management problems, which detract from a straight-forward success.

LARGE PROJECTS

It will be recalled that the smallest sized projects tend to become the computer department itself. At the other extreme, large projects could have their own dedicated computer installation, and they too may tend to resemble a management services division, whose annual budget may exceed $3 million.

Another analogy between the smallest and the largest projects is that, in both cases, the lines of responsibility tend to be more clear-cut, than in the tenuous small-to-medium sized project, which shares the computer department and line resources, and has many dotted line responsibilities.

Medium-sized and larger projects, especially those developing integrated systems could have the problem of handling numerous nodes or interactions, which means extensive negotiations with many line departments, several other projects, and several departments and functions within the computer department. Another factor in medium-to-large projects developing integrated systems is that they will have to test their integration links with other application systems. This requires more time, greater effort, and the necessity to agree test results with numerous line user and computer people.

Mainly the systems analysts are affected by these overheads, which are manifest at the design and testing stages. The presence of say 15 more interactions, could well double the total required systems effort, compared to a similar sized programming load carried out by a different project with very few interactions.

A similar effect of size occurs in respect of the project's support and special testing groups, which can account for over 50% of a very large project's total manpower, in contrast with small projects where staff automatically provide their own support.

CHAPTER SUMMARY

This chapter examines the factors that affect the organization and structure of projects, and how these are reflected in an evolving organizational plan. It starts by examining the composition of a project's staff, and then shows how to plan for the normal divergence between the numbers of staff and skills required, and what is actually available. If a project comprises more than about 6 people, supervisory hierarchies are generally required with the formation of teams. These teams may be functionally orientated or contain people with like skills. The planned organization of the project should incorporate all the project's work streams, i.e. *all* the necessary people affecting the development process.

Unlike a normal chain of command, an explanation is given as to why a project manager has a unique management problem in effecting his authority over staff who are supposed to be under his control. This is followed by a section that elaborates on the internal politics within a project, and illustrates how various management styles affect project staff in different ways. In particular, a distinction is made between the management of creative tasks and routine tasks, as well as a comparison between a democratic management approach as opposed to an autocratic approach.

Finally, a juxtaposition is made between department and project organization. The changing nature of a project's structure is emphasized, as it relates to the ever-changing problems, needs, and skills employed. Examples are given of possible structures of medium sized projects at different phases of development. The characteristics and difficulties of both small and large projects are highlighted.

Chapter 12

People management

This chapter develops further the personnel aspects of DP work in general and projects in particular. Manpower is not treated as a resource, but as individuals requiring skilled management. Starting at the top, we examine desirable qualities required for the head of the information systems department, and follow this with an analysis of his departmental managers and team leaders, including the project managers' qualities.

Traditional methods of motivating DP staff are augmented by some additional observations, and one section looks at possible ways managers within a DP installation may, if necessary, improve morale. Practical advice relevant to DP, is given on such topics as corporate personnel policies, staff deployment, career development, training, recruitment and appraisals, i.e. most aspects of man management.

QUALITIES FOR MANAGERS IN DP

Many of the desired qualities for various managers within information systems, including project managers and team leaders, may equally apply to management in general, not necessarily DP. As with any discussion relating to personal qualities, the arguments are highly subjective and difficult to prove conclusively. However, this section could form a basis for self-analysis, and may be of assistance by indicating which factors should be considered when appointing or appraising managers.

The head of the computer department

What are the particular attributes required by a head of information systems, management services, or a data processing manager (or whatever the equivalent title?). A successful approach is often where this manager may be on the board, and runs his division as a benevolent dictator. Although he is a computer professional and knows what needs to be done (without relying too heavily on other people's expertise, or requiring committees to make decisions for him) he should, on the one hand, be user orientated but, on the other, firm when committing his DP resources. He should be a 'front man' not too involved with day-to-day matters, and it often helps if he is an 'ideas man'.

Particular qualities directly related to the job obviously depend on the size of the installation and what it is attempting to achieve in its use of DP technology. Historically, in the early years of DP, a straightforward knowledge of computing was the obvious prime requirement. To-day, there may additionally, be new areas of responsibility within the realm of management services. These may relate to the organization's communications in its widest sense, including computerized telephone exchanges, facsimile transmission, and distributed computing, as well as to advanced office equipment, which may incorporate micro computers, and in some installations photo typesetting or Prestel/viewdata systems, etc. In fact, the head of management services could be talking to the same supplier on different subjects. It is the fortunate manager, though, that can claim in-depth experience in all these areas.

As well as his DP experience, the head of management services should possess a general business and/or a particular industry experience. He should be able to talk management's language, and initiate strategic developments of information systems that pre-empt competitors in the market place. This balance needs to be carefully considered, because too much of a business emphasis often proves disadvantageous. A primary DP experience is essential:

(a) to initiate and control the organization's high investment in developing new systems, (which requires a deep knowledge of development techniques),
(b) to protect the organization's (substantial) DP assets (which are in the form of hardware and live working systems);
(c) because the largest part of a management services budget usually relates to the operations side, (which in turn, requires a fairly detailed appreciation of the technical aspects of hardware, system software, communication lines etc).

In fact, the latter point may be a powerful political lever, and is demonstrated in that many heads of computer departments have been promoted via management of the DP operations department.

One of the features of the job is the management of change, and he must be actively geared to cope with this. Although amendments are continuously occurring in every department of every organization (e.g. markets vary, production techniques alter etc.), changes in DP seem to occur at a greater rate than elsewhere. The causes of this may be considered under five headings, the first of which relates to *technology*. Just keeping up with new hardware devices, items of software, or even fresh suppliers is practically a full time job: the DP industry grows so rapidly! Selecting the most appropriate and cost effective hardware devices, or items of software or supplier(s) is even more difficult. New *techniques* abound, ranging from data bases and distributed data processing, to the use of structured methodologies, prototyping, fourth generation languages, or the automatic generation of systems. Trends in industry, and new *business objectives* for the organization generally mean changes to both existing and new systems, apart from possible re-organizations inside and outside the computer department. Innovative *ideas* or new *user personnel* also cause continual requests for changes to systems requirements. Last, but by no means least, *government* and *legislative* changes can cause major amendments to an organization's DP. Keeping a tight rein on all these mushrooming changes requires a calm, rational, objective personality.

One of the qualities a head of management services should possess is the ability to communicate, both with the users (in their language), and with his DP technicians in theirs. This ability should ideally manifest itself in the creation of respect for the head of management services by both the DP staff and the line users. In fact, all levels of user management should positively want him to help them.

As our man is, in fact, running a business with a significant budget, he should have the flair for being motivated by profit. Observation suggests that many of the most successful DP installations are those that are not only profit centres, but also compete for business with outside service bureaux, software houses, or consultancies. Measuring his effectiveness in business management is straightforward if the head of DP is operating within a profit centre, but if his brief is just to recover costs, the main criteria for his assessment is the satisfaction of users. This, in some organizations, can be highly subjective.

If, (as in numerous cases) he hopes to become a director or vice president, representing the organization's DP on the main board of the organization, this ambition could in many organizations, prove to be an obstacle, requiring additional abilities. He may need to overcome the natural barrier of the current board members, who may treat him as a specialist, and may not accept him as a general manager of a business.

Managers within the computer department

Moving down one or more levels, some observations are made about the qualities of the other managers and supervisors in the DP department.

General experience

As information systems become more of a strategic weapon rather than an administrative tool, DP management's role has to change as well. More emphasis is required on solving business problems. The traditional view of the DP manager is that he is happier when providing technical and programming solutions. Observation indicates that it is often more fruitful if a department, project or team is led by a well-experienced professional computer manager, who has worked in the industry long enough to acquire all the qualities and experience necessary to direct the many skills involved in making his department or project function smoothly. Many successful computer managers strike a fifty/fifty balance between this tangible and intangible computer experience, and a user orientation, and thus gain the respect of all parties. In selecting a computer manager, a slight bias towards DP management experience seems, in the writer's opinion to be preferable.

A manager should not be just a consultant or technical expert made up to manager. This sometimes occurs in an organization where the career development paths are very limited, and technical skills may not be adequately rewarded other than by calling the specialist 'a manager'.

Higher levels of management cannot, in general, ascertain directly what the 'workers at the coal face' are achieving. Consequently these managers, especially if they lack in-depth experience in information systems, tend to judge productivity on how early people arrive for work, how late they stay, how much apparent overtime they work, whether their heads are down working, or if they seem to chat. It is easy to gain the wrong impression from such superficial views of DP work. The late arriver who may be chatting might be the most effective team member, who was up all night testing, and is explaining the problems to the rest of the team.

A similar problem is the poor manager (for example, a person given responsibility for an unfamiliar area) who is unsure of what to manage, so he controls bureaucratic factors, such as tidy desks, prompt arrival to work, smart attire, reducing expense claims, etc. Such managers often avoid involvement in the productive work in hand. The above traits usually demotivate and are counter-productive to achieving high output from staff.

A shield

A good manager should shield his staff from pressures from above (and not just pass down problems). He should be seen to look after his staff and support them whenever possible, and he should provide a quick response to staff problems (both work and personal).

Delegation

A manager should be able to delegate responsibilities, and then allow his staff to be judged on their performance. Eventually, a manager should promote himself out of his own job, by making himself dispensable. The latter point may be a hallmark of an ambitious manager who wishes to achieve promotion. His staff will benefit because the deputy to the manager could take his place when the manager is promoted. Obviously, this is beneficial for both manager and staff, as there will be promotions along the chain and the staff's enthusiasm will reflect in their performance and achievement. The only 'fly in the ointment' is whether the organization should be able to absorb all these promotions!

Respect

Personal observation indicates that a manager should gain the respect of his staff as a consequence of his ability, rather than attempt to gain authority just as a result of his genial personality or friendly approach. However, a combination of both aspects is advisable. To be successful, the manager should appear to be strong, and must be firm in keeping to any decisions made, as well as exuding confidence regarding them. At the first signs of 'liberty-taking'; irregular attendance; or not 'pulling his weight', an individual must be stopped immediately, and the underlying cause established.

Long hours/effectiveness

A successful manager does not always have to work long hours, although many choose to. Often a high proportion of a manager's work is eventually proved to have been wasted. For example, he may be unnecessarily worrying about the lowest levels of detail, or after checking a competent supervisor's work he subsequently finds it was satisfactory. He may even produce contingency considerations that never materialize. In most cases only a few minutes of long meetings or seminars are relevant or useful to the problems in hand. The art of good management is to select carefully activities for maximum effectiveness.

Communication

When a manager is dealing with his staff, or attempting to persuade people not under his direct control, he should not be impatient or attempt to give orders. The other person's view is usually valid or based on wrong information caused by a lack of communication. In either case he will resent being dictated to. Communication, in general, is especially important, as so many computer personnel talk jargon and are unable to relate to the users in their own terms.

When attempting to resolve problems, decisions may rarely be seen in objective black and white terms. This may apply to the whole range of problems—from the smallest queries to major disputes. Usually, there are merits in the arguments of both sides. The more experienced a manager, the more impartial he may become. In fact, the only thing he is certain about, is that he is becoming indecisive! However, the manager still needs to convey to his staff an air of confidence. A vacillating manager may be symptomatic of him being taken over by events, and his job being placed at risk.

Mature

A computer manager should be sufficiently mature to be unbiased towards any particular techniques or type of hardware. This is difficult in practice, because the majority of computer personnel can have had only personal experience with a few computers and a relatively limited number of applications. Consequently, people in DP tend to relate back to their own experience.

Tough

A manager should be able to accept personal disappointments without becoming demoralized and demotivated.

Realistic

A manager must be prepared to accept unpleasant facts of life even when they do not concur with his own thinking.

Committed

A manager must not only accept, but be committed to the goals and the management style within his organization. Likewise, being a 'company man' usually pays off. 'Fighting the system' is counterproductive, but is unfortunately common in computer professionals.

The project manager

Apart from the above general management qualities, project managers need additional characteristics in order to achieve their prime role, which is producing results on time.

Determination

A project manager must ensure that deadlines are kept and the project is on target. He must be single-minded and determined; not allowing anything to deviate his project from its objectives. Only a change in fundamental corporate policy, or a subsequent disaster to a poorly specified, badly designed, or inadequately justified project, should affect the project manager's single-mindedness in respect of his project. This quality is the opposite to that required by a line-manager or say, the systems development manager.

Flexibility/Adaptability

On the other hand, a project manager should be able to carry through changes in requirements without loss of drive, even though these changes may render redundant, work already accomplished.

Negotiator

The ability to persuade and communicate both inside and outside his project should enable the manager to negotiate the necessary trade-offs and compromises that are the inevitable part of computer projects.

Planner

The project manager must be able to plan in great detail the systems development aspects of the project. He must be ready to re-plan, and have sufficient depth of strategic experience to understand the consequences of his re-planning on the rest of the project, including a comprehension of any resultant interactions. This ability for the project manager to be ready to implement changes in plan is particularly essential for research projects, when it is easy to go down blind alleys. He must minimize the risk when assessing different approaches that the project may take.

Psychology

A project manager should consider his staff's personal preferences, as in general, these could be at variance with the actual project. In the rush to get things done, jobs can tend to be assigned, irrespective of personal feelings and career ambitions. As the project manager requires maximum output from his staff, he should *not legislate against human nature*, but *use* human nature to the advantage of the project. In other words, if he takes time to understand the motivations and interests of each individual, (both short and long-term), he can plan out tasks in conjunction with these individuals, and keep them highly motivated. In addition, to motivate people, obviously he must understand what motivates them; he must transmit a sense of purpose in order to instil a satisfied feeling of direction and of their own usefulness; and he should be honest with his staff.

Administrator

Finally, this 'perfect project manager' should be a good administrator, to keep control over all aspects of his project, and be able to monitor progress of all departments, people, and sub-contractors. This quality includes the ability to organize, including keeping in continual, first hand contact with people by visiting the relevant departments, and encouraging project staff to discuss ideas in an informal manner.

MOTIVATING STAFF

A prime DP management responsibility is man management, which in turn requires an understanding of motivation and motivating computer people, in particular. This subject has received much attention in various publications, and below are summarized, as bald statements, some of the factors involved in general work and in DP work in particular, that the author has found most relevant. Consideration should be given as to how to convert these academic ideals into practical actions by management for both their own benefit, as well as that of their staff. It is taken as axiomatic that, for the best work output (as measured in quality, speed, originality, benefit to the organization, etc.), staff need to be well-motivated. If not, poor documentation and shoddy unprofessional standards may result. In fact, project leaders, analysts, or programmers may avoid documentation in order to use a subtle form of blackmail against their company. This tends to make them indispensable, preserve their jobs, and use their position as a lever to increase their salaries or their status. It may be argued that a conscientious but demotivated person (who may be trapped, for financial reasons, in a large institution) will still produce good work. However, good motivation in this example produces similar results but earlier.

A list of motivating factors

. Staff require an opportunity to use their knowledge, skills, and abilities to the fullest extent.
. Specialists and other technical staff usually possess a desire to learn, wishing to improve their skills in order to keep abreast of new products and ideas.
. Interesting work obviously improves job satisfaction.
. Staff like to feel that they are doing a worthwhile job, preferably one that is also essential to the organization.
. Recognition of effort is important for job satisfaction.
. People feel a sense of accomplishment if they have done a job well.
. Technical achievement is usually high up on the list of DP staffs' ideals.
. People tend to be more satisfied if they are working in small organizations.
. Working near the top of the management hierarchy is more satisfying.
. In general, self-employed people appear happier in their jobs.
. Lack of confidence and lack of respect for one's manager, could tend to demotivate staff, as could poor standards of supervision. Staff like to see that a manager knows what he is doing.
. Staff require to be given a certain amount of responsibility, and like to make decisions, when applicable.
. It is satisfying for staff to be able to see where they, and their department or project, are going, and that the overall strategy is correct.
. Individuals like to assess their own chances for advancement; being happier in a growth orientated environment.
. People prefer jobs where they have a choice of work, coupled with an element of independence.
. Staff are happiest when they have plenty of work to keep them fully occupied. Few people, in DP or otherwise, are really satisfied when under-utilized.
. Staff seem to take some pride in becoming identified within a group, be it the organization, the computer department, their project, or their team. They will defend their unit from outsiders, and protect their colleagues.

The above are primary positive motivating factors, whilst below are negative factors which may not necessarily improve motivation, but might cause demotivation if they exist.

. Salary is obviously a high priority with staff, and an individual's salary must be comparable with salaries for similar jobs within the computer industry. The organization must be seen to have a good salary record.
. Job security can be a worrying and distractive factor for staff, if, for example, the organization has a history of redundancy.
. Staff are conscious of status, and this requires an individual be given a job title; placed in a publicized structure; and is aware of his position in the hierarchy.

. The organization's policy and administration can range from being institutionalized or traditional, with formal rigid procedures, to being relaxed and easy-going, with a certain amount of freedom to adopt individual ideas. People may prefer either extreme or the shades in between. This factor needs to be considered when assigning or recruiting staff.
. Poor working conditions can suppress output, although good conditions will not necessarily improve motivation. Included in this category are the state of desks, offices, noise, telephones, heat, light, etc.
. Jobs requiring long hours of work rarely deter people who are otherwise satisfied.
. Having to travel to and from work is something people tend to accept without too much concern.
. Adverse social and business personal relationships might tend to demotivate. For example when clashing personalities work together, or if the department has a cold and impersonal atmosphere.
. An individual may have problems in his personal life, which could affect his job performance. If possible, the manager should offer counsel or support.

HOW TO IMPROVE JOB SATISFACTION AND STAFF MOTIVATION

It is one thing to read (and comprehend) a list of factors, like those above, that purport to motivate staff. However, this is oceans apart from a manager actually doing something about improving job satisfaction (and the ensuing improved motivation), which should hopefully result in greater effectiveness and better productivity.

Many managers, by their nature or lack of training, are insensitive to the need to improve motivation in their areas. Some feel that their priority as a manager is ensuring that their staff are at all times kept working hard at the job in hand. Staff must be seen to be productive: work output is paramount. Others claim, that as they are so snowed under with work and business pressures, they cannot take the time out for the 'luxuries' of attempting to improve their staff's job satisfaction. Some well-intentioned managers may have made an attempt at improving motivation, but soon realized that their efforts are in vain.

Basically, the problem is that management actions in this area of improving job satisfaction are not just like switching on a light. It may require fundamental changes to the 'fabric' of the organization, including alterations to management structure and possibly the replacement of certain managers. It also requires a gradual change in attitudes of mind at all levels. In some instances, the task may be nearly impossible: how does one motivate a person sweeping a shop-floor?

This section attempts therefore, to bring together a selection of relevant recommendations. Some of these are elaborated in a different context elsewhere in this book, and it shall be seen how they also relate to improving the motivation of staff who are involved in systems development. This list is by no means exhaustive but purely illustrative.

Making the best use of abilities

Computing is in the 'brains business' and associated staff generally are anxious to execute demanding tasks. They are, therefore, reluctant to become engaged on repetitive or low-skill assignments. Several topics have related to making the best use of people's abilities. The recommended structure of the computer department (as in Chapter 3) is one prime example. In particular, the establishment of specialist pools with career managers, ensures that abilities are both developed and utilized to the full. The desire of DP specialists to keep up with new ideas so that they are able to tackle high-technology problems, requires an element of training, which can take the form of formal courses or seminars, as well as 'on the job' experience. Subsequent sections in this chapter on staff training and staff appraisals are also geared to the optimization of abilities (but also within the constraints of the job to be done), as is the recommended method (in Chapter 10) of planning project skills and the method of assigning and scheduling work to project staff. In addition, Chapter 11, concerning project organization is aimed at providing the right people, with the appropriate skills at the correct time.

Interest in Work

Suggestions for keeping staff interested in their work include them using (where relevant) the latest technologies and techniques. This in turn requires an awareness of what is happening in the DP industry. Achieving this is not as easy as it appears (as most salesmen of hardware, software, or DP services will readily testify!). Where possible, the work itself should be innovative or involve recent technology in order to improve job interest. This may necessitate having to use a higher risk end-product technology if a 'safe' batch system was originally being contemplated. If the planned work in hand does not lend itself to this, a possible compromise might be to set-up a (part-time if necessary) research section to examine the relevance of, for example, microcomputers to the organization, or the cost benefits of developing communication based systems.

In some cases, loss of job interest may be caused by having to work on system maintenance simultaneously with systems development, with the former usually having a higher priority and distracting from an even work flow on the latter. Many ideas have been given for resolving this problem, especially in Chapter 3.

Worthwhile job

People like to think that their work is worthwhile, and they do not wish to be considered as an overhead to the organization. Similarly, their department should not be viewed as ineffective within the organization. It should not be too difficult (in theory) for DP management to demonstrate that the work on which their development staff is engaged is essential to the organization. This may be achieved, in part, by keeping open good communication with the users, and by DP staff having first-hand contact with the users' difficulties, and hence seeing whether their end-product will in fact be worthwhile. The other part of demonstrating that a job is worthwhile is not only by carrying out thorough cost justifications of projects, but to make sure this is done *visibly for all* levels of staff working on the project, with clearly defined benefits highlighted. Having initially justified to staff how *their* work is vital, a psychological spin-off from the business reviews (conducted by senior management at the end of each phase of the project) is that project staff can be continually reminded that their work is essential to the organization.

Recognition of effort

This leads on to the general question of 'recognition of effort' being a contributory factor to job satisfaction. A formal appraisal system may be relevant, but is somewhat limited in this context, because it usually occurs only once a year. Recognition of an individual's efforts needs to be more spontaneous and frequent and should not only be implied, but, when appropriate, an individual should be told by his manager that he is appreciated. Similarly, computer staff require to receive some respect for the skills they possess. This could manifest itself by their advice being taken (when appropriate). Recognition may be especially difficult to achieve if there is a long project with no tangible end-product for 3 years. The strong emphasis placed on the use of milestones is also of relevance. Achieving results, or passing milestones encourages pride in one's work, and produces a sense of accomplishment coupled with the satisfaction of seeing a job completed, being of use, and working efficiently. Another way of looking at this aspect is that success breeds success, and it may therefore be advisable to have to complete satisfactorily many short duration projects or milestones, rather than lengthy ones.

The size of an organization and job satisfaction

Many people appear to be satisfied with their jobs if they work for a small organization. Obviously the march of time cannot be stopped and companies cannot be prevented from growing or merging. Nor can the tendency be stopped towards bigger national and international under-takings, which in turn require large computing facilities, (e.g. in banking, weather forecasting, civil engineering, nuclear physics, aeronautics, etc.). How then can a manager in a large organization use this preference for smallness, to improve job satisfaction?

One way is to utilize the project concept (as recommended in this book) to its fullest meaning, which also includes breaking-up very large projects into successive smaller ones. The people within these type of projects see a (relatively) small, compact, independent group, highly effective, with a profit motive. In other words, this situation is attempting to mirror a small independent firm.

Another way of creating 'smallness' may be facilitated by introducing distributed computing into a large organization. By devolving, to the periphery, the responsibility for the development, implementation, or the live running of systems, smaller units will be created with more say over their own systems and processing requirements, and over how they will manage the development of their systems.

Self-employed and job satisfaction

The observation that self-employed people have a greater job satisfaction may at first sight imply that the practice of engaging contract programmers or analysts should be actively encouraged. However, this may be a case of the staff being happier, but the development work and the project may suffer. Common objections to contract staff include the lack of commitment to the organization, difficulty in taking over their work after they leave, and in making them work the times when they are most needed. This approach is not, therefore, recommended, even though situations are known to exist where, because of (adverse) labour laws and a desire to reduce 'head-counts' on the payroll, a computer department may have more self-employed staff than company employees.

Near the top

Job satisfaction often improves the nearer one reaches to the top of the hierarchy, presumably because of closer apparent control over one's own destiny. The project concept can, once again, be relevant in this context of improving job satisfaction, where a self-contained project, comprising a relatively few levels of management, often reports near to the organization's top executives. In this environment, project staff and team managers, being very close to a 'powerful' project manager who may appear to have a 'carte blanche', may feel less of a little cog in a big wheel than, say, operatives in a very large monolithic department.

Respect for the boss

Respect for the boss can be gained in several ways. First, has the right man been appointed? The previous sections dealing with the qualities of managers in DP may be of assistance when answering this question. These included comments on ideals for heads of management services, system development managers, project managers, team leaders, etc. A fairly common problem in DP is that a manager with inappropriate experience is appointed within the management hierarchy. This tends to be sensed readily and causes demotivation.

Poor supervision might demotivate, and so it is necessary for a manager to make sure that things are done professionally with the adoption of correct attitudes of mind to work.

A further factor which may cause disrespect for one's boss may arise in those cases where senior management visibly does not understand DP, nor comprehends their own role in project control. A long, slow, uphill climb is often necessary by all levels of managers in the computer department, to provide the necessary education.

The need for strategic planning as a motivator

The purpose of strategy in this motivation context is to drive one's team to attain the maximum of achievement by setting longer term goals which enable them to see where they are going. By the very nature of their jobs, computer analysts and programmers are usually reasonably intelligent, logical, and creative (as are many specialists). Their egos and their incentives should be stimulated by realistic and worthwhile strategic goals, which in turn, improves the motivation for their assigned tasks. It is desirable for this factor relating to strategy and motivation to be appreciated by a computer manager who should produce long term and in depth plans. It is inadvisable to rely on keeping staff busy with ad hoc work. These strategies need not only relate to successful projects (which eventually turn out as having had good estimates and kept to targets) but might also relate to strategically improving user co-operation, or to providing improved corporate personnel policies which are more relevant for DP and project staff.

Chances of promotion

For an individual to be able to see his chances for promotion, a career development strategy is required. The earlier recommendation of making special career managers responsible for career development, not project managers, is also relevant. However, an individual should be able to ascertain indentifiable prospects, and this includes a career path within the organization, the computer department, the project, as well as within his team. Poor performers holding key positions are often a demotivating factor, as these people may appear to hold back promotion chances of high-fliers.

A staff appraisal procedure is discussed later in this chapter and some of the ideas in it may be relevant to making the prospects of promotion more apparent. Seeing is believing, and so it is necessary to create a history of good promotions. One way of doing this is by generating growth and using one's initiative to establish new ventures (e.g. go professionally into the service bureau market), or set-up new departments (e.g. one that assesses and installs office automation facilities).

Staff development

The obvious reason for considering staff development is to keep them abreast of relevant technological changes, and for them to acquire appropriate skills for the benefit of the department or project. This interpretation is more akin to training, but is only part of the requirement. To obtain the most out of a useful professional computer man, as with many similar specialists, he needs to be 'drawn along by a carrot dangling in front him'. This 'carrot', which must be seen, takes the form of greater responsibility; bigger projects; more interesting or advanced applications or promotion. It is up to the skilful manager to carry out a balancing act between the development needs of each of his staff, and the project's or department's requirements. For example, in some cases, it may be necessary to avoid an individual becoming stuck in one particular job or skill. This may be important in those situations when there is no-one to replace him, and his particular knowledge. This person may see no way out, and may tend to become demotivated. Sensible recruiting and movements of people will prevent this situation occurring. Alternatively, it may be appropriate to provide supervisory experience as part of the computer staff's development plan. Sensible recruiting or job rotation may provide juniors for the established staff to supervise, the latter, becoming qualified for their own promotion.

Career development

A career development plan should be produced jointly between each man and his (career) manager. First, this should comprise a list of the relevant formal organization progression grades (or promotional titles) a particular person wishes to attain in the long term. The salary ranges associated with these grades should also be included (although this may be taboo in many organizations). A list should then be drawn up of the relevant skills needed to attain the next level of promotion (in approximate chronological sequence). This list can then be implemented by stating how the experience is to be achieved in practice, by the individual, and what his specific responsibilities will be. Finally, an approximate training plan can be devised to enable him to fulfil these duties. However, all this assumes an overall strategy to build on, with the management of the computer department knowing where they are going and being in control of events.

Career training

There is a tendency for some people to equate training to education and courses. There is more to training than just courses. On-the-job experience and relevant supervision is another element. Another aspect is matching the immediate department's or project's tasks with the total career development plan previously discussed. Formal training should support this plan, but training is expensive, so it is important to match booked courses against both the individual's personal requirements, and the project's or department's needs. Often courses prove to be irrelevant or a waste of time to the individuals involved, because they are out-of-step with their career plans. How many DP staff are appeased and go on irrelevant, fashionable database or real-time courses? Or how many consultants, who may not be natural management material, are sent on project management courses, as no other career development course can be found?

Choice of work

Giving people a choice of work, with an element of independence, obviously depends on the type of work in hand. Someone has to do all of it; even the dreary tasks! However, the recommended method of planning and assigning project work may be of assistance in spreading the load as appropriately as possible. More generally though, the old cliche of a manager delegating responsibility is just one aspect of this. In a similar vein the boss not continually looking over his staff's shoulders is also relevant advice.

Plenty of work

'Hard work hurts no-one,' and it may seem difficult to dissatisfy staff by giving them insufficient work. However, a programmer waiting to use a program specification which is late, or an analyst waiting for the results of his system test (which is held up because of the computer's poor turn-round), will readily vouch for the apparent inevitability of forced idleness. The recommendations in Chapter 13 on project control may be relevant, as is the general advice on minimizing departmental interactions by incorporating the relevant people into a project. From a negative point of view, to a certain extent keeping staff very busy with tight deadlines, prevents demotivation because they do not have the time to think about anything else but work.

Group identity

The fairly strong desire of people to be associated with a group may be used quite effectively in the project concept. Ploys based on this psychology are elaborated in many parts of this book. In fact several recommendations relating to project administration are based on a visible project identity, an impressive project name, and even a symbol associated with the project.

Least important factors

If a manager has to make a choice between several possible alternatives that might improve job satisfaction, which factors seem less important?

Spending money on improving the physical working conditions and the comfort of offices, although socially desirable, may not buy much in the way of increased productivity or improved job satisfaction. (It is probably purely co-incidence, but the author's most stimulating assignments have been in very poor offices which were eventually condemned or due for demolition, whilst the reverse has applied to assignments in the most modern or well furnished offices).

In general, DP staff, especially those brought up in project work, are used to panics in order to achieve deadlines. Compared to many other industries, DP staff are very flexible in their working habits. For example, long hours of work appear to upset few people (especially once they are used to it), so consequently, a manager need not worry too much about asking staff to put in extra hours to meet deadlines or carry out over-night testing etc.

Having to travel to and from work does not appear to concern people too much. So asking staff, especially younger personnel, to work in a roving consultancy or a trouble shooting role, or installing a distributed system, all of which may necessitate visiting geographically spread sites, should not prove to be too much of a problem.

Conclusions on improving job satisfaction

We have seen that improving job satisfaction may necessitate all levels of management address a whole range of issues. These may span from the structure of the computer department, as determined by the head of management services, to the quality of supervision by team leaders. In fact, Figure 12.1 is an attempt to illustrate, for a selection of factors discussed in this section, the most appropriate manager(s) who may be able to do something about implementing the relevant recommendations. It should be apparent that improving job satisfaction is not easy. Apart from such trivia as avoiding continually looking over staffs' shoulders, there are only a few things any one individual manager can perform in isolation. In fact many improvements involve senior non DP management. What is more usually required is a combined effort by all levels of management to changing the fabric of the organization, as alluded to at the beginning of this section.

GENERAL AND CORPORATE PERSONNEL POLICIES AND TECHNIQUES

The following are further observations relating to man management, but are of a more general nature and impinge on the organization as a whole.

The role of DP staff as a motivator

The average person in DP often appears to be disgruntled with his lot. This job dissatisfaction could be due to the fact that, as computing is much younger than many other professions, it is less well-defined, and accordingly its ideas are not always accepted. Other groups of business specialists, such as accountants, production controllers, actuaries, etc. have a historically accepted job-definition, function and reporting structure within organizations.

Figure table — LEVEL OF MANAGEMENT vs. FACTORS AFFECTING JOB SATISFACTION:

Team leaders	Career managers	Project manager	Systems development manager	Head of computer department	Senior (non DP) management	Factors affecting job satisfaction	Factor
				*		Computer department structure	ABILITY
	*	*	*	*		Use of career managers	
		*	*			Project skills analysis and planning	
*		*	*			Assigning and scheduling project tasks	
			*			Project structures and organization	
	*					Training in new techniques and technologies	
*	*					Appraisals for formalizing abilities	
			*			Using latest techniques and technologies	INTEREST
			*		*	Innovative systems *vs.* reliable projects	
				*		Research groups for new ideas	
				*		Separate maintenance work	
*		*			*	Communication of users' benefits	WORTHWHILE
			*	*	*	Cost justification of projects	
			*	*	*	Phase end business reviews and feedback	
*	*	*	*	*	*	Giving praise	RECOGNITION
*		*	*			Taking advice	
	*					Appraisals/sense of accomplishment	
*		*				Use of milestones to breed success	
			*	*	*	Projects to generate smaller units	SMALLNESS
			*	*		Distributed computing	
		*	*	*	*	Projects and few levels of management	NEAR TOP
		*	*	*		Passing down levels of responsibility	
*	*		*	*		Input to corporate/business plans	
*	*			*		Right qualities of appointed managers	RESPECT FOR BOSS
						Professional supervision	
					*	Senior management not understanding DP	
		*	*		*	Planned phased project work	STRATEGIC PLANNING
			*		*	Avoid being event driven	
				*	*	Corporate personnel policies for DP	
*	*	*				Avoid short term *ad hoc* assignments	
			*		*	User co-operation in DP	
			*	*	*	DP career development strategy	CHANCES OF PROMOTION IN ORGANIZATION
			*	*		Use of career managers	
			*	*		Establish career paths	
			*	*		Poor performers blocking career paths	
	*		*	*	*	Appraisals and formalizing opportunities	
			*	*	*	History of growth and new ventures	
	*	*	*			Balancing work with staff's requirements	PERSONAL CAREER DEVELOPMENT
	*		*	*		Job rotation	
	*	*	*	*	*	Balanced recruiting policy	
	*					Personal career plans	
	*		*			Skills/experience requirements	
	*	*	*			Relevant training plans	
*	*	*	*			Consultative planning and assigning work	CHOICE OF WORK
*	*	*	*	*		Manager delegating work	
*	*	*	*	*		Avoiding looking over staffs' shoulders	
*		*	*	*		Project control	PLENTY OF WORK
			*	*		Minimize interactions and dependencies	
*		*				Setting tight deadlines	
*	*	*				Keep busy with *ad hoc* work	
		*	*			Project administration techniques	GROUP IDENTITY
		*	*			Project logo, central files, etc.	
			*	*	*	Project team concept	
			*	*	*	Salary in step with DP industry	LEAST IMPORTANT FACTORS
			*	*	*	Offices and general working conditions	
			*	*	*	Security	
	*	*	*	*		Status, title, and hierarchy	

Figure 12.1 Who might improve job satisfaction

An example of how a person's role affects his work relates to systems analysts who are often trained by the computing industry

(a) to believe they are the managers of programmers and other project staff or
(b) to fill a much more important and strategic *business* role than merely serving the programmers with specifications.

The art of man management in this context is to face the situation head on, and avoid possible demotivation of any particular member of staff via discussions aimed at tempering expectancy with the practical realities of the installation.

While on the subject of the role of systems analysts, it is sometimes necessary to question their apparent absolute power which may be exercised when designing systems *for other people* to work and live with. In this age of industrial democracy, it may be claimed, what right has the analyst (who is often young or at a relatively low level in the organization's hierarchy) to be so presumptuous as to decide how a group of people (i.e. all the staff in the user departments) will work? Surely, it may be argued, even the user clerks have a right to influence and to determine their optimum work pattern. They also may require a say in how they are organized and structured. Sometimes, the outputs from the computer system and their sequence, determine how the user department is organized, not the other way round. Where appropriate, the role of the systems analyst should take this into account, but the mechanics of its implementation depend upon corporate attitudes, the responsiveness of the users, and the relationships between the DP department and the users.

Corporate personnel policies for project staff

Introducing a project management philosophy is not easy. It is necessary for organizations who adopt this approach, first to introduce special personnel policies that will enable them to attract, mobilize, and retain the necessary high calibre project staff and project managers.

Project staff

For example, staff may need to be held in a pool to allow flexibility in assigning and releasing them from projects. This pool should hold them in a *constructive* way between assignments to different projects. Employing contract staff for a fixed duration may be the only way to staff single projects in organizations not contemplating any growth in DP. In this case, the organization's remuneration policy and its terms of employment may have to differ for these people. Project staff may be required to work, when necessary, long hours or at weekends. For many projects, there is a disruption to home life which can be further aggravated by travel. These irregular working conditions may require policy decisions which allow flexibility in giving time-off in lieu, or in paying disturbance allowances, or in granting overtime payments. This leads on to the question of incentive bonuses, based on achievement of target, for project staff. This is an accepted method of motivating staff to achieve dead-lines. As many of these factors may be at variance with a company's policy for line department staff, these personnel conflicts should be resolved at senior management level.

Project managers

In general, it is not usually successful to employ contract project managers. It should, therefore, be beneficial for organizations who are employing project managers, to adopt career paths for them. This, in turn, means the introduction of several grades of promotion each reflecting different levels of complexity of project management. Appropriate training is also required, which ties up with this approach to their careers. After a project has been completed, the project manager returns to a pool, but a personnel problem may exist, because there is no other suitable project for the unengaged project manager. Career development in-fills are, therefore, required in a planned manner.

Recruitment of staff

Balance of experience and background

When recruiting, it could prove beneficial for the manager to strike a balance between *internally* recruited users (who may have little computer expertise, but should preferably be dynamic) and *externally* recruited professional computer people (possibly not having the relevant industry knowledge). Similarly, it may be advisable that a balance is struck between *senior* and *junior* staff, to enable promotions to take place readily. Lastly, a suitable combination could be appropriate between *service* orientated people recruited from hardware or software suppliers, consultancies or service bureaux, and people recruited from *computer user* installations. These people need not necessarily have experience of the computer being used within the installation or of the applications being developed. The exact ratios of personnel will be dictated by the actual projects and the jobs to be done, as well as the current state of the DP manpower recruitment market.

A department, or large project, with the above cross-section of staff, could benefit by striking a happy medium between producing a technically introvert, in-bred computer man, and possibly, a more healthy dynamic situation provided by cross-fertilization and influx of fresh ideas and an awareness of computing in the outside world. This also tends to eliminate the technique orientated approach often associated with individual computing people; for example, preference for a certain software package, or data validation being performed in a set manner on a mainframe rather than by local data entry equipment.

In all cases, a compromise should exist between a project's requirements and the overall computer department's staffing philosophy. One important reason is that at the end of a project, it's staff usually return to the pool, and they must be suitable for employment on another project.

The mechanics

Usually, a project will be staffed from within the computer department and the user departments. Sometimes this may involve relevant people from associated companies. This staffing process takes place in conjunction with senior line management and the management within the computer department. In certain cases, it may be possible to obtain staff from the hardware or software suppliers, on a temporary basis, or to employ contract programmers via an agency. However, it may be necessary to recruit externally and to resort to advertising in the national press or to approach staff recruitment agencies.

A golden rule when recruiting computer staff is to 'do it yourself' and not to depend exclusively on the personnel department. It is unreasonable to expect a personnel department to be aware of individual requirements for staff, the type of people to recruit, the idiosyncrasies of the computer job market, or the job specification in question. The personnel department unknowingly may put the wrong connotation on advertisements, supply applicants with the wrong or misleading information, and because of pressures of work from other departments delay sending out letters of offer.

Typically, one may receive upwards of 70 replies to national advertisements and to interview approximately 20 promising applicants. One can then find that the standard of applicants is much lower than imagined, and only two or three people will prove suitable, but are considering other offers. This is a fact of life that must be appreciated if an expansion is planned requiring a substantial recruiting drive. The management involved should allow a considerable amount of time for this exercise, expecially if high quality staff are required. In fact, the task is not only time-consuming and tedious, but the success rate could be low; the process demoralizing; and the end result may be unsatisfactory. Installations able to afford a departmental support group, could well benefit if recruitment is made their responsibility, with the relevant managers in the computer department only carrying out the final interviews for those promising applicants filtered out.

Bearing in mind the low hit rates, and the considerable management over-heads, usually a good case can be made for employing a professional recruitment firm to undertake the basic advertising and filtering. Management effort can then be concentrated on selecting from a short list. Figure 12.2 is a practical, tested checklist that could assist in recruitment.

Management's problems do not end here! If the manager (or department) is successful in recruiting large numbers of staff, there is then the problem of assimilation. Considerable expenditure is required to train new staff for both the job and the organization, and it can take several months before they are fully productive and motivated.

Years experience (in different DP technical skills)
Size of computer configurations worked on
Technical experience in DP products, languages, operating systems, and techniques.
Types of DP standards used
Formal technical DP training received

Business experience   —   types of industry
                                —   types of business functions
Formal commercial and business training received
Experience in negotiating with senior user line management
Application systems worked on
Size of projects worked on
Project development phases worked on

Formal management training received
Years experience in management (line or functional)
Management of who and what
Number of staff managed and their levels
Budget responsibility

Existing position in current employment, illustrated with a hierarchy chart
Why the applicant wishes to leave his present job
Salary and fringe benefits   —   now
                                —   expected

Notice period
General appearance
Ability to communicate and inspire confidence
Experience in giving training and instruction
Number of previous jobs and their frequency of change

Figure 12.2 A recruitment checklist

Staff appraisal

One aspect of staff career development is the formal appraisal, which can be used to highlight strengths and weaknesses in order to utilize strengths or improve weaknesses. There should be *no surprises* at the formal appraisal, because all the relevant factors should have been discussed on numerous occasions throughout the rest of the year. In fact, if the manager steers the appraisal correctly, the person being appraised should list all his strengths and weaknesses without any prompting. The practical consequences however, are often limited because it could be difficult to make noticeable improvements to weaknesses. If the person being appraised cannot communicate proficiently either in writing or verbally, any number of training courses will not cure the problem completely. The manager should, in this case, deploy him accordingly. Another example might be a person unable to keep 'many balls in the air' and unable to work well under strain. In this case, if he thinks the person worth keeping, the manager should give him only one full-time activity that does not involve many users or interacting computer projects.

An enlightened manager may take the above ideas a stage further by analysing the adverse effects caused by *himself* on the person in question. The *uncertainty principle* can, to an extent, be applied to human relations. This means that an observation by a manager when trying to ascertain his staff's ability, affects this measurement by his own (adverse) personality traits. An extreme example of this is a clash of personalities causing a particular member of staff to be unhappy and demotivated. A lesser example is differing opinions on an adopted technique. Consequently, the performance and achievements of that member of staff may be way below what he would have attained under a different manager. During an appraisal (and throughout the rest of the year) a manager must look to see if he is reflected in his staff's performance. He needs to establish the underlying cause for problems and consider if they are a result of his own bad management, or even that of the organization itself.

Limitation of career development planning

It has previously been suggested that encouraging career development plans for each member of staff is of benefit—especially as a means for improving motivation. This statement needs qualification. In some situations, this approach to management may be well-intentioned and seems good in theory, but in practice may go too far, and adversely affect both the organization as well as some individuals.

Irrelevant situations

Often, departments need many people to perform mundane or repetitive work. There is little point in developing staff in such a department so that it comprises all 'chiefs' undertaking stimulating work, but having no 'workers'. The net result may be disillusionment with the organization. Alternatively, there may be no mutual benefit obtained in encouraging some people to develop their careers away from routine, clerical, or administrative jobs. This especially applies where people are happy with their work routine and do not seek advancement. The security of a constant and predictable job may, indeed, be a motivator. Many programmers, for example, are quite content to code and do not want to supervise. Some people do not want to be pressurized into thinking about their career development, and in fact, positively resent this interference. They may simply be unambitious, or do not wish to move geographically or to a different part of the organization. In general, the personal reasons for this state of mind are limitless. A few ambitious senior managers seem unable to accept this, expecting everyone to be as enthusiastic about career development as they are themselves.

Corporate systems for career development

Taken to its extreme, a situation may arise with career development planning, whereby an organization's main measure of each member of staff's performance is proportional to his or her own promotional prospects. Someone who, it is estimated, may be recommended for promotion within one year is 'better' and receives a greater percentage salary increase than a person who, it is similarly estimated, may be recommended for promotion in two years' time. In fact, in these situations, the staff appraisals may be geared to promotions, with no way of giving recognition to the invaluable 'plodder'. Alternatively a formal 'career development system' with special forms may be introduced in order to encourage job moves. Job enrichment and utilizing staff's talents to the full, are associated claimed benefits. However, in this case, where it is necessary to complete these special career forms, it is not unknown for staff and their managers to invent possible moves because these may be judged, within the organization, as 'good' for career development. This corporate process may also become, by necessity, unselective. It is difficult to have some people in the system, but not others. Consequently, examples can be quoted of people over 60 years' old who are approaching retirement, or of cleaning personnel being asked to consider their careers.

Dashing staff's expectations

If staff are interested in career development, expectations may be built up of imminent upgradings, or of new technical experience, or of challenging new areas of work. Usually, these expectations cannot be met in weeks, but may take many months or years to effect, if at all.

If an employee wishes to change jobs within the organization (even without an associated upgrade), his current department may be reluctant to release him until a suitable replacement has been found. Alternatively, the person in question may not have the necessary professional qualifications, or levels of experience for the desired job. Frequently, an ambitious person, but with limited ability, believes that his own experience and attitude to work justifies his rapid promotion. However, the image he portrays to the rest of the organization, coupled with the more direct assessment by his superiors, destines him to more limited corporate prospects. Given a career development system, this type of person may become more engrossed in his personal future than in applying himself to the benefit of the organization. His work output may become deflected from achievements in his current work, but instead expended on planning his career. The net effect could be a more disgruntled employee than if career development ideas were not encouraged in the first place.

If an employee's career development plan proposes an upgrade sometime in the future, the probability of this promotion actually occurring diminishes the nearer the top of the ladder he climbs. Not everyone can be senior management. An organization's management hierarchy consists of the normal pyramid; there are simply less jobs nearer the top.

In addition to these factors, in an economic down-turn, or a contracting industry, people may be more worried about retaining their jobs than with promotions. In this example, as indeed with those referred to above, an unnecessary build up of hopes may be dashed.

The need for some form of career development planning

Career development planning is not being denigrated in this section, only its limitations are being illustrated somewhat dramatically. Development of 'high fliers' is obviously essential in order to retain them and to use their talents effectively. In this connection, the earlier section on motivation is relevant where corporate committees or individual managers affect career changes as and when appropriate. At the other extreme, moving people about may become necessary in order to avoid them becoming 'stale' after several years in one job. Some people may lie somewhere in the middle between these two needs. Career development guidance and counselling may be appropriate in these cases. Suitable areas of work may be mutually ascertained, where their personal strengths may be utilized and their weaknesses not highly exposed.

In a similar vein, career planning at the lower staff levels is much easier than for senior managers, because more potential opportunities exist, which offer greater flexibility and more scope for realistic planning. This philosophy may lead to a practical compromise whereby the careers of the more junior levels of staff are actively planned and encouraged. Once given a good start by the organization, the middle and senior levels of staff, so far as their careers are concerned, are to a certain extent left to their own devices.

In summarizing, caution, selectivity, and relevance is being advocated, otherwise this exercise may become counter-productive. Career development planning, as has been demonstrated, may result in demotivation, rather than the expected motivation.

Management by objectives

A management technique that has been in vogue for several years is management by objectives. Each person throughout the organization is set specific purposes and objectives, which preferably are quantified and relate to the organization's business plan. These objectives are passed down the hierarchy, being expanded to the appropriate level of detail, so that the objectives of the people working at the 'coal-face' reflect the implementation of the organization's business plan. Additionally, an individual's objectives may become augmented with parochial or local departmental objectives, as well as personnel orientated objectives aimed at self-betterment. In many organizations, the first part of a formal appraisal document is a statement of all these objectives.

A practical snag with management by objectives is that certain individuals may become demotivated by its introduction, as they feel some of their initiative is being removed, and they are being placed in a straight-jacket. Also it is often difficult to pass down meaningful objectives. More important though, performance may be reduced and complacency introduced; which is the exact opposite of what is intended! This may best be illustrated by an example of a fairly common type of objective, whereby an area manager must improve volume growth (i.e. over and above inflation) by 10% p.a., or a financial controller expects any project to achieve a minimum of 15% return on capital employed. In some cases, these objectives may be easily achieved by the manager setting himself a finite amount of work, just sufficient to meet his objectives, possibly with a little to spare. He can then move on to other ancillary or supportive activities.

Compare this with a self-motivated manager, or even a self-employed business man, who is not blinkered by a growth target of 10% p.a. As far as he may be concerned, the sky is the limit. The market in his area may be able to absorb 30% growth, and he may work to this objective without even imagining that a 'constraint' of 10% could have been introduced. In fact, two different managers working in these two different environments may talk a different language and not understand each other's method of working. For example, the manager who has only worked in a management by objectives environment, cannot comprehend why the other manager spends most of his time *optimizing* the profitability of a new venture, and is not content in stopping when he has planned for the nominal 15% return.

CHAPTER SUMMARY

The main emphasis, prior to this chapter, has been on work as opposed to people. This follows the philosophy that if work dictates are not put first, there will not be any jobs, nor the need to employ people! However, people considerations should not follow too far behind; without good people the jobs cannot be achieved. This chapter attaches great importance to the actual managers and technical staff at all levels, and attempts to show how good management can combine a correct attitude to work with personal preferences in order to produce well motivated staff.

It is first necessary to have the right man in the right job. Starting with the head of the computer department, numerous desirable qualities are elaborated. This is followed by a similar treatment for other managers within the installation, including the special attributes required for a successful project manager.

A great emphasis is placed on the motivation of staff and many factors are examined, both from the theoretical and practical viewpoints. Having itemized these, the difficult subject is tackled of what management actions are required to improve job satisfaction and motivation. To achieve this, numerous concepts and techniques expounded in other chapters, possibly in another context, have been brought together to show how they may equally apply to improving motivation. An attempt has also been made to illustrate which level of management within an organization can implement each recommendation. It is apparent, not unsurprisingly, that one manager may find it difficult to make dramatic improvements in morale or job satisfaction by himself. The whole organization is involved.

A concluding section covers general and corporate personnel policies and techniques. Topics covered include the role of DP staff, the difficulties of establishing a personnel framework for project working, ideas on recruiting, staff appraisals, and on management by objectives.

Chapter 13

Project control

Having at great length planned the work-load, assigned people to the tasks, and examined how best to motivate them, the outcome of all these concepts are combined by way of project control. First, an analysis is conducted of what is project control, why it is only a sub-set of project management, who is responsible for project control, and why each level of management sees project control in a different light. Various control techniques are covered, together with recommendations on their relevance to different types of management's plans. The 'knotty', but universal problem of measuring progress is tackled, and this leads to specifying the requirements of quantitative project control systems. Examples of these are given together with advice on what to do when difficulties occur, and on the subject of written upwards reporting.

WHAT IS PROJECT CONTROL?

Before examining what is being controlled, let us first consider the meaning of *project management* in its widest sense. In order to manage successfully a corporate project, it has been necessary to encompass a wide range of concepts that include the following formidable list: the structure and role of the computer department, the structure of the project within the organization, the reviewing role of senior management, costs, benefits and budgets, development in formal phases, end-product technology, development techniques, development standards, quality control, the approach to testing, planning methodologies, man management, training, documentation, project organization, support, administration, changes control, contingency planning, etc. These aspects, and more, are management considerations that span the duration of a project in both depth and breadth. This is what is meant by *project management*.

Management can be defined as: planning, assigning tasks, monitoring, comparing against prescribed standards of work quality, recording progress, highlighting variances, controlling, re-planning and re-scheduling when appropriate. Project management in particular, means applying this sequence of management tasks to each item on the above extensive list of important considerations which affect projects. This definition of management leads us to define control (and project control in particular) as the sub-set of the above definition of project management which relates to 'the awareness of progress and the taking of alternative action as necessary'.

In practice, this definition of project control may become further reduced in scope because:

(a) Different levels of management are responsible for various aspects of control, i.e. any one level of manager sees project control in a different light from another.
(b) Only some items in the range of concepts listed above under the project management heading require sophisticated control.
(c) The key requirement of measuring *progress* (which is necessary before one is able to exercise control) is not an easy or absolute measurement.
(d) In many organizations, the term 'project control' is synonymous with a clerical or mechanised system, which requires input forms to record work undertaken, and produces output reports for management's attention.

If the original question, 'What is project control?', is now asked, a valid reply in one installation might be simply 'a project control system which records the expenditure of manpower, resources and costs'. The approach adopted in this chapter is to examine the factors which contribute towards project control in its widest sense, so that individual managers within an installation can extract those aspects relevant to their own needs.

WHO IS RESPONSIBLE FOR PROJECT CONTROL?

In a small installation, where the data processing manager performs a major part of a project's management, his responsibility for project control is reasonably clear-cut. The main area of doubt is around senior management's or user management's responsibility in controlling the project. On the other hand, the situation in a very large installation is far from clear-cut, with a hierarchy of management encompassing supervisors, team leaders, programming managers, project managers, a systems development manager, a head of management services, user management, steering committees, etc. In fact, the control aspects are so variable that each installation tends to find its own natural state by filling management gaps or delegating responsibilities depending on personalities and circumstances. What is important, though, is (a) ensuring that all the project management and associated control is, in fact, carried out, (b) appreciating that the control requirements for different levels of management will vary considerably and (c) understanding that the project control emphasis may well alter as the project progresses. (e.g. controlling testing requires a different approach to the control of a feasibility study).

A simplistic example of the diversity of project control may be that the financial director is interested in budgetary control (and therefore requires detailed financial information regarding costs for development); the senior line user manager might be concerned about the cost benefits for his proposed computerized system (and therefore requires detailed performance projections of the end-product); the project manager, who may be judged primarily on his ability to meet target dates, might be involved in measuring and controlling any slippage in time; the systems development manager may be interested in adherence to standards (and will be interested in the quality control reporting); and a programming team leader may be perturbed by apparent slow coding rates (and might require productivity information).

CONTROL TECHNIQUES

Not necessarily PERT

Project control might conjure up visions of vast PERT networks requiring regular meetings with all participants to update these networks. Although this technique was discussed in relation to planning, it is suggested that it may not always be appropriate for project control purposes, but possibly better suited for the planning stage, when clarifying proposed work. Although there can be little dispute about the power of network techniques for projects in general, its main benefit for the control of interactions may be more relevant to engineering types of development projects. In practice, the problems of interactions in DP projects are better resolved in other, more personal ways.

It is not uncommon for up to 10% of development effort being absorbed in establishing a complex network, and then keeping it updated, corrected and meaningful. As PERT is orientated towards the elapsed-time of tasks, or events in time, it is not always easy to control the productivity or performance of individual members of staff on a weekly basis. Similarly, unscheduled or non-project work is difficult to measure. If PERT appears to be needed for control purposes it might indicate that the computer project could be too complex, and it may be better to divide it into several smaller phased projects.

In practice, PERT, for controlling all stages of a computer project, may be difficult to use, set up, update and to understand, even if a computer PERT system is utilised. It could confuse the line users, and it is impersonalized. A project manager who depends on PERT may tend to rely on it to the detriment of carrying out his job properly. Subsequently, PERT outputs may only advise the manager of the consequences of his poor management.

An example of the misuse of PERT

The UK subsidiary of an American parent company was instructed to use a PERT package to control important development projects. The first project to fall within this ruling probably benefited whilst the network was being set up, as this exercise clarified thinking about the necessary tasks ahead. This PERT package was run weekly on the installation's computer, and the outputs were received by senior management, as well as sent to the parent company in the United States. After about six months, the project's end-date was still shown as the next April. During the previous December, the DPM, without consultation, confidently committed the project to this April end date. The project members were furious because they knew April had always been impossible, and they would be at least four month's late. The reasons for this discrepancy were manifold:

(a) as some departments did not benefit, they were not fully committed to supplying accurate input to the PERT package.

(b) in general, people were reluctant to consider, let alone amend, start and end dates of each future activity (i.e. those activities not yet started were not re-estimated).

(c) As work progressed, many new activities became necessary, and many of the old ones became superseded or combined with others. Not all of these activities were reflected in the network.

(d) The review committee did not want to alarm senior management with apparent early slippages because they thought they would recover—in spite of the network.

(e) System testing was behind schedule because the errors being found aborted the system. It was impossible to start proper system testing without the outputs. No one was willing to hazard a guess as to when the system would be sufficiently clean to enable systems testing to commence.

A moral of this example, is that project control (of in-house development projects at any rate) should be from within, at the nuts and bolts level; not from the outside looking in, or by assuming that an end-date must be the gospel truth just because it appears on a computer print-out.

Weekly progress meetings

Another myth of project control (in DP) is to adopt weekly progress meetings as a means of keeping senior management informed of progress. At these meetings problems are discussed, but important events do not tend to take place immediately prior to them. In addition, progress requires detailed measurement and cannot be gauged adequately by the process of weekly meetings. The point is that the project manager should control every day, not just once a week. Events should be monitored on the dates they should occur, with continuous informal discussions with all relevant parties.

Not necessarily bar-charts

As with PERT, a bar-chart technique may be useful when planning, but not necessarily for subsequent management control. An example is given below of a small project responsible for implementing a marketing system, which initially was controlled using conventional bar-charts. This project, because it had proved difficult to control, was chosen deliberately to illustrate the problems. As measured by the criteria relating to project grading, the size of this project was small, except for the 13 nodes of interactions, and a total of 32 individuals. None of these interacting departments or individuals were under the direct responsibility of the project manager, nor were they dedicated full time to this

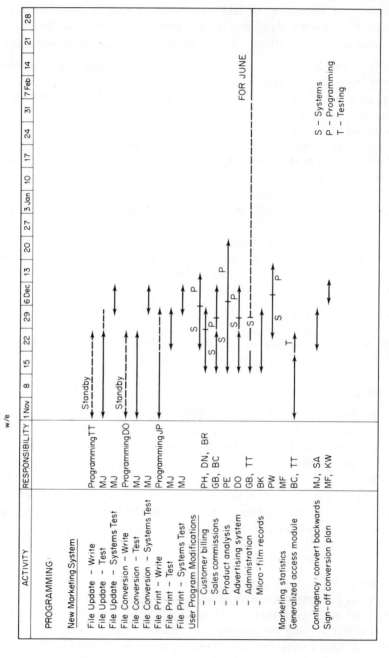

Figure 13.1   An example of a bar chart for project control

project. Figure 13.1 on the previous page is a small detail of a set of bar charts drawn up by the systems team leader. A three-month period is shown and only the programming activities are indicated (not the other project work streams). This could have been any bar-chart, as the argument still applies.

Although very useful when planning, this bar-chart was felt to be inadequate for control purposes and, because of slippage, had to be revised four times within the first two weeks. The great difficulty was knowing how far along the line each activity had progressed. The final version of the bar-chart was as refined as possible, but it still proved difficult to measure how each person was progressing. Consequently, after only a few weeks this approach for controlling the project was abandoned.

CONTROLLING DIFFERENT ASPECTS OF MANAGEMENT'S PLANS

Having explained what project control is not, the remainder of this chapter discusses some practical project control ideas that might be employed. Consideration of the many facets of project management reveals that there are different methods of control required for various types of plans. In addition, there are several degrees of difficulty to the control problem, and, by combining these two points, the individual plans can be grouped accordingly.

Group 1: control by inspection

In the course of project management, plans may well have been produced relating to such areas as: project organization, training, documentation, change control, and post project evaluation. The project control requirement for these plans might be a relatively simple inspection by management, who may compare, for example, a document's format or the method of operating changes control, to the installation's data processing standards; or by comparing the training a user department received to the original (or revised) plans. This is the easiest form of project control, requires no quantified measurement, and conceptually is akin to a manager controlling that his staff arrive for work.

Group 2: control using simple quantified data

A similar comment applies to the plans relating to such items as manpower, support, testing, resources and contingency. In these cases, control is slightly more complicated, because quantified data (e.g. machine time) is required to ensure that the planning is appropriate. This type of control is akin to a manager ensuring that his staff work a set number of hours per week. Significant deviations from these plans could cause a depletion or saturation of resources, which would bring an automatic response from the manager responsible for the functions affected, and thus simplify control (e.g. testing has not started because of a lack of manpower, or a support team is snowed under with work).

Group 3: control of budgets (financial or budgetory control)

In Chapter 4 covering budgets and the financial aspects of DP, it has been shown in some detail that financial control involves different areas to project control. One, for example, measures how much a person costs the organization, the other determines how gainfully employed and effective he is. Thus, financial control compliments project control and is not a substitute for it. In the writer's opinion the project manager does not usually derive much benefit from financial control, it is mainly for senior management, who should couple it with the assessment of the end-product's financial benefits and returns.

Characteristically, project control should take place daily and requires a fast response. Financial control is usually more sedate; possibly tending towards a ritual based around monthly budget variance reports.

Group 4: control of quality

The quality of the product under development requires monitoring, both from a technical DP, and from a user business aspect. The explicit identification of the main project work streams is often invaluable because automatic quality control of the end-product could be established at every phase and milestone by ensuring that each of the work streams formally signs off his approval (e.g. the user signing off his agreement to his user requirements). End-product performance comes into this category, with say, the control of program size, of response times to transactions input to the system, or of disk usage, being exercised by DP operations or a control team. It is important that this is not attempted at the end of the project prior to the system going live, but continuously during the systems development.

In principle, this approach allows management to control the product's development and delivery. Again, standards and check lists are invaluable.

Group 5: control and the measurement of progress

Measuring progress against what has actually been achieved at the end of each development phase, and against intermediary milestones, as detailed in the project's development plan, is usually the major project control consideration. This aspect of project control is now referred to as a project control system. As before, control of the work against pre-set standards is an essential method of ascertaining progress. Knowing, for example, that 69 man days effort are required to complete a task, document or phase is of little use without knowledge of what will be produced in 69 days, and the acceptability of the work.

WHAT IS PROGRESS?

One of the most common expressions used in practical project control is the word 'progress'. Before exercising control, any level of management wants to ask: 'How far have we got? and: 'How far to go?'. Unfortunately, progress is nearly impossible to define because it is not an absolute measurement as is mass, or length, or temperature. Consequently, progress is a mythical measure and it is necessary to substitute more tangible units when deciding if a project is progressing well or otherwise.

Common substitutes are man days effort expended and costs expended. However, it hardly needs mentioning that one million dollars can be spent with no progress being made. Even if one adds an expectancy factor (i.e. measuring and controlling against planned man days per month, or cost per phase) it is not much better, because the quality aspect needs to be defined. If one defines progress as the completion of previously defined steps (i.e. passing quantified milestones), the measurement of progress appears more tangible and meaningful. In fact, this approach is implied when advocating the use of system development phases for control purposes at the project level, and using events and milestones at the individual or team level. However, the disadvantage of doing this is that progress is measured in jerks, progress measurement is pessimistic in that it ignores work started on the next phase or milestone, and it is difficult to forecast completion dates. If, for example, the first phase was completed to plan does that mean that the next six phases will also be completed to plan? This illustrates that, without care, progress might become an historical measurement, causing glee to disbelievers of project control who might re-quote that 'history is bunk'.

Yet another practical consideration is that, if a project is progressing 'badly', a common method of control is to continue as before, but reduce the facilities and features of the end-product under development. Subsequent measurement of the project might prove it to be progressing 'well'.

In replying to the question, 'What is progress?' the answer appears to be a somewhat elusive measure which requires quantification in other units. These units can only be ascertained accurately after a pre-defined part of the end-product has been built, and this must have been achieved within a specified time. This light-hearted look at progress illustrates that it needs to be treated with caution by all levels of management.

MILESTONES

The key to a project control system is an *achievement orientated* approach with careful monitoring of precise milestones, at the project as well as at the individual's level. The basic theory is that if milestones are being achieved to target, costs take care of themselves. If milestones are achieved on target dates, but costs are increasing at a greater rate than anticipated, the original planning may have been poor. In this case, a solution is to re-assess and re-justify the project, subsequently either cancelling it (even though the project manager and his team have achieved their effort and schedule related targets) or proceeding as re-planned.

Milestones were previously referred to during the final stage in planning. The context then was that the project at the highest levels, and the individuals at the lowest levels, were aware of what the estimates referred to and what was expected of them. It is now appropriate to take up this concept in the complementary context of monitoring milestones for project control purposes, i.e. as continual check-points during the project that must be reached by specified dates, if it is to achieve the intended delivery dates of the end-product. By definition, the start and end dates of each phase are fundamental milestones. For smaller projects (with durations between six to nine months) these phase check points could be sufficient. For larger projects, additional check points are required. At the project level, these should occur at about monthly intervals, and should be signed off by both the users and the technical computer management responsible for the project.

Milestones at an individual's level should occur at approximately fortnightly intervals. Attempting to monitor more frequently may be counterproductive. At the other extreme, monitoring progress at periods greater than one month could be dangerous. It could be easier to quantify planning and monitoring milestones if:

(a) a management by objectives approach is used;
(b) performance yardsticks are available.

In these cases, staff could be used to a more formalized staff/manager control relationship.

Precise milestones usually require a considerable amount of thought by the project manager and his planners. For a naturally long activity (e.g. six months coding of one program) precise, intermediate milestones may be difficult to set, and senior management may not have any tangible control. In these types of activities, it may prove better strategic management to divide the job into simpler, more definable steps having possibly a less efficient system, but with less risk involved. If a methodology, based on data structures, is being used, and on-line development aids being adopted, precise milestones might be the number of data definitions agreed, progress in agreeing data entity charts, pictorial processes agreed, and progress in mapping data against processes.

Apart from the obvious benefits in project control, this approach also has the additional advantage that, at each milestone, all the project's personnel can see clearly the tangible results of their efforts and it should be possible to have this acknowledged by both user and computer management. If on the other hand, a milestone is missed, a measure of outstanding work may be required to assess the state of an activity and to enable a revised end date to be planned. The checklist below may be a useful aid when setting practical milestones, at the project level.

EXAMPLES OF KEY MILESTONES DURING DEVELOPMENT

1. Investigation, and feasibility study report completed to an agreed format, and signed off by all involved parties on a specific date.

2. Agreement on an initial development plan (including man-days effort, a schedule of dates and resources), by all project work streams by a specified date.
3. Justification for the project obtained by a set date.
4. User-orientated data structure, completed by a definite data, and to a specified format, with agreement obtained from all involved parties.
5. All project work streams agreeing to the user requirements document and signing it off.
6. Data capture methods including, if appropriate, a pilot study being devised, and formal agreement obtained to clerical procedures.
7. Formal agreement to new file layouts and data descriptions, including file creation specifications, and file controls.
8. The systems design specifications (including formal agreement on the system controls, and of test data logic) completed. .
9. Conversion philosophy defined in sufficient detail to gain agreement from all parties by a specified date.
10. System test plan drawn up and agreed by a specific date.
11. Freeze accepted by all parties, because they agree with the specifications.
12. Updated development plan agreed by all parties by a verified date.
13. Program specifications for specific sub-systems formally agreed and signed off (if third generation programming methodologies are being used).
14. A specified number of program modules coded with clean complications and clean tests.
15. Operational procedures agreed.
16. Signing-off of the completion of the preparation of systems test data by the line users.
17. Program testing and module linkage completed for a specified number of programs by a certain date.
18. Successful completion of system tests, and results signed off by line user (s).
19. Integration tests signed off and agreed by all parties.
20. Volume data, and file tests with users' agreement to outputs.
21. Acceptance tests, user procedures, and training agreed by the user (s).
22. Take-on completed, with all controls relating to conversion agreed.
23. Trial running completed, with the results signed off by the line user (s).
24. Initial user training completed to the line users' satisfaction.
25. Date the system is made operationally live: phased implementation starting for other areas, products, or facilities.

THE REQUIREMENTS OF A BASIC PROJECT CONTROL SYSTEM

An important factor requiring consideration is the *balance* between the management of *quality* control in the project's method of working and the quantified *measurement* of progress against target. In general, a greater emphasis on the former project management aspects reduces the need for an extensive and sophisticated quantified method of measuring progress. An extreme, but important example of this philosophy, is that during the later part of the project's life cycle, target completion dates can become wildly optimistic if a high number of errors is found during testing. Effective quality control earlier in the project, is a better management concern than attempting in a sophisticated manner, to measure, predict and control end dates at this late stage.

As will be apparent, there is no one method of project control, and each organization requires an individual system which depends on its size and experience in using data processing techniques. Any project control system and the information it produces, should be appropriate to the project and its problems, and ideally, be relevant at all levels receiving and inputting information. Above all, the purpose and usefulness of the information being produced must be ascertained as there may be a tendency, initially, to go for an over-kill. The check-list below may be of assistance when assessing the features and the requirements for a particular project control system.

1. An ideal project control system should be compatible with all of management's tasks, i.e. planning, assigning tasks, monitoring, recording progress, controlling and re-scheduling.
2. The normal development procedures and standards associated with any data processing department or computer project should be incorporated in the system with control exercised against them.
3. Firm control should be exercised on a phase basis with subsidiary milestones used during each phase.
4. For each phase, firm estimates in man days are required of the work content for all known tasks. Reference to the standards manual may be appropriate at this point.
5. These man day estimates should be assigned to known manpower, and scheduled over the phase to give actual completion dates. Allowance for all overheads should be made, which should include both *non-project* activities (e.g. leave, sickness, administration, etc.) and general *non-specific* project activities (e.g. team meetings, reviewing other teams' work, reading project documents). In fact, a schedule of activities, tasks and milestones could be provided for each individual as a formal method of assigning jobs. It also could be used as a reviewable working document.

The above five requirements are compatible with the ideas in Chapter 10 on planning.

6. A procedure is required that enables achievement to be recorded in a chronological manner, so that it can be monitored and reviewed by various levels of management.
7. The project control system may include an independent body of reviewers for the impartial review of progress. In particular, this body would review the consequences of variance.
8. An oral and written reporting procedure might be required at weekly, fortnightly or monthly intervals, together with an appropriate circulation list.

9. Formal signing off forms may be necessary at the time when major milestones are reached, e.g. after important documents have been approved, or when completed programs have met their design requirements.
10. As a project control system is the same as any other business system, implementation effort is required, as are samples of forms and procedures, as well as training in their use.

AN EXAMPLE (IN OUTLINE) OF A BASIC PROJECT CONTROL SYSTEM

The practical objectives

A project manager of a typical small-to-medium system development project, having worked through the above check-list of requirements, may come to the conclusion that his personal objectives for a project control system are that it should be a mechanism for: (a) keeping more senior (line and DP) management (who are less close to the work being performed) aware of progress and difficulties, (b) predicting reliable end dates for them, and (c) committing his team leaders to keep to mutually agreed milestones.

Quality control would occur by a combination of (1) a control team (comprising proven technically-competent staff), (2) trusting his team leaders to keep a tight grip, (3) the project work streams signing off their agreement to each completed phase or important milestone, and (4) entrusting control of the end-product's performance to the DP operations department. Monthly reports for financial control by senior management would be produced by the organization's own budgeting system.

Senior management's control would exist by means of business reviews at phase ends and information for this needs to be recorded. The objective (a), stated above, of keeping management informed between phases, could be achieved by fortnightly reports by the project manager of progress against milestones. A system (in outline) based on these objectives is now given.

Controlling via milestones

Having established key project milestones as described earlier, the next level of detail can be illustrated with the same project as before (see Figure 13.1). It will be recalled that this project failed in its attempt at using bar charts for project control, because the key concept missing from the bar charts, was a list of activities for each individual and a suitable set of quantified milestones. A sound principle to establish is that *individual people* should be controlled and *not* intangible activities, teams, projects, or departments. Accordingly, the activity schedule produced as firm estimates during project planning, may not be sufficient for project control. What may be more practical, is a people schedule which shows every individual, his expected output and target dates. Figures 13.2 and 13.3 (although simplified) illustrate how this can be done during a part of the programming phase. Also shown is how the analysts linked with the programmers, at the interface between the end of design and program-

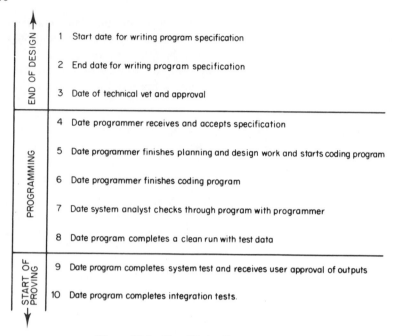

Figure 13.2   Simplified milestones in Figure 13.3

ming, and between programming and proving. Figure 13.2 simplifies comprehension by defining the 10 milestones represented along the top row of Figures 13.3. For this project, this proved to be a far more satisfactory method of project control—even if it meant more effort by the project manager in thinking through in detail each step of every activity.

Figure 13.4 is an example from another project, where managers in an experienced installation could take the process one stage further, by making the people and milestone schedule a reviewable working document, as well as using it as above. In this case, each activity has 5 *review* dates for each milestone. The original planned *target* dates for each milestone are shown at the top of each line. At each review the *actual* status is recorded below the milestone, and if necessary, *revised* schedules for the milestone completion dates are made.

This information could be subsequently collated and condensed, so that a project management overview could be built up into a two-dimensional chart, with one axis representing explicit key project milestones, (e.g. at monthly intervals) and the other axis representing explicitly stated project work streams. As the project proceeds, this chart of progress, formally agreed by all relevant parties, can be updated, thereby ensuring nothing is overlooked, and reducing the chance of errors in the project's plans or in the product being developed. Figure 13.5 is an example of this approach, where five project work streams are illustrated. The project has completed two major milestones and has made inroads to the next three. The project manager can use this to chase up the laggards, and to demonstrate overall progress to his superiors.

This approach to project control, in conjunction with the many other

ACTIVITIES BY PEOPLE / MILESTONES	1	2	3	4	5	6	7	8	9	10
MJ										
File update							22 Nov		28 Nov	6 Dec
File convert							22 Nov		28 Nov	6 Dec
File print							15 Nov		6 Dec	10 Dec
Contingency conversion	3 Dec	6 Dec	10 Dec				17 Dec		19 Dec	23 Dec
TT										
File update				1 Oct	4 Oct	20 Nov	22 Nov	5 Dec		
Administration				3 Dec	5 Dec	11 Dec		13 Dec		
Access module					1 Nov	12 Nov		22 Nov		
DO										
File conversion				5 Oct	7 Oct	22 Nov	25 Nov	3 Dec	5 Dec	6 Dec
Advertising system				25 Nov	29 Nov	5 Dec	5 Dec	9 Dec	10 Dec	12 Dec
JP										
File Print				23 Oct	23 Oct	22 Nov	25 Nov	3 Dec	6 Dec	9 Dec
PH										
Customer billing	11 Nov	22 Nov	25 Nov				13 Dec		18 Dec	20 Dec
DN										
Customer billing				29 Nov	2 Dec	13 Dec	13 Dec	16 Dec		
BR										
Customer billing				29 Nov	2 Dec	16 Dec	16 Dec	19 Dec	23 Dec	24 Dec

Figure 13.3   People schedule with milestones

associated concepts mentioned earlier in this section, is a good introduction to controlling by milestones, especially for smaller projects. It tends to be a conservative method of showing progress, in that items are indicated only after completion; no credit is implied for partial completion. It is also end-date orientated, which in practice is all that matters. For a large project, or if progress is wildly out of control, this system will detect slippage early, but there may be difficulty in determining the cumulative effect of slippage, and in predicting the final end date. Another problem in some installations may be that the expenditure of man days effort is not an integral part of this project control system. However, the desirability of this is not essential, as its effectiveness in the context of overall control is probably over-rated, as shall soon be seen.

AN EXAMPLE (IN OUTLINE) OF A QUANTITATIVE PROJECT CONTROL SYSTEM

The next level of sophistication would be to introduce a more quantified system involving man days effort. This would include formal time recording by each

NAME : A Ross

PROJECT PHASE : System design

ACTIVITY	REVIEW DATES	1	2	3	4	5	6	7	8	9	
1	14 Apr 75	12 May	20 May	30 May							P
User		C 10 May									A
requirements											RP
	12 May		25 May	3 Jun							A
			4 queries								RP
	25 May		28 May	5 Jun							A
											RP
2	14 Apr 75	30 Jun	12 Jul	27 Jul	5 Aug						P
		3 more pages									A
											RP
Clerical	30 Jun	10 July	20 Jul	3 Aug	15 Aug						A
procedures											RP
	10 July	C 8 Jul	Form not tested	5 Aug	20 Aug						A
			25 Jul								RP
	25 July		C 24 Jul	Proposal not agreed	25 Aug						A
											RP
	5 Aug				20 Jun						A
											RP
7	14 Apr 75	6 May	20 May	5 Jun	20 Jun	5 July	16 Jul	28 Jul			P
		3 out of 5 files									A
Sub-system											RP
master	6 May	10 May	20May/50fields								A
files											RP
	20 May										A
											RP
											P
											A
											RP

MILESTONES

P = Planned; A = Actual; RP = Revised plan

Figure 13.4   People and milestone schedule

PROJECT TEAM B

MAIN PROJECT WORK STREAMS	DESIGN MILESTONES										PROGRAMMING MILESTONES										PROVING MILESTONES				
	1	2	3	4	5	6	7	8	9	10	11	12	13	14	15	16	17	18	19	20	21	22	23	24	25
Line users																									
Function 1	C	C	C											NA	NA										
Function 2																									
Other projects																									
X	C	C	C	C					NA							NA									
Y		C	C	C	C									NA											
Systems	C	C	C	C	C																				
Programming	NA	C	C																						
DP operations:–																									
Hardware	C	C																							
System software																									
Communication lines																									

CHRONOLOGICAL AND SEQUENTIAL PHASES

C = Completed   NA = Not applicable

Figure 13.5 Project overview

project member at an activity level, coupled with weekly forecasts of the effort required to complete each task. However, before rushing ahead, let us be very sure of our objectives, and relate this to what can be achieved in practice and the accuracy and effectiveness of the net result.

Apart from compatibility with the previous ideas on the milestone approach to project control, the prime objective should be to forecast accurately the project's end-date; all else is incidental. Although there are numerous project control systems in use (both clerical and computer based), few seem to predict reliable or consistent end-dates. Before examining one system that works quite well, let us look at its fundamentals.

Figure 13.6 is a pictorial representation of a planned end-date for the completion of a system development phase. The firm estimate of man days

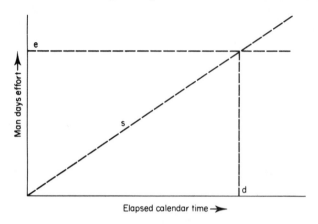

Figure 13.6   Planned end date

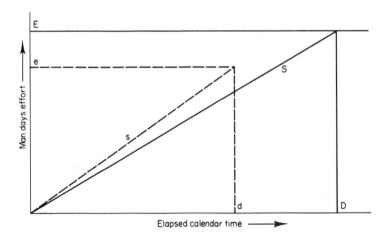

Figure 13.7   Actual end date

effort for the phase (e) is represented by the dotted horizontal line. How this estimate is produced was explained in Chapter 10 on project planning, as was the scheduling of this manpower. In this illustration, the number of people over the duration of the phase is assumed constant, as is their net availability after deducting holidays and non-project work, etc. This rate of applying the manpower (i.e. the schedule) is represented by the diagonal line (s). Where lines (e) and (s) intersect gives the end date for the phase, (d). It is usually easier to work in terms of week numbers.

This is fine in theory. What happens in the most adverse case is illustrated in Figure 13.7. At the end of the phase or project, the original estimate of man days effort is found to have been too low, and the final effort expended (E) is represented by the upper solid horizontal line. Coupled with this, the actual levels of manpower, and/or their net availability was less than planned. This lower rate of applying manpower is represented by the solid diagonal line (S). Where lines (E) and (S) intersect gives the final completion date (D). Figure 13.6 illustrates the starting plan, whilst Figure 13.7 is the final position. What happens in between, i.e. whilst the project or phase is in progress? An actual example is shown in Figure 13.8. Estimates, which in this case were revised weekly, of the development effort required for completion fluctuate, whilst a plot of the actual cumulative man days effort expended is more steady and predictable.

Returning from this digression in Euclidean geometry, to practical project

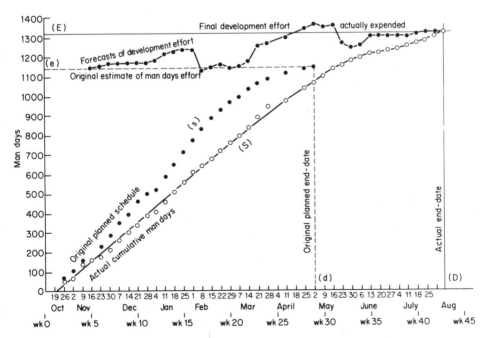

Figure 13.8 Graph of planned and actual progress

312

control systems, we conclude that to achieve the prime objective, (which is the ability to forecast accurately the project's end-date) a procedure is required so that at any time during a project, a completion date may be forecast based on:

(a) The trend in the (weekly) increases or decreases of forecast man days for completing tasks during a phase, compared to original estimates at the time of planning (i.e. dynamically allowing for the latest estimates of man days effort required to complete each task).
(b) The actual rate of applying manpower after allowing for leave, sickness, administration and other overheads (i.e. dynamically allowing for the latest situation in scheduling staff to project tasks).

To achieve this, it is necessary to record weekly progress at the level of each individual in terms of:

(a) a forecast of the number of man-days effort still required to complete all tasks for the entire phase, irrespective of the original estimate.
(b) a record of the man-days effort actually expended each week on relevant project work.

Figure 13.9 illustrates an actual forecast made relatively early on (at week 16) for the same project as shown in Figure 13.8. It is apparent that the revised end-date (week 40), although way behind the original target (week 29) was fairly good, when compared to the actual result in Figure 13.8 (which was

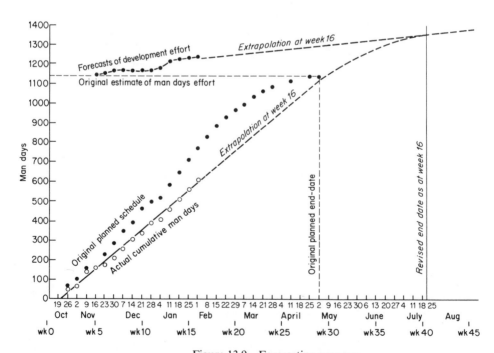

Figure 13.9   Forecasting progress

week 43). It may be of interest to note, that the wavering forecast of development effort in Figure 13.8, occurred immediately after this forecast was made. The ensuing rumpus caused by senior management's reaction to the predicted slippage, caused an artificial under-estimate of the amount of work outstanding. It took nearly 2 months for the project control system to return to a 'natural' state.

Summarizing then, this approach to project control enables management to be able to see whether the project is ahead of or behind schedule, and if so management should see why either because:

(a) Technical *achievement* problems, or poor estimates, are resulting in a greater or lesser number of man-days being required?
and/or
(b) The rate of *applying* manpower is greater or less than scheduled? There might be two reasons for this. The number of people allocated could be as planned, but the direct or indirect project overhead activities are not as expected. Alternatively, in a multi-project environment, insufficient people may be allocated because other projects are retaining them.

In this way, management is made aware of the problems and are vividly shown the resulting effects. What they intend to do about it is discussed elsewhere.

OTHER PROJECT CONTROL SYSTEMS

If an installation has numerous projects, each with many people, each person having numerous activities, and many activities are carried out by more than one person, a computerized project control system may be required to collate and condense the information relating to progress at the lowest level. Project control reports may be produced which are relevant to all management levels. In addition, the monitoring procedure may automatically incorporate some facilities to allow performance measurement to be made, not only for control purposes, but also to allow a historical build-up of data, which may be useful for future planning or for revising current estimates. This measurement and control may be used to produce performance yardsticks, which might include program coding rates, machine time usage, etc.

However, a very careful study should be made before adopting a computerized project control system. Like all other computer systems, they will need development time and effort expended on such things as—evaluation, package selection, systems, and programming work to make necessary modifications, system testing, and user training (which in this case are the project and other DP staff). The system will also need operational scheduling, incur the normal DP running costs including input and output stationery, require special programming and systems resources to run the system including collection and distribution of all inputs and outputs, and to correct the usual errors and make changes in the data. Last but not least, like all other systems, there is usually continuous maintenance work to be undertaken, as well as overcoming faults in the software.

Apart from the above resource overheads, more fundamental questions should first be resolved. Will the system actually provide a means for project control by using a milestone approach? Many systems require time expended to be recorded against tasks, each of which may have a lengthy duration. This may allow a more elastic interpretation of both the input and output sides of the system, and is not as precise as using a milestone, which should be a specific event in time (i.e. having no duration).

Will the system be able to predict end-dates intelligently, based on the dual trends to date of (a) the forecast man days effort to complete the project and (b) the net productivity of the manpower assigned to the project? Many systems cannot do this; others just add the current position to the original target date, e.g. if the project appears to be 2 weeks late at a specific run date, the reported end date is 2 weeks later. This approach is often too optimistic for slippages.

Another problem that may arise, is that like most computer systems, they do not have the same flexibility as a clerical system. Taken to the absurd limit, the voluminous procedures associated with some such systems seem to lead the reader into believing that 'all sick leave must be booked at least two weeks in advance on a form B3!'. This formal rigidity may sometimes prove infuriating, especially when changes in plan need to be reflected in the project control system. Additionally, being a computerized system, numerous output reports are usually available. In some cases, so much data is printed, that the various levels of management become snowed under with data. This has been known to turn some managers away from using the outputs of the system for control purposes. In these cases, the data accumulated may eventually be of more use for historical records, or for extrapolating future end dates, rather than for actually controlling the project now. In general, these and other systems require a lengthy procedures manual to explain them fully. Bearing in mind the recommended emphasis on quality rather than progress measurement, more complex project control systems are not detailed here.

UPWARD ACHIEVEMENT REPORTING

The approach to the project control system described in the previous examples, requires *achievement orientated* reporting (i.e. emphasizing progress in meeting milestones) not only by all parties in the project to the project manager, but also by the project manager to his superiors and senior line management. Line management should have a separate document listing the agreed *significant* milestones, and it should be made the responsibility of the project manager to report to his superiors on each achievement or failure. Rather than wait for the monthly or weekly progress report, the project manager should approach senior management as soon as possible, informing them of such achievement or failure. The project manager should seek management's views and suggest possible solutions that require management's directions.

REPORTING TO THE PROJECT MANAGER

The reporting to the project manager by all parties involved may be on similar lines to that described above. However, if there are many people on a project, it may be beneficial to have a weekly achievement reporting form completed by each individual (see Figure 13.10). The idea is for the individual only to record *achievements*, not to record diary notes or events. This is easier said than done, especially if the individual has carried out a tremendous amount of well-intentioned work but has not achieved anything. However, an attempt should be made to establish an achievement-orientated frame of mind within the project or department. This approach should not only reflect the reporting, but more important, affect the individual's achievement-orientated approach to his daily work. It should be stressed that this written reporting is no substitute for the project manager to maintain continually informal verbal communication with his staff.

```
               THE LENDING LIBRARY PROJECT
 ┌──────────────────────────────────┬──────────────────┐
 │   WEEKLY  ACHIEVEMENTS REPORT     │ Week ending Friday│
 ├──────────────────────────────────┴──────────────────┤
 │ Name:                                                │
 ├──────────────────────────────────────────────────────┤
 │              Achievements/progress                   │
 │                                                      │
 │                                                      │
 │                                                      │
 │                                                      │
 │                                                      │
 │              Plans/problems                          │
 │                                                      │
 │                                                      │
 │                                                      │
 ├──────────────┬───────────────────────────────────────┤
 │              │ Signed:                               │
 └──────────────┴───────────────────────────────────────┘
```

Figure 13.10 An example of a project reporting form

WHEN DIFFICULTIES OCCUR

In computing, events rarely occur as planned; eventually something goes wrong. The difference between a good and bad manager is the ratio of successes to failures for planned project activities. It is important to note, that when matters go wrong (e.g. technical problems build up, or delays occur because of individuals not under the direct responsibility of the project manager) the manager should rely on *self-help*. When a crucial decision must be made, this may coincide with even more critical events occupying the time of senior management, which affect the entire organization and not just the project. The manager should expect to resolve the matter himself, and justify his subsequent actions later to his superiors, who would expect this as part of the project manager's job, and the reason he is paid a relatively high salary. In reporting difficulties to his many supervising managers, the project manager should, at the same time, list the possible alternatives as a solution, together with his suggested best option.

As the nature of the project cuts across the organization's defined line structure, in some formal organizations problem areas usually arise outside the systems development jurisdiction. This means that the project manager may have to request assistance from his equivalent level in the line user departments or in the management services division. If this fails, the project manager must approach the systems development manager, who then contacts the director of management services. He in turn goes to the board with his problem which, with their approval, can then go down the line structure to the appropriate department and level causing the problem.

The usual, but effective, established methods for overcoming project problem areas are: working overtime, brain-storming, moving to a different environment (e.g. a hotel conference room) until the solution has been found, or pouring in appropriate resources.

TERMS OF REFERENCE

The last topic in this section on project control relates to terms of reference. In some installations, it may be found that if terms of reference are required it may be an indication of poor communications existing within the project. A snag with terms of reference is that however precise and explicit one makes them, the recipient frequently misunderstands. To minimize this difficulty, terms of reference should be in four distinct sections:

1. The first section should state specifically the *purpose* of the particular job, and it frequently might include the words 'In order to'.
2. A statement is required as to whom the individual reports.
3. The next section should list out the tasks required and some recommended lines of attack.
4. The last section is probably the most important and lists all the expected

results, all the measures on which the individual is going to be assessed, schedule date and all specific milestones.

As always in all communications, these terms of reference should be developed jointly between the manager and the individual, and they should contain *no surprises* and confirm what the individual already knows.

CHAPTER SUMMARY

The organization in general, and a project in particular, has determined its concept of the required end-product, and has drawn up numerous associated plans which indicate how this end-product will be built. By means of a project control system, the organization must now consider how these plans will be monitored and controlled during the project's extensive development time.

All levels of management affected by the proposed application system are responsible for project control, which tends to establish itself around a political equilibrium. It is important to realize that a project control system must cater for each manager's particular areas of concern. However, there are several common techniques used for project control that may not always be suitable. In addition, different aspects of project work require different approaches to control. These may range from simple control by inspection that an action has been taken, to sophisticated quantified measurement of progress, and from financial control of the development process to quality control of the end-product.

The main emphasis of a project control system is usually on the measurement of progress, but caution is recommended when attempting to ascertain progress, and equate it to costs or man days expended. Even stating that 90% of a task is completed does not help precision. Quality and end-product considerations are paramount. This philosophy leads to an achievement orientated approach to project control via the use of quantified milestones, both at the project level and down to the individual's level. In this way, precise points in time are given a greater importance than incomplete tasks spanning a finite, but possible indeterminate duration.

The requirements of a project control system are that it should enable management to carry out its functions of planning, assigning tasks, monitoring, controlling and rescheduling when a variance is detected. It is suggested that an emphasis on the management of quality reduces the need for sophistication in attempting to quantify progress to date and the amount of work outstanding.

In general, each installation evolves its own system for project control. Smaller projects may just use the installation's DP standards and project control system. Larger projects might either form an appreciable part of the organization's computer development, or have significantly different requirements for project control. In both these cases, the project might need to develop and implement its own project control system.

An example of a basic project control system is given which encourages each individual person to achieve his target dates, and hence the project to meet its targets. This approach can then be augmented by a more quantitative project control system for measuring progress, and an example is given of predicting the all important end date. More complex or computerized control systems are discussed, but caution is necessary to ensure that their advantages outweigh the disadvantages.

A distinction is made between activity reporting (i.e. diary entries) and the more preferable achievement-orientated reporting for both internal and external briefing of each level of management. When difficulties occur a project manager, in general, should rely on self-help, but informing his seniors subsequently of his actions and the reasons for them. Advice is also given on the use of terms of reference and their role in project control.

Chapter 14

Dp/User relationships and the conclusion

This concluding chapter brings together some of the more important themes running through this book, and suggests how the DP professional can improve professionalism and introduce these improvements to his own organization.

SUMMARY OF THE SOLUTION

The aim of this book has been to help the reader to derive a philosophy for the successful marriage of computing and business needs. The key lies with DP management, their expertise, and gaining co-operation from the numerous user managers involved in development projects. General areas requiring attention have included:

1. senior management's involvement and commitment.
2. the management of computer departments, and systems development in particular.
3. the relation of the computer department to the rest of the organization.
4. the introduction of project management techniques that span the organization and the computer department.
5. the integration of a sophisticated project budgeting philosophy into the corporate financial control system.
6. the running of a project as a profitable business exercise.
7. the motivation of staff associated with the development of computerized systems.
8. the use of beneficial techniques and standards to facilitate the development process.

These subjects are closely interrelated and important enough to be considered at the heart of the organization, in order that sensible attitudes to computing may prevail.

Starting at the top, a laudable idea worthy of attention relates to senior management's involvement. An organization will benefit from a greater sense of corporate responsibility for its computer projects. This entails user line management having more confidence in, and a desire to become involved in their corporate computing (but not too involved, thereby demotivating their computer management). By senior management taking an interest in their computing, enlightened DP management usually will be more than

319

320

pleased. No longer would they have to contend with one or two vociferous line managers who could dictate the priorities of the computer department and the computing application systems being developed.

At the next level, a computer department fulfils two important functions. These are:

(a) the running of *production* work (live computerized systems), which is vital to the prosperity of an organization and

(b) the *development* of new application systems (which are subsequently run as production work).

It is usual that the structure of the computing department should reflect these two distinct purposes. Next to the running of live systems, the systems development projects should be among the most important considerations in computer departments. All other non-project activities can then be organized as support functions so that they improve efficiency, and help meet the needs of successful projects. Figure 14.1, which represents a total organization, illustrates the recommended conceptual relationships. The top box represents the computer department (which comprises DP operations, projects and support functions), whilst the lower box represents the users who interact daily with DP operations on a departmental basis. The projects, which span

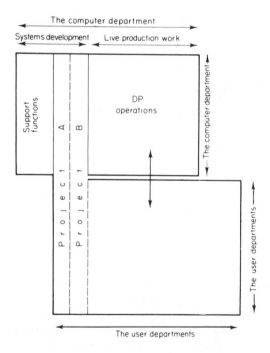

Figure 14.1 The conceptual relationship between the line users, the computer department, and projects

both boxes (and are assisted by the support functions) cut across the traditional departmental boundaries.

Although this book deals primarily with computer projects, it also covers other aspects of managing computers. It has indicated how some of the conflicts arising between individual line users, the computer department, and those engaged in project development, may be resolved in the best interests of the organization. Indeed, one of its main objectives is to demonstrate how the line users and the computer department should work closely together, as well as showing how the proposed system should be justified at the corporate level, and how a sophisticated project management approach, which involves the relevant line function, should be introduced, in order to implement successfully substantial computer applications. Project management is a proven way of achieving satisfaction from heavy investment in installing new computer applications.

Although some of the organization's needs can be met by resorting to systems that call for little computational skill (e.g. printing a one-off report), in general, computer department staff are skilled, intelligent people who create complex logic to feed into a dumb computer. The main aspects here are the people and the abstract processes they create. These hidden assets, in the form of program code, can be measured in millions of dollars, even in an organization of average size. If these logically and analytically skilled staff are to be employed, management must appreciate the motivation they require. This book recommends ways of managing and motivating computer personnel, for the benefit of the manager and the organization.

A PROFESSIONAL ANALOGY

In this section, the important topic of professionalism is coupled with the relationship between users and the computer department. Typical problem areas are highlighted including responsibilities, and possible solutions.

A computer department and development projects only exist for the line users' benefit (not the other way round!), and they should, therefore, be user-orientated. However, a compromise must exist between good DP practice and user pressures for cutting corners to produce quick results, or developing unjustifiable features for a system. A good analogy of mutual confidence and respect between the computer department and their users may be with the general professional approach adopted by solicitors or accountants with their clients, where the client gives instructions, and it is up to him whether or not to accept the advice given. However, if the solicitors or accountants disagree with their client's proposed plan of action, the solicitors or accountants usually can bring sufficient persuasive pressure to bear, so that their advice is eventually taken. This chapter could, therefore, be subtitled 'how computer departments and individual projects should treat their user clients'.

This analogy may be extended to accommodate a further complication. The 'professional' computer department is usually part of the same company as the line users, and conceptually, the computing staff are no different to other company specialists (e.g. accountants, marketing consultants, actuaries, etc.). Why should these other corporate specialists be treated any differently from DP specialists, or have less difficulty in exercising their corporate support role? If the relationship between DP staff and their users is a problem in an organization, it may be because computing is relatively new and its role frequently is not established or accepted. It may also be that DP is not a self-contained department (unlike say a self-contained internal legal department), but cuts across most facets of an organization. All these reasons add up to potential areas of conflict, and so several common causes of friction and practical ways of eliminating it are considered, towards the end of this chapter.

END USER COMPUTING

Bringing computing nearer to the end user is an inevitable process that has been gaining momentum. To meet this trend, an increasing percentage of information systems departments are installing some kind of support group to assist users in their own computing. Information centres are a popular example of this. The vast wealth of DP expertise, learned practically, over many years, would be wasted if users re-invented the wheel every time they started their own computer application. For example, a first time personal computer user (who possibly imagines his application system is easy) is sooner or later bound to come across such common DP problems as recovery, testing, maintenance, poor documentation, taking over the system when staff leave, etc. Large numbers of users in an organization may require training and guidance. This needs to be originated, controlled, co-ordinated and managed by an information systems department which is sensitive to the users' needs, and to what they perceive in the personal computer market-place. At the same time, users may need forceful persuasion that personal computers are not the panacea for all problems and applications.

If the trend is placing more computer processing power into the hands of the user, what can the user do with it? The simplest applications are word processing on a personal computer, with say, secretaries keying large volumes of text, whilst managers correct or make their own amendments, and produce their own reports. Using spread sheets and graphics for such things as budgets, or departmental performance statistics is the next level of complexity. Data manipulation is another possibility, with the data possibly being extracted from the corporate mainframe, and the user producing his own tailor-made report using report writer software. This can lead to local DP applications, either as a stand-alone system, or as a small back-end system using the corporate mainframe data-base. Personal computers are by no means the only way of achieving end-user computing. Decision support software run by the user via mainframe terminals is an effective approach. Financial modelling would be an example of this.

One problem with easily accessible end-user processing power is that both small and large businesses can suffer from too much sophistication. For example, investment justifications can become bogged down in detail, as the software tools allow management to think of every conceivable problem and simulate the resultant effects on costs. As a result, problems become highlighted, the worst case tends to be considered, and little gets through the cost justification process. Computer printouts tend to be treated as gospel truth, even if the figures and conclusions are dubious. Competitors, making more emotional decisions, go ahead with a similar acquisition or investment, and find that, in practice, the return on their investment was better than the 'Jeremiahs' sitting in front of screens originally stated.

End-user computing started with clerks and possibly secretaries operating DP systems via terminals. This on-going process is creeping higher up the corporate ladder as managers, directors, vice presidents, etc. use computing tools directly. However, in many examples, from one-man businesses to large organizations a conflict arises, because these users are not employed to program or perform systems work. They are there to manage the business. Stories abound of too much management effort wasted on getting microcomputer systems written and working. Motivation is extremely high, with in some cases, senior management up half the night, enjoying the challenge. Unfortunately, as such effort is not being spent on running the business, such managers may fall between two stools. The business aspects suffer, and poor end-user developed systems are produced, which in some cases result in a return to clerical systems!

Up to now, the discussions have related to local, stand-alone, even small business end-user computing. To conclude this subject, a brief examination will be made into how end-user computing can be adopted as a method of tackling the frequently quoted corporate DP back-log, and how it can complement the traditional systems development life cycle. Under the initiation and control of the information systems department, users can be given appropriate tools to assist and facilitate the development process. Such tools may be fourth generation languages, friendly data dictionaries, or screen and menu generators. In a similar vein, techniques such as user involvement in prototyping, or access to local hardware and software may enable users to produce their own reports from corporate mainframe databases without the inevitable wait for the traditional DP department. All of these topics have already been covered elsewhere in this book. The point being made here is that even though many of the tools mentioned above may not be very user friendly, the DP professional can still give users more involvement. For example, data dictionaries can be notoriously non-user friendly. However, software operated by the systems analyst, for drawing entity charts and data structures, can be automatically linked to a data dictionary. Users can easily identify themselves with the pictorial representations of their business, and by working closely with these motivated users, the systems analyst can speed up his analysis work, improve its accuracy, and improve his user's commitment to the system. Similarly, only a small percentage of corporate applications are better developed by the users (using, say, a fourth generation language) working in isolation from the information systems department. A better management approach is to let users, in a controlled iterative fashion, under the guidance of the information systems department, produce quick mock-up working models of the system they require. After they have ironed out most of the problems, and the users have discovered what they actually want from the system, the final production version of the system can be written with more traditional DP methods and languages. Once again, by adopting such an approach, the involved end user is taking some of the load off the information systems department, helping the analysts in clarifying the system, and bringing forward the end date by which the system is correctly specified and thus improving the efficiency of the systems development process.

AVOIDING COMMON AREAS OF CONFLICT

Putting one's own house in order

Before one can criticize users, or attempt to improve relationships with them, it is first necessary to put one's own house in order. In other words, the users must see professionally managed and tightly controlled development pro-jects, they must see effective support for these projects from the rest of the computer department, and they must be aware that the DP operation's depart-ment are running the users' live systems slickly, accurately and on time. It is hoped that these topics have already been sufficiently well covered.

If a project is controlled, it will appear to the outsider that everything is in order. If the line users see confusion with problems everywhere coupled with delays, they cannot be expected to be reasonable. In general, an objective might be to introduce a frame of mind into project staff which strives to ensure that users should see events happen when they are supposed to, and when they do occur that the outputs produced are accurate and as anticipated by the users.

Avoid firefighting and being event driven

A useful concept to establish is that of *no firefighting*. The alternative usually means a state of continuous friction with the users or operations department continually on the telephone or sending memoranda to development staff, because problems keep occurring. No sooner is one problem settled than another problem replaces it, and consequently there is little time for proper strategic systems development.

Computer specialists may become demoralized if the project or department becomes *event driven* in this fashion, as opposed to being the master of its own destiny. If a project manager is unfortunate enough to take over a 'sour' pro-ject, it could take him a long time to improve this situation, because of adverse inherited attitudes and the host of outstanding problems. However, it should be quickly established with all parties, that this firefighting state should not be the norm, but should be replaced by the gradual introduction of strategic management and improved methods of working.

Corporate, or integrated systems vs. local ones

There sometimes may be a major conflict between the users' wishes, other projects, and the rest of the organization. What may be beneficial for the organization may not be best for an individual user. For example, it may be more satisfactory to the organization for a computerized application to be implemented, over a period of several years, as part of an integrated system involving many steps (which appear unnecessary to a specific line user). The specific user, on the other hand, may wish to implement a similar application in several months, and not include these additional steps. In practice, the systems development manager or perhaps the project manager may have to carry out a balancing act, even if theoretically, this problem should be resolved by a corporate strategic decision. It is no good avoiding the issue, otherwise development might go ahead with a reluctant and uncommitted user adversely affecting a small but key area of the total system. Senior (non DP) management may have to be lobbied in order to resolve these political type of problems.

Defining the end-product

Users are notorious for not knowing what they want. This image is often a little unfair. Even for a simple system, it is usually very difficult for anyone (including systems analysts) to define, in logical, unambiguous, precise terms exactly what processes and outputs they require. For a complex or completely new system, it is virtually impossible to know in advance, with absolute certainty, what one wants. The mind just does not work like a programmed computer! A mixture of intuition and evolution is perhaps nearer the truth. It is so much easier if some sort of system is already working. By suggesting successive improvements to this embryonic system in an iterative manner, one is more certain of determining the precise user requirements.

How can this be done in practice? In many installations, the conventional approach to systems development does not help. Either:

(a) the user requirements phase is made the responsibility of the users. In this environment the computer department waits until it has received a written definition of the users' requirements. The consideration of utilizing the latest technologies is not encouraged nor are the professional talents of the systems analysts fully employed. They are unable to act as a catalyst when the users are formulating their ideas, or to document the users' requirements to a high standard (for which they, and not the users', have been trained).

or (b) the development process is separated into rigid self-contained steps. After the feasibility study comes 'the systems analysis phase' (which concludes with the user requirements document), and this is followed by the 'system design phase'. It is exceedingly difficult to perform systems analysis in isolation. Having in mind some idea of the final system makes analysis so much easier.

In both of the above approaches, the user is forced to state categorically what he requires, and possibly even sign his acceptance to it, before he has actually seen and 'felt' anything.

An alternative method in many situations is to treat the user requirements phase and the design phase more sympathetically. The user should receive something tangible which relates to the eventual end-product. He can then review it, suggest improvements, clarify his ideas, and gradually firm up on his requirements. At each step of this evolving process, the systems analyst can apply his analytical and design talents also to suggesting improvements, and to documenting the requirements for the end-product. Adopting this philosophy means that the users should see a model of their eventual system. This may be in the guise of detailed mock-ups of inputs, screen layouts, and output reports. It may be possible to arrange for some data to be processed clerically, so that the dummy reports have some reality. In some cases, cheap microcomputers may be used to perform the processing, or quite likely to simulate VDU screen formats, and interactive working by user department staff. Similarly, word processing equipment may be used to simulate coding forms, or output reports. By these means, evolutionary changes are easily made. For maximum effectiveness the users need actually to use the outputs in conditions that are as realistic as possible. In this way, they can determine whether, in practice, they actually do need each prospective report.

Responsibility for data

Even after a project has been completed successfully, and the live running of the application system handed over to the computer operations department, conflict may arise over the system itself. A common reason is that the responsibilities between the data processing department and the line user departments may not have been clearly defined and spelt out. It is essential that prior to the application being handed over, agreement is reached between the users and the computer operations department as to their respective responsibilities for the running of the application system. The golden rules which must be agreed from the beginning are:

The user creates the data

The data processing department processes the data

The user department checks and uses the data.

i.e. the user is responsible for his data. Although this sounds obvious it does not apply in all organizations. However, a distributed processing approach to the system design, or a screen based transaction processing system might have the added advantage of automatically producing the correct responsibility. The user, in this case, having local responsibility for the input and ouput of his own data.

In general though a simple example of this policy of responsibility is that, if a user updates a record, he should check if that update is as he expects. A consequence is that user departments need their own input and output control resources, which should be set up as early as possible, working full-time on this function, and be fully educated about the controls in the system. Although to a certain extent this occurs in practice with the users setting up a data control function as a natural task, extra line responsibilities are being emphasized. Additional resources and controls are required to double-check considerable amounts of daily data; both after coding/data entry, and after the data is returned from the computer. In fact, update reports from the computer should include details of the before and after state of master file records, for both successful transactions, as well as error or invalid transactions.

Errors

There should be a distinction made to the users between (1) errors coming to light during systems development (e.g. as a *normal* result of the several forms of testing), (2) operational errors caused by the operations department or users whilst running a live production system, (3) errors occurring whilst undertaking maintenance of a system after it has gone live, and (4) latent random errors in a live system which, because of system design errors, cause wrong processing or even total inoperability.

These different types of errors may cause endless confusion with some users, which manifest themselves in different ways. For example, as the development project tends to become a focal point for an application, it may be blamed for all these errors. A project may not just start and stop, but implements a stage of an application, and then develops it further. The problems discussed here are especially relevant with development work occurring during these further development stages. This can cause significant conflict between users and development staff, as well as between development staff and the DP operations department. It is quite normal for the technical staff in a systems development project to become demoralized by being involved with operational errors after a system, or stage of a system has gone live. It is up to the computer department staff in general, and the project manager in particular, to educate the user departments as to the effects of each type of error and who, in the installation, should be approached for fixing these errors.

The project manager and his staff, should warn the inexperienced user well in advance, of errors arising out of normal development testing. Many users have been known to panic on seeing many errors arising during systems testing. It does not help if new errors appear to arise after old ones have been cleared up.

Prior to live running, the users should be advised by project staff, as well as a representative of the DP operations department, about possible examples of operational errors, which might include: the misalignment of paper, or the wrong files being used, the incorrect data batches being read, duplicate batches being used, operational delays occurring, machine troubles existing, or control errors giving incorrect processing. Hopefully these should have been catered for, so if operational errors do occur, recovery is easy and the user should resolve them directly with the appropriate liaison function within the DP operations department.

To avoid excessive errors occurring when the system is eventually live, managers should ensure thorough testing of the end-product during system development or maintenance, even if this means a delay in the date the system goes live. After this date, a target might be that no more than one major system development error occurs every 4 to 6 months, most of the other problems being of an operational nature.

The project manager and his staff should warn the line users in advance about these latent development errors which will happen, even months after thorough tests, parallel runs and final acceptance. These errors may be caused by the systems analysts, or may be oversights in the system. Development analysts and programmers may be prepared to accept these problems as their concern more readily than operational problems.

This distinction between errors is not black and white, and as the project manager is the focal point for a computer system he probably will become involved with both sorts of error. A major improvement might occur if separate managers are responsible for development and production work. This means that all live systems and their maintenance are the responsibility of the DP operations department, which does not report to a system development manager or his equivalent. Formal acceptance testing by the DP operations department may signify the hand-over point.

DISSEMINATING DATA PROCESSING IDEAS

Where does management end? Unlike a book, there is no start, middle and finish to management. Even the piece of string in the proverbial question 'how long is a piece of string?' has, conceptually, at any rate, two finite ends, even if there is an indeterminate length. As management is limitless without a beginning, duration, or end, concluding this text on management is logically difficult and somewhat arbitrary. Up to now, numerous suggestions have been made regarding improvements to DP. This section, by way of a conclusion, briefly outlines an approach for actually introducing some of the recommendations made in this book, and for disseminating data processing concepts within an organization. It is suggested that the onus rests on the DP practitioner himself, who may find it useful to use some of the following ideas.

Marketing orientated

The information systems department should be extrovert, selling itself to the line users and creating a continuous dialogue. It must be stressed that the 'selling' is a softsell, where the projects and the systems development manager go out to users to find their 'market needs' and requirements, and thereby keep one step ahead of user requests. Obviously, it is better if these computer people understand the organization's business, as well as the latest technology, and originate ideas in key areas.

Softly, softly

Disseminating ideas outside the DP department (as well as inside) should be a gradual calculated process. DP management should attempt to gain *confidence* from the rest of the organization in its DP, by achieving successful *results*: and it is worth concentrating on four specific areas.

. All projects should work in a *professional* manner—this means adhering to the normal accepted computer standards within the computer industry.

. The projects should be *credible* at all times, and many sound ideas may need to be enforced, subtly, or otherwise, in order to achieve a successful implementation.

. Good *planning* is essential for success. This leads to realistic control and the necessity to chase people to meet target dates.

. The *minimum risk* philosophy should permeate throughout all projects, so as to ensure that more deadlines are met than are missed.

Entrepreneurial and flexible

None of these goals can be achieved without staff. A good way to obtain the best ideas from computer personnel is to give them a certain amount of freedom to bring out their creative abilities in their jobs. This psychological approach is necessary to motivate computer people (as with any specialist), and obtain maximum output from them. An extension to this, is not to have too rigid standards, procedures and organization, and thereby not stifle creativity and decrease motivation within the computer department.

By way of summarizing, a manager should attempt to influence corporate staff by *evolving attitudes of mind*. This process can be thought of as a step function, where the bottom step represents old and existing attitudes. After a short period of time, the new attitudes, which have been introduced by the manager (represented by the top step) should have become accepted subconsciously. Psychologically, the same state of individual freedom exists as before, but the work output is at a higher level of sophistication.

APPENDIXES

Appendix 1

The reasons for introducing an application system

Listed below are reasons why an organization may wish to introduce a computerized application system. The intention is usually to increase profitability. Some applications may achieve this by saving costs (e.g. by reducing levels of manpower, or by saving office accommodation). Different applications relate to the other side of the equation and increase the value of the system to the organization; and others help to generate additional business. However, not all application systems fit neatly into one of these categories, and sometimes there simply is no alternative to a computerized solution.

Reduced manpower

Reducing manpower costs in a line department function may be possible by performing some of the function automatically via a computer system. For example, an enquiry system which allows a rapid access to data on many files, enables a clerk to handle many more transactions in a shorter period of time. Spin-offs from these types of application include fewer supervisory staff, reduced administration services such as typing and filing, less overtime costs, and a reduction in office accommodation.

However, the benefits associated with such applications may require closer scrutiny or need qualification. Usually, not all of the business function is replaced by a computerized system. Often, it could require the same or additional skilled line user staff to operate the system. This staff may also have to handle alternative and more complex queries. Union pressures might prevent any reductions in manning levels. Additional (and expensive) technical computer programmers, operators, analysts, data entry operators, etc. may be required to develop and run the application system.

A possible reason for introducing such a computerized application system is to alleviate labour shortages. Usually this reflects a general labour problem in the organization, not only relating to one function in a line department. Consequently, any clerical staff displaced by a computer application system often are required elsewhere in the organization to be deployed on (1) more rewarding, or (2) more important decision-making tasks, or (3) new problem areas, or (4) less mechanized functions. An exception to this could occur if the introduction of the application system coincides with a down-turn in the economic business cycle. In this case, clerical staff may not be found alternative employment in the organization, and labour savings would indeed be made. It is debatable whether the computer system or the business climate does, in fact, reduce the labour costs!

Accordingly, a computer application system may indicate an apparent saving in staff numbers, but the total net effect on the organization may not show a significant reduction in manpower costs. Therefore, corporate decisions (not computer department or isolated line department decisions) usually are required for substantial applications that are claiming improved productivity.

Improved productivity

Maintaining staff numbers, but improving their productivity is a common benefit from using computers. Managers, salesmen, clerical staff, etc. could all benefit from a reduced administration overhead by using even the simplest spreadsheet, word processing, or data manipulation facility.

Strategic competitive edge

Computing is no longer perceived as a corporate background activity which relates to the improvement of administration. Information systems should be regarded as good strategic weapons for improving the organization's competitive edge, in such corporate functions as marketing, sales, customer service, product development, and financial management.

By selecting from computerized name and address files, it is possible to produce the optimum target audience for mail shots, or produce prospect lists for salesmen to improve their effectiveness. Giving salesmen portable computers may enable them to provide faster quotations, and enter orders directly, quicker and more accurately. This may result in less errors, earlier deliveries, less paperwork, as well as more loyal customers. In some industries it may be possible for customers to interrogate the relevant parts of the corporate data base to track the status of their orders. This also improves customer service and loyalty, and may be taken one stage further by giving the customer the facility to communicate his orders, and relieve him of producing the paperwork for order entry, despatch, stock-out discrepancies, etc. Such a facility would lock in customers, and prevent them from placing business with competitors.

By encouraging customer feedback and queries (e.g. hot-line support, free phone service, pre-paid mail cards) it is possible to hold files of queries and complaints which could lead to ideas for product improvements or new products. By building up customer profiles, (e.g. age, family size, geographic location, income bracket) it is possible to obtain improved marketing intelligence and make product changes for specific market niches.

For many industries, cash management is important. Banks allowing such organizations to access them via a computer link, can not only attract extra (low cost) business, but the corporate financial controllers can, for example, benefit from minimized loan interest, maximized deposit interest, or advance notification of direct debit or standing order receipts.

Learning new skills is an ever-increasing problem for most organization's employees. Training workers using video discs, or microcomputers is an effective low cost method. Similar techniques, or in-house electronic publishing can be adopted to produce product or standards manuals.

Reducing office equipment costs

It may be possible to reduce non-manpower costs in a line department function by a computerized system replacing clerical machines such as typewriters, calculators, stationery, files, and cabinets etc., as well as general information accessing and handling costs. This is usually a tangible benefit, relatively easy to quantify, although often not significant to the total corporate profitability.

No alternative solutions

A computerized system might allow increased volumes of business to be processed, when skilled labour is difficult to recruit, train or retain, and especially if the work is dull and repetitive. A further aspect is that it may not be possible for large volumes of transactions to be handled clerically with sufficient speed or accuracy, and this may be coupled with the need to cover a large geographic area. Data transmission techniques may be appropriate here, and well developed banking systems are an example of this. In general, this volume problem, which could adversely affect the objectives of a growing organization, is relatively easy to identify and justify, (although the solution may be expensive and not easy to develop).

Peak-load processing

Reducing the cost of peak-load processing may be made possible by eliminating, for example, the need for temporary staff at the month's end, or the necessity for making overtime payments. In this case, management decisions could be local and tactical, rather than corporate and strategic.

Accuracy

If inaccurate data is a problem, a computer system could help in two ways. First, improvements in processing accuracy and consistency are likely. Probably, more important though, errors in data may be reduced significantly by only working from source documents and by placing the data-entry function and its *responsibility* at the actual location of the user. Again, communication based or distributed systems facilitate this.

Better customer service

Introducing a computer application system may provide an improved service to customers, by promptly handling their enquiries. In a highly competitive industry this may be vital, and if the organization is dispersed the desired service levels may not be attainable without communication systems and online processing of transactions. This category of benefits might also include the rapid processing of customer's orders, or stock status queries, or the prompt despatch of spares, but the benefits, although apparent, are not always easy to *quantify*. What value should one attach to less lost customers? What will be the percentage increase in market share from such systems?

Improving cash flows

The increased speed in processing computerized order/sales, distribution and accounting systems enable invoices to be dispatched earlier, and this may improve cash flow. However, submitting statements several days earlier might not produce the expected benefits in improved cash flow or reduced debtors, if, for example, unrelated factors, such as a national credit squeeze, cause delays in payment of bills.

Improving management information and control

A system may improve line performance from better management decisions based on new, or hitherto unobtainable, facts. This covers a very wide area. Examples of these applications could result in improved cost control, increased stock turnover, less work in progress, reduced distribution costs, fewer production delays, stimulated sales from sales statistics or marketing information, or the use of management science techniques requiring complex calculations.

This category may be difficult to justify initially (e.g. by how much will work in progress be reduced?), but it can produce significant benefits as it attacks the heart of corporate problem areas. The far reaching consequences of these applications, therefore, usually require corporate decisions for their go-ahead.

Reducing levels of stock

An important case of better customer service, and improving management control is the reduction in the frequency of stock-outs, and reducing inventory levels by introducing order entry, stock control, production control, or even point-of-sale systems. These systems would be beneficial in both manufacturing and distribution industries, and in particular, communication based systems would be applicable for organizations with fast-moving perishable stocks held at many locations. Spin-offs may also result in reduced administration costs, and less storage space and warehousing costs being required.

Appendix 2

General terms of reference for project managers

Job Purpose

1. To lead a project and be responsible for the strategy, tactics, and overall approach, so that the project is not *event-driven*, but is guided by *strategic management*
2. To initiate, and subsequently motivate, the systems development aspects of the project, to the benefit of the organization.
3. To be responsible for all aspects of the successful implementation of the application system in accordance with the time-scales, performance, and systems requirements agreed with the user.
4. To provide technical and technical management advice to the project.
5. To improve the users' computing competence and their ability to use the system effectively.
6. To carry out the above within the limits of the agreed budget.
7. To ensure that the above are carried out in an efficient and professional manner.
8. To train project staff in both technical and project management skills.

Reporting

The project manager will have responsibilities to the following people:

1. He will report with a full-line responsibility to the systems development manager (or his equivalent) for :—

   (a) Discharging his obligations for managing the project to the satisfaction of the users, as well as the rest of the organization.
   (b) Advising the systems development manager on the technical viability and consequences of any future variations or additions to the originally agreed project.
   (c) Establishing functional links within the organization both within the computer department and the line user departments.

2. The project manager will look to the career managers (system, programming, O and M, operational, and technical) as well as to the relevant line managers for assistance in providing:
   (a) Support resources to staff the project.

(b) The appraisal review and career development of project staff in the longer term.

(c) Technical guidance.

The project manager will, in turn, be responsible for keeping the above managers informed on the availability of staff and the progress of the project.

3. The project manager will report as required to the organization's project review committee.

4. He will also report to specified user executives

Sub tasks, expected results, and their measures

1. To plan all aspects of the project, identify all activities, their timescales, the risks, any requisite back-up plans and all the resources necessary to implement the system, after obtaining agreement with the appropriate management.

   The above plan is to be integrated into the overall plan for the organization.

2. To closely monitor these plans, and control variances.

3. To establish and operate a procedure for controlling changes to the end-product's specification.

4. To prepare a project budget covering the total project from conception to completion, and then to operate within this budget once agreed by the relevant line user managers.

5. To define and obtain sufficient resources of suitable quality via the DP and user management, and subsequently manage these resources.

6. To recruit and if necessary, train the members of the project, and to carry out, in co-operation with the career managers, appraisals of the staff whenever necessary. Also to be responsible for developing the skills and abilities of the members of the project in accordance with their talents and project requirements.

7. To influence the staffing, structure, and operation of the computer department, where appropriate, to achieve the necessary capability and competence for running the system.

8. To develop the best possible understanding of the users' requirements, so as to ensure that they have been correctly interpreted and that the system is capable of carrying out these requirements.

9. To develop a co-operative spirit with the users.

10. To keep the users advised of progress and problem areas.

11. To ensure that the users receive sufficient training, and are competent to run their system.

12. To establish acceptance criteria with the users and to have this agreed with the appropriate management within the computer department. To then ensure that the computer system passes the acceptance tests to the agreed time.

13. To check that all necessary standard hardware and software products

are ordered and any special requirements raised. To progress carefully the delivery of both hardware and software necessary for the successful implementation of the project.

14. To keep the computer operations department fully informed of expected changes in hardware usage requirements.

15. To ensure that all necessary accommodation for project staff is provided and fitted out appropriately at the relevant user premises.

16. To ensure that suitable areas provided by the users are properly prepared to receive computer hardware, e.g. communication terminals.

Appendix 3

System development phases

It is virtually impossible to manage effectively, a systems development project without a deep understanding of the phases necessary for the development of an application system. The following is a brief, but practical description of one method of grouping development work into phases.

Initial appraisal

The initial appraisal (sometimes termed a pre-project business survey) is the first phase in the development cycle, and is usually a very brief method of formally initiating development. The original ideas for a computer application system and the inspiration could have originated from within the computer department or the users.

The work carried out in this phase, involves identifying the needs of the organization, followed by a general appraisal of the business procedures, the scope, constraints, and problems in a particular area. This in turn leads to an investigation of the type of application system that is required. The lead business orientated systems analysts (or even manager) performing this survey, should produce for senior management, a report setting out in very broad terms, a statement of requirements, alternatives, benefits, and estimated costs. This document, which need only comprise a few pages, could recommend that a clerical system would suffice, or that no further development work should take place, or that further systems analysts be assigned to carry out a more detailed feasibility study.

By the end of this phase sufficient work should have been carried out, for senior management to justify further development effort, and proceed confidently to establish a project by issuing a formal project initiation 'brief' that contains the project's terms of reference, scope, and objectives.

The personnel assigned to this phase often find the work enjoyable, because of the broad open ended brief, the general business administration aspects, and the lack of pressures, as usually there are no imminent implementation target dates.

The feasibility study phase

This phase is a joint user and DP responsibility which develops the ideas in more depth, proves them workable or otherwise, and identifies and evaluates alternatives. It includes determining the benefits and costs of the different ways of developing the system, and the subsequent ongoing running expenses of the application on the computer, together with the savings that could be achieved by the implementation of the proposed system. Estimates of resource requirements and an overall timetable for development also need to be produced. The process can be compared to model building. By the end of this phase, management should have a shrewd idea whether the proposed application system is viable, and be acquainted with a feasible design based on the best alternative solution to the business problem. This is summarized for senior management in a feasibility report (sometimes termed a system proposal document), issued by the business and technical systems analysts carrying out this work. Management can now make its second justification decision whether to proceed further, by issuing appropriate terms of reference and setting budget limits.

A disastrous management error is sometimes made at this point. Owing to business pressures, and the desire to produce a tangible end-product (in the form of program code), it is assumed that as a feasible design now exists, sufficient systems analysis and system design work must have been completed. This, unfortunately, results in the next two phases being skimped or omitted.

The user requirements phase (sometimes termed the functional requirement, or systems analysis phase)

This phase lays three foundations: for fact finding and business analysis, for logical systems design, and for project resource planning. The first purpose of this phase is to produce the user requirements document (also known as the business functional requirement, or the system definition), which is user orientated with little computer terminology. It contains the business functions and commercial requirements of the proposed system, and describes in detail the facilities required by the users. This is the primary reference document for designing the end-product, and this stage can be likened to preparing a blue-print and describing what will be built. Systems analysts (or business analysts) should prepare this document. A good indication to management that analysis is proceeding satisfactorily is that the systems analysts should be spending most of their time with the users.

The line users have an important responsibility in determining their requirements, as they must provide the DP personnel with a clear, detailed and complete definition of their needs. The systems analysts act as a catalyst, suggesting technological solutions and formally documenting requirements. They can assist by recommending input and output formats that would be most helpful, system controls that would improve accuracy, or more efficient features in the proposed system. The resultant user requirements document needs to contain sufficient information for the users to sign off their agreement and commitment to the facilities they expect to receive.

The second main purpose of this phase is to convert the user requirements into an overall, or logical design document, describing *how* the system for the proposed application will do what has been specified in the previous part of the phase. This document should define logically (i.e. in business terms) all input transaction types, all outputs, all screens, and all processes, together with such quantified information as the anticipated volumes of each item, response times, and how fast the system needs to be processed. (At this stage, it is sensible to ignore such physical considerations as programs, files, screen maps, etc.) A data model of the system is also produced during this phase. It is also necessary to lay down a strategy for conversion from the existing system. It may prove beneficial whilst formulating the users' ideas, to run a mock-up of the proposed system, and gradually evolve precise requirements.

Apart from thorough fact-finding, systems analysis, and documenting findings, this phase is characterized by considerable planning of manpower, resources, and schedules. This, the third main purpose of this phase, enables a project development plan to be produced to demonstrate how the system will be developed. The necessary skills for this phase could include business orientated systems analysis and systems design, technical systems design, and project planning. In a small project, one person may possess all these skills.

The end of this phase is an important check-point for senior user managers. It will enable them to decide formally whether or not to proceed with designing and installing the system. This justification which is the third in an escalating sequence of control, will contain all the cost benefits and savings resulting from expenditure on the hardware, software, development, and running costs. Included in the justification is the budget for the duration of the rest of the project, and the development plan. This justification stage also includes numerous discussions and meetings between all interested parties, with possibly the decision for the project's go-ahead being made at board level, especially for larger projects.

The technical system design phase

Having defined the system in terms of business requirements, the purpose of the technical system design phase is to specify a total computer system which meets the analysed requirements. This is obviously the responsibility of the DP specialists assigned to the project (system designers, analysts, senior programmers, and operations staff). In general, this phase can be interesting to work on, but it can sometimes be very tedious. Much creative design work is possible, and this may be stimulating and intellectually satisfying. However much laborious calculation and assessment of alternative designs is essential, in order to optimize the design.

If the system under development is replacing an existing system, the conversion process may present serious difficulties. Often the solution to the problem substantially affects the development process and the schedule for implementing the new system.

Most commercial systems require master, transient, reference, and other files, and usually they are designed at this stage. However, in certain circumstances, existing or modified files may be utilized. In some projects, the file design is an important consideration, requiring a team to analyse scientifically the organization's data. Also designed are details of all inputs, outputs, processing rules, tables, the break down into subsystems, back-up and restart requirements, all interfaces with the users and other systems, and all controls and audit trails. The system designer also optimize the end-product's throughput, processing speed, response times, file processing times, CPU store and backing store requirements.

If not already started during systems analysis, a pilot study might be necessary to measure clerical error rates in the proposed data capture method. Similarly, samples of data may be analysed from existing computer systems, which will feed data into the system under development. These analyses do not occur frequently, and may be classed as an expensive luxury. However, often they are useful.

Testing and clerical input are usually left until much later in the project, but invite disaster if (a) data input programs are written before the data coding has been finalized professionally or (b) test data logic proves that the system specification is incorrect. It is far safer if detailed plans for system and user testing are made now.

To conclude the work of designing the system, a document which is computer-orientated is produced, that sets out in technical detail how the computer system will work. This usually comprises system flow charts, record layouts, transaction details, etc. The project manager and systems staff should then ensure, by discussion and explanation, that the user personnel understand it in principle. It is mainly technical skill in systems design that is required in this phase, but program design skills are certainly an advantage.

Once the design of the system is finalized, all changes to both the user requirement and the technical design specification by any department should be frozen. This is essential if the subsequent programs are to be completed on time. Any changes made after this stage must go through a formal cost justification procedure. It is often easier to sell the word 'stabilization' than the emotive word 'freeze'. Confirmation can then be given to the users that non-justified amendments can be made during post-live maintenance.

As is apparent, a tremendous amount of work should be carried out at the design phase. In fact, as much work as possible should go into the design phase and be agreed, before commencing the program design and programming phases. In this way, development costs will be minimized, difficulties reduced, and above all the likelihood of serious managerial error eliminated. Unfortunately, in many organizations this does not normally occur, because important conceptual changes and detailed amendments are made right up to the end of development. There is then the obvious waste of programming and other resources, with the inevitable delays whilst solutions are being found.

The program specification phase

The purpose of the program specification phase is to produce the lowest levels of detailed design for the new system, to structure each program, to determine modules where appropriate, and to produce firm and detailed documentation to enable the application programs to be designed. This work is based on the technical system design specification, and a detailed program specification is produced for each program or module within the system. The intention is to have a program specification phase, followed by a program design phase. This reflects the logical sequence of first stating what must be done in the program specification, and then how the processing will be achieved in the subsequent program design.

Skills for this phase tend to vary between installations, and to be supplied by either systems analysts or programmers. A program development plan, and a program test plan are also produced as well as program libraries. In general, management need to make a conscious effort to prevent a head-long rush into coding, before programs have been fully designed.

Around this time, the project is at its half-way point in terms of manpower, expenditure, peak staff numbers, and duration. A check-list below indicates what should have been known, and documented by the end of system design.

THE STATE OF KNOWLEDGE BY THE END OF SYSTEM DESIGN

The business aims and purpose of the new system.
Current procedures, problems, statistics, forecasts.
Detailed design of the new system including system flow-charts.
Outputs — actual samples, screen layouts, interactive prompts, transaction error reports, use, volumes, distributions.
Inputs — actual samples, screen layouts, interactive prompts, data coding considerations, data coding trials, transaction types, volumes, responsibility for creating data.
Message combinations, sizes, statistics, and profiles.
Validation rules, error messages.
Parameters.
Hardware requirements—processor storage, file storage, peripherals.
Software requirements both standard and non-standard.
Communications network and terminals.
Hard copy requirements. Pre-printed stationery.
Throughput.
Response times.
Reliability of total system.

Recovery from failure requirements.

Fallback facilities.

Simulation of the proposed total system (if applicable).

File structure.

File data content.

File processing methods.

Security, privacy.

Processing details, common routines, calculations.

Daily, weekly, monthly, quarterly, annual, and *ad hoc* runs.

Interfaces with the database and TP software.

Controls — data, files, system, clerical and computer.

Programs to be created, sizes, run frequencies.

Existing programs that will be effected.

Effect on other systems.

Detailed implementation schedule and resources.

Sub-contracting requirements.

Conversion procedure.

Systems test data.

Acceptance criteria.

Areas requiring corporate policy decisions.

System development plan.

Project budget.

Benefit of the proposed application.

Possible ideas for future stages of development.

The programming phase

The programming phase is the actual production of the computer programs. Some authorities advocate splitting this phase into two or three, viz. design coding and program testing. However, the cut-off point between these often defies definition, and usually, the same team of people are responsible for both producing and testing their code. One combined phase may, therefore, be preferable in practice. (It is difficult enough to enforce a few phases without having to introduce some more.)

Program design from the program specifications includes defining each program's structure down to the lowest level, designing work files, and specifying common modules, etc. In practice, the level of detail documented depends on the experience of the person(s) responsible for coding. The full range of programming skills and experience is required for this phase, the senior programmers possibly being responsible for the more complex or control modules, and the juniors for coding the simpler routines. Within this phase, the programming staff usually require some management 'prodding' to adhere to a fairly rigid set of standards and conventions (particular to each installation) and to produce *intelligible* program documentation.

During this phase, it is the first time in the project that any real contact is made with the computer. As it is virtually impossible to obtain an error-free program, the actual errors in the program logic will be apparent. After compiling a correct program, controlled and extensive test data (which has been prepared by the programmers) will be fed in to make sure that it is really right.

In the case of modular programming, 'bug-free' modules, which are now being produced, can be scheduled and linked together to test the interfaces between adjacent modules, and can then be tested subsequently to form a complete program. Eventually, adjacent programs can be tested for correct linkages by passing data through all programs in a suite. The system then works as far as the programmers can tell!

The proving phase

The purpose of this phase is to prove that the system works correctly, first from the viewpoint of the system's designers, and then from that of the users of the system. This leads some installations to split the proving into two or three separate phases. In practice, it is probably preferable to have one combined phase, even if separate teams, or even departments are involved. The initial work in this phase links all the programs in the system for continuity; more serious errors of logic should be found by the systems analysts from the controlled and extensive test data being used. It is now that the pressure builds up. In badly organized projects, deficiencies will be highlighted and program specifications changed daily. This phase also enables the computer operations department to check out its role in running the programs, data, and files.

The next step which applies only to integrated systems, makes it possible to test the application system with all its interacting systems (and possibly other development projects) by controlled and extensive test data. After proving that the application system satisfactorily integrates with the minimum sized test data, volume tests can be made with large quantities of realistic data. Also it is possible at this stage to highlight systems defects and determine if the data throughput is slower than planned.

It is essential for the line user departments to vet and approve the input data, the print-outs, and listings of data files that have been created, or converted. These activities comprise acceptance tests whereby the users can accept formally the whole system and its facilities. However, this process can be very difficult to define precisely, because of the numerous factors and unforeseen circumstances that can occur when the system has been implemented fully. In the case of hardware orientated projects and especially when the communication systems are complex, this stage can be an anxious one for the computer supplier and customer, as it may be several months before the customer feels he can accept the system.

The need for a clearly defined user requirement, the adherence to the freeze, and formally agreed user-orientated milestones will become apparent at this stage.

The final step in the proving phase is to test the change-over from an existing system to the new application system, and formal proof that the new system is correct may be obtained by several methods. One method, called parallel running, entails running the old and new systems side by side and comparing the outputs. An alternative approach may be extended pilot running, or introducing a model office.

The installation phase

The purpose of the installation phase is to plan, order and install all hardware, terminals and communication lines, in order to give the users a live working system that has already been proved correct. Because of the duration of the tasks, this implementation phase is lengthy, runs concurrently with many of the preceding phases, and may commence after the conversion and implementation planning has taken place during the system design phase. It may even start earlier if there is a long lead time for, say, communication lines. The installation phase consists of two distinct aspects, viz; conversion and implementation. In fact, a case could readily be made for two separate phases, especially if the complexity of the conversion problem warrants the development of a system within itself.

Conversion is unique for any project and although only a one-time effort, the difficulties associated with it are often high up on the list of management's headaches. Included are one-off file conversions or data capture, and the creation of new files, in order to set up the basic data for the application system to use and update subsequently. Frequently, many records of existing clerical data have to be gathered and corrected during this phase before live production running can occur.

Implementation involves much clerical work to be carried out by the users, and O and M skills may be required. Forms and stationery are proofed and printed, user manuals are written, special procedures are developed where they are needed for conversion and/or parallel running, and user training is undertaken.

At long last the users receive something useful from the computer! Although output was received during the previous phases, it consisted of either test data or samples of old data, and the computer application system may not so far have seemed to be producing useful results. It might take over two years to put all branches on to say, a banking, or public utilities communications system with a national spread of terminals.

During this period, the phased education of all the people who will be using the system should take place. This training could be given by the systems analysts, by O and M analysts, or by the personnel department's special training unit. The training could take the form of both explanatory lectures and programmed instruction (PI) texts. The latter may include sample document-ation, work-flow diagrams, examples, and the control methods. Special demonstrations for terminal users could be required, which will require relevant demonstration programs to be written by the project programmers.

To conclude implementation, the application system can now be accepted by, and formally handed over to, the data processing operations department to run on a repetitive 'factory production' basis. This marks the formal ending of the project.

Post-project evaluation (Post-implementation review)

This phase comprises a post-installation audit of the application system, as well as a management analysis of lessons learned that could be useful in the future. Two reviews are possible, one prior to the dispersal of the project (a review of the project management aspects), the other after about 6 months live running (which is a review of the actual system). The former evaluation could be carried out by the project manager and his team. In practice, this evaluation is rarely conducted, but if a post-project evaluation plan exists from the beginning, there is a greater chance that it will take place. At the review, it is necessary to look at the successes and failures, and the problems that have arisen. For future reference the following statistics on the project's performance should be recorded:

(1) The manpower estimates should be compared with actual man days effort and skills used by the project.
(2) The amount of machine time that was used for testing should be recorded.
(3) Total overall costs should be analysed.
(4) The reasons for variances against plan should be highlighted.
(5) What the project would have done differently with hindsight, in relation to the project management aspects, the technical aspects, and in the development techniques used.
(6) Productivity figures and program sizes for future planning purposes.
(7) General improvements to the computer department, in its relationship with the users, and in its DP procedures.

At all events, a review three to six months after the system has gone live should be carried out, but by an *independent* body. This body should assess whether or not the projected costs and benefits are being realized, whether the system requirements have been achieved, and identify weaknesses in the system. The checklist below may be of use when a manager is defining the scope of a post-implementation review.

THE SCOPE OF A POST-IMPLEMENTATION REVIEW

THE STATE OF DOCUMENTATION
Systems, programming, operational, user procedures.

TESTING
Test packs available for maintenance.
Test data, expected results, and test logs.

ERRORS TO DATE DURING LIVE RUNNING

An analysis of all errors found to date, the type of error, the department or program responsible, their cause, and current status.

USER ASPECTS

The users' impressions of the system, user problems, input and output usage, benefits derived from the system, user deficiencies/training needs.

SYSTEM REVIEW

Review of the design and operation of the system including strengths and weaknesses, controls and audit trail, the interface of the system with other systems.

DATA CAPTURE AND CONVERSION

Review of the data capture to date, and the plans for any remaining data capture.

COMPUTER OPERATIONS

The effectiveness of how the total system is run by the operations department.

COST EFFECTIVENESS

Determine if the current total running costs warrant the derived benefits.

RECOMMENDATIONS FOR THE SYSTEM

What should be done to make the system water-tight, and to improve its effectiveness, e.g. enhancements to the system, operational changes, any additional requirements for data integrity, documentation, testing, facilities, controls, user training, user procedures, personnel, etc.

In general, this project review is usually found interesting by the experienced person(s) assigned. This is not only because there may be few pressures for completion, but because the wide brief given to the reviewer invariably enables him to find many defects and recommendations for improvements.

Maintenance (amendments)

The changes requested after the formal freeze, but not authorized during changes control, can be incorporated during maintenance. Possibly the delay to the project caused by these business and data processing amendments could not be accepted earlier. Short projects can now be set up to introduce small improvements to the user facilities, and to 'tune' the system.

The development cycle may now return back to the beginning for developing the next stage of the application system.

Appendix 4

A checklist of system controls

Data control counts

the counting of records, or hash totals of numeric fields, or accumulated $ values.

(1) counting items present on receipt of data and comparing the totals to figures previously calculated and recorded elsewhere and by a different method. (e.g. batch headers which give the total number of associated cards, or a file trailer giving the total number of records on file).

(2) counting items into every program, and comparing these input totals to the corresponding output totals from the program at the end of processing (e.g. 10 records input. 5 went to file A, 3 went to file B, and 2 records amended file C).

Data control checks

(1) checking that today's brought forward totals are identical to yesterday's carry forward totals.

(2) checking that the physical count of records, when reading a file, agrees with the totals on the control record (produced when the file was last created).

(3) checking that the number of transactions input as recorded on the user department's register, equals the number of transactions processed by the system.

(4) checking that carry forward totals written by the end of a run, equal the brought forward totals at the start of the run plus amendments.

On-line data entry

conventional batch totals and batch controls are inapplicable. All errors should be logged for subsequent 'batch' monitoring and control over the terminal operators. The system

350

	should, periodically, be self balancing, with checks and balances at the end of each day for each terminal.
Real time error trapping and correction	notify the terminal operators of any error, at the end of each transaction, or an earlier logical entry point.
File version	checking file headers and carrying out operating system checks for latest or correct versions.
Standing data amendment	ensuring restricted access to transaction input forms. Supervisor to check amendments in and out, to minimize fraud. All amendments should be printed—microfilmed, with nil reports highlighted.
Printed output	an automatically produced distribution list of expected reports, and the number of pages. This may be compared to the pile of reports awaiting dispatch.
Cheque printing	see that there are adequate name and address restrictions. The clerk raising a cheque should not have access to it after it has been printed. Controlling access to pre-printed cheque stationery, which preferably should be unsigned. Ensure security is exercised over cheque numbers and their subsequent clearance. Where possible, avoid raising cheques clerically, but preferably use an independent cheque printing system with cheque requests originating from other systems.
Data formats for financially sensitive outputs	print leading zeros for critical financial fields, values, dates and times to reduce the temptation for fraud.
Double update control	preventing the same batch or transaction being processed twice, by use of a batch number register, or additional update checks.
Clerical operations	preventing two transactions, by different clerks, from updating the same record on file without both parties being made aware.
Input data validation	detect all errors. Check *all* fields (not only up to an error field). Print in words (not code letters) the reason for an error. Print in order of error importance, for rapid correction of major errors.
Check digits	highlighting certain data errors on input, e.g. transposition errors, (but not necessarily all transcription errors).

Overlay update control	ensuring prevention of a second master file change to a specific record from overlaying the first change during that run.
Error control	holding all errors and accounting for them.
Check point restart	see that restart points exist and are in the right places (e.g. at the end of each file volume, or after a specified time measured in records processed).
Reasonableness checks	where a control is impossible to quantify precisely, but an order of magnitude appears correct (e.g. average purchase value for a customer's order, or commissions paid against turnover with various commission rates and discounts).
Internal activity or process control	controlling a process rather than data (e.g. generating reminder letters by a certain date) by use of independent control logic.
Financial reconciliation	controlling say, cash received to outstanding invoices, during the actual program run.
Audit trail	to answer the questions, 'to where did a transaction go?' and, 'from where did a transaction come?'. The elements of an audit trail consist of source documents, batch registers, a cash allocation list, a suspense file ons list and offs list, a successful updates list containing the source of each transaction during that run. Each element should contain the run date, time, program, run number, and file version used. Audit trails should be held by responsible managers, and if not printed, held on magnetic tape or microfilmed.
Privacy and access to data	restricting access, both physically and technically, passwords, transaction types restricted to specified departments or grades.
Security of files and programs (e.g. against fire, loss, damage)	copies to be stored in a different building to the computer.
Clerical data control checks within computer operations	employing responsible clerks to vet computer input, and log its receipt.
The creation of program run numbers	to avoid unauthorized runs.
Unscheduled runs and the distribution of output	the system should log all outputs.
The use of numbered pages on the console control log	to avoid unauthorized amendments and runs.

Program amendments,
and their authorization

Data entry

keep source documents that authorize program amendments.

control that the number and value of input items relates to the number of source documents.

Appendix 5

Detailed testing techniques

5.1 TECHNIQUES TO FACILITATE TESTING

Criteria for the evaluation of useful techniques

The criteria for adopting techniques, useful for testing, are that the techniques must ensure that every condition is tested, and that all necessary test data is produced, but the quantity of test data, and the number of tests are kept to a minimum. This will minimize the requirements for manpower and machine time.

Project stage, and development phase dependence

Techniques useful for testing are mainly relevant at different development phases. For example, module testing has different requirements to user acceptance testing. It is also possible that, for a large project, implemented over several stages, various techniques may be applicable. For example, one project stage may involve adding modules to existing programs, and the testing requirements could, therefore, differ from the testing of completely original programs that were implemented in an earlier stage. The following sections discuss testing techniques relevant to each development phase.

5.2 TECHNIQUES FOR TESTING RELEVANT TO THE SYSTEM DESIGN PHASE

The five types of testing, being *planned* during system design (i.e. suite, sub-system, integrated, acceptance and pilot tests) may each require different approaches and techniques. In particular, acceptance tests should use a different approach to the systems tests performed earlier. Sometimes, the selection of system testing techniques may have to reflect the design techniques adopted.

The steps detailed over the next few pages are a systematic method of producing test data and expected results for use during suite, sub-system, and integrated system testing (i.e. not necessarily for acceptance or pilot tests). Each step for preparing test data and planning the system test runs could be carried out by people with a progressively lower skill level. These steps involve:

overall strategic planning
determining high level test conditions

developing them into detailed conditions
planning the actual system test runs
planning the clerical tests

Each of these is now discussed in turn.

Overall Strategic Planning

Testing by path

One method is to systematically produce the test conditions, the test data and perform the tests down each *path* of the overall system. A program, on say five paths, would be tested separately at least five times. A combined test of all paths simultaneously is finally necessary. The main difficulty is to define actually what is a 'path', especially in an integrated system, and to ensure that *all* paths are identified. A path can be identified by using the system specification as a working document and marking off those sections, paragraphs, or sentences that require to be tested. This document can be further used to monitor testing, by marking up all conditions that are under test, and that have been tested and are correct. (The alternative is to draw out another document!). Having found every path, basic test data is drawn up which tests the route down every path and hence should prove that the overall system works.

The detailed, invisible processing can now be checked by identifying all the paths a transaction may take, and attempting to prepare as many versions of a transaction as required to test all processing. The final step in each path is to identify the processing which produces print lines, and to ensure that variations of each transaction type find the path to trigger each type of print line.

This approach is very thorough, and provides a method to demonstrate that everything has been tested. However, it usually consumes great effort and produces much test data. Because program, as well as system conditions are being considered, some duplication occurs of program test data.

Testing by program

Another approach is to systematically trace through the system, program by program, both to produce test data and when performing the tests. As each program is initially treated as a 'black box' it should be relatively easy to ensure that all inputs, outputs and processes are considered with minimal oversights. However, as with path testing, this technique is one of the best approaches, but requires a great deal of effort compared to other techniques. All *intermediate* files are required to be set up, together with expected results, and duplication of program tests and program linking might occur.

Testing by report

Using this technique each line of every report is considered, with little emphasis being placed on *program* conditions. The test data is produced and the tests are run systematically, report by report. The final step is to run the test data so that all reports and all possible variations within each report, are produced during one run of the system.

The advantage is that the output is well tested, but not necessarily all inputs and processing options. In practice, this method is used as a by-product of other methods, or as a secondary method, but most probably in conjunction with the following method.

Testing by transaction type

Having identified each transaction type and its consequential effect in the system, each transaction type is tested separately. All transaction types are eventually run together. The advantages are that each transaction is clearly defined, they can be grouped (by batches), and their general effect can be assessed readily. The error conditions are also clearly defined and the controls can be checked.

This technique is useful for testing the data input, and processing aspects of the system. It is the corollary of the above method of report testing, and the two techniques could be used together as a recommended compromise approach to system testing, especially if minimizing effort is an important factor.

Testing by function

An alternative approach is that each system function is tested separately. 'A function' could be defined as a DP or business function, or refer to a facility, or relate to the requirements of a section of a department, or relate to a group of transaction types.

This method could be appropriate to define different steps in the overall testing sequence, e.g. to define a sub-system test or a user acceptance test.

Testing by department

A method of testing (especially for acceptance tests) may be appropriate, that entails separate runs for each department (or section of a department). This approach is one aspect of 'testing by function' defined above, and could be appropriate for testing systems which cut across many divisions and departments.

Integrated systems

For a very large integrated system an additional initial step may be necessary to break up the testing into smaller steps.

Figure A.1 gives a strategic testing hierarchy for a specific system. As is apparent, four levels are considered. This, like many of the other techniques, could also be considered as top-down testing.

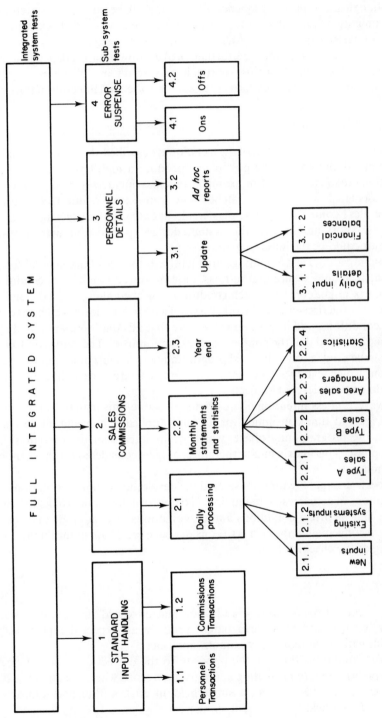

Figure A.1 An example of a strategic testing hierarchy for an integrated system

Although the eventual sequence of testing will be suite, sub-system, and then integrated tests, at this overall planning stage we work backwards and break down the integrated system tests into independent sub-system tests. These sub-systems can then be further broken down into independent units for testing. Not adopting this approach may result in difficulties occurring when attempting to produce correct test data for the final integration tests.

High-level conditions

Having selected one (or more) of the techniques described above and determined a strategy, it should now be possible to produce a high level list of all basic conditions requiring tests. For example, this may include every type of condition associated with inputs (batches and transactions); interfaces with reference files; controls; reports; master file updates; output files and run frequencies. Working through the system design specification with a system flowchart could be the initial step to take.

Assuming all the test conditions are identified, the use of decision tables or a test matrix should ensure that test cases are produced to check all conditions. The matrix might consist of each condition described along one axis, and test cases or transactions along the other axis. Ticks will indicate which cases test which conditions, and inspection will ensure that all conditions are tested by at least one case, and that the number of cases is minimized. The matrix or decision table can be used, as on structured programming, to enable one diagram to take decisions which lead to a lower level and so on. Therefore, each diagram should be dealing at one level or subject.

However, unless intentionally restricted in scope, this matrix could become very large and time-consuming, or it could duplicate the program designer's tests in the programming phase, which occur later than the current system design phase. This matrix might, therefore, only be considered for the high-level conditions.

Successive stages are now considered for developing detailed conditions into descriptions of actual test data required. To improve the chances of listing all the correct and incorrect conditions and combinations of conditions that require testing, a convenient approach is to consider each condition in turn under every heading of the checklist below.

Single Conditions:

(a) Basic correct *conditions* (e.g. add a new master record, update an outstanding balance, accept a clean batch, produce an expected report, accept fields with minimum and maximum sizes, etc.).
(b) *Error* conditions that are the opposite to the correct conditions in paragraph (a) above (e.g. creating a new master record when one already exists, an error in a batch total, a single field in error within one transaction, amending a field to its current status).

(c) *Other error* conditions (e.g. a parameter error, a non-existent transaction type relating to an existing correct record, a monthly report on a daily run, a duplicate but otherwise correct transaction).

Multiple Conditions:

(d) *Combinations* of *correct* conditions (e.g. add a new record after the last master record on file, apply two different amendments to the same record, input several valid transaction types from an approved originator).
(e) *Error* conditions of *combinations* relating to paragraph (d) above (e.g. two or more errors on one transaction, delete a master record that is not on file but whose key is greater than the last master record, two amendments to a missing master record, a duplicate of an error transaction, a combination of valid transaction types relating to one master record but one field is in error).
(f) Other *combination errors* (e.g. a parameter error at month end, a non-existent transaction on a missing master record, a continuation card not relating to the previous card, a non-existent transaction type relating to an incorrect record).

Detailed conditions

A checklist

Under each heading of the high level list of conditions, and using the above checklist, it is possible to produce a low level list of detailed test conditions at the transaction, file, report, record, and field levels, using information contained in the system specification. As an additional aid, the following checklist may prove helpful when determining the basic conditions for fully testing batch and transaction inputs, prior to and during their update of a master file. (To this checklist should be added DP tests, such as checking for file contention, recovery, etc.)

A CHECKLIST OF CONDITIONS FOR TESTING INPUTS

1. Batch control errors in input transaction data

No batch header for the first batch of input data.

No batch header for a batch in the middle of several input batches.

A batch header without a batch identification number.

A batch with duplicate batch headers.

Two batches with a duplicate batch number.

A batch header but no data in the batch.

A count error between the number of transactions in the batch, and the count on the batch header.

A missing batch item count on the batch header.

A $ value control error between the total $ value of a field within the batch, and the control value on the batch header.

A zero or space control $ value on the batch header when transactions in the batch do not have a $ value field.

A batch header with a missing $ value control when transactions in the batch involve money.

A count and a $ value control error between the transactions in the batch, and the count and value controls on the batch header.

Mixed transaction types in one batch when system controls require separate batching of transaction types.

Mixed transactions in one batch when system controls require the separation of batches into transactions that create new master file records, and transactions that only amend existing master records.

Mixed transactions of credits and debits in one batch, when system controls require separate batches.

Missing batch identification number on a transaction within a batch.

More than one batch identification batch number on transactions within one batch.

An unrecognizable record terminator for one transaction in a batch.

Combinations of the above types of batch control errors.

2. Types of input transaction test data

A. CLEAN TRANSACTIONS WITH SINGLE TEST CONDITIONS ONLY — EXAMPLES

Stand-alone checking

	EXAMPLES
Formats, ranges and values of each field correct.	Valid fields and values for each type of transaction.
Intra card (or segment) logic is correct.	Values of dependent fields are compatible.
Inter card (or segment) logic is correct.	A common transaction reference, and correct card numbers.

Validation against reference file(s)

	The branch or agent or product exists on the reference files used for validation.

Valid data when updating master file(s)

Correct access to a master record.	A transaction's key is *present* on the master file for amendments/deletions.
Adding a new master record with no duplication of keys.	The transaction's key is *not* on the master file already.
No duplication of existing data.	Not attempting to amend master record data to the same values.
Correct values on a transaction.	A payment is equal to the amount outstanding on the master transaction.
Correctly amending history data on a master record.	Accessing the correct level of personnel, or payment history.
Very high and very low values.	Payments received of $0.01, or cheques for values of $100,000.
Ability to handle credits and debits.	Credit notes, or refunds of −$0.005.

B. TRANSACTIONS WITH A SINGLE ERROR ONLY — EXAMPLES

An error in stand-alone checking

	EXAMPLES
A non-existent transaction type.	Where transaction types are not in pre-set positions and require identification.
A missing transaction type identifier.	

Cards out of sequence	Cards in a batch, cards within a multi-card transaction.
The identifier of a key field is unrecognizable.	Where a key field is not always in a pre-set position.
Part of the transaction's key is missing.	The check digit, or a prefix character is omitted.
Duplicate transactions.	Two identical transactions for the same master record.
A value is present but its significance is not known.	A transaction comprising several optional fields, but a field identifier has been omitted.
A missing field terminator.	One field runs into the next without any obvious separation.
A data field with blank contents but its identifier is present.	Input format has not changed for different transaction type.
Data present in fields where it should be absent.	Wrong input format on VDU screen for the transaction in question.
Data in fields which are not relevant to a transaction type.	Adding a field identifier and data to the wrong transaction type.
A non-existent field identifier on an input transaction.	A keying error.
Validation fails for one field only, against predetermined alpha, numeric or special characters.	The usual rules for data validation.
Particular check on $\emptyset$0, I1, Z2, S5.	The usual ambiguous mis-coding experienced with data.
Invalid range of an alpha or numeric field.	Minimum and maximum values are exceeded.
A field does not equal the alpha or numeric pre-set values	Field value not equal to one of a set of values.
Dates are too early or too late.	People whose date of birth does not agree with their age, an actual delivery on a future date, or a date prior to a product's launch.
A field with zero value: should it be zero filled or blank.	Leaving an irrelevant field blank, when the program expects it to be zero filled.
An optional field with no contents.	Absent value equals 0 or blank.
Wrong arithmetic on input.	An incorrect build up of several fields to a net value.
Bad data entry or key-punching.	Misalignment of columns, over-punching.
Error in editing against reference file(s)	The branch or the agent or the product appearing on a transaction is *not* on the reference file.

An error in a transaction which becomes apparent when updating master file(s)

Attempting to access a master record which does not exist.	The key of a transaction causing an amendment or deletion is *not present* on a master file record.
Create a duplicate master record.	The key for a transaction to create a record is already *on* the master file.
A duplicate transaction.	Amending a field to the same value as already exists on a master file.
A value error on a transaction	A payment which is not equal to the amount outstanding on the master record.
A history amendment error.	Accessing the incorrect level of personnel or payment history. (e.g. accessing the third payment instead of the fourth).

EXAMPLES

C. CLEAN TRANSACTIONS WITH MULTIPLE CONDITIONS

Stand-alone checking is correct

Keys of several transactions are not in sequence.	The usual random sequence of clerical transactions on input.
2 different valid transactions for the same master record.	A name and address change accompanied by a cash receipt for a bill.
Several valid transaction types from an approved originator.	Security cleared transactions types for a specific password.

Valid processing when updating master file(s)

Inter-transaction logic is correct.	Set up an agent and pay his commission during the same input.
	Records on the master file, or segments within a record are in sequence.
Correct sequence of records.	Add a new record after the last master record on file.

D. TRANSACTIONS WITH MULTIPLE ERRORS

Multiple stand-alone errors

Multiple errors when editing against references files
Multiple logic errors apparent at update

Combinations of stand-alone, reference and update errors
Any combination of errors in section B or D
Unreasonable checks fail.

EXAMPLES

A missing data field and its identifiers.
A duplicate of an error transaction.
A non-existent transaction for a missing master record.
A non-existent item for a non-existent product.
Delete a master record that is not on file, but whose key is greater than the last master record.
Two amendments to a missing master record.

The total commission paid at the end of a run appears significantly unrelated to the orders received.

In order to minimize duplication, it may also be necessary at this stage to list the more vital fields for system testing and, to state the assumptions made of those tests to be carried out during program tests (e.g. range, format, presence or absence of each field).

Having listed all conditions, it may now be desirable to write a test *description* of each type of error using sufficient detail for someone else, if necessary, to code the actual data. It is also often useful, to produce a list of record code numbers for each test, a summary of the relevant data fields, and indicating whether it is an invalid or clean input transaction, if its master record is on file(s), and if it appears as an output record. This may prove helpful during the actual testing and when checking outputs.

Compatibility

A common difficulty is producing test data that is compatible within the system. This may manifest itself in several ways. The fields comprising an individual input transaction may need to tie up with each other (an intra record problem), or they need to be compatible with fields in other transactions (an inter record problem). Similarly, there must be compatibility between input transactions and master file records. One small change in one field of test data might require, say, five further changes in other data items. Without due care, this situation may result in having to make five test shots to clear errors as they come to light, because *all* five fields were not changed correctly. A most difficult problem to overcome is first establishing, and then maintaining, compatibility as changes in test data occur to intermediary files set up to test separate programs.

The way round the latter problem is not to do testing that way! If possible, it is simpler to carry out complete system tests via the input programs(s) and build up master files in stages during the testing. In this way, compatibility is obtained automatically (assuming the programs work!). It may also be beneficial to extend the standards relating to design documentation, so that the logical values for each field *within the total system* are readily obtainable from a suitably formated document. This means not only defining each field in isolation (which is usual for individual program specifications), but also defining inter record and intra record dependencies (which are not usually so well documented for an entire system). This problem might also be minimized by using a data administration program to establish dependencies.

Expected results

At this stage, a high level list of *expected results* (reports and files) should be produced. The above plan together with the system flowchart and the specification are required to list, say, the appropriate error messages. However, in many cases, a reasonable practical approach could be to run tests first, with scant prior detail of outputs, and then examine the results against the inputs to determine if the test was successful.

By this stage it should have been possible to create test data for master, reference and intermediate files, as well as to create compatible input transaction data.

Preparation for system test runs

Having prepared test records, they can be assembled into test files for use in specific test cycles. This forms a test run plan, so that for each stage and test cycle it is apparent which record was input, the expected results, and which files were used. The optimum *sequence* of test runs may be different from the sequence of inputs and expected output that have been coded to date. It is, therefore, necessary to ensure that the coded test case data, and the corresponding coded actual expected results are in the same sequence at the time of running the tests. In addition, the testing sequence should progress logically. This means that it is quicker in time and easier on the mind to run 3 simple tests, knowing that each of the previous tests were correct, than to run one complete test where the conditions being tested rely on other untested conditions.

It is also necessary to be able to carry on testing:

(a) If a program is completed later than scheduled;
(b) If a program is not available because errors are being corrected;
(c) If an error is found and the system test stops.

Strategic files within the system, e.g. at the start of each suite or sub-system, (which could be groups of 3 to 6 programs) are, therefore, required to be set up in advance, but would be produced automatically if expected results are set up for each intermediary file.

As the testing escalates, test packs that were initially used for separate tests will gradually become combined (e.g. correct batches, then error batches, then combination batches, then several transaction types, etc.). It is necessary to document how individual test packs and individual expected results are systematically consolidated into an eventual test pack for the total system.

During the systems testing, test files are required to be set up, and during the latter part of system testing, volume and cyclic data is required. These could be time-consuming tasks, and if an automated method of generating data is used, it is preferable to tie the generated data to the expected results. Working backwards, by carrying out the tests and then examining the printed output and comparing it to the generated input, is a valid approach.

The final step in producing test data is to convert the descriptions of tests into actual *coded data* suitable for computer input. An appropriate coding/ punching document should be used with a cross reference to the test description list. For less complex systems, it may be possible to dispense with descriptions of test cases, and code actual records and data fields directly.

Sometimes it is necessary to code the *detailed expected results* from the high level descriptions produced previously. The detailed system specification and file layout charts will also be required. If outputs are sorted, or are not in the original input test sequence, an extra planning step is needed. A useful idea is to compile a list of expected testing controls that can be compared to the system control totals, e.g. the number of test transactions that should be accepted and rejected. It then will be easier to ascertain if a test run was successful, and if not, what transaction types are causing problems.

Planning the clerical tests

During the latter part of integrated system testing and user acceptance testing, clerical tests, on both inputs and outputs, can be planned and performed either by:

(a) using the system for several weeks, and then working through the (draft) procedure manual page by page and comparing it to what actually occurred. Unused pages can be reviewed subsequently and tested.
(b) inputting each transaction type, and using each computer print-out, and then comparing with the (draft) procedure manual.

The second approach has the advantage of detecting omissions, but both techniques are probably required to test everything systematically.

User acceptance tests

When negotiating acceptance criteria with the user departments, and when they are producing their test data subsequently, the updated user requirement document should be used, and preferably not the system design document (which is used by the system testers). This assumes that a detailed user requirement has been produced with detailed inputs and outputs. User testing should adopt a different approach from systems testing, even though the test plan may have a similar format, using similar forms and testing logs. It is the responsibility of the development team to check the feasibility, effectiveness and completeness of the users' test plan. For example, the users may be attempting to undertake too much, or they may be contemplating using too many (live) records, or producing too many print lines.

In the case of integrated systems involving many line user departments, it may be necessary to negotiate with each department separately, and for each department to produce its own relevant test data (with systems analysts closely involved). At the eventual run time, some of this test data may need to be combined in order for the system to run.

Recapitulation

We have now concluded all the planning and preparation work that should occur during the system design phase, and for the system tests which are eventually performed in the proving phase. A daunting amount of material has been presented in this section, which primarily is aimed at suggesting a systematic method of producing efficient test data and documenting which item of

test data is testing which condition. Time spent on this planning and preparation is usually found to be well spent when actual tests are being performed.
However, starting planning *too early* will usually mean that there will be more
specification changes to comprehend, accompanied by more alterations to the
prepared test data. In addition, too much planning may demotivate the people
responsible for testing who are probably 'raring to go' and intend to use an
ad hoc approach to the proving phase.

5.3 TECHNIQUES FOR TESTING RELEVANT TO PROGRAM DESIGN AND PROGRAMMING

The planning and production of test data for program testing could use the
same sequence of techniques as described above for system tests. If many
modules are involved, a greater emphasis should be placed on the optimum
testing sequence for each module, and consequently, the necessary sequence
and duration for coding each module in time for its testing should be
ascertained.

If a design technique based on data structures is used for program and
module design, then program tests could also be based on data structures.
If pseudo code or a design language is used to produce structured program
modules, the program designer can simultaneously produce a checklist of
program test conditions every time he reaches one of the three basic system
logic elements. If systems test data has already been produced, the program
designer can check it to ensure completeness, notify the system testers of
omissions, and select all system test data relevant to his own program tests.

The area between 'techniques' and 'recommended tasks' overlaps for
program design and programming, and much material has already been
covered in the earlier parts of this appendix. However, the following are additional techniques:

Test logs

A test log, that cross references to the test data chart used for planning tests,
is required for recording the actual tests, their dates, the type of test, machine
time used, and the outcome. One test log per module is convenient during
module testing, and one test log per program (including setting up test files)
during program testing.

The purpose of the log is:

(1) to control the history of each module and program;
(2) to check the completeness of the testing against the original test plan;
(3) to measure staff performance of coding, testing, and accuracy. This analysis
    can be made over the following heading, and used by the installation's
    managers, the project manager and team leaders for future planning and
    target setting:

Module/Program : Name	Programming : Complexity	Number of : Statements	Number of : Compiles
Number of : Test Shots	Machine : Time used	Man Days : Effort	Elapsed : Time	Programmer and years' experience

Test code

A common technique is to insert special program code which facilitates testing; for example, by printing out intermediary steps in the processing, thereby indicating that all paths have been processed.

Top-down testing

Advantages

Traditionally, program and system tests become extended when excessive bugs are found at a late stage, and rectifying them then is costly and time-consuming. Compared to conventional programming and testing methods, top-down testing, where groups of dependent modules are tested systematically down the various levels of the hierarchy, should reduce errors arising from specification problems. If errors do occur, they should manifest themselves much earlier in the project's testing sequence, when the early but partial test results can be examined by systems testers and even the users. Similarly, general program coding errors are trapped earlier, because the module testing and linking process is so planned that from the outset, simulated files and inter-linking modules are always present, even if the final version has not been completed.

An additional advantage claimed for top-down testing is that it tends to halve the computer time requirement of the programming phase, compared to other testing methods. This is because less errors are found in tested modules during link testing, and consequently, there is less need to re-test and re-link amended modules.

Disadvantages

The disadvantages are that the 'top-down' method of testing requires the tests to be performed in a definite sequence. Delays at any level will automatically cause delays at lower levels, since it is necessary for all higher level modules to be functioning correctly before testing on any subordinate modules can commence. Consequently, a burden is imposed on the scheduler, who is attempting to schedule modules for testing in the correct sequence, and at the same time schedule the rectification of established errors.

A minor disadvantage is the need to provide simulators and stubs for missing modules, to enable the top-down testing to be effected. Another disadvantage, this time more major, of top-down testing is that initial tests can produce false hopes, when the simplified logic works correctly, but the later systems complexity produces many errors.

The project manager may find that top-down testing is often more appropriate for testing 'legs' of programs, or testing small programs, or simple programs (e.g. prints), or when one programmer is writing and testing one structured program or one suite of programs.

Bottom-up testing

Bottom-up testing is where individual modules are produced and tested randomly and in isolation, often starting at the bottom level of the hierarchy. Thus, the final program is built module by module, and subsequently, the whole program is tested in isolation. The use of a test harness simplifies the testing and linking of modules if bottom-up testing is adopted.

This approach is more commonly used on large or complex programs (e.g. updates). The project manager and his team leaders could prefer it because it greatly reduces the scheduling difficulties of producing and testing modules in the correct sequence, and it eliminates time wasted whilst waiting for other modules to be completed.

5.4 TECHNIQUES FOR TESTING RELEVANT TO THE PROVING PHASE

The main technique for proving is to follow the plans created in the system design phase! This ground has already been well covered; the following additional techniques may be found useful.

When to start proving

A positive effort should be made to start system testing as *late* as possible. This may seem crazy advice, because it puts more pressures on the people responsible for testing, who become squeezed up to the target dates for going live. However, the benefits of this approach are that (a) the programming phase (for the suite in question) can be completed properly with thorough program, and program link tests. (b) complete suites will be received by the systems testers and not programs in dribs and drabs, this means that (c) the system testers avoid testing single programs (and therefore, avoid duplicating program tests), and can be confident to start with *systems* testing without having to plan for testing each program. This means that (d) *much less* test data is required for system testing as opposed to testing separate programs. (This applies to input transaction files, test master files, but mainly to intermediary test files). (e) It is easier to produce *initially* test data which is also suitable for subsequent integrated systems tests. (In practice, this objective cannot be achieved with the larger quantity of program orientated data, because the latter usually changes substantially from errors in one's own test data, from specification errors, and from additional test requirements that come to light during testing). (f) It is much easier, using actual end-product programs, to produce valid files of transaction test data that are compatible, at update, to valid test files of master records.

Technical system summary for preparing tests

In order to speed up the production of JCL decks and to facilitate the actual testing, a technical summary of the system may prove useful, which comprises:

(a) A system flowchart.
(b) A chart of *all* error messages in each program. (This is invaluable for saving time when test runs abort).
(c) For each program, detailed input and output file information containing file name(s), record length, block size, record format, write permit ring, if record counts include headers and trailers, file organization, maximum possible volumes, and parameters.

Changing or improving test data

Test data needs continual changes to it. When amending (or creating) test files it is preferable to use up-to-date file layouts, either from the data dictionary or from the latest program compilation.

Preferably, test packs (data and JCL) should not be modified. A better method is to duplicate the test pack first, then amend the data or JCL of the copy and retain safely the original. Incidentally, card decks come into their own in this situation. Testers in installations wholly with VDU input, paper tape, or key to disk input may become envious of old fashioned cards!

After a text-run has been completed, the test pack should not be destroyed. Program fixes and on-off conditions can always then be re-tested. If additional test data is required (e.g. to test new or previously unplanned conditions) it is often preferable to do it by adding separate files, and/or extra cylces. This not only improves control over testing, but it should be easier to reconcile the new system control totals to the old.

Back-up and recovery of test beds

It is advisable to take sufficient back-ups of transaction files, master and reference files, and dumps of expected results files. A sensible procedure is to test out recovery before it is required, especially for index sequential files, preferably as the final step in the job setting up the files. If recovery is not tested at the outset, it is often never tested until recovery is required, by which time if it fails it is too late.

User acceptance techniques

The auditors should, at least, form a passive part of the acceptance tests, by reviewing all plans, test data, and ouput, thereby ensuring the system has been thoroughly tested.

Prior to the start of user acceptance tests, the users should be familiarized with the system by being shown system testing inputs and outputs. In the case of systems with several users, acceptance tests for all departments are usually run at the same time, and consequently, the users will receive their outputs at the same time (often first thing each morning). They all will then require a testing liaison person from the DP department simultaneously to resolve queries or to whom they can report errors. It might be a useful management decision to assign one person to each user department during acceptance. This person could come from either the development or testing teams.

Index